THE FEAR OF CONSPIRACY

IMAGES OF UN-AMERICAN
SUBVERSION FROM
THE REVOLUTION
TO THE PRESENT

THE FEAR OF CONSPIRACY

IMAGES OF UN-AMERICAN SUBVERSION FROM THE REVOLUTION TO THE PRESENT

EDITED WITH COMMENTARY BY

DAVID BRION DAVIS

CORNELL UNIVERSITY PRESS | ITHACA AND LONDON

Copyright © 1971 by Cornell University

All rights reserved. Except for brief quotations in a review, this book, or parts thereof, must not be reproduced in any form without permission in writing from the publisher. For information address Cornell University Press, 124 Roberts Place, Ithaca, New York 14850.

First published 1971

International Standard Book Number 0-8014-0598-X
Library of Congress Catalog Card Number 70-127775

Printed in the United States of America by Vail-Ballou Press, Inc.

To Martha Elizabeth

It will throw additional light . . . to go back and run the mind over the string of historical facts already stated. Several things will now appear less dark and mysterious than they did when they were transpiring. The people [in the Territories, according to the Kansas-Nebraska Bill] were to be left "perfectly free," "subject only to the Constitution." What the Constitution had to do with it outsiders could not then see. Plainly enough now, it was an exactly fitted niche for the Dred Scott decision to afterward come in, and declare the perfect freedom of the people to be just no freedom at all. . . .

We cannot absolutely know that all these exact adaptations are the result of preconcert. But when we see a lot of framed timbers, different portions of which we know have been gotten out at different times and places and by different workmen,—Stephen, Franklin, Roger, and James, for instance, —and we see these timbers joined together, and see they exactly make the frame of a house or a mill, all the tenons and mortises exactly fitting, and all the lengths and proportions of the different pieces exactly adapted to their respective places, and not a piece too many or too few, not omitting even scaffolding—or, if a single piece be lacking, we see the place in the frame exactly fitted and prepared yet to bring such piece in—in such a case we find it impossible not to believe that Stephen and Franklin and Roger and James all understood one another from the beginning, and all worked upon a common plan or draft drawn up before the first blow was struck.

ABRAHAM LINCOLN
Speech at Springfield, June 16, 1858

Acknowledgments

For some years past the late Richard Hofstadter and I have borrowed from each other on the general subject of the paranoid style and movements of countersubversion. I am most grateful to him for suggesting a number of valuable sources for this book as well as for his general encouragement. I am also indebted to Gerald E. Stearn, who first suggested the idea of a collection of documents on conspiracy. I am also extremely grateful to Joel Bernard, one of my former students at Cornell, whose aid in gathering and sifting materials makes him virtually a co-editor.

DAVID BRION DAVIS

December 1970

Contents

Introduction

Although the United States has had more than its share of wars, riots, and assassinations, the standard surveys of American history present a picture of general stability, sobriety, and even blandness. In contrast to the history of other nations, that of America, in the standard view, exhibits strong institutional continuity, a relative lack of class conflict, and a remarkable capacity for pragmatic compromise.

But the historian's perspective tends to be calmer and more equable than the perspective of history's actors and creators. Statistical analysis of election results may flatten out political differences which once aroused intense emotions. If the United States has enjoyed uncommon security from the time of independence, the American people have also been subjected to continual alarms and warnings of imminent catastrophe. As the selections in this book make clear, many Americans have been curiously obsessed with the contingency of their experiment with freedom. From the time that free institutions miraculously survived the subversive plots of the British crown, they have supposedly been threatened by a long succession of dark conspiratorial powers. Since alarmists have portrayed each subversive force as posing an unprecedented danger, and have accordingly pictured the past as a time of idyllic harmony, it is easy to overlook the continuity in American movements of countersubversion and the characteristics common to them.

The purpose of this book is to identify an important phenomenon in American thought which has often been obscured by efforts to achieve an objective and balanced picture of "reality." By focusing on the exaggerated ways Americans have often *perceived* reality, I am not proposing a new interpretation of American history. It must be emphasized at the outset that this book provides an opportunity to view the major events of American history through a special and highly distorted lens. Like other unusual lenses, this one enables the viewer to see configurations that are hidden from normal vision. I am not implying that all the individuals represented in the book suffered from "abnormal vision" but am simply referring to the overall impression that the selections convey.

Material of this kind presents formidable problems of interpretation. It would have been easier to compile an anthology of writings from the lunatic fringe, allowing the reader (and editor) to assume a superior stance of normality and rationality. But if we have learned nothing else from modern psychiatry, we should by now be aware of the infinite gradations between "normal" and "abnormal" behavior. If there is any historical significance to what Richard Hofstadter has termed "the paranoid style," it lies precisely in the intersection of private and collective fantasies. The word "paranoid" is therefore highly misleading unless we acknowledge that we all have our paranoid moments, and that the fear of conspiracy is sometimes reasonable and may also serve important social functions. Dr. Howard Feinstein, a psychiatrist who closely observed and studied the cataclysmic events of April 1969 on the Cornell University campus, concluded that the paranoid style became rampant among students and faculty because "for many, it was less frightening to believe in hostile conspirators than it was to face the fact that no one was in control." °

Of course one can raise the obvious objection that there have been genuine conspiracies from the time of Benedict Arnold to the current campus revolts. It might be possible, given sufficient time and patience, to rank movements of countersubversion on a scale of relative realism and fantasy. Thus the anti-Masons would appear to have been more autistic than the later abolitionists, who had some empirical basis for their perception of a Slave Power conspiracy and who were in fact harassed in the North by carefully organized mobs. Certainly we should resist any temptation to conflate all warnings of conspiracy into a single "American paranoid mind." It would also be a mistake to assume that the fear of subversion is always generated by internal, psychological needs. Most of the men represented in this book were responding to highly disturbing events; and their perceptions, even when wild distortions of reality, were not necessarily unreasonable interpretations of available information. Collective beliefs in conspiracy have usually embodied or given expression to genuine social conflict.

There are limitations, however, to any schematic attempt to distinguish realistic from unrealistic suspicions of conspiratorial subversion. In the first place, even the most realistic guardians and watchmen

° Howard M. Feinstein, "April 1969: A Celebration of the Mass," in *Divided We Stand: Reflections on the Crisis at Cornell,* ed. by Cushing Strout and David I. Grossvogel (Garden City, N.Y.: Doubleday & Co. Inc., 1970), p. 110.

have been prone to exaggeration and have adopted muted versions of the characteristic paranoid themes. Second, throughout our history there has been a striking discrepancy between the pitiful weakness and incompetence of most conspirators and the willingness of many Americans to believe that a powerful, monolithic, and virtually infallible organization was about to overthrow the Republic. Third, there has been a continuity in the imagery of subversion that bears no necessary relation to any given enemy. Thus in the following selections we shall frequently encounter Trojan horses, entering wedges, blueprints for the destruction of liberty, and lists of names of supposedly loyal leaders who are exposed as the tools of a hostile power. This interchangeability of images and metaphors suggests that the phenomenon of countersubversion might be studied as a special language or cultural form, apart from any preconceptions of its truth or falsity. Finally, we should note the tendency of such rhetoric to polarize actual conflict in conspiratorial terms. For example, colonial charges of a British ministerial plot were answered by British charges of a colonial revolutionary plot. A similar escalation of fear and suspicion developed between Federalists and Republicans, between abolitionists and anti-abolitionists, and between big business and organized labor. In numerous instances, accusations of conspiracy have proved to be self-fulfilling or have resulted in the adoption by counterconspirators of conspiratorial techniques.

Another problem arises from the universality of nativist or countersubversive movements. Most of the traits of the paranoid style can be found in the millenarian religious sects of medieval Europe, in the Reformation and Counter-Reformation, in the Boxer movement in China, and in various primitive societies resisting modernization, to cite only a few examples. It is probable that every society contains certain personality types who are inclined to blame disrupting change on secret, diabolical forces and who gain hearers at times of particular stress.

There are good reasons, however, for studying American ideas of subversion so long as one gives adequate attention to chronology and changing situations. In more traditional and hierarchical societies, conspiracies may have been attributed to witches and heretics, to wicked courtiers, to disaffected nobles, or to fanatics who deluded and inflamed the lower classes. But once such subversives were exposed, they could clearly be regarded as outlaws who endangered established orders, estates, and institutions. Necessarily, the threat of conspiratorial subversion acquired new meaning in a nation born in revolution and based on the sovereignty of the people. American crusades against subversion have never been the monopoly of a single social class or ideology, but have been readily appropriated by highly diverse groups. Thus both abolitionists and slaveholders could picture themselves as upholding traditional values against un-American conspiracies. In the 1930's the "radio priest," Father Charles E. Coughlin, echoed many of the fears and concerns of the violently anti-Catholic Ku Klux Klan. Sometimes the fear of conspiracy has been used as an excuse for repression and tighter social discipline; sometimes it has been associated with movements for expanding human liberties. But the belief in widespread conspiracy has always been a challenge to the comforting view that the American people, despite their minor differences, share a common loyalty and a consensus of basic commitments and values.

This is not to say that Americans have been more suspicious than other people or that American civilization has been blighted by some paranoia that has mysteriously infected every group of newcomers. Rather, we need to remind ourselves that America has long been seen as a distinctive society and that Americans, regardless of their religion or their social origins, have faced certain common problems and situations. As Alexis de Tocqueville observed in his classic *Democracy in America*, the American was inclined to adopt "great numbers of theories, on philosophy, morals, and politics, without inquiry, upon public trust." A relative "equality of condition," by which Tocqueville meant a lack of fixed and accepted inequalities, produced a state of uncertainty, aspiration, and suspicion: "As men grow more alike, each man feels himself weaker in regard to all the rest; as he discerns nothing by which he is considerably raised above them or distinguished from them, he mistrusts himself as soon as they assail him." This continuing condition of social fluidity and personal insecurity made Americans especially susceptible to the belief that appearances were deceiving, that things were not what they seemed to be. In a nation in which every man is supposed to be on the make, there is an overriding fear of being taken in.

The American economy may never have conformed to Adam Smith's model of laissez-faire competition, but the American creed incorporated Smith's suspicion of "combinations" for private economic advantage. From the standpoint of laissez-faire philosophy, any collective action—such as that of a labor union, for example—

smacked of conspiracy. In a nation that lacked any tradition of privileged orders or large, monopolistic companies, there was a particular fear of secret alliances that might give certain groups unfair advantage in the race for economic and political power. Nineteenth-century Americans insisted that worldly opportunity, like God's grace, should be open to all men and not arbitrarily dispensed or withheld by a self-appointed elite. For it was only in a context of free opportunity that the fruits of competition could be endowed with the highest moral value. In America, therefore, the idea of conspiracy has generally suggested shady dealing, the stacking of cards in a game that was supposed to be governed by the sacred laws of nature. So long as equality has endured as a viable ideal, it has encouraged Americans to interpret gross inequalities as evidence of hidden and illegitimate power.

It would require another book to provide even a barely adequate framework for classifying and interpreting American movements of countersubversion. Here we can only suggest a number of broad distinctions that should be kept in mind, and then sketch several patterns of thematic continuity which run through the selected readings.

One way of distinguishing different categories of countersubversives is to look at the sources of real or suspected danger. Thus we can identify the defenders of various threatened establishments from the New England Federalists of the 1790's to the businessmen leaders of the Liberty League in the 1930's. For them the charge of conspiratorial subversion may have been a strategic device to convince potential supporters that any threat to their own power imperiled the social order. A quite different category would include men who were being displaced or put in new positions of dependency, and who protested that their oppression was the result of conspiracy. There were others who expressed more diffuse anxieties over social or cultural change. A final grouping might be made of Americans whose fears were triggered by foreign revolution or tyrannical reaction and who searched for domestic counterparts on the assumption that fires may be avoided if one looks out for flying sparks.

Another way of classifying countersubversives would be by personality type. Some of the selections are the products of inflamed minds that exhibit an extreme degree of suspiciousness and gullibility. These alarmists often perceive a given conspiracy as a personal threat. They frequently assume a messianic role of "saving the nation." They indulge in the wildest fantasies and offer a single explanation for a multitude of disparate events. This relatively pure form of the paranoid style is often associated with a displaced or embattled group which suddenly becomes aware of the gap between its own traditional way of life and a "new America" of outrageous beliefs, styles, and values. A second category would include writers who are more personally detached but who are profoundly concerned over some specific threat to traditional values or class structure. A third type would be the political or religious leaders who seem to adopt conspiratorial rhetoric largely as a tactical weapon. Finally, one might distinguish those writers who simply hit upon the idea of conspiracy as the most reasonable explanation for a progression of facts and events.

While it is well to keep such theoretical distinctions in mind, we should also remember the limitations of any static scheme of classification. In practice, the categories we have described merge and overlap, especially as we trace the development of any specific movement of countersubversion. Moreover, the most extreme or "paranoid" cases often indicate the evolving tendencies of a radicalizing movement. (Thus the "extreme" abolitionist view of the Slave Power conspiracy in 1840 had become a Republican platitude by 1860; over a century later the same pattern would be repeated by the proponents of Black Power.)

Quite apart from differences in personality and social situation, the selections suggest thematic continuities which shed considerable light on that murky but irrepressible question: what is "the American identity"? No doubt such themes could be defined in various ways, but I shall content myself with a brief summary of six clusters of ideas.

The first concerns the menace of a hostile foreign power, the prototype of which was Catholic Europe of the Counter-Reformation. As devout Protestants in a world divided by religious and ideological conflict, the American colonists inevitably looked upon the Catholic Church as the source of a worldwide conspiracy against liberty. They defined their own society as a purified and de-Romanized extension of England, and thus as the polar opposite of Catholic Europe. They prided themselves upon being the target which European despots would most like to destroy, and considered the Jesuits the very model of conspiratorial subversives. As the Ebenezer Baldwin selection (1774) makes clear, the Quebec Act allowed a transference of traditional fears of French Catholic intrigue to the new plots of the British government. The mother country had betrayed the cause of Protestantism and liberty and had thus become the vehicle for the Pope's designs against America, the last true outpost of Christian freedom. By the 1790's the classic Jesuitical foe had been transmogrified into the godless Illuminism of the French Revolution.

From a superficial point of view it would appear there could be no greater disparity than that between Catholic royalists and Jacobin Illuminati, between reactionary princes and socialist revolutionaries, or between fascist dictators and Communist subversives. But Americans from the 1790's to the mid-twentieth century have frequently discerned a subtle connection between radical and reactionary designs to destroy the world's model of Christian liberty. Thus New England Federalists charged that the domestic Democratic-Republican societies were revolutionary cells planted by French Jacobins who were themselves the tools of Jesuit intrigue. Anti-abolitionists portrayed the antislavery societies as engines of revolution manipulated by British aristocrats who cunningly promoted Negro emancipation as a means of undermining the bastion of liberty. Josiah Strong exposed the unsuspected connections between Catholic immigration and the spread of revolutionary socialism. Father Charles E. Coughlin tried to explain his consistency in attacking the Tory bankers and capitalists of England, the American New Deal, and international Communism. Various names and labels might disguise the Great American Enemy, but his objectives and tactics remained the same.

It is true, of course, that Europe has often been torn by actual conspiracies and counterconspiracies. Literal-minded Americans have been able to quote the ominous words of revolutionary anarchists or of reactionary Catholic sovereigns in order to prove that there were dangerous forces abroad that were absolutely antithetical to American institutions and the American way of life. It seems unlikely that any movement of countersubversion could have lasted very long unless its warnings carried some credibility and gave expression to some genuine conflict. But the point to be emphasized is that Americans have long been disposed to *search* for subversive enemies and to construct terrifying dangers from fragmentary and highly circumstantial evidence. American alarmists had come close to inventing an image of international Communism well before such an enemy existed. By the 1950's the nation's foreign policy seemed to presuppose that a single Communist enemy was responsible for every protest movement or revolutionary uprising in the world. The significant question is why Americans have been so inclined to conceptualize their relationship with the rest of the world in conspiratorial terms. If images of subversion reveal changing needs and tensions, we need to look closely at what Americans have thought they needed most to fear as well as at the values and institutions that they have seen as primarily endangered. In this way, pictures of conspiracy may give us access to a kind of internal history of American minds as the new and expanding nation groped for a sense of national identity.

It is a truism that the fluidity of American society has tended to detach individuals from traditional groups and classes. While such uprooting has opened new paths of opportunity, it has often been accompanied by feelings of guilt, isolation, and insecurity. Perhaps it is only a current fashion to find "identity crises" at the root of every social problem. Nevertheless, we need to recognize the special needs and tensions that first arose when personal identity became linked primarily with economic achievement. According to American egalitarian theory, an individual's ultimate worth had nothing to do with family, education, religious denomination, or membership in fraternal societies. Through much of American history, the criterion of material achievement has seemed to be a liberating and leveling force. Yet material achievement has commonly provoked new rivalries and social conflicts, and has also suggested a pursuit of pure self-interest without regard for the public welfare. In a nation dedicated to self-government, there seemed to be no checks on individualism or "mammonism."

The second theme originates with the conviction that only Protestant Christianity could guarantee orderly change by balancing individual liberty with public virtue. A thread which runs through much of the literature of countersubversion is the argument that any threat to American Protestantism is a threat to freedom, order, and morality. Lyman Beecher, who was alarmed by the increasingly competitive, acquisitive society of the 1830's, warned that unless the West was rapidly Christianized its population would become "a poor, uneducated reckless mass of infuriated animalism." In 1831, at the beginning of the age of enterprise, he expressed anxiety over the growing "diversity of local interests, the power of selfishness, and the fury of sectional jealousy and hate." Characteristically, he also called for a closing of ranks against an atheistic conspiracy which would "dissolve society, and turn out the whole family of human animals into one common field of unbridled appetite and lust." In a competitive and individualistic society, crusades against subversion could at once become a substitute for the communal solidarity of the church and the means of defining a higher national purpose. As a secular reinforcement of religious revivals, they could help to counteract the effects of materialism and moral lethargy.

One suspects that if Beecher could survey twentieth-century America, he would conclude that his missionary campaign had failed, that his worst fears had been fulfilled. There is a note of swelling desperation among his ideological descendants from Josiah Strong to John A. Stormer. In the ante-bellum years there was little *direct* challenge to Protestant orthodoxy, and even a Lyman Beecher could hardly blame Unitarians and Catholics for all the social and cultural dislocations that weakened belief in traditional verities and ways of life. But by the time of the First World War, when the American Defense Society defined Protestant Christianity as the core of "one hundred percent Americanism," Beecher's ethic was being challenged by a multitude of supposedly alien and "modernist" influences which were attributed to the Hun, the international Jew, or the Bolshevik. In so far as Protestant fundamentalism has been seen as the only force that could stabilize and redeem American society, its decline in national importance has produced an increasingly fanatical and embittered backlash. There is a striking contrast between Beecher's robust confidence in Protestant America and the panicky vigilantism of the American Protective League.° If we accept the premises of Beecher's crusade to "save the West," we end up with the despair of John A. Stormer's recent testament, *The Death of a Nation.*

But there has also been a radical, sectarian strain in the history of countersubversion. A third theme evolves from the ancient idea of Christianity as the poor man's kingdom. In the selection by Abraham Bishop, a New England Jeffersonian, we have an early specimen of populist indignation over a new self-appointed elite of "great" men who claim a monopoly over religious and political power. The object of the New England Establishment, according to Bishop, was to wait until the egalitarian ardor of the Revolution had waned and then to "reduce the people to the European standard of dependence." A similar notion of a hidden aristocracy, lulling and duping the common people, re-emerges in the anti-Masonic, Jacksonian, and Populist movements. As a challenge to existing institutions and establishments, such protests provided some men with new avenues to power and prestige.

° Not to be confused with the American Protective Association.

But the very ease of launching movements of social protest created anxieties of a different kind. Anti-abolitionists were chiefly alarmed by the ability of the American Anti-Slavery Society to print and disseminate unprecedented numbers of cheap publications. Improvements in printing technology and in advertising and propaganda techniques increasingly raised the specter of manipulated opinion and of the sudden emergence of new pressure groups. Since the American identity has so often been defined as a state of mind which any immigrant is free to adopt, it also followed that traditional values and loyalties could be lightly discarded in the competitive marketplace of ideas. The fourth theme, then, concerns the problem of assuring public consensus and solidarity in the face of uncontrolled, irreverent, and questioning media, and among a people who value novelty and experimentation. Often this conflict came down to an attempt by established leaders to defend their local authority against the encroaching influence of national media. And local lawyers, political bosses, and clergymen have often interpreted nationalizing pressures in terms of conspiracy. We can see this pattern, for example, in local efforts to discredit abolitionist literature and in modern reactionary attacks on the alleged left-wing conspiracy of the eastern publishers and journalists.

A fifth idea that reappears in many of the selections is the fear of betraying the priceless heritage won by the Founding Fathers. As phrased by Frederick Robinson, an ardent Jacksonian (1834), the Founders had purchased political rights and an equality of privileges which their descendants had neither the intelligence to appreciate nor the courage to protect. Lyman Beecher feared that "corrupting abundance" had sapped the Americans' will to pursue their great destiny. Henry Ford's *Dearborn Independent* accused the Jews of conspiring to "frivolize" the minds and tastes of the people by intoxicating them with changing styles and fashions and by enticing them to buy vain luxuries. The discovery of a national conspiracy could counteract the corrosive effects of affluence and lethargy by allowing the people to re-enact the primal drama of patriotism. It is hardly accidental that, in 1799, Fisher Ames called for a new generation of Minute Men to rise against the Jacobins, or that the same image was invoked by the anti-Masons, anti-abolitionists, and anti-Catholics. In the 1880's a secret group of New York City Minute Men plotted against the Papists. And of course in our own time the heart-stirring name has been appropriated by militant right-wing extremists.

The desire to recover an imperiled heritage through self-purification is related to the final theme, which is the belief in America's mission to emancipate mankind. Many of the selections in this book reveal a striking correlation between fears of conspiracy and American aspirations to national greatness. It is almost as if the nation's grandiose mission to liberate and democratize the world could only be confirmed by proving the maliciousness and power of a clandestine enemy. We may recall similar patterns in the history of religion as well as in more recent secular quests for the millennium. A transcendent cause that demands communal commitment and self-sacrifice may well require a satanic force against which to struggle, whether it is the devil himself, infidels and heretics, or "bourgeois deviationists" who have been unfaithful to the words of Chairman Mao. Of course this similarity of pattern does not imply a similarity in values or aspirations. For Americans, the sense of an endangered national mission has been historically related to ambivalent attitudes toward the Old World. America's special mission had originated in an escape from Old World oppression. Not only did a flow of immigrants keep alive the notion of America as a land of unlimited hope and opportunity, but the discouraging history of European revolutions reinforced the image of the Old World as a place where liberty was always lost. America could fulfill her high destiny of ultimately saving the world only by remaining apart from the world and by somehow avoiding the cycle of declension, corruption, disunity, and dictatorship that seemed to be the fate of all other peoples. This central concept re-emerges in a variety of forms from Jeffersonian democrats and religious revivalists to Josiah Strong, the Populists, and Senator Joseph McCarthy.

Our final theme has clearly brought us back to the first theme of a hostile foreign power, and obviously no scheme of classification can do justice to such complex interrelationships of ideas. We can do no more here than point to certain general configurations and problems of interpretation. Specific background and questions of interpretation will be presented in the headnotes and introductions to each section.

A final word should be said on the process of selection. Since the main purpose of this book is to use images of conspiracy and subversion as a means of studying American tensions, values, and expectations, I have generally excluded conspiracies, real or imaginary, that were of little ideological significance. The conspiracies of Aaron Burr, of the Molly Maguires, or President Grant's cronies, or even of criminal associations from John A. Murrell's river pirates to the Cosa Nostra, for example, have offered little challenge to America's institutions and way of life. Unlike the Communists, the Slave Power, or the republican Illuminati, such conspirators have not been accused of plotting the total corruption of moral values and the overthrow of the entire social order. Their ambitions were personal, and they were content with personal profit.

While some of the writers included are intelligent and others are stupid, some are well informed and others are ignorant, collectively they represent relatively "pure" examples of the conspiratorial mentality. Similar patterns of thought have occasionally been mixed with the rhetoric of party politics. But the viability of the American political system might be jeopardized if there were not strict limits on accusing one's opponents of subversion. The paranoid style has frequently arisen as a reaction *against* the expediency and compromise of conventional politics. But a mixture of the two is inherently unstable, since a crusade against subversion, if contrived for purely political purposes, usually ends up in a compromise with the supposed subversives.

In editing these documents I have tried to preserve the original spelling and punctuation except for obvious typographical errors and occasional minor changes in the interest of clarity.

D. B. D.

THE FEAR OF CONSPIRACY

IMAGES OF UN-AMERICAN SUBVERSION FROM THE REVOLUTION TO THE PRESENT

1. Orientation and Theory

ALTHOUGH HISTORIANS have devoted considerable attention
to various nativist movements against religious and ethnic minorities,
relatively little has been written on the more generalized and sometimes related phenomenon of crusades against supposedly subversive,
conspiratorial forces. It needs to be re-emphasized that Americans
have not been unique in their tendency to perceive conspiracies
where none exist or to exaggerate the power and danger of actual
conspiratorial groups. Indeed, in recent years Europeans have shown
themselves more prone to assume immediately and without evidence
that any political assassination *must* be the product of a far-reaching
plot. But if Americans have often expressed faith in the ability of
their political institutions to withstand fortuitous calamities, they
have also exhibited a profound sense of insecurity regarding the
strength of public virtue and the permanence of their traditional way
of life. Perhaps because American identity has usually been defined
as a state of mind rather than as a familial heritage, Americans have
been susceptible to the fear that their neighbors' minds were being
seduced by the devil, that their free institutions were being infiltrated
by enemies in disguise, and that a hidden society, opposed to every
principle of democracy and Christianity, was growing within the very
tissues of the existing social order. The image of a vast subversive
force subtly appropriating and transforming American institutions
might well reflect anxiety over the problem of preserving a consistent
sense of national identity in the face of rapid social change. In other
words, it is possible that men might find reassurance in blaming un-
settling change on a secret, satanic force and trying to restore a sense
of communal solidarity by a struggle against internal enemies. While
such theories are frankly speculative in character, they provide one
means of approaching a neglected but highly significant aspect of
American thought and behavior. The following selections provide an
overview of the movements against subversion which have recurred
throughout American history. They also point to concerns and themes
common to these movements, and suggest some of the social and ideological functions of alarmist literature.

The Paranoid Style
in American Politics

RICHARD HOFSTADTER

Richard Hofstadter, who was DeWitt Clinton Professor of American History at Columbia University, was one of the first scholars to draw attention to the periodic obsession with conspiracy and subversion in American political life. His delineation of the "paranoid style," a term which he carefully defined and qualified, was first presented in 1963 as a Herbert Spencer Lecture at Oxford and then appeared as an article in Harper's *Magazine before being published in 1965 as the title essay of a book.*

Although American political life has rarely been touched by the most acute varieties of class conflict, it has served again and again as an arena for uncommonly angry minds. Today this fact is most evident on the extreme right wing, which has shown, particularly in the Goldwater movement, how much political leverage can be got out of the animosities and passions of a small minority. Behind such movements there is a style of mind, not always right-wing in its affiliations, that has a long and varied history. I call it the paranoid style simply because no other word adequately evokes the qualities of heated exaggeration, suspiciousness, and conspiratorial fantasy that I have in mind. In using the expression "paranoid style," I am not speaking in a clinical sense, but borrowing a clinical term for other purposes. I have neither the competence nor the desire to classify any figures of the past or present as certifiable lunatics. In fact, the idea of the paranoid style would have little contemporary relevance or historical value if it were applied only to people with profoundly disturbed minds. It is the use of paranoid modes of expression by more or less normal people that makes the phenomenon significant.

When I speak of the paranoid style, I use the term much as a historian of art might speak of the baroque or the mannerist style. It is, above all, a way of seeing the world and of expressing oneself. Webster defines paranoia, the clinical entity, as a chronic mental disorder characterized by systematized delusions of persecution and of one's own greatness. In the paranoid style, as I conceive it, the feeling of persecution is central, and it is indeed systematized in grandiose theories of conspiracy. But there is a vital difference between the paranoid spokesman in politics and the clinical paranoiac: although they both tend to be overheated, oversuspicious, overaggressive, grandiose, and apocalyptic in expression, the clinical paranoid sees the hostile and conspiratorial world in which he feels himself to be living as directed specifically *against him;* whereas the spokesman of the paranoid style finds it directed against a nation, a culture, a way of life whose fate affects not himself alone but millions of others. Insofar as he does not usually see himself singled out as the individual victim of a personal conspiracy, he is somewhat more rational and much more disinterested. His sense that his political passions are unselfish and patriotic, in fact, goes far to intensify his feeling of righteousness and his moral indignation.

Of course, the term "paranoid style" is pejorative, and it is meant to be; the paranoid style has a greater affinity for bad causes than good. But nothing entirely prevents a sound program or a sound issue from being advocated in the paranoid style, and it is admittedly impossible to settle the merits of an argument because we think we hear in its presentation the characteristic paranoid accents. Style has to do with the way in which ideas are believed and advocated rather than with the truth or falsity of their content. . . .

A distorted style is, then, a possible signal that may alert us to a distorted judgment, just as in art an ugly style is a cue to fundamental defects of taste. What interests me here is the possibility of using political rhetoric to get at political pathology. One of the most impressive facts about the paranoid style, in this connection, is that it represents an old and recurrent mode of expression in our public life which has frequently been linked with movements of suspicious discontent and whose content remains much the same even when it is adopted by men of distinctly different purposes. Our experience suggests too that, while it comes in waves of different intensity, it appears to be all but ineradicable.

I choose American history to illustrate the paranoid style only because I happen to be an Americanist, and it is for me a choice of convenience. But the phenomenon is no more limited to American experience than it is to our contemporaries. Notions about an all-embracing conspiracy on the part of Jesuits or Freemasons, international capitalists, international Jews, or Communists are familiar phenomena in many countries throughout modern history. One need only think of the response to President Kennedy's assassination in Europe to be reminded that Americans have no monopoly of the gift for paranoid improvisation. More important, the single case in modern history in which one might say that the paranoid style has had a consummatory triumph occurred not in the United States but in Germany. It is a common ingredient of fascism, and of frustrated nationalisms, though it appeals to many who are hardly fascists and it can frequently be seen in the left-wing press. The famous Stalin purge trials incorporated, in a supposedly juridical form, a wildly imaginative and devastating exercise in the paranoid style. In America it has been the preferred style only of *minority* movements. It can be argued, of course, that certain features of our history have given the paranoid style more scope and force among us than it has had in many other countries of the Western world. My intention here, however, is not to make such comparative judgments but simply to establish the reality of the style and to illustrate its frequent historical recurrence.

We may begin with a few American examples. Here is Senator McCarthy, speaking in June 1951 about the parlous situation of the United States:

> How can we account for our present situation unless we believe that men high in this government are concerting to deliver us to disaster? This must be the product of a great conspiracy, a conspiracy on a scale so immense as to dwarf any previous such venture in the history of man. A conspiracy of infamy so black that, when it is finally exposed, its principals shall be forever deserving of the maledictions of all honest men. . . . What can be made of this unbroken series of decisions and acts contributing to the strategy of defeat? They cannot be attributed to incompetence. . . . The laws of probability would dictate that part of . . . [the] decisions would serve this country's interest.[1]

Now let us turn back fifty years to a manifesto signed in 1895 by a number of leaders of the Populist party:

> As early as 1865–66 a conspiracy was entered into between the gold gamblers of Europe and America. . . . For nearly thirty years these con-

[1] *Congressional Record*, 82nd Cong., 1st sess. (June 14, 1951), p. 6602; for a similar passage, see McCarthy's book *McCarthyism: The Fight for America* (New York, 1952), p. 2.

spirators have kept the people quarreling over less important matters, while they have pursued with unrelenting zeal their one central purpose. . . . Every device of treachery, every resource of statecraft, and every artifice known to the secret cabals of the international gold ring are being made use of to deal a blow to the prosperity of the people and the financial and commercial independence of the country.[2]

Next, a Texas newspaper article of 1855:

. . . It is a notorious fact that the Monarchs of Europe and the Pope of Rome are at this very moment plotting our destruction and threatening the extinction of our political, civil, and religious institutions. We have the best reasons for believing that corruption has found its way into our Executive Chamber, and that our Executive head is tainted with the infectious venom of Catholicism. . . . The Pope has recently sent his ambassador of state to this country on a secret commission, the effect of which is an extraordinary boldness of the Catholic Church throughout the United States. . . . These minions of the Pope are boldly insulting our Senators; reprimanding our Statesmen; propagating the adulterous union of Church and state; abusing with foul calumny all governments but Catholic; and spewing out the bitterest execrations on all Protestantism. The Catholics in the United States receive from abroad more than $200,000 annually for the propagation of their creed. Add to this the vast revenue collected here. . . .[3]

Finally, this from a sermon preached in Massachusetts in 1798:

Secret and systematic means have been adopted and pursued, with zeal and activity, by wicked and artful men, in foreign countries, to undermine the foundations of this Religion [Christianity], and to overthrow its Altars, and thus to deprive the world of its benign influence on society. . . . These impious conspirators and philosophists have completely effected their purposes in a large portion of Europe, and boast of their means of accomplishing their plans in all parts of Christendom, glory in the certainty of their success, and set opposition at defiance. . . .[4]

[2] The manifesto is reprinted in Frank McVey, "The Populist Movement," *Economic Studies*, I (August 1896), 201–202; the platform of the Populist party for 1892 asserts: "A vast conspiracy against mankind has been organized on two continents, and it is rapidly taking possession of the world. If not met and overthrown at once, it forbodes terrible social convulsions, the destruction of civilization, or the establishment of an absolute despotism."

[3] Quoted by Sister Paul of the Cross McGrath, *Political Nativism in Texas, 1825–1860* (Washington, 1930), pp. 114–115, from *Texas State Times*, September 15, 1855.

[4] Jedidiah Morse, *A Sermon Preached at Charlestown, November 29, 1798 . . .* (Worcester, Mass., 1799), pp. 20–21.

These quotations, taken from intervals of half a century, give the keynote of the style of thought. In the history of the United States one finds it, for example, in the anti-Masonic movement, the nativist and anti-Catholic movement, in certain spokesmen for abolitionism who regarded the United States as being in the grip of a slaveholders' conspiracy, in many writers alarmed by Mormonism, in some Greenback and Populist writers who constructed a great conspiracy of international bankers, in the exposure of a munitions makers' conspiracy of the First World War, in the popular left-wing press, in the contemporary American right wing, and on both sides of the race controversy today, among White Citizens Councils and Black Muslims. . . .

Let us now abstract the basic elements in the paranoid style. The central image is that of a vast and sinister conspiracy, a gigantic and yet subtle machinery of influence set in motion to undermine and destroy a way of life. One may object that there *are* conspiratorial acts in history, and there is nothing paranoid about taking note of them. This is true. All political behavior requires strategy, many strategic acts depend for their effect upon a period of secrecy, and anything that is secret may be described, often with but little exaggeration, as conspiratorial. The distinguishing thing about the paranoid style is not that its exponents see conspiracies or plots here and there in history, but that they regard a "vast" or "gigantic" conspiracy as *the motive force* in historical events. History *is* a conspiracy, set in motion by demonic forces of almost transcendent power, and what is felt to be needed to defeat it is not the usual methods of political give-and-take, but an all-out crusade. The paranoid spokesman sees the fate of this conspiracy in apocalyptic terms—he traffics in the birth and death of whole worlds, whole political orders, whole systems of human values. He is always manning the barricades of civilization. He constantly lives at a turning point: it is now or never in organizing resistance to conspiracy. Time is forever just running out. Like religious millenarians, he expresses the anxiety of those who are living through the last days and he is sometimes disposed to set a date for the apocalypse. . . .

As a member of the avant-garde who is capable of perceiving the conspiracy before it is fully obvious to an as yet unaroused public, the paranoid is a militant leader. He does not see social conflict as something to be mediated and compromised, in the manner of the working politician. Since what is at stake is always a conflict between absolute good and absolute evil, the quality needed is not a willingness to compromise but the will to fight things out to a finish. Nothing but complete victory will do. Since the enemy is thought of as being totally evil and totally unappeasable, he must be totally eliminated—if not from the world, at least from the theater of operations to which the paranoid directs his attention. This demand for unqualified victories leads to the formulation of hopelessly demanding and unrealistic goals, and since these goals are not even remotely attainable, failure constantly heightens the paranoid's frustration. Even partial success leaves him with the same sense of powerlessness with which he began, and this in turn only strengthens his awareness of the vast and terrifying quality of the enemy he opposes. . . .

A final aspect of the paranoid style is related to that quality of pedantry to which I have already referred. One of the impressive things about paranoid literature is precisely the elaborate concern with demonstration it almost invariably shows. One should not be misled by the fantastic conclusions that are so characteristic of this political style into imagining that it is not, so to speak, argued out along factual lines. The very fantastic character of its conclusions leads to heroic strivings for "evidence" to prove that the unbelievable is the only thing that can be believed. Of course, there are highbrow, lowbrow, and middlebrow paranoids, as there are likely to be in any political tendency, and paranoid movements from the Middle Ages onward have had a magnetic attraction for demi-intellectuals. But respectable paranoid literature not only starts from certain moral commitments that can be justified to many non-paranoids but also carefully and all but obsessively accumulates "evidence." Paranoid writing begins with certain defensible judgments. There *was* something to be said for the anti-Masons. After all, a secret society composed of influential men bound by special obligations could conceivably pose some kind of threat to the civil order in which they were suspended. There was also something to be said for the Protestant principles of individuality and freedom, as well as for the nativist desire to develop in North America a homogeneous civilization. Again, in our time innumerable decisions of the Second World War and the cold war can be faulted, and it is easy for the suspicious to believe that such decisions are not simply the mistakes of well-meaning men but the plans of traitors.

The typical procedure of the higher paranoid scholarship is to start with such defensible assumptions and with a careful accumulation of facts, or at least of what appear to be facts, and to marshal these facts toward an overwhelming "proof" of the particular conspiracy that is to be established. It is nothing if not coherent—in fact, the paranoid mentality is far more coherent than the real world, since it leaves no room for mistakes, failures, or ambiguities. It is, if not wholly rational, at least intensely rationalistic; it believes that it is up against an enemy who is as infallibly rational as he is totally evil, and it seeks to match his imputed total competence with its own, leaving nothing unexplained and comprehending all of reality in one over-reaching, consistent theory. It is nothing if not "scholarly" in technique. . . .

What distinguishes the paranoid style is not, then, the absence of verifiable facts (though it is occasionally true that in his extravagant passion for facts the paranoid occasionally manufactures them), but rather the curious leap in imagination that is always made at some critical point in the recital of events. . . .

Since I have drawn so heavily on American examples, I would like to emphasize again that the paranoid style is an international phenomenon. Nor is it confined to modern times. Studying the millennial sects of Europe from the eleventh to the sixteenth century, Norman Cohn finds, in his brilliant book *The Pursuit of the Millennium*, a persistent psychological complex that closely resembles what I have been considering—a style made up of certain marked preoccupations and fantasies: "the megalomanic view of oneself as the Elect, wholly good, abominably persecuted yet assured of ultimate triumph; the attribution of gigantic and demonic powers to the adversary; the refusal to accept the ineluctable limitations and imperfections of human existence, such as transience, dissention, conflict, fallibility whether intellectual or moral; the obsession with inerrable prophecies . . . systematized misinterpretations, always gross and often grotesque . . . ruthlessness directed towards an end which by its very nature cannot be realised—towards a total and final solution such as cannot be attained at any actual time or in any concrete situation, but only in the timeless and autistic realm of phantasy." [5]

The recurrence of the paranoid style over a long span of time and in different places suggests that a mentality disposed to see the world in the paranoid's way may always be present in some considerable minority of the population. But the fact that movements employing the paranoid style are not constant but come in successive episodic

[5] *The Pursuit of the Millennium* (London, 1957), pp. 309–310; see also pp. 58–74.

waves suggests that the paranoid disposition is mobilized into action chiefly by social conflicts that involve ultimate schemes of values and that bring fundamental fears and hatreds, rather than negotiable interests, into political action. Catastrophe or the fear of catastrophe is most likely to elicit the syndrome of paranoid rhetoric.

In American experience, ethnic and religious conflicts, with their threat of the submergence of whole systems of values, have plainly been the major focus for militant and suspicious minds of this sort, but elsewhere class conflicts have also mobilized such energies. The paranoid tendency is aroused by a confrontation of opposed interests which are (or are felt to be) totally irreconcilable, and thus by nature not susceptible to the normal political processes of bargain and compromise. The situation becomes worse when the representatives of a particular political interest—perhaps because of the very unrealistic and unrealizable nature of their demands—cannot make themselves felt in the political process. Feeling that they have no access to political bargaining or the making of decisions, they find their original conception of the world of power as omnipotent, sinister, and malicious fully confirmed. They see only the consequences of power—and this through distorting lenses—and have little chance to observe its actual machinery.

Some Themes of Countersubversion: An Analysis of Anti-Masonic, Anti-Catholic, and Anti-Mormon Literature

DAVID BRION DAVIS

While the following article focuses on three specific movements of "countersubversion" in the mid-nineteenth century, the reconstructed images of a conspiratorial power bear a striking resemblance to earlier and later expressions of what Hofstadter terms the "paranoid style." Whether we are justi-

From David Brion Davis, "Some Themes of Countersubversion: An Analysis of Anti-Masonic, Anti-Catholic, and Anti-Mormon Literature," *The Mississippi Valley Historical Review*, XLVII (September 1960), 205–224. Copyright, 1960, by the Mississippi Valley Historical Association (now the Organization of American Historians); reprinted without footnotes by permission of the editor of the *Journal of American History*.

fied in thinking of a continuous American tradition of "countersubversion" is open to question. The reader should be alert to subtle changes in the image of the subversive enemy and to the possibility that such changes reflect the different fears, values, and aspirations of various social groups and classes.

During the second quarter of the nineteenth century, when danger of foreign invasion appeared increasingly remote, Americans were told by various respected leaders that Freemasons had infiltrated the government and had seized control of the courts, that Mormons were undermining political and economic freedom in the West, and that Roman Catholic priests, receiving instructions from Rome, had made frightening progress in a plot to subject the nation to popish despotism. This fear of internal subversion was channeled into a number of powerful countermovements which attracted wide public support. The literature produced by these movements evoked images of a great American enemy that closely resembled traditional European stereotypes of conspiracy and subversion. In Europe, however, the idea of subversion implied a threat to the established order—to the king, the Church, or the ruling aristocracy—rather than to ideals or a way of life. If free Americans borrowed their images of subversion from frightened kings and uneasy aristocrats, these images had to be shaped and blended to fit American conditions. The movements would have to come from the people, and the themes of countersubversion would be likely to reflect their fears, prejudices, hopes, and perhaps even unconscious desires.

There are obvious dangers in treating such reactions against imagined subversion as part of a single tendency or spirit of an age. Anti-Catholicism was nourished by ethnic conflict and uneasiness over immigration to the expanding cities of the Northeast; anti-Mormonism arose largely from a contest for economic and political power between western settlers and a group that voluntarily withdrew from society and claimed the undivided allegiance of its members. Anti-Masonry, on the other hand, was directed against a group thoroughly integrated in American society and did not reflect a clear division of economic, religious, or political interests. Moreover, anti-Masonry gained power in the late 1820's and soon spent its energies as it became absorbed in national politics; anti-Catholicism reached its maximum force in national politics a full generation later; anti-Mormonism, though increasing in intensity in the 1850's, became an important national issue only after the Civil War. These movements seem even more widely separated when we note that Freemasonry was traditionally associated with anti-Catholicism and that Mormonism itself absorbed considerable anti-Masonic and anti-Catholic sentiment.

Despite such obvious differences, there were certain similarities in these campaigns against subversion. All three gained widespread support in the northeastern states within the space of a generation; anti-Masonry and anti-Catholicism resulted in the sudden emergence of separate political parties; and in 1856 the new Republican party explicitly condemned the Mormons' most controversial institution. The movements of countersubversion differed markedly in historical origin, but as the image of an un-American conspiracy took form in the nativist press, in sensational exposés, in the countless fantasies of treason and mysterious criminality, the lines separating Mason, Catholic, and Mormon became almost indistinguishable. . . .

If Masons, Catholics, and Mormons bore little resemblance to one another in actuality, as imagined enemies they merged into a nearly common stereotype. Behind specious professions of philanthropy or religious sentiment, nativists [1] discerned a group of unscrupulous leaders plotting to subvert the American social order. Though rank-and-file members were not individually evil, they were blinded and corrupted by a persuasive ideology that justified treason and gross immorality in the interest of the subversive group. Trapped in the meshes of a machine-like organization, deluded by a false sense of loyalty and moral obligation, these dupes followed orders like professional soldiers and labored unknowingly to abolish free society, to enslave their fellow men, and to overthrow divine principles of law and justice. Should an occasional member free himself from bondage to superstition and fraudulent authority, he could still be disciplined by the threat of death or dreadful tortures. There were no limits to the ambitious designs of leaders equipped with such organizations. According to nativist prophets, they chose to subvert American society because control of America meant control of the world's destiny.

Some of these beliefs were common in earlier and later European interpretations of conspiracy. American images of Masonic, Catholic, and Mormon subversion were no doubt a compound of traditional myths concerning Jacobite agents, scheming Jesuits, and fanatical

[1] Though the term "nativist" is usually limited to opponents of immigration, it is used here to include anti-Masons and anti-Mormons. This seems justified in view of the fact that these alarmists saw themselves as defenders of native traditions and identified Masonry and Mormonism with forces alien to American life.

heretics, and of dark legends involving the Holy Vehme and Rosicru-
cians. What distinguished the stereotypes of Mason, Catholic, and
Mormon was the way in which they were seen to embody those traits
that were precise antitheses of American ideals. The subversive group
was essentially an inverted image of Jacksonian democracy and the
cult of the common man; as such it not only challenged the dominant
values but stimulated those suppressed needs and yearnings that are
unfulfilled in a mobile, rootless, and individualistic society. It was
therefore both frightening and fascinating.

It is well known that expansion and material progress in the Jacksonian era evoked a fervid optimism and that nationalists became in-
toxicated with visions of America's millennial glory. The simultaneous
growth of prosperity and social democracy seemed to prove that
Providence would bless a nation that allowed her citizens maximum
liberty. When each individual was left free to pursue happiness in his
own way, unhampered by the tyranny of custom or special privilege,
justice and well-being would inevitably emerge. But if a doctrine of
laissez-faire individualism seemed to promise material expansion and
prosperity, it also raised disturbing problems. As one early anti-Mormon writer expressed it: What was to prevent liberty and popular
sovereignty from sweeping away "the old landmarks of Christendom,
and the glorious old common law of our fathers"? How was the individual to preserve a sense of continuity with the past, or identify himself with a given cause or tradition? What, indeed, was to insure a
common loyalty and a fundamental unity among the people?

Such questions acquired a special urgency as economic growth intensified mobility, destroyed old ways of life, and transformed traditional symbols of status and prestige. Though most Americans took
pride in their material progress, they also expressed a yearning for reassurance and security, for unity in some cause transcending individual self-interest. This need for meaningful group activity was filled in
part by religious revivals, reform movements, and a proliferation of
fraternal orders and associations. In politics Americans tended to assume the posture of what Marvin Meyers has termed "venturesome
conservatives," mitigating their acquisitive impulses by an appeal for
unity against extraneous forces that allegedly threatened a noble heritage of republican ideals. Without abandoning a belief in progress
through laissez-faire individualism, the Jacksonians achieved a sense
of unity and righteousness by styling themselves as restorers of tradition. Perhaps no theme is so evident in the Jacksonian era as the

strained attempt to provide America with a glorious heritage and a noble destiny. With only a loose and often ephemeral attachment to places and institutions, many Americans felt a compelling need to articulate their loyalties, to prove their faith, and to demonstrate their allegiance to certain ideals and institutions. By so doing they acquired a sense of self-identity and personal direction in an otherwise rootless and shifting environment.

But was abstract nationalism sufficient to reassure a nation strained by sectional conflict, divided by an increasing number of sects and associations, and perplexed by the unexpected consequences of rapid growth? One might desire to protect the Republic against her enemies, to preserve the glorious traditions of the Founders, and to help insure continued expansion and prosperity, but first it was necessary to discover an enemy by distinguishing subversion from simple diversity. If Freemasons seemed to predominate in the economic and political life of a given area, was one's joining them shrewd business judgment or a betrayal of republican tradition? Should Maryland citizens heed the warnings of anti-Masonic itinerants, or conclude that anti-Masonry was itself a conspiracy hatched by scheming Yankees? Were Roman Catholics plotting to destroy public schools and a free press, the twin guardians of American democracy, or were they exercising democratic rights of self-expression and self-protection? Did equality of opportunity and equality before the law mean that Americans should accept the land claims of Mormons or tolerate as jurors men who "swear that they have wrought miracles and supernatural cures"? Or should one agree with the Reverend Finis Ewing that "the 'Mormons' are the common enemies of mankind and ought to be destroyed"?

Few men questioned traditional beliefs in freedom of conscience and the right of association. Yet what was to prevent "all the errors and worn out theories of the Old World, of schisms in the early Church, the monkish age and the rationalistic period," from flourishing in such salubrious air? Nativists often praised the work of benevolent societies, but they were disturbed by the thought that monstrous conspiracies might also "show kindness and patriotism, when it is necessary for their better concealment; and oftentimes do much good for the sole purpose of getting a better opportunity to do evil." When confronted by so many sects and associations, how was the patriot to distinguish the loyal from the disloyal? It was clear that mere disagreement over theology or economic policy was invalid as a test, since honest men disputed over the significance of baptism or the wisdom of protective tariffs. But neither could one rely on expressions of allegiance to common democratic principles, since subversives would cunningly profess to believe in freedom and toleration of dissent as long as they remained a powerless minority.

As nativists studied this troubling question, they discovered that most groups and denominations claimed only a partial loyalty from their members, freely subordinating themselves to the higher and more abstract demands of the Constitution, Christianity, and American public opinion. Moreover, they openly exposed their objects and activities to public scrutiny and exercised little discrimination in enlisting members. Some groups, however, dominated a larger portion of their members' lives, demanded unlimited allegiance as a condition of membership, and excluded certain activities from the gaze of a curious public.

Of all governments, said Richard Rush, ours was the one with most to fear from secret societies, since popular sovereignty by its very nature required perfect freedom of public inquiry and judgment. In a virtuous republic why should anyone fear publicity or desire to conceal activities, unless those activities were somehow contrary to the public interest? When no one could be quite sure what the public interest was, and when no one could take for granted a secure and well-defined place in the social order, it was most difficult to acknowledge legitimate spheres of privacy. Most Americans of the Jacksonian era appeared willing to tolerate diversity and even eccentricity, but when they saw themselves excluded and even barred from witnessing certain proceedings, they imagined a "mystic power" conspiring to enslave them. . . .

The distinguishing mark of Masonic, Catholic, and Mormon conspiracies was a secrecy that cloaked the members' unconditional loyalty to an autonomous body. Since the organizations had corrupted the private moral judgment of their members, Americans could not rely on the ordinary forces of progress to spread truth and enlightenment among their ranks. Yet the affairs of such organizations were not outside the jurisdiction of democratic government, for no body politic could be asked to tolerate a power that was designed to destroy it. Once the true nature of subversive groups was thoroughly understood, the alternatives were as clear as life and death. How could democracy and Catholicism coexist when, as Edward Beecher warned, "The systems are diametrically opposed: one must and will

exterminate the other"? Because Freemasons had so deeply penetrated state and national governments, only drastic remedies could
restore the nation to its democratic purity. And later, Americans
faced an "irrepressible conflict" with Mormonism, for it was said that
either free instititions or Mormon despotism must ultimately annihilate the other.

We may well ask why nativists magnified the division between unpopular minorities and the American public, so that Masons, Catholics, and Mormons seemed so menacing that they could not be
accorded the usual rights and privileges of a free society. Obviously
the literature of countersubversion reflected concrete rivalries and
conflicts of interest between competing groups, but it is important to
note that the subversive bore no racial or ethnic stigma and was not
even accused of inherent depravity. Since group membership was a
matter of intellectual and emotional loyalty, no *physical* barrier prevented a Mason, Catholic, or Mormon from apostatizing and joining
the dominant in-group, providing always that he escaped assassination from his previous masters. This suggests that countersubversion
was more than a rationale for group rivalry and was related to the
general problem of ideological unity and diversity in a free society.
When a "system of delusion" insulated members of a group from the
unifying and disciplining force of public opinion, there was no authority to command an allegiance to common principles. This was
why oaths of loyalty assumed great importance for nativists. Though
the ex-Catholic William Hogan stated repeatedly that Jesuit spies respected no oaths except those to the Church, he inconsistently told
Masons and Odd Fellows that they could prevent infiltration by requiring new members to swear they were not Catholics. It was precisely the absence of distinguishing outward traits that made the
enemy so dangerous, and true loyalty so difficult to prove.

When the images of different enemies conform to a similar pattern,
it is highly probable that this pattern reflects important tensions
within a given culture. The themes of nativist literature suggest that
its authors simplified problems of personal insecurity and adjustment
to bewildering social change by trying to unite Americans of diverse
political, religious, and economic interests against a common enemy.
Just as revivalists sought to stimulate Christian fellowship by awakening men to the horrors of sin, so nativists used apocalyptic images to
ignite human passions, destroy selfish indifference, and join patriots
in a cohesive brotherhood. Such themes were only faintly secularized.

When God saw his "lov'd Columbia" imperiled by the hideous monster of Freemasonry, He realized that only a martyr's blood could rouse the hearts of the people and save them from bondage to the Prince of Darkness. By having God will Morgan's death, this anti-Mason showed he was more concerned with national virtue and unity than with Freemasonry, which was only a providential instrument for testing republican strength. . . .

Without explicitly rejecting the philosophy of laissez-faire individualism, with its toleration of dissent and innovation, nativist literature conveyed a sense of common dedication to a noble cause and sacred tradition. Though the nation had begun with the blessings of God and with the noblest institutions known to man, the people had somehow become selfish and complacent, divided by petty disputes, and insensitive to signs of danger. In his sermons attacking such self-interest, such indifference to public concerns, and such a lack of devotion to common ideals and sentiments, the nativist revealed the true source of his anguish. Indeed, he seemed at times to recognize an almost beneficent side to subversive organizations, since they joined the nation in a glorious crusade and thus kept it from moral and social disintegration.

The exposure of subversion was a means of promoting unity, but it also served to clarify national values and provide the individual ego with a sense of high moral sanction and imputed righteousness. Nativists identified themselves repeatedly with a strangely incoherent tradition in which images of Pilgrims, Minute Men, Founding Fathers, and true Christians appeared in a confusing montage. Opposed to this heritage of stability and perfect integrity, to this society founded on the highest principles of divine and natural law, were organizations formed by the grossest frauds and impostures, and based on the wickedest impulses of human nature. Bitterly refuting Masonic claims to ancient tradition and Christian sanction, anti-Masons charged that the Order was of recent origin, that it was shaped by Jews, Jesuits, and French atheists as an engine for spreading infidelity, and that it was employed by kings and aristocrats to undermine republican institutions. If the illustrious Franklin and Washington had been duped by Masonry, this only proved how treacherous was its appeal and how subtly persuasive were its pretensions. Though the Catholic Church had an undeniable claim to tradition, nativists argued that it had originated in stupendous frauds and forgeries "in comparison with which the forgeries of Mormonism are completely thrown into the shade." Yet anti-Mormons saw an even more sinister conspiracy based on the "shrewd cunning" of Joseph Smith, who convinced gullible souls that he conversed with angels and received direct revelations from the Lord.

By emphasizing the fraudulent character of their opponents' claims, nativists sought to establish the legitimacy and just authority of American institutions. Masonic rituals, Roman Catholic sacraments, and Mormon revelations were preposterous hoaxes used to delude naïve or superstitious minds; but public schools, a free press, and jury trials were eternally valid prerequisites for a free and virtuous society.

Moreover, the finest values of an enlightened nation stood out in bold relief when contrasted with the corrupting tendencies of subversive groups. Perversion of the sexual instinct seemed inevitably to accompany religious error. Deprived of the tender affections of normal married love, shut off from the elevating sentiments of fatherhood, Catholic priests looked on women only as insensitive objects for the gratification of their frustrated desires. In similar fashion polygamy struck at the heart of a morality based on the inspiring influence of woman's affections: "It renders man coarse, tyrannical, brutal, and heartless. It deals death to all sentiments of true manhood. It enslaves and ruins woman. It crucifies every God-given feeling of her nature." Some anti-Mormons concluded that plural marriage could only have been established among foreigners who had never learned to respect women. But the more common explanation was that the false ideology of Mormonism had deadened the moral sense and liberated man's wild sexual impulse from the normal restraints of civilization. Such degradation of women and corruption of man served to highlight the importance of democratic marriage, a respect for women, and careful cultivation of the finer sensibilities.

But if nativist literature was a medium for articulating common values and exhorting individuals to transcend self-interest and join in a dedicated union against evil, it also performed a more subtle function. Why, we may ask, did nativist literature dwell so persistently on themes of brutal sadism and sexual immorality? Why did its authors describe sin in such minute details, endowing even the worst offenses of their enemies with a certain fascinating appeal?

Freemasons, it was said, could commit any crime and indulge any passion when "upon the square," and Catholics and Mormons were even less inhibited by internal moral restraints. Nativists expressed horror over this freedom from conscience and conventional morality, but they could not conceal a throbbing note of envy. What was it like to be a member of a cohesive brotherhood that casually abrogated the laws of God and man, enforcing unity and obedience with dark and mysterious powers? As nativists speculated on this question, they projected their own fears and desires into a fantasy of licentious orgies and a fearful punishments.

Such a projection of forbidden desires can be seen in the exaggeration of the stereotyped enemy's powers, which made him appear at times as a virtual superman. Catholic and Mormon leaders, never hindered by conscience or respect for traditional morality, were curiously superior to ordinary Americans in cunning, in exercising power over others, and especially in captivating gullible women. It was an ancient theme of anti-Catholic literature that friars and priests were somehow more potent and sexually attractive than married laymen, and were thus astonishingly successful at seducing supposedly virtuous wives. Americans were cautioned repeatedly that no priest recognized Protestant marriages as valid, and might consider any wife legitimate prey. . . .

While nativists affirmed their faith in Protestant monogamy, they obviously took pleasure in imagining the variety of sexual experience supposedly available to their enemies. By picturing themselves exposed to similar temptations, they assumed they could know how priests and Mormons actually sinned. Imagine, said innumerable anti-Catholic writers, a beautiful young woman kneeling before an ardent young priest in a deserted room. As she confesses, he leans over, looking into her eyes, until their heads are nearly touching. Day after day she reveals to him her innermost secrets, secrets she would not think of unveiling to her parents, her dearest friends, or even her suitor. By skillful questioning the priest fills her mind with immodest and even sensual ideas, "until this wretch has worked up her passions to a tension almost snapping, and then becomes his easy prey." How could any man resist such provocative temptations, and how could any girl's virtue withstand such a test?

We should recall that this literature was written in a period of increasing anxiety and uncertainty over sexual values and the proper role of woman. As ministers and journalists pointed with alarm at the spread of prostitution, the incidence of divorce, and the lax and hypocritical morality of the growing cities, a discussion of licentious subversives offered a convenient means for the projection of guilt as well as desire. The sins of individuals, or of the nation as a whole, could be pushed off upon the shoulders of the enemy and there punished in righteous anger. . . .

Though the enemy's sexual freedom might at first seem enticing, it was always made repugnant in the end by associations with perversion or brutal cruelty. Both Catholics and Mormons were accused of practicing nearly every form of incest. The persistent emphasis on this theme might indicate deep-rooted feelings of fear and guilt, but it also helped demonstrate, on a more objective level, the loathsome consequences of unrestrained lust. Sheer brutality and a delight in human suffering were supposed to be the even more horrible results of sexual depravity. Masons disemboweled or slit the throats of their victims; Catholics cut unborn infants from their mothers' wombs and threw them to the dogs before their parents' eyes; Mormons raped and lashed recalcitrant women, or seared their mouths with red-hot irons. This obsession with details of sadism, which reached pathological proportions in much of the literature, showed a furious determination to purge the enemy of every admirable quality. The imagined enemy might serve at first as an outlet for forbidden desires, but nativist authors escaped from guilt by finally making him an agent of unmitigated aggression. In such a role the subversive seemed to deserve both righteous anger and the most terrible punishments.

The nativist escape from guilt was more clearly revealed in the themes of confession and conversion. For most American Protestants the crucial step in anyone's life was a profession of true faith resulting from a genuine religious experience. Only when a man became conscious of his inner guilt, when he struggled against the temptations of Satan, could he prepare his soul for the infusion of the regenerative spirit. Those most deeply involved in sin often made the most dramatic conversions. It is not surprising that conversion to nativism followed the same pattern, since nativists sought unity and moral certainty in the regenerative spirit of nationalism. Men who had been associated in some way with un-American conspiracies were not only capable of spectacular confessions of guilt, but were best equipped to expose the insidious work of supposedly harmless organizations. Even those who lacked such an exciting history of corruption usually made some confession of guilt, though it might involve only a previous indifference to subversive groups. Like ardent Christians, nativists searched in their own experiences for the meanings of sin, delusion, awakening to truth, and liberation from spiritual bondage. These personal confessions proved that one had recognized and conquered evil, and also served as ritual cleansings preparatory to full acceptance in a group of dedicated patriots.

Anti-Masons were perhaps the ones most given to confessions of guilt and most alert to subtle distinctions of loyalty and disloyalty. Many leaders of this movement, expressing guilt over their own "shameful experience and knowledge" of Masonry, felt a compelling obligation to exhort their former associates to "come out, and be separate from masonic abominations." Even when an anti-Mason could say with John Quincy Adams that "I am not, never was, and never shall be a Freemason," he would often admit that he had once admired the Order, or had even considered applying for admission. . . .

Such self-dramatization reached extravagant heights in the ranting confessions of many apostate Catholics and Mormons. Maria Monk and her various imitators told of shocking encounters with sin in its most sensational forms, of bondage to vice and superstition, and of melodramatic escapes from popish despotism. A host of "ex-Mormon wives" described their gradual recognition of Mormon frauds and iniquities, the anguish and misery of plural marriage, and their breathtaking flights over deserts or mountains. The female apostate was especially vulnerable to vengeful retaliation, since she could easily be kidnapped by crafty priests and nuns, or dreadfully punished by Brigham Young's Destroying Angels. At the very least, her reputation could be smirched by foul lies and insinuations. But her willingness to risk honor and life for the sake of her country and for the dignity of all womankind was eloquent proof of her redemption. What man could be assured of so noble a role?

The apostate's pose sometimes assumed paranoid dimensions. William Hogan warned that only the former priest could properly gauge the Catholic threat to American liberties and saw himself as providentially appointed to save his Protestant countrymen. "For twenty years," he wrote, "I have warned them of approaching danger, but their politicians were deaf, and their Protestant theologians remained religiously coiled up in fancied security, overrating their own powers and undervaluing that of Papists." Pursued by vengeful Jesuits, denounced and calumniated for alleged crimes, Hogan pictured imself single-handedly defending American freedom: "No one, before me, dared to encounter their scurrilous abuse. I resolved to silence them; and I have done so. The very mention of my name is a terror to them now." After surviving the worst of Catholic persecution, Hogan claimed to have at last aroused his countrymen and to have reduced the hierarchy to abject terror.

As the nativist searched for participation in a noble cause, for unity in a group sanctioned by tradition and authority, he professed a belief in democracy and equal rights. Yet in his very zeal for freedom he curiously assumed many of the characteristics of the imagined enemy. By condemning the subversive's fanatical allegiance to an ideology, he affirmed a similarly uncritical acceptance of a different ideology; by attacking the subversive's intolerance of dissent, he worked to eliminate dissent and diversity of opinion; by censuring the subversive for alleged licentiousness, he engaged in sensual fantasies; by criticizing the subversive's loyalty to an organization, he sought to prove his unconditional loyalty to the established order. The nativist moved even further in the direction of his enemies when he formed tightly knit societies and parties which were often secret and which subordinated the individual to the single purpose of the group. Though the nativists generally agreed that the worst evil of subversives was their subordination of means to ends, they themselves recommend the most radical means to purge the nation of troublesome groups and to enforce unquestioned loyalty to the state.

In his image of an evil group conspiring against the nation's welfare, and in his vision of a glorious millennium that was to dawn after the enemy's defeat, the nativist found satisfaction for many desires. His own interests became legitimate and dignified by fusion with the national interest, and various opponents became loosely associated with the un-American conspiracy. Thus Freemasonry in New York State was linked in the nativist mind with economic and political interests that were thought to discriminate against certain groups and regions; southerners imagined a union of abolitionists and Catholics to promote unrest and rebellion among slaves; gentile businessmen in Utah merged anti-Mormonism with plans for exploiting mines and lands.

Then too the nativist could style himself as a restorer of the past, as a defender of a stable order against disturbing changes, and at the same time proclaim his faith in future progress. By focusing his attention on the imaginary threat of a secret conspiracy, he found an outlet for many irrational impulses, yet professed his loyalty to the ideals of equal rights and government by law. He paid lip service to the doctrine of laissez-faire individualism, but preached selfless dedication to a transcendent cause. The imposing threat of subversion justified a group loyalty and subordination of the individual that would otherwise have been unacceptable. In a rootless environment shaken by bewildering social change the nativist found unity and meaning by conspiring against imaginary conspiracies.

2. Conspiracy in the American Revolution (1763–1783)

HISTORIANS HAVE generally been content to treat the American Revolution as a conflict with economic, political, social, and constitutional dimensions, and have tended to dismiss as "mere rhetoric," the more extreme fears and accusations of the colonists. Yet as Bernard Bailyn has recently shown, in his *Ideological Origins of the American Revolution,* the Americans had inherited a Whig interpretation of British history which largely hinged on the concept of conspiracy. Thus the Glorious Revolution of 1688 was thought to have saved British liberty from the plots of the Stuart royal family and their Catholic (and French) allies; the Revolution of 1688 had then been betrayed by scheming factions within Parliament. By the 1760's American colonists were throughly familiar with the idea that seemingly innocuous and unrelated acts of legislation might be parts of a systematic plan to subvert traditional liberties and concentrate power in the hands of an aristocratic oligarchy. Innumerable sermons and pamphlets warned of the slavery that would inevitably follow if the first encroachments on freedom were not successfully resisted. In reading the protest literature of the Revolutionary era, one is struck by the far-reaching implications of the belief that the nation's liberty, its very existence, had depended on the exposure of a conspiratorial plot. Is it possible that the circumstances of the Revolution conditioned Americans to think of resistance to a dark subversive force as the essential ingredient of their national identity?

A Note on Conspiracy

BERNARD BAILYN

Bernard Bailyn, a professor of history at Harvard University, has argued that the idea of political conspiracy was taken with deadly seriousness and

Reprinted, without most of the footnotes, by permission of the publishers from pp. 144, 152, 156–159 of Bernard Bailyn, *The Ideological Origins of the Ameri-*

played a crucial ideological role in the American Revolution. He shows that both Englishmen and Americans were susceptible to suspicions of conspiracy, and that such suspicions were not unreasonable in the light of their fragmentary knowledge and the assumptions of traditional political theory.

. . . The conviction on the part of the Revolutionary leaders that they were faced with a deliberate conspiracy to destroy the balance of the constitution and eliminate their freedom had deep and widespread roots—roots elaborately embedded in Anglo-American political culture. How far back in time one may trace these roots it is difficult to say, but I have attempted . . . to show in considerable detail elsewhere [1] that the configuration of attitudes and ideas that would constitute the Revolutionary ideology was present a half century before there was an actual Revolution, and that among the dominant elements in this pattern were the fear of corruption—of its anticonstitutional destructiveness—and of the menace of a ministerial conspiracy. At the very first signs of conflict between the colonies and the administration in the early 1760's the question of motivation was openly broached and the imputation of secret purposes discussed. Early in the controversy antiadministration leaders like Oxenbridge Thacher could only "suppose" for the sake of discussion "that no design is formed to enslave them," while pro-administration partisans, like Martin Howard, Jr., were forced to refute the charge of design. To be sure, the conviction that the colonies, and England itself, were faced with a deliberate, anti-libertarian design grew most quickly where the polarization of politics was most extreme and where radical leaders were least inhibited in expressing and reinforcing general apprehensions. But in some degree it was present everywhere; it was almost universally shared by sympathizers of the American cause. The views of John Dickinson are particularly interesting, not merely because, though the most cautious and reluctant of Revolutionary leaders, he so forcefully conveyed the idea of conspiracy, but because he understood so well the psychological and political effects of thinking in precisely these conspiratorial terms. Reviewing the crisis of Charles I's reign, he pointed out that

acts that might *by themselves* have been upon many considerations excused or extenuated derived a contagious malignancy and odium from other acts

can Revolution (Cambridge, Mass.: The Belknap Press of Harvard University Press), copyright, 1967, by the President and Fellows of Harvard College.
    [1] *The Origins of American Politics* (N.Y., 1968).

with which they were connected. They were not regarded according to the simple force of each but as parts of a system of oppression. Every one, therefore, however small in itself, became alarming as an additional evidence of tyrannical designs. It was in vain for prudent and moderate men to insist that there was no necessity to abolish royalty. Nothing less than the utter destruction of the monarchy could satisfy those who *had* suffered and thought they had reason to believe they always *should* suffer under it. The consequences of these mutual distrusts are well known.

The explosion of long-smoldering fears of ministerial conspiracy was by no means an exclusively American phenomenon. It was experienced in England too, in a variety of ways, by a wide range of the English political public. Under George III, George Rudé has pointed out, it was

widely believed . . . that the influence of the Crown was being used to staff the administration with new Favourites and "King's Friends," who formed a secret Closet party, beyond the control of Parliament and guided behind the scenes by the sinister combination of the Earl of Bute (who had resigned office in 1763) and the Princess Dowager of Wales. Opponents of the new system talked darkly of a repetition of "the end of Charles II's reign"—and such talk was not confined to the circles of the Duke of Newcastle and others, who might be inclined to identify the eclipse of their own public authority with that of the national interest.

Such expressions, Rudé concludes, "were common currency and abound throughout this period both in the press, in Burke's *Thoughts on the Present Discontents* (1770), in personal correspondence, pamphlet literature and speeches in Parliament."[2] Burke's *Thoughts* is particularly relevant to the American situation, for the apprehension that dominates that piece is in essence interchangeable with that of innumerable Revolutionary writers. Its argument that Parliament was on the brink of falling "under the control of an unscrupulous gang of would-be despots" who would destroy the constitution "was sufficiently widely believed," Ian Christie has written, "to give momentum in due course to a radical movement in the metropolis."[3] The specific identification in *Thoughts* of the conspiratorial cabal at work was distinctively Burke's, but those who most vehemently disagreed with him about the source and nature of the conspiracy were no less convinced that a conspiratorial cabal of some sort was in fact at work. . . .

[2] George Rudé, *Wilkes and Liberty* (Oxford, 1962), p. 186.
[3] Ian R. Christie, *Wilkes, Wyvill and Reform* (London, 1962), p. 32. . . .

Not everyone, of course, even within opposition circles, agreed that there was a deliberate design to overthrow the balance of the constitution; fewer still agreed with the republican radicals that the Coercive Acts were intended to "enslave America; and the same minister who means to enslave them would, if he had an opportunity, enslave England." Yet Lord Dartmouth felt it necessary to refute that charge specifically, and while it is true, as Christie has explained, that "abundant evidence now available about the activities of court and government enables historians to dismiss this fear as a chimera," it is nevertheless also true that there was a "contemporary belief in such a threat," a belief that was associated with the American crisis and that proved to be "a powerful stimulus to demands for reform" in English domestic affairs. . . .

The opponents of the Revolution—the administration itself—were as convinced as were the leaders of the Revolutionary movement that they were themselves the victims of conspiratorial designs. Officials in the colonies, and their superiors in England, were persuaded as the crisis deepened that they were confronted by an active conspiracy of intriguing men whose professions masked their true intentions. As early as 1760 Governor Bernard of Massachusetts had concluded that a "faction" had organized a conspiracy against the customs administration, and by the end of the decade he and others in similar positions (including that "arch-conspirator" Thomas Hutchinson) had little doubt that at the root of all the trouble in the colonies was the maneuvering of a secret, power-hungry cabal that professed loyalty to England while assiduously working to destroy the bonds of authority and force a rupture between England and her colonies.

The charge was quickly echoed in England. The Massachusetts Convention of 1768 elicited from the House of Lords resolutions based on the belief that "wicked and designing men" in the colonies were "evidently manifesting a design . . . to set up a new and unconstitutional authority independent of the crown of England." Such dangerous charges, tantamount to treason but objectively indistinguishable from faction—which was itself, in eighteenth-century terms, merely the superlative form of party—had been a source of concern in the colonies since the start of the controversy. Under Grenville, Arthur Lee wrote, "every expression of discontent . . . was imputed to a desire in those colonies to dissolve all connection with Britain; every tumult here was inflamed into rebellion." The fear that colonial leaders nursed secret ambitions that they masked, with greater or lesser success, by continuing professions of loyalty grew as the crisis deepened. If in 1771 Hutchinson, an equal with his arch-enemies the Adamses in detecting secret purposes behind open professions, could report with relief that "the faction in this province against the government is dying," he still felt it necessary to add "but it dies hard." After the Tea Party such cautious optimism faded, and officials confirmed once and for all their belief that malevolent factions were implacably at work seeking to satisfy hidden ambitions and to destroy the ties to England. . . .

The accusations of conspiratorial designs did not cease with the pamphlet series touched off by the Declaration [of Independence], nor even with the American successes in battle. They merely shifted their forms, and began a process of adaptation that has allowed them to survive into our own time. Just as radical pamphleteers in England, patriot historians in America, and such Whig leaders as the younger Pitt continued after the war to blame the Revolution on the deliberate malevolence of the administrations of the 1760's and 1770's, so loyalists like Galloway and Thomas Jones continued to "expose" the Americans' conspiracy; continued to argue that no error had been committed by the government of George III in not conceding more to America since the colonists had been secretly determined from the start to cast off their dependence upon England; continued too to link the rebels with opposition factions in England; and began, in the nadir of military defeat, darkly to suggest that the strangely defeated commander in chief, Sir William Howe, was himself not above suspicion of secret collaboration with the faction that had carried out so successfully the long-planned design of independence.

These wartime and postwar accusations were both an end and a beginning—an end of the main phase of the ideological Revolution and the beginning of its transmutation into historiography. Charges of conspiratorial design settled easily into a structure of historical interpretation, on the one hand by Hutchinson, in the manuscript third volume of his *History of . . . Massachusetts-Bay* (published 1828); by Peter Oliver, in his frenzied *Origin & Progress of the American Rebellion* (1781, published 1961); by Thomas Jones, in his *History of New York during the Revolutionary War* (1780–1790, published 1879); by Jonathan Boucher, in the book-length Introduction of his *View of the Causes and Consequences of the American Revolution* (1797);—and on the other hand by Mercy Otis Warren, in her three-volume *History of the . . . American Revolution* (1805); by David

Ramsay, in his *History of the American Revolution* (1789); and by patriot historians of individual states: Belknap, Burk, Trumbull, Ramsay. These are the histories of participants, or near-participants: heroic histories, highly personified and highly moral, in which the conspiratorial arguments propounded during the Revolution are the essential stuff of explanation. These views, caricatured and mythologized in such immortal potboilers as Weems' *Washington*, survived almost unaltered through the next generation—survived, indeed, through the next two generations—to enter in a new guise into the assumptions of twentieth-century scholarship. The "progressive" historians of the early twentieth century and their successors of the post-World War I era adopted unknowingly the Tory interpretation in writing off the Revolutionary leaders' professed fears of "slavery" and of conspiratorial designs as what by then had come to be known as propaganda. They implied when they did not state explicitly that these extravagant, seemingly paranoiac fears were deliberately devised for the purpose of controlling the minds of a presumably passive populace in order to accomplish predetermined ends—Independence and in many cases personal advancement—that were not openly professed. No Tory or administration apologist during the Revolution itself ever assumed more casually than did such distinguished modern scholars as Philip Davidson and John C. Miller that the fears expressed by the Revolutionary leadership were factitious instruments deliberately devised to manipulate an otherwise inert public opinion. Conversely, nowhere in the patriot literature of the Revolution proper is there a more elaborate effort to prove that there was in actuality a ministerial conspiracy—a plot of King's friends aimed at victimizing the colonists—than that made by Oliver Dickerson in his *Navigation Acts and the American Revolution* (1951).

But the eighteenth century was an age of ideology; the beliefs and fears expressed on one side of the Revolutionary controversy were as sincere as those expressed on the other. The result, anticipated by Burke as early as 1769, was an "escalation" of distrust toward a disastrous deadlock: "The Americans," Burke said, "have made a discovery, or think they have made one, that we mean to oppress them: we have made a discovery, or think we have made one, that they intend to rise in rebellion against us . . . we know not how to advance; they know not how to retreat . . . Some party must give way."

The American Alarm (1773)

JOHN ALLEN

John Allen was a Baptist minister who was imprisoned as a debtor before finally leaving England for America in 1769. Four years later he won considerable acclaim in Boston for his tracts supporting the American cause against Great Britain. As a recent immigrant and representative of the English tradition of Dissent, Allen could assimilate American grievances with the older religious struggle against arbitrary power and monolithic establishments.

This ministerial power, are a union of gentlemen, both of Lords and Commons, who, it is to be feared, that few of them fear GOD, or regard Man. These are (unhappy for the people) favoured to be around the King, as his council, favourites and flatterers; and they not acting as the guardians of the British Crown, and the *rights of the people,* but acting in the affairs of the nation by their despotic will, making it the rule of authority and power: The people are justly alarmed at their actions, since they must intend thereby such a change in government, that must effectually destroy their rights, if not produce an entire revolution of the whole State. For their power and interest is so great, that they can, and do procure whatever laws they please; having, (by power, interest, and the application of the people's money, to *placemen,* and *pensioners,*) the whole legislative authority at their command. So that it is plain . . . that the rights of the people are ruined, and destroyed by ministerial *tyrannical* authority. . . .

Was this all, *Gentlemen,* I would, with sympathy of soul, be solemnly silent in tears, for the breaches, inrodes, and growing ruins of England: But as it is too notorious before GOD, and Man, that this is nearly thy case, Oh America, that the British ministerial power, by an unjust sovereignty, they claim over you, have already destroyed your rights!—Thrown down your liberties!—Despised your charter!—Deprived you of your spirit of trade, nay, of your lives!!! But what is

From [John Allen], *The American Alarm, or the Bostonian Plea, for the Rights, and Liberties, of the People* . . . (Boston, 1773), pp. 9–11, 17–18.

worse, they are now aiming at the final overthrow of all your RIGHTS as a people; did I say *aiming?* Have they *not already* destroyed the ancient rights of your *forefathers,* which was the life and glory of America? Namely, the power of making your own laws, and right of disposing your own money? This natural right, the British ministry have violently attacked, and done their utmost to destroy. . . .

Therefore, with all the tremendousness of danger, with all the solemnities of fear, with all the pathos of affection let me intreat you as men of refined, and ready understanding, to see that your rights, your lives, your lands, are all in danger; your rights, as you are taxed without your consent; your lives, as witness the bloody massacre in your streets. . . .

Rouse! Stand! *And take the* ALARM! You are now in eminent danger of losing (after many other losses) the life, soul, and *capitol* of all your right and liberties: Namely, the power of not only *making, placing,* or *paying* your own GOVERNOR, but now of paying your JUDGES, who are, or should be, the *guardians* of your laws, and the *pillars* of your political life. The plan is laid, the foundation is fixed, to make them dependent for place and payment, upon the arbitrary will, and power of the British ministry; upon that power that has for years been seeking the destruction of your RIGHTS. If you suffer this, then farewell the olive branch that has so sweetly spread; and the peaceful Dove that has hovered so long over you; for then you and your children are *Slaves* at once. Then *taxation* on *taxation* will follow, until your lands become seizable by your TASKMASTERS, under pretence of LAW.

The Heavy Grievances
the Colonies Labor Under (1774)

EBENEZER BALDWIN

The Reverend Ebenezer Baldwin developed a number of themes which would run through much of the alarmist literature of the following century:

From Ebenezer Baldwin, An Appendix, Stating the Heavy Grievances the Colonies Labour Under From Several Late Acts of the British Parliament, and Shewing What We Have Just Reason to Fear the Consequences of These Measures Will Be (New Haven, 1774), pp. 66–68, 74–75.

the Protestant fear of Catholic expansion; the conviction that the West was threatened by alien and hostile forces; the suspicion of bureaucracy and "big government"; the belief that the forms of a free government were no protection against scheming men, and that a failure to unite against subversion would lead to mass enslavement and to sexual as well as economic exploitation.

Again the *Quebec government act* the colonies have just reason to complain of. First as it establishes the *popish* religion: by the articles of capitulation the inhabitants of Canada were indeed to have a toleration, but not an establishment. But *popery* is now established, tythes are collected by law for its support; which shews such a disregard for the *protestant* religion as we never should expect in the reign of one of the house of *Hanover*, who were called to the British throne to be guardians of the protestant religion. And tho' there are thousands of English settled in that province, yet no provision is made for the support of a protestant clergy; there is only a reserve, that the king may make such provision, if he sees fit. Now when such favour is shewn to the bloody religion of Rome, it argues either a *favourable* disposition in the parliament towards that religion; or that it is done, in order to carry on some other *favourite* scheme. Again trials by juries are abolished by this act: which is injurious, at least to the English inhabitants, who under the faith of a royal proclamation, promising English privileges, have settled there. As the government of Canada is now entirely after the model of the arbitrary government of France, 'tis to be feared this is designed as a precedent for what is to be done in the other colonies; or at least we may suppose without much conjecture, that the French inhabitants of Canada are gratified with an establishment of *popery* and a restoration of their former laws; to engage them to be *true* to the ministry in any future struggles with the colonies: A military government is continued there; that they may always have a good body of troops at hand, to join the Canadians and Indians to pour down upon the back of us, if the ministry should find occasion to use them. And that this *French* arbitrary government may take in as much of America as possible, its limits are extended southward to the Ohio, and westward to the Mississippi: so that it comprehends an extent of territory almost as large as all the other provinces. When this vast extent of territory comes to be filled up with inhabitants, near half America will be under this arbitrary *French* government. So that upon the whole the Quebec act doubtless wears as threatening an aspect upon Americans as any act that hath been passed by the British parliament. Thus I have hinted to you some of the principal grievances which the Americans judge they labour under from the *late* acts of the British parliament.

Indulge me a little longer while I endeavour to point out what we have *just* reason to fear the consequences of these measures will be. If we view the whole of the conduct of the ministry and parliament, I do not see how any one can doubt but that there is a settled fix'd plan for *enslaving* the colonies, or bringing them under arbitrary government, and indeed the nation too. The present parliament have ever been (by all accounts) more devoted to the interest of the ministry, than perhaps ever a parliament were. Now notwithstanding the excellency of the British constitution, if the ministry can secure a majority in parliament, who will come into all their measures, will vote as they bid them; they may rule as absolutely as they do in *France* or *Spain*, yea as in *Turkey* or *India:* And this seems to be the present plan to secure a majority of parliament, and thus enslave the nation with their own consent. The more places or pensions the ministry have in their gift; the more easily can they *bribe* a majority of parliament, by bestowing those places on them or their friends. This makes them erect so many new and unnecessary offices in America, even so as to swallow up the whole of the revenue. . . . This doubtless is the great thing the ministry are driving at, to establish arbitrary government with the consent of parliament: And to keep the people of England still, the first exertions of this power are upon the colonies. . . .

View now the situation of America: loaded with taxes from the British parliament, as heavy as she can possibly support under,—our lands charged with the most exorbitant quit rents,—these taxes collected by foreigners, steeled against any impressions from our groans or complaints, with all the rapaciousness of Roman publicans—our charters taken away—our assemblies annihilated,—governors and councils, appointed by royal authority without any concurrence of the people, enacting such laws as their sovereign pleasure shall dictate—judges appointed from the same source, without any check from juries carrying their arbitrary laws into execution,—the lives and property of Americans entirely at the disposal of officers more than three thousand miles removed from any power to control them—armies of soldiers quartered among the inhabitants, who know the horrid purpose for which they are stationed, in the colonies,—to subjugate and bear down the inhabitants—who know what a chance they stand for impunity, tho' they commit the greatest excesses. These will be ready, not only to execute every arbitrary mandate of their despotic masters; but self-moved (if like others of their profession) to commit every outrage upon the defenceless inhabitants.—Robberies, rapes, murders, etc. will be but the wanton sport of such wretches without restraint let loose upon us.—These will be at hand by force and arms to quell every rising murmur, to crush every rising groan or complaint e'er it be uttered. And whenever the iron hand of oppression shall excite opposition or raise insurrections among the people: (which will ever be the case under arbitrary and despotic government, till long use has rendered their necks callous and insensible to the galling yoke) Blood-thirsty soldiers will be let loose upon them. Those who survive their murdering hands and have the misfortune to be taken captive by them, will soon be dragged, by the sentence of more merciless judges, to the place of execution.—Nothing shall then be heard of but executions, forfeitures of estates, families reduced to beggary, orphans crying for bread, and such like scenes of distress. . . . . What free-born Englishman can view such a state of abject slavery as this, tho' at the greatest distance, without having his blood boil with indignation?

There Has Been a Regular, Systematic Plan (1774)

GEORGE WASHINGTON

Ebenezer Baldwin's lurid fantasies of British military occupation represent the pure paranoid style, much as Richard Hofstadter has described it. Clearly there was little in common between extremists like Baldwin and men as judicious and realistic as George Washington. No one would suggest that Baldwin and Washington shared the same "style." Yet Washington perceived the objectionable acts of Parliament as part of a systematic plan for enslaving America. His notion of "enslaving" drew immediacy from the visible example of Negro slaves, who seemed to have been rendered abject and defenseless through long "custom." This association of ideas suggests that the fear of conspiracy could reflect a deeper fear of retribution, and thus an uncertainty over the moral basis of American society.

From John C. Fitzpatrick, ed., *The Writings of George Washington from the Original Manuscript Sources, 1745–1799*, III (Washington, n.d.), 241–242.

Satisfied, then, that the acts of a British Parliament are no longer governed by the principles of justice, that it is trampling upon the valuable rights of Americans, confirmed to them by charter and the constitution they themselves boast of, and convinced beyond the smallest doubt, that these measures are the result of deliberation, and attempted to be carried into execution by the hand of power, is it a time to trifle, or risk our cause upon petitions, which with difficulty obtain access, and afterwards are thrown by with the utmost contempt? . . . I could wish, I own, that the dispute had been left to posterity to determine, but the crisis is arrived when we must assert our rights, or submit to every imposition, that can be heaped upon us, till custom and use shall make us as tame and abject slaves, as the blacks we rule over with such arbitrary sway. . . . I am as fully convinced, as I am of my own existence, that there has been a regular, systematic plan formed to enforce [the acts], and that nothing but unanimity in the colonies (a stroke they did not expect) and firmness, can prevent it.

3. Ideological Responses to the French Revolution (1795–1802)

PRIOR TO the French Revolution, Americans tended to conceptualize political conspiracy in terms of selfish factions of public officials seeking personal power and wealth by manipulating the machinery of government. But in the 1790's the cataclysm in France raised the spectre of a mass assault on inherited property and privilege, and thus on the social foundations of established power structures. In both England and America it soon became clear that the philosophic principles of the French Revolution directly challenged the religious and political ideologies that sanctioned the existing social order. The alarm of conservatives was most acute in England, where the Pitt administration violently suppressed agitation for democratic reform. This was done partly in the name of national defence, as Britain and France became enmeshed in a bitter and prolonged war. In America the Federalists quickly appropriated British propaganda and sought to identify their opponents, led by Madison and Jefferson, with the egalitarian and anticlerical principles of the French Revolution. The image of a revolutionary conspiracy directed by a foreign power became a key weapon for defending the status quo and discrediting political opposition.

The series of bewildering events in France which began with the fall of the Bastille and culminated in the execution of the king and the Reign of Terror seemed to defy explanation unless one assumed, in the words of the Abbé Barruel, "plots long hatched and deeply premeditated." Barruel, a French ex-Jesuit who lived in England, helped to popularize the view that every stage of the Revolution had been planned and implemented by secret societies, largely Freemasonic in origin, as part of a master conspiracy to overthrow Christianity and legitimate government. Although Barruel's work was translated and published in America, a Scottish scientist named John Robison was probably more influential in spreading the fear of a secret conspiratorial organization which aimed at subverting the established governments of the world. Robison had been a Freemason and had visited various Masonic lodges on the Continent, where the Order had acquired a more radical character in opposition to despotic governments. Robison had become alarmed by Masonic "innovations" and by supposed evidence that many lodges had been infiltrated by Jesuits, deists, and heretical sectarians. After a close study of various obscure documents, he concluded in 1797 that Freemasonry had finally been taken over and exploited by the secret Order of Illuminati who sought to destroy Christianity and overturn all the governments of Europe, and who had in fact engineered the French Revolution. In Robison's inflamed mind, the Illuminati appeared as the most dangerous conceivable enemy to British Protestantism: they combined the secular rationalism of the left-wing Enlightenment with all the diabolical traits once ascribed to the Catholic Counter-Reformation.

Robison's book was reprinted in New York, and in 1798 and 1799 leading members of the New England clergy propagated his thesis as a means of defending the Alien and Sedition Acts, combating Jeffersonian Republicans, and attacking religious apathy and creeping rationalism. It should be emphasized that in this case a specific social group adopted Robison's paranoid style partly for its strategic value in helping them maintain their leadership role. But there is no reason to doubt that the conservatives' fears were genuine or that the conspiratorial view of politics gave ideological expression to significant conflicts in social and political values. During the 1790's the United States struggled, as the modern world's first "new nation," to define its national purpose and work out its basic policies in the face of European revolution and global war. This formative decade was also punctuated by a series of sharp crises, from the defiant challenges of Citizen Genêt and the Whisky Rebellion to the XYZ Affair and an undeclared naval war with France. As we shall see in the highly revealing selection by Abraham Bishop, Jeffersonian Republicans could also appropriate the paranoid style and accuse their Federalist opponents of betraying the promise of the American Revolution and of conspiring to lead America back to a despotic union of church and state like those in Europe. This tendency to exaggerate political differences and to portray one's opponents as dangerous subversives soon gave way to a more pragmatic and compromising approach which has generally characterized American politics. Yet in many respects the conspiratorial fantasies of the 1790's articulated important beliefs and attitudes concerning national identity and the relation of

America to the rest of the world. In seeking to conceptualize the Great American Enemy, men like Abraham Bishop and Jedidiah Morse followed modes of thought that strikingly foreshadow the Populists' image of Wall Street and the modern conservatives' image of international Communism.

Proofs of a Conspiracy (1797)

JOHN ROBISON

Although John Robison was not an American, he served as a bridge between English and American concepts of conspiracy, and had an enormous influence on Federalist writers and on the later anti-Masonic movement. Robison was anything but an ignorant fanatic. He was a professor of science (natural philosophy) at the University of Edinburg and secretary to the Royal Society of Edinburgh. His book exhibits the careful massing of evidence, the plausible scholarship, and the quick jump to breathtaking conclusions which Richard Hofstadter has described as among the hallmarks of the paranoid style. There is a note of modernity to Robison's protest against a movement governed by the belief that a noble end justifies any means. He also anticipated later patterns of thought when he sensed that systems of ethics could become ideological weapons, and that tests of loyalty should concern one's commitment to "approved principles" rather than to specific leaders or groups.

There is actually no evidence that the Order of the Illuminati was anything more than a short-lived organization dedicated to the humanitarian and rationalistic principles of the Enlightenment. It was certainly not responsible for the French Revolution. On the other hand, there can be no doubt that in the years preceding Robison's book, the repressive measures of the British government had provoked conspiratorial movements among pro-French radicals and oppressed English workers. By defining all social protest as subversive, the Pitt administration drove protest under ground. Pitt's spies and informers gathered extensive evidence on some of the "Secret Assemblies" that worried John Robison. Robison's theories must therefore be understood as a somewhat hysterical and reactionary response to genuine social unrest. It is significant that Robison, as a defender of the ex-

From John Robison, *Proofs of a Conspiracy Against All the Religions and Governments of Europe, Carried on in the Secret Meetings of Free Masons, Illuminati, and Reading Societies* (Edinburgh, 1797), pp. 15–16, 106–107, 205–206, 209–210, 358, 374–375, 405–406, 437, 468–469, 476–479, 486.

isting order, was especially fearful that revolutionary ideas were contaminating the young. The same apprehension would later be shared by American anti-abolitionists and anti-Communists.

The Association of which I have been speaking is the Order of IL-LUMINATI, founded, in 1775, by Dr. Adam Weishaupt, professor of Canon law in the university of Ingolstadt, and abolished in 1786 by the Elector of Bavaria, but revived immediately after, under another name, and in a different form, all over Germany. It was again detected, and seemingly broken up; but it had by this time taken so deep root that it still subsists without being detected, and has spread into all countries of Europe. It took its first rise among the Free Masons, but is totally different from Free Masonry. It was not, however, the mere protection gained by the secrecy of the Lodges that gave occasion to it, but it arose naturally from the corruptions that had gradually crept into that fraternity, the violence of the party spirit which pervaded it, and from the total uncertainty and darkness that hangs over the whole of that mysterious Association. . . .

The Order was said to abjure Christianity, and to refuse admission into the higher degrees to all who adhered to any of the three confessions. Sensual pleasures were restored to the rank they held in the Epicurean philosophy. Self-murder was justified on Stoical principles. In the Lodges death was declared an eternal sleep; patriotism and loyalty were called narrow-minded prejudices, and incompatible with universal benevolence; continual declamations were made on liberty and equality as the unalienable rights of man. The baneful influence of accumulated property was declared an insurmountable obstacle to the happiness of any nation whose chief laws were framed for its protection and increase. Nothing was so frequently discoursed of as the propriety of employing, for a good purpose, the means which the wicked employed for evil purposes; and it was taught, that the preponderancy of good in the ultimate result consecrated every mean employed; and that wisdom and virtue consisted in properly determining this balance. This appeared big with danger; because it appeared that nothing would be scrupled at, if we could make it appear that the Order could derive advantage from it, because the great object of the Order was held as superior to every consideration. . . .

The great aim professed by the Order is to *make men happy;* and the means professed to be employed, as the only and surely effective, is *making them good;* and this is to be brought about by *enlightening the mind,* and *freeing it from the dominion of superstition and preju-dices.* This purpose is effected by its *producing a just and steady mo-rality.* This done, and becoming universal, there can be little doubt but that the peace of society will be the consequence,—that govern-ment, subordination, and all the disagreeable coercions of civil gov-ernments will be unnecessary,—and that society may go on peace-ably in a state of perfect liberty and equality. . . . The [true] aim of the Order is not to enlighten the mind of man, and show him his moral obligations, and by the practice of his duties to make society peaceable . . . but to get rid of the coercion which must be employed in place of Morality, that the innocent rich may be robbed with im-punity by the idle and profligate poor. . . . Their first and immediate aim is to get the possession of riches, power, and influence, without industry; and, to accomplish this, they want to abolish Christianity; and then dissolute manners and universal profligacy will procure them the adherence of all the wicked, and enable them to overturn all the civil governments of Europe; after which they will think of far-ther conquests, and extend their operations to the other quarters of the globe, till they have reduced mankind to the state of one undistin-guishable chaotic mass. . . .

That the Illuminati and other hidden Cosmo-political societies had some influence in bringing about the French Revolution, or at least in accelerating it, can hardly be doubted. . . . Nothing can more con-vincingly demonstrate the early intentions of a party, and this a great party, in France to overturn the constitution completely, and plant a democracy or oligarchy on its ruins. The Illuminati had no other ob-ject. They accounted all Princes usurpers and tyrants, and all privi-leged orders as their abettors. They intended to establish a govern-ment of Morality, as they called it, . . . where talents and character (to be estimated by their own scale, and by themselves) should alone lead to preferment. They meant to abolish the laws which protected property accumulated by long continued and successful industry, and to prevent for the future any such accumulation. They intended to es-tablish universal Liberty and Equality, the imprescriptible Rights of Man. . . . And, as necessary preparations for all this, they intended to root out all religion and ordinary morality, and even to break the bonds of domestic life, by destroying the veneration for marriage-vows, and by taking the education of children out of the hands of the parents. *This was all that the Illuminati could teach,* and THIS WAS PRECISELY WHAT FRANCE HAS DONE. . . .

Thus were the Lodges of France converted in a very short time into a set of secret affiliated societies, corresponding with the mother Lodges of Paris, receiving from thence their principles and instructions, and ready to rise up at once when called upon, to carry on the great work of overturning the state.

Hence it has arisen that the French aimed, in the very beginning, at overturning the whole world. In all the revolutions of other countries, the schemes and plots have extended no farther than the nation where they took their rise. But here we have seen that they take in the whole world. They have repeatedly declared this in their manifestos, and they have declared it by their conduct. This is the very aim of the Illuminati.—Hence too may be explained how the revolution took place almost in a moment in every part of France. The revolutionary societies were early formed, and were working in secret before the opening of the National Assembly, and the whole nation changed, and changed again, and again, as if by beat of drum. Those duly initiated in this mystery of iniquity were ready everywhere at a call. And we see Weishaupt's wish accomplished in an unexpected degree, and the debates in a club giving laws to solemn assemblies of the nation, and all France bending the neck to the city of Paris. The members of the club are Illuminati, and so are a great part of their correspondents. . . . The famous Jacobin Club was just one of these Lodges as has been already observed. . . .

France has given an awful lesson to surrounding nations, by shewing them what is the natural effect of shaking off the religious principle, and the veneration for that pure morality which characterises Christianity. By a decree of the Convention (June 6, 1794), it is declared, that there is nothing criminal in the promiscuous commerce of the sexes, and therefore nothing that derogates from the female character, when woman forgets that she is the depositary of all domestic satisfaction,—that her honour is the sacred bond of social life. . . .

Nothing is so dangerous as a mystic Association. The object remaining a secret in the hands of the managers, the rest simply put a ring in their own noses, by which they may be led about at pleasure; and still panting after the secret, they are the better pleased the less they see of their way. A mystical object enables the leader to shift his ground as he pleases, and to accommodate himself to every current fashion or prejudice. This again gives him almost unlimited power; for he can make use of these prejudices to lead men by troops. He finds them already associated by their prejudices, and waiting for a leader to concentrate their strength and set them in motion. And once great bodies of men are set in motion, with a creature of their fancy for a guide, even the engineer himself cannot say, "Thus far shalt thou go and no farther."

We may also gather from what we have seen, that all declamations on universal philanthropy are dangerous. Their natural immediate effect on the mind is to increase the discontents of the unfortunate, and of those in the laborious ranks of life. No one, even of the Illuminators, will deny that these ranks must be filled, if society exists in any degree of cultivation whatever, and that there will always be a greater number of men who have no farther prospect. Surely it is unkind to put such men continually in mind of a state in which they might be at their ease. . . .

When we see how eagerly the Illuminati endeavoured to insinuate their Brethren into all offices which gave them influence on the public mind, and particularly into seminaries of education, we should be particularly careful to prevent them, and ought to examine with anxious attention the manner of thinking of all who offer themselves for teachers of youth. There is no part of the secret correspondence of Spartacus [Weishaupt] and his Associates, in which we see more varied and artful methods for securing pupils, than in his own conduct respecting the students in the University, and the injunctions he gives to others. . . . We may be certain, that the zeal of Cosmo-politism will operate in the same way in other men, and we ought therefore to be solicitous to have all that are the instructors of youth, persons of the most decent manners. . . . Weishaupt undoubtedly thought that the principles of civil anarchy would be easiest inculcated on minds that had already shaken off the restraints of Religion, and entered into habits of sensual indulgence. We shall be safe if we trust his judgment in this matter.—We should be particularly observant of the character and principles of *Men of Talents*, who offer themselves for these offices, because *their* influence must be very great. Indeed this anxiety should extend to all offices which in any way give the holders any remarkable influence on the minds of considerable numbers. Such should always be filled by men of immaculate characters and approved principles; and, in times like the present, where the most essential questions are the subjects of frequent discussion, we should always consider with some distrust the men who are very cautious in declaring their opinions on these questions.

It is a great misfortune undoubtedly to feel ourselves in a situation which makes us damp the enjoyments of life with so much suspicion. But the history of mankind shows us that many great revolutions have been produced by remote and apparently frivolous causes. . . . Nor can it be said that these are vain fears. We know that the enemy is working among us, and that there are many appearances in these kingdoms which strongly resemble the contrivance of this dangerous Association. We know that before the Order of Illuminati was broken up by the Elector of Bavaria, there were several Lodges in Britain, and we may be certain that they are not all broken up. . . . I am very well informed that there are several thousands of subscribing Brethren in London alone, and we can hardly doubt but that many of that number are well advanced. The vocabulary also of the Illuminati is current in certain societies among us. . . . Seeing that there are such grounds of apprehension, I think that we have cause to be on our guard, and that every man who has enjoyed the sweets of British liberty should be very anxious indeed to preserve it. We should discourage all secret assemblies, which afford opportunities to the disaffected, and all conversations which foster any notions of political perfection, and create hankerings after unattainable happiness. These only increase the discontents of the unfortunate, the idle, and the worthless. —Above all, we should be careful to discourage and check immorality and licentiousness in every shape. For this will of itself subvert every government, and will subject us to the vile tyranny of the mob.

If there has ever been a season in which it was proper to call upon the public instructors of the nation to exert themselves in the cause of Religion and of Virtue, it is surely the present.

An American Thanksgiving for Divine Favor (1795)

DAVID OSGOOD

The year 1794 was one of the most critical in American history. Harassed by mounting opposition to the Hamiltonian program, Washington's second

From David Osgood, A *Discourse, Delivered February 19, 1795, The Day Set Apart by the President for a General Thanksgiving Through the United States* (Boston, 1795), pp. 11–12, 14–15, 18–19.

administration also faced an armed rebellion in western Pennsylvania, Indian uprisings encouraged by the British who still occupied posts in the old Northwest, and the threat of outright war with England. For New England Federalists and orthodox clergymen the picture was further darkened by the spread of secular rationalism and republicanism in the colleges, where students had begun preaching the doctrines of Voltaire and Thomas Paine. But by February 1795, when the Reverend David Osgood delivered the following speech of thanksgiving in Medford, Massachusetts, the Northwestern Indians had been decisively beaten by Anthony Wayne, John Jay had negotiated a treaty with England (the terms of which were still unknown), and the Whisky Rebellion had been crushed. Osgood's discourse is notable for its statement of America's unique blessings and for its conservative view of the American Revolution, which is sharply contrasted with the upheavals in France. While Osgood sounds a cautiously optimistic note, praising Washington for his firmness in suppressing the Whisky Rebellion, he suggests that America's divine favor depends on maintaining the status quo and repelling foreign influence. Such views created a congenial climate for John Robison's theories of conspiracy.

The manner in which we were brought thus to unite, cannot be remembered without emotions of thankfulness to that Being who has the hearts of all men in his hand. In violence, in usurpation, or conquest, most other governments have originated. Rarely has any nation ever renounced tyranny, and obtained a free government without civil war and bloodshed. But in this country, the important acquisition was made without any great struggle, or violent commotion. Our national birth, indeed, was attended with a long and severe travail: Our emancipation from a foreign country and independence, were the price of much blood and treasure. But our free constitutions of government—all harmoniously uniting in a general one, were the result of free debate and mature deliberation. By reason and argument alone were they effected. The grand instrument of our union was constructed by the most eminent sages of America. Its contents were afterwards thoroughly discussed in state-conventions, chosen for the purpose. In this way, it obtained the sanction of the whole nation. Happy experience has proved it to be a master-piece of human wisdom and policy. It is however so framed, as to admit, at any time hereafter, such improvements as the increase of knowledge and farther experience may recommend. But, at present, imagination cannot conceive of more equal principles of liberty, or more ample privileges, civil and religious, than are here established. What other nation, ancient or modern, has been equally fortunate and happy? . . .

If we look abroad, and consider the present state of the world—if we compare the little disquietudes occasioned by parties among ourselves, with the real and wasting miseries which afflict so many other nations—the burdens imposed upon them—the oppressions committed by the great on all the lower classes of the community—the rapacity of rulers, favourites, and pensioners—all devouring the fruits of laborious diligence; if we take into our view, the dangers to which personal liberty and safety are exposed under all arbitrary governments; and the many melancholy instances which such governments exhibit, of persons suddenly driven from their families and possessions into solitary banishment, or hurried into dungeons and places of cruel confinement and seclusion from all the blessings and comforts of life—suffering all this for weeks and months together, without any knowledge of the crimes of which they are accused, or of the persons of their accusers—if, in these respects, we compare our situation with that of most other nations, we may learn how much the distinction is in our favour, and the obligations we are under to an indulgent providence. *Surely He hath not dealt so with any nation.* How many millions of our fellow-men sigh for the blessings which we enjoy, without the most distant hope of ever obtaining them? . . .

During the reign of a ferocious and atheistical anarchy in France, its authors formed the design of bringing other nations to fraternize with them in their infernal principles and conduct. With this view, their emissaries spread themselves in every country open to their admission. In the neighbouring state of Geneva, these agents were horribly successful in overthrowing a free government but lately established, and in bringing on, in imitation of what had happened in their own country, one revolution after another; till at length, all law and liberty, learning and religion, together with the property and lives of the worthiest citizens, were suddenly prostrated in a wild uproar of ignorance, guilt, and barbarism. Geneva, says the narrator of these events, "Geneva is lost without resource, in respect to religion, to morals, to the fine arts, to trade, to liberty, and above all, to internal peace,—for the present generation, it can only be a residence of hatred and vengeance."

The same spirit and some of the identical agents, found their way into these states, and began *here* their fraternizing system. . . . Under the influence of their suddenly diffused principles and our own passions, roused by unprovoked injuries, we seemed, for a time, to be rapidly borne away, as by a strong current, towards that sea of troubles on which so many other nations are still tossed. Our preservation, under Providence, seems to have been principally owing to the wisdom and firmness of the President. He originated and directed those counsels which have hitherto saved us, and which afford an increasing prospect of continued safety.

The Present Dangers and Consequent Duties of the Citizens (1799)

JEDIDIAH MORSE

In 1798 and 1799 the international crisis evoked hysteria among American conservatives. French military triumphs appeared to signal the downfall of Christian civilization in Europe; the raids of French privateers on American shipping, coupled with humiliating treatment of the American minister and an attempt to bribe special envoys (the XYZ Affair), aroused a sense of national outrage. By the Alien and Sedition Acts the Federalists sought to suppress political opposition and to stamp out lingering sympathy for the principles of the French Revolution. Throughout the Northeast, clergymen warned of declining faith and morals and of the spread of atheism and infidelity.

Jedidiah Morse, who was destined to be remembered as the father of Samuel F. B. Morse, the inventor of the telegraph, was famous in his day as a geographer and Congregationalist minister. One of the leaders of the New England Establishment, Morse was a close friend of Federalist politicians like Oliver Wolcott, the Secretary of the Treasury. In a sermon delivered at Boston's New North Church on May 9, 1798, Morse called attention to John Robison's recently published Proofs of a Conspiracy *and charged that the Illuminati had already begun to subvert American society. While Morse quoted Robison at length and gave voice to a similar ideology, there were important differences between the positions of conservatives in Britain and America. In Britain one could assume that any attack upon religion threatened the established union of church and state. But in America, a revolution had been justified by the natural-rights philosophy, which further sanctioned social forces that had long encouraged religious toleration and the*

From Jedidiah Morse, *A Sermon, Exhibiting the Present Dangers, and Consequent Duties of the Citizens of the United States of America. Delivered at Charlestown, April 25, 1799. The Day of the National Fast* (Charlestown, Mass., 1799) pp. 10–11, 15–17, 18–20, 22–23.

separation of church and state. Despite the official support of religion in New England and the prestige which the Congregationalist clergy had won by their active role in the Revolution, ministers like Morse were under increasing pressure to justify their involvement in politics. It is clear that Morse seized upon the specter of the Illuminati as a means of uniting the people against a common enemy and restoring the power and prestige which the clergy had enjoyed during the Revolution. Indeed, he saw "the dreadful fire of Illuminatism" as in some sense "permitted" by an omniscient God in order to awaken people to their duties as citizens. As Morse continued his crusade against the domestic Illuminati, he compiled and published detailed documents to answer critics who charged that he had furnished no evidence of the conspiracy. Early in 1799 he delivered another sermon, from which this excerpt is taken, and presented elaborate "proof" that the Illuminati had infiltrated the Democratic-Republican Societies (or clubs) which supported Thomas Jefferson.

Our dangers are of two kinds, those which affect our religion, and those which affect our government. They are, however, so closely allied that they cannot, with propriety, be separated. The foundations which support the interests of Christianity, are also necessary to support a free and equal government like our own. In all those countries where there is little or no religion, or a very gross and corrupt one, as in Mahometan and Pagan countries, there you will find, with scarcely a single exception, arbitrary and tyrannical governments, gross ignorance and wickedness, and deplorable wretchedness among the people. To the kindly influence of Christianity we owe that degree of civil freedom, and political and social happiness which mankind now enjoy. In proportion as the genuine effects of Christianity are diminished in any nation, either through unbelief, or the corruption of its doctrines, or the neglect of its institutions; in the same proportion will the people of that nation recede from the blessings of genuine freedom, and approximate the miseries of complete despotism. I hold this to be a truth confirmed by experience. If so, it follows, that all efforts made to destroy the foundations of our holy religion, ultimately tend to the subversion also of our political freedom and happiness. Whenever the pillars of Christianity shall be overthrown, our present republican forms of government, and all the blessings which flow from them, must fall with them.

. . . It has long been suspected that *Secret Societies*, under the influence and direction of France, holding principles subversive of our religion and government, existed somewhere in this country. This suspicion was cautiously suggested from this desk, on the day of the last National Fast, with a view to excite a just alarm, and to put you on your guard against their secret artifices. Evidence that this suspicion was well founded, has since been accumulating, and I have now in my possession complete and indubitable proof that such societies do exist, and have for many years existed, in the United States. I have, my brethren, an official, authenticated list of the names, ages, places of nativity, professions, etc. of the officers and members of a Society of *Illuminati*, (or as they are now more generally and properly styled *Illuminees*) consisting of *one hundred* members, instituted in Virginia, by the *Grand Orient* of FRANCE. This society has a deputy, whose name is on the list, who resides at the Mother Society in France, to communicate from thence all needful information and instruction. . . . The members are chiefly Emigrants from France and St. Domingo, with the addition of a few Americans, and some from almost all the nations of Europe. A letter which enclosed this list, an authentic copy of which I also possess, contains evidence of the existence of a society of the like nature, and probably of more ancient date, at *New-York*, out of which have sprung *fourteen* others, scattered we know not where over the United States. Two societies of the same kind, but of an inferior order, have been instituted by the society first mentioned, one in Virginia, and the other at St. Domingo. How many of equal rank they have established among us I am not informed.

You will perceive, my brethren, from this concise statement of facts, that we have in truth secret enemies, not a few, scattered through our country; how many and, except in three or four instances, in what places we know not; enemies whose professed design is to subvert and overturn our holy religion and our free and excellent government. And the pernicious fruits of their insidious and secret efforts, must be visible to every eye not obstinately closed or blinded by prejudice. Among these fruits may be reckoned our unhappy and threatening political divisions; the unceasing abuse of our wise and faithful rulers; the virulent opposition to some of the laws of our country, and the measures of the Supreme Executive; the Pennsylvania insurrection; the industrous circulation of baneful and corrupting books, and the consequent wonderful spread of infidelity, impiety and immorality; the arts made use of to revive ancient prejudices, and cherish party spirit, by concealing or disguising the truth, and propagating falsehoods; and lastly, the apparently systematic endeavours made to destroy, not only the influence and support, but the official existence of the Clergy. . . .

And what have they [the Clergy] done to provoke this hostility? Why they have *"preached politics."* This, so far as I know, is the principal, if not the only, charge alleged against them. But is this any new crime? No; it is as old as Christianity; nay it is as old as the priesthood itself. . . . And yet, for doing what only twenty years ago they were called upon to perform as a *duty*, they are now censured and abused, and represented as an expensive, useless, nay even, noxious body of men. In some of our newspapers, which are read by too many with more avidity, and more faith than the Holy Bible, they are continually reproached and vilified; and every low artifice is used to lessen their influence and usefulness; and what is deeply to be lamented, this poison is greedily swallowed, and assiduously disseminated by some even, who profess to be the warm friends and supporters of Christianity, and of the Christian Ministry. Little are these good people aware of what they are doing. Little do they believe that, blinded by their prejudices, they are in fact aiding with all their influence, the adversaries of religion in subverting its foundations; that they are acting a part directly contrary to their prayers and their professions. I would to GOD the veil might be speedily torn from the eyes of such Christians, as are ignorantly assisting to pull down the pillars which support the Christian fabric, lest they too late deplore their folly amidst its ruins!

The contest which now engages the attention, and fills with fearful apprehensions all the civilized world, is singular in its kind. "It is a contest of liberty against despotism; of property against rapine; of religion against impiety; of civilized society against the destroyers of all social order. These terms feebly express the calamities which the principles and the arms of France have produced in their baleful progress; and which the wounds of a bleeding world will attest." *

* Quotation from Mallet DuPan, *History of the Destruction of the Helvetic Union.*—ED.

A Warning to Harvard Seniors against World Revolution (1798)

DAVID TAPPAN

Soon after Morse's first sermon on the Illuminati, David Tappan, the Hollis Professor of Divinity at Harvard, addressed the departing senior class on the dangers of democratic ideology. As future doctors, lawyers, and ministers, the students would be in a strategic position to defend traditional standards and to protect the American people from foreign delusions. In Tappan's eyes, the United States had the all-important mission of thwarting world revolution and ultimately of saving the world from atheism and moral ruin.

As the present crisis of human affairs is very solemn and eventful; as we, in common with our fellow citizens, feel a lively interest in it; and as this University is soon to resign a considerable number of her sons to the service of their country and mankind; I cannot but seize this affecting opportunity, to address to them and the students at large some observations and counsels, suggested chiefly by the present state of the world. . . .

I think it highly expedient . . . to remind you of a more recent system, which affects the . . . aspect of extreme and universal good-will, and has for its ostensible object THE REGENERATION OF AN OPPRESSED WORLD TO THE BLISSFUL ENJOYMENT OF EQUAL LIBERTY.

You know that those who led in the French Revolution early held out, at least in a partial degree, this fraternal intention; and that their successors are to this moment affectedly prosecuting it with their utmost policy and force. Mr. Robison, Professor of Natural Philosophy, and Secretary to the Royal Society of Edinburgh, in a work recently published, has endeavoured to trace the principles and measures of France to a more early, profound, and extensive source than has been generally supposed. After long possessing, as he asserts, uncommon means of information, and exploring the subject with the most inquisitive and laborious attention, he gives the public a minute account of

From David Tappan, *A Discourse Delivered in the Chapel of Harvard College, June 19, 1798* (Boston, 1798), pp. 3, 13–20, 22, 27–28.

a society, calling itself the ILLUMINATI, which was founded in Germany by Dr. Adam Weishaupt in 1775, and under the mask of universal philanthropy has been aiming at complete dominion over the minds and bodies of mankind. . . . This society, according to our author, under various names and forms, in the course of a few years secretly extended its branches through a great part of Europe, and even into America. The aim of its members is to enlist, in every country, such as have frequently declared themselves discontented with the usual institutions; to acquire the direction of education, of church management, of the professional chair, and of the pulpit; to bring their opinions into fashion by every art, and to spread them among young people by the help of young writers; to get under their influence reading and debating societies, reviewers, booksellers and postmasters, journalists or editors of newspapers and other periodical publications; and to insinuate some of their fraternity into all offices of instruction, honor, profit, and influence, in literary, civil, and religious institutions. As it is one of their favorite maxims, that "the end sanctifies the means," they have nothing to restrain them from pushing their plans by the vilest methods. . . .

Accordingly, the avowed sentiments, objects, and even language of the French government have, from the beginning of the revolution, remarkably coincided with those of this brotherhood. In 1792, their National Convention by a solemn decree OFFERED HELP AND FRATERNITY TO ALL PEOPLE. In 1793, they expressly decreed, that the object of their war against surrounding countries was THE ANNIHILATION OF ALL PRIVILEGES, WAR WITH THE PALACES, PEACE WITH THE COTTAGES. This decree was ordered to be translated into all languages, and dispersed into all the neighbouring countries. In execution of this system, their agents or armies have uniformly excited discontent, if not insurrection, in every nation which they meant to fraternize or subdue; and by the aid or under the cover of this, have compelled the invaded people, at the point of the bayonet, to accept the offered boon of liberty and equality!

They have also exactly copied the scheme of the Illuminati with respect to religion and morality. As early as 1792, a proposition was made in their Convention, and received with loud and general applause, for ABOLISHING THE ALTARS OF GOD. Their legislature likewise early set aside the christian era, and by substituting decades in place of weeks artfully contrived to destroy the observation and even memory of the christian sabbath. They also decreed that *death was an everlasting sleep,* and ordered an inscription to this effect to be placed in capitals at the entrance of their grave yards. In 1793, the Convention solemnly renounced both the belief of a God and the immortality of the soul, asserted that all religions were the daughters of ignorance and pride, decreed the publication of these sentiments in all languages, and assumed the sublime function of diffusing truth over the whole earth. The avowed moral principles and conduct of regenerated France are also a faithful copy of Illuminatism: they are such as brutalize the human character, and prostrate the safety, beauty and happiness of human society.

I cannot forbear adding that the supposition of so deep and extensive a conspiracy against government and religion as our author attempts to prove, easily accounts for the rapid progress of impious and disorganizing principles, and the wonderful success of the French arms and intrigues, in various and distant parts of the world; for that ardent and obstinate devotion to the principles and measures of a hostile and abandoned foreign power, which still characterizes some intelligent and even native Americans, and some high or influential characters in our national councils; for the zealous, persevering support and circulation of certain newspapers and other productions, which are uniformly devoted to malignant falsehood, calumny, and sedition, which aim or directly tend to undermine the religious and moral, as well as civil institutions, principles and habits of our country, to destroy the character and official existence of its present rulers and clergy, and to establish on their ruins the dreadful reign of infidelity and confusion. If these and similar facts do not evince so early and broad a system of wickedness as this writer supposes (the truth of which in *all* its extent the speaker is not prepared to support); yet they indicate a real and most alarming plan of hostility against the dearest interests of man; and thus lay an ample foundation for those remarks and counsels, which are to finish this discourse.

One obvious and important inference is, that fervent professions of general philanthropy, or splendid and passionate harangues on universal freedom and equality, are too often either fanciful or hypocritical, and for the most part productive of evil effects. They are fanciful, as they hold out a pleasing abstract idea, a beautiful phantom, which does not apply to the present frame and condition of man; and substitute a metaphysical, speculative, and artificial benevolence, which has no real, definite object and use, in place of those natural and important duties, which we owe to ourselves, our families, and our country. . . .

The same lesson is further enforced by the immoral lives of these modern reformers. The founder and principal members of the illuminated brotherhood, while deluding mankind with a beautiful picture of virtue, rescued from the defiling embraces of superstition, were themselves stained with vices of the most gross, savage, and monstrous complexion. It is a remarkable fact, that the most distinguished promoters of this new morality both in France and Germany, are either licentious and prostituted clergymen, who had solemnly professed to believe and sworn to inculcate the doctrines of christianity, or men in other departments, whose characters were a reproach to human nature. . . .

As the local situation and other signal advantages of our favored land seem to point her out as the destined barrier against the threatened universal inundation of irreligious and political fanaticism; so the firm and united stand of her enlightened youth in favor of the opposite principles may ultimately rescue and bless the world. This is a species of universal philanthropy, which is solid and noble, and which I earnestly recommend to your emulous pursuit.

In this way you may effectually counterwork the subtle policy of the common enemies of God and man. While they are seeking to brutalize the world by exterminating the weekly sabbath and christian instructors; you are invited, and indeed have virtually sworn, to oppose this infernal artifice by supporting these great pillars of social order. While they are outraging female modesty and dignity, prostrating the venerable rites of marriage, debasing the important and endearing connexions of husband, son, and brother, reducing both men and women to worse than brutal impurity and barbarism, forming both into a motley compound of the swine and the tiger, and at last consigning them, with kindred beasts, to eternal sleep and putrefaction; while this is the boasted work of modern reformers, be it yours to assert the dignity of man, to guard and improve the delicacy and worth of the female character, to exemplify the fairest portraits of domestic virtue and happiness, to exhibit, in their most alluring forms, the devout and benevolent christian Pastor, the strictly just as well as able Lawyer, the equally humane and skillful Physician, the inflexible Friend and Patriot, the beneficent Leader and Pattern of mankind.

Laocoon (1799)

FISHER AMES

Federalist politicians gave powerful support to the clergy's crusade against subversion. Fisher Ames, an eminent Massachusetts lawyer and statesman, had advocated stern repression of Shays' Rebellion in 1786 and strongly backed the Sedition Act twelve years later. A celebrated orator in the national Congress, Ames warmly supported Hamilton's program and Jay's Treaty. He became increasingly obsessed with the perils generated by the French Revolution, and invoked the characteristic image of Minute Men rallying to defend American liberty against Jacobian subversives.

It is not doing justice to licentiousness to compare it to a wind which ravages the surface of the earth; it is an earthquake that loosens its foundations, burying in an hour the accumulated wealth and wisdom of ages. Those who, after the calamity, would reconstruct the edifice of the public liberty, will be scarcely able to find the model of the artificers, or even the ruins. . . . This is not exaggerated description. Behold France, that open hell, still ringing with agonies and blasphemies, still smoking with sufferings and crimes, in which we see their state of torment, and perhaps our future state. There we see the wretchedness and degradation of a people, who once had the offer of liberty, but have trifled it away; and there we have seen crimes so monstrous, that, even after we know they have been perpetrated, they still seem incredible.

If, however, the real people will wake, when their own government is in danger; if, like a body of minute-men, they will rally in its defence, we may long preserve our excellent system unimpaired in the degree of its liberty; we may preserve every thing but our tranquillity.

It is however difficult, if not impossible, to excite and maintain as much zeal and ardor in defence of government, as will animate the jacobins for its subversion; for to them action is ease, to us it is effort; to be at rest costs them more constraint, than us to stir. The machinery of our zeal is wrought by a feeble and intermitting momentum, and is impeded by its own friction; their rage beats like the pulse of life, and to stop it would be mortal. Like the whirlwind,

From Seth Ames, ed., *Works of Fisher Ames*, II (Boston, 1854), 112, 114–115.

it clears away obstacles, and gathers speed in its progress. . . .

It must be remembered, too, that public opinion is the great auxiliary of good government. Where can its weight fall so properly as on the conspirators who disturb its tranquillity and plot its subversion? The man who, from passion or folly, or bad company, happens to believe, that liberty will rise when government sinks, may be less criminal, but little less contemptible, for his sincerity. If a madman should poison a spring, because he fancies that all who drink and die will go to heaven and be happy, is he to be soothed and indulged? Will you let him have his way? Are you not to tell those who are thirsty, and about to drink the poisonous water, that it is death? Will it be against "candor and decency" to tell them that the man is mad? The gentle critics on the style of federal writers would have that scorn withheld, which is almost the only thing that actually restrains the jacobins from mischief; that scorn, which makes those who might be misled ashamed to join them. The factious have the cunning to say, that the bitterness of their spirit is owing to the harsh and acrimonious treatment they receive; as if reproach had made them jacobins; whereas it is jacobinism that extorts reproach. Our government has not armies, nor a hierarchy, nor an extensive patronage. Instead of these auxiliaries of other governments, let it have the sword of public opinion drawn in its defence, and not only drawn but whetted by satire to an edge to hew its adversaries down. Let jacobin vice be seen as a monster, and let not a mock candor pity, till we embrace it. Other governments may stand, though not very steadily, if public opinion be only neuter; but our system has so little intrinsic energy, that this soul of the republic's soul must not only approve but cooperate. The vain, the timid, and trimming must be made by examples to see that scorn smites, and blasts, and withers like lightning the knaves that mislead them. Then let the misled many come off and leave the party if they will; if not, let them club it with them for the infamy.

A frame of government less free and popular might perhaps have been left to take some care of itself; but the people choose to have it as it is, and therefore they must not complain of the burden, but come forward and support it; it has not strength to stand alone without such help from the wise and honest citizens. The time to do this, is at the elections. There, if anywhere, the sovereignty of the citizen is to be exercised; and there the privilege is open to the most excessive and most fatal abuse.

A Republican View of
Federalist Conspiracy (1802)

ABRAHAM BISHOP

Although Abraham Bishop was born in Connecticut and went to Yale, he was an ardent Jeffersonian who looked upon Hamilton's funding system as "the radical cause of our evils, the political fall, which subjected us to the loss of an American Eden." In Bishop's eyes the new Eden had been achieved by the American Revolution. The Federalists and their clerical supporters had then plotted to betray the Revolution and to assume the despotic role once held by Englishmen, knowing that "royalty can never be again sustained in our world without a correspondent dominion of force." Bishop did more than turn the tables against the Federalist detectors of conspiracy, whom he accused of conspiring to overthrow popular liberty and the true spirit of Christianity. In exposing the machinations of a "power elite," he enunciated themes that would run through Jacksonian, anti-Masonic, Populist, and New Leftist views of subversion. Bishop's typology of a Great Betrayal, a moral declension, and a restoration of earlier purity rested on a profoundly significant theory of the history of human redemption. The Federalist apostasy followed by the triumph of Jefferson as savior of democracy was simply a modern version of the cycle of religious decline and rebirth which had begun with the ancient Hebrews. Bishop's image of history was essentially that of the radical sectarian who is unalterably opposed to all institutions and all establishments, especially to established ties between church and state. President Jefferson rewarded Bishop by making him collector of the port of New Haven, an act which infuriated local merchants who considered him a licentious radical.

To compass a revolution in the public mind was a necessary task. Various arts were improved; but among them none so leading as Professor Robison's proofs of a conspiracy. This Scotch royalist had dis-

---

From Abraham Bishop, *Proofs of a Conspiracy Against Christianity, and the Government of the United States; Exhibited in Several Views of the Union of Church and State in New England* (Hartford, 1802), pp. 60–61, 70–71, 76–77, 86–88, 99, 110–112, 117–119, 124–125.

covered that a few obscure instructors in Germany, who had nothing on earth to gain but the knowledge of truth and the approbation of their employers, were in fact associated with some new orders of masons, and that these, connected with designing men in other parts of the world, were conspiring to destroy christianity, *by establishing a system of morals.* . . .

This miserable mixture of falsehood and folly was greedily seized by our unionists [Federalists] in this country, and instant pains were taken to domesticate and apply the Professor's facts and doctrine. The facts Dr. Morse found in a great number of masonic societies here—but as an important fact was wanting, viz. *the actual existence of these societies,* the unionists affected to charge the facts on all the leading republicans in the country. . . . Under this order of things Mr. Jefferson was said to be the great illuminat of this country, and doubtless a correspondent of Weishaupt. He had declared that the laws of society ought not to control the consciences of men— therefore he was an atheist; he was attached to the French cause, therefore loved anarchy and approved of all the cruelties reported of that nation: All his friends, in approving him, approved every sentiment, which he was said to entertain.

Thus a humble class of men, who enjoyed no power in society, and who merely wished for the civil and religious liberty, which they had dearly earned, were suddenly converted into a set of illuminatists, conspirators against christianity, anarchists and infidel philosophers. Barruel, an emigrant papist, heightened this triumph of the unionists by shewing that the early protestant martyrs were disorganizers, and that infidels and revolutionists were hand in hand to destroy christianity. This infidel philosophy then spread its wings and was found to be of monstrous extent. It was now discovered by our political clergy, that all the heathen philosophers, the deists of Europe, the illuminatists, and all the bad men of every age in the world, and all the republicans here were in a league against God, against morality of every description, against divine truth, and that the whole force of federalism must be mustered against such a daring combination. . . . The grossest barbarities, the wildest theories, even the cruelties of Robespierre and the atheism of Danton were charged on us. . . .

The man, who *really* believed that the houses of worship and bibles were to be burnt, if Mr. Jefferson should be president, did right in opposing his election.—The clergyman, who *really* believed that Robison and Barruel had published the truth and that all republicans were infidels, destitute of morals, seeking for universal confusion, would naturally have been alarmed, and when his powerful brethren, *who knew all this to be political fraud,* told him that it was all true, it was *natural* for him to pray against such men, to preach against them, to attend proxies and to stimulate his people to vote against them, and even to read *forged* letters from his desk, if he believed them to be genuine. . . . Sorely has society suffered by such men. It is difficult to separate between the leaders and followers of this profession; but wherever you find, in New-England, a clergyman, whose chosen society is among infidel civilians, and whose greatest delight has been to spread the alarm of infidel philosophy against the republicans, he is a conspirator against christianity; the New-Testament is full of reproofs for him, and there is a loud call to him to repent and believe the gospel. . . . Christianity was brought forward as the poor man's kingdom, and the singularity of its policy is not confined to the mere choice of subjects. Its invariable opposition to men's pride and wishes, together with the occasions and means which the unionists have improved to assimilate this to their own kingdoms may be usefully traced. If we divide the history of man into three great periods, viz. from the giving of the law at Mount Sinai to the coming of the Saviour—from the death of the apostles to the reformation—from that to the present day, we shall find him [man] at the close of each of these periods possessing the same character, originating in the same passions and in an uniform cause.

Fondness for idol-worship and a religion consistent with human depravity are noticeable in the Jews, to whom the law was revealed. Those, who could bow to the works of their own hands, must have been sorely disappointed at receiving a law, which demanded exclusive worship to the only invisible God, which forbad every vice and commanded every moral virtue. Following their own propensities, they soon changed the glory of the incorruptible God into an image made like unto corruptible man, and at the beginning of the second period we find them abounding in forms, but destitute of substance —having a convenient religion for this world, just suited to the ambition of the rulers. The invisible object of worship was again announced, the law and the true worship revived, a new and living way opened, but this was a declaration of war against all which was esteemed great and good in that day. The new religion took effect; but at the opening of the third period, we find it wholly changed, and the wise, mighty and noble who were not called, to have taken the ground, which was to have been occupied by the weak, and the poor. The reformation restored this religion to its first principles, and the present view exhibits all which is visible of this kingdom under the control of kings and their courts, high priests and rulers, drawing millions from the people by the force of law, disposing of titles and attending armies in the field—the forms carefully retained; but the substance lost, and men are now as fond of images made like unto corruptible man as they ever were, and of having a religion of their own making.

Our unionists have not only formed this conspiracy in view of all these preceding ones, but with actual knowledge that similar unions of church and state for the same secular purposes are operating in other nations, and in order that no doubt of the existence of this conspiracy might exist, one entire political party in New-England forms the corporate body of church and state union. The Jews and Catholics claimed that they had all the religion of the day: Ours put in the same claim with equal justice—each has been careful to retain the name and forms, to derive all the earthly profits, and each has constituted a great political party. . . .

To retain the *forms* of christianity is indispensible to the political objects of our unionists; hence they avail themselves of a fact, which long experience has established, viz. that it is easier *to profess to believe* than to practise, and that a religion of faith is on this account the most popular and most easy to be promoted. Men love cheap ways of gaining honor on earth and glory in heaven. Hence the artful unionist, finding that his neighbors love the world, forms up a religion apparently on the gospel, but in no respect conformed to its temper, and offers this as christianity, even joins in its ordinances, talks loudly of its excellence, thunders against his opponents, and thus enlists a great portion of passion in its favor—learns its votaries to curse instead of blessing—to persecute instead of convincing—to talk of infidelity rather than to practise morality—to avenge instead of forgiving—and thus to erect a system of INFIDEL PHILOSOPHY on the benevolent religion of Jesus. This precisely the state of things which the unionists have produced in New-England. . . .

Never before this, since the creation of the world, could such a charge of conspiracy have been made without certain hazard to the accuser. Men full of power could safely charge conspiracy on their opponents and if they did not acquiesce in it, could send an army with the logic of kings to enforce it; but at the present moment the serpent has lost his sting, and the devourer's teeth are broken, and we are at liberty to examine those accounts, which ages of terror have suppressed.

The first article for adjustment rests on the question, why federalists as such should conspire against christianity, and why republicans as such should wish to detect and repel the conspiracy? I have anticipated, in part, the solution of this question, but it remains to remark that as republicanism is the poor man's government, so christianity is the poor man's religion—and if the religion will not soften the heart, yet it may check the force, and in any case it will give patience to endure whatever political evils the powerful enemies of the common people can devise.

It has been natural for federalists in every age of the christian church to retain the forms of christianity, even to abound in them, because these forms would turn to their account, but to conspire against the substance, because it opposed their policy, and thus doing they were not in hazard as respected the concerns of this world, because they had the power of making laws and could guard their claims conclusively. He, who has the control of armies and Bastilles can dispense with the laws of religion; but the poor subject, whose all depends on the caprice of such lords, is willing to have the aid of religion, because even if it does not protect his rights, it will punish his oppressor. Our federalists when full of power must necessarily have hated that spiritual influence, which was opposed to all their systems of war and wealth. . . . No federalist understood the *real tendency* of his party, if he devoutly wished for the prevalence of pure and undefiled religion.

It was perfectly natural for republicans *as such* to wish for the destruction of false religion, for the humiliation of the political clergy, and for an end of an aristocratic government; but let me ask, what earthly motive could they have for wishing the destruction of christianity? Civil power was wholly in federal hands and did those wish to free their opponents from restraint—and that these should be let loose on them with all their passions, especially after having seen their temper? You may suppose republicans to be infidels or atheists, yet you will allow that some of them understood well their political interests, and could it be their interest that a religion, which is said to inculcate peace, humility and universal benevolence should be abolished? . . .

Where powerful causes coincide, their natural effect becomes inevitable. I have adverted to ancient connections between similar causes and effects, and for the purposes of the present disclosure have relied on the natural enmity of man to christianity, on the natural course, which this enmity has taken in New-England, and on the general facts illustrating the change of this enmity into *conspiracy*, under the influence of political motives. The names of *all* the unionists might easily have been furnished, with notes under the head of each, shewing his connection with the conspiracy, and the season and motives of his joining it, and the profits, which he has received from it. . . . The zeal in one class of men to have dominion over the rest has appeared in every country. It is inseparable from the hearts of proud men. Those, who seek this dominion will always deny it. Call them monarchists or hierarchs, they disclaim your terms; but in every nation, where there are men, this spirit walks in darkness as a pestilence— and though its operations are subtle, yet in every country you may as surely find its origin in an union of church and state, as you may trace vegetation to the earth. . . .

Taking nature for our guide we shall find the unionists conspiring against the poor man's government under the influence of the same passions, which led them to conspire against the poor man's religion.

The history of the world presents two classes of men, as distinct in their motives and means, as if they were of an entire different species of being, and formed of different materials.

1st. The body of mankind, honest and industrious, contented with a little, laboring hard to support a class of men, who are always promising to bring them to a degree of happiness and independence, which they have never seen and never will see, if they trust such promises; fighting when they are told that religion or their rights are in danger; trembling before court-martials; mounting the scaffold, when the pride of a courtier or the petulance of a midshipman requires it; dying when they are bid to die; drawn by the force of fraud, falsehood and passion, from the mild government of their heavenly Father, under the dominion of men, who fear no power but that of death, and no enemies but the intrepid asserters of the eternal rights of men.

2d. The lordly tyrants of the world, known by different titles: *the well-born*, scorning the lowly task of the Saviour, who had a feeling of human infirmity, because he took upon him our natures. These great men know not the value of labor nor the stings of poverty, nor the sense of danger, nor the tenderness of affection, which binds together those, whose sphere of action is limited. These tyrants bind heavy burdens on the people; talk of millions of debt with as little concern as the people do of pence; declare war with perfect composure, and assume on themselves to answer for the blood of the slain, as if they considered the books of record to be forever closed, and as if a season would never arrive, when the sea would give up its dead. They enter peaceable families and drag their hopes into the field; desolate villages and destroy their thousands, and when vengeance says it is enough, they pray that swords may be turned into ploughshares and spears into pruning-hooks, and that nations may learn war no more. The war serves as an apology for an increase of taxation, and having before taxed all which the labor of man produces, they tax the light which heaven bestows, and if discontent arises by reason of oppression, another war is declared in order to hush the tumult.

Thus wars are excited under pretence of serving the kingdom of peace, and all the rights of mankind are violated under a pretence of advancing those rights. Every thing has always been in danger; these men have affected to avert the danger, and the state of things has, under their management, been always growing worse: yet these pilots, who are always steering among the rocks, are still at helm, and multitudes of listless men, whose all is at stake, say, "let the ship sink, we are only passengers"—and this stupid confidence is among the "*steady habits*," which receive the constant eulogy of the great men.

Such is the history of the world—on the one hand an easy, unsuspicious confidence, and on the other a bold and daring assumption of all power, human and divine: and through these two causes the earth has been filled with artificial miseries, and the souls of those, who have been slain, have been crying, "How long, O Lord, dost thou not judge and avenge our blood on them that dwell on the earth?"

When our declaration of independence was penned, all these facts were known and recognized by our people, and Britain was expressly charged with tyranny, and we called ourselves the oppressed. In that day we were resolved to be free and to have a republican government, in which the people were for once to be sovereign, and to take in charge their own rights. By the government, against which I claim that the unionists have conspired, is intended the government for which our revolution was effected; not that republic, which under Mr. Adams, meant anything or nothing; nor any particular set of men, composing an administration; but *that political system, which has been always denominated republican.*—By the conspiracy charged is intended that portion and kind of enmity against such a government, (arising from the same motives, and conducted by as insidious means) which animated the court of St. James and the British army to conspire against our independence. . . .

At the peace of 1783 we had completed the first point of our revolution, viz. an establishment of our independence, and at this moment it was natural to reflect on the advantages, which, as a nation, we might derive from it. We were far distant from the kingdoms of Europe, those theatres, where religion and humanity had been always outraged by civil and ecclesiastical tyrants; those theatres, where the common people had been made to act the part of beasts of burden, where ribbons were esteemed more than lives, where men were boasting of their pedigree, where rank depended on birth, and where heaven was banished from earth, as much as the depravity of man could banish it. We were redeemed from crowns and the pageants who wear them, and had an extended country, to which we might invite the oppressed of the old world. This was a season of enthusiasm, and (as the event has proved) of strong illusions. Man is never more ennobled than when, reflecting on his virtuous struggles, he resolves that the world shall enjoy the benefit of them, and is never in greater danger of disappointment, than when he entrusts the execution of his benevolent projects to those, who despise his motives.

In the season which we are contemplating, much was said of *the majesty of the people,* a set of terms, which the unionists then despised, and which one of their number (a clergyman) lately termed, the majesty of the *mob;*—but in those days it was understood that the people, who had gained all the power, who did all the labor, and on whom would depend the whole support of government, should, in their corporate capacity, be regarded with respect. They never conceived in that day that a being of their own creation [John Adams] should talk of "humbling them in dust and ashes"—that little beings of their creation [Federalist Congressmen] should vote away their money by millions, contrary to their known mind and will, and call it "a trifle"—that beings of their creation should, without any reference to them, draw them into alliance with all the abandonment against which they had been fighting for years—that the aliens, whom they had invited, should be banished, and that they should be imprisoned for questioning the propriety of such conduct. . . .

Had a government been formed at this season, it would have involved all the principles of the revolution—no tory nor monarchist would have had a seat in the convention—no plan of a *limited monarchy* would have been brought forward—no provision would have been made for diplomatic agencies—no great national plans provided for. . . . How would a legislature, sitting at that time, have succeeded in establishing a funding system, to deprive the soldier, whose wound was yet bleeding, of his hard earnt commutation? How would the proposal of a British treaty have been received? Our unionists well knew that the ardors of the revolution must abate, before they could advance with their systems. The pretence that the country was not prepared for a regular government is idle: they were prepared for peace, for order, for economy, for political equality, for toleration, and for support of an administration, which was seriously in favor of such a government; but they were not prepared to sacrifice at a stroke the fruits of a revolution. They were not prepared to bid an eternal adieu to the hopes, which had sustained them through an eight years war. . . .

At the season which we contemplate, our people knew all these things, and the impressions of the people were known to the leaders; but theirs was a course of national glory, and the season had not arrived for laying the foundation of it. If a pure republic is ever established, it must be at a time, when the public mind is not corrupted; when it has virtue enough to sacrifice the tempting baubles of present splendor to the substantial interest of the present and future generations. The principle of virtue may be generated in a single mind by reason of reflection; but public virtue results from some occasion powerful enough to overwhelm the passions, and this virtue will abate, as it advances from its producing cause. To the revolutionary eye of the people, it was clear that to a nation the avoidance of evil communications, the habits of economy, peace and humanity, with moderate wishes, were as necessary as to an individual: that the plans of monarchs and the principles of republicanism could not coincide, and that any attempt to enjoy the blessings of the last, under the auspices of the first, must be unsuccessful.

The unionists well knew that the public memory soon fails; that public passion, when ceased to be blown, soon expires, and that a few years would change the aspect, and therefore delayed to come forward with the great plans which were to annihilate the principles of the revolution; to domesticate the power which we had acquired; to reduce the people to the European standard of dependence, and to elevate themselves above all control, except the nominal power of elections, in which their management was to deprive the people of volition and choice. . . .

When Britain offered as the wager of battle on the question, "Whether he who earnt bread should eat it," the *people* of America deliberately decided to accept it, and it was the *people*, represented in congress, who declared our independence, and the title of an American republic will always be, "We the people of the United States." By that revolution the people recovered from the contempt and humiliation in which they had been held, regained their majesty and assumed to transmit this character to posterity.

The establishment of the simple proposition, "that he who earnt bread should eat it," changed the whole face of society and the people were to issue the allowances instead of receiving them from their lords. The consequence of experiment on it would have been the ruin of all, who calculated to live and be wealthy without rendering services to society. . . . An experiment on such an unfashionable revolutionary sentiment would have shocked every delicate nerve and alarmed every man, who dreaded equality with his fellow-mortals as a premature death.

But mere personal freedom was not the only object: the mind of man had been enslaved for centuries, and its strongest fetters had been put on by the clergy. Toleration became a favorite theme and the people resolved that religion was a connection between God and man; that as every man was to render account for himself he ought to think and decide for himself, and that the mind ought always to be balanced by the greatest weight of evidence.—This was a point of resolution, which church and state could not endure. An experiment of this would have destroyed all dignities in the church, have exploded all establishments, and have reduced even the most powerful of the clergy to the simple elements of sense and usefulness. Hard lot indeed that a dominion over the conscience, which had been gained by the labor of a century, should be wholly lost, and that common people should read and expound their bibles! This would be . . . destroying a kind of influence, which our American nobles would need for the re-establishment of the old order of things; for amidst all the ardors of the revolution every subtle unionist kept sight of the doctrines of the old school, and resolved that when a proper season should arrive, the people of this country should be as the people of other countries, the nation should be as great as other nations, and our leaders in church and state like those of other countries.

The people had seen that religion and liberty had always been in danger, and that this danger *arose wholly* from the fact that those, who excited alarms about them, had their exclusive management . . . and to the doctrines of passive obedience and non-resistance they opposed the manly sentiment, "THAT REBELLION AGAINST TYRANTS IS OBEDIENCE TO GOD."

Such revolutionary sentiments appeared rational in the days of the revolution; they were well understood by the people; they were all susceptible of practice; but the application of them would have been ruin to our unionists, the champions of the throne and the altar. They hated such sentiments with a cordial hatred, and from this hatred they were led to those measures, which have degraded the people more rapidly than their most sanguine hopes could have calculated, and these measures have assumed the form of a conspiracy in that very union of church and state.

4. New Threats to
Internal Security (1825–1860)

ECONOMIC HISTORIANS describe the period from the late
1820's to the Civil War as one of accelerating and cumulative change.
Social and political attitudes were necessarily affected by the rapid
settlement and cultivation of the Mississippi Valley, by the "transportation revolution" that helped create and integrate national markets,
by the arrival of millions of immigrants from Europe, and by the
growth of manufacturing and the emergence of large cities. While it
would be futile to search for direct one-to-one relationships between
rapid economic development and new social movements, it was
surely no accident that the period from 1825 to 1860 saw a mush-
rooming of radical reform movements, of various cults and isms, and
of crusades against supposed subversives. Indeed, the political history
of the so-called Middle Period was bounded by sudden eruptions of
the paranoid style which dramatically transformed the existing party
structure.

The character of American politics after 1832 owed much to innovations introduced by the anti-Masonic movement. As Lee Benson
has suggested in his important study, *The Concept of Jacksonian Democracy*, it was the Anti-Masonic party that first won a widespread
popular following by attacking special privilege and by demanding
full equality of opportunity for all citizens. The anti-Masonic attack
on the unfair advantages enjoyed by a rising "aristocracy" had much
in common with the spirit and rhetoric of the New York Working
Men's party; and, in fact, the two movements partly coalesced in
1829–1830. Because it was difficult to sustain public excitement over
alleged Masonic subversion, in the absence of convincing evidence or
of ethnic or class conflict, the more politically astute leaders of the
Anti-Masonic party focused increasing attention on economic reforms
and finally on the usurpations of power by "King Andrew" Jackson.
But though there was thus some continuity between anti-Masonry
and the Whig party, it was the Jacksonian Democrats who adopted
the anti-Masons' egalitarian rhetoric, their hostility to monopolistic

privilege, and their appeal to the ballot box as the ultimate arbiter. The Jacksonians also portrayed the Second Bank of the United States as a "Monster Institution" whose conspiracies and iniquities rivaled those of Freemasonry.

Paradoxically, the anti-Masonic movement ushered in a period of political balance between two relatively stable national parties. In the early 1850's, however, anti-Catholicism helped to destroy the equilibrium and to reintroduce ideology in place of pragmatic compromise. Unlike anti-Masonry, anti-Catholicism was not a sudden or short-lived outburst of popular hysteria. By the early 1830's a growing influx of Catholic immigrants alarmed many leaders of the Protestant Establishment and rekindled suspicions and fears that went back to the Reformation. Ethnic conflict in the northeastern cities periodically exploded into mob violence; by the early 1840's Catholics and Protestants were engaged in a bitter struggle over the relation of religion to tax-supported education. Although members of the two denominations were divided by tangible conflicts of interest, Protestant writers exhibited all the traits of the paranoid style, picturing the Catholic Church as the very archetype of the "Monster Institution" contrived to subvert liberty in every part of the world. The widespread conviction that the Church inevitably opposed democracy and civil liberty was strengthened by the reactionary role of the European Church in the revolutions of 1848. Even in America, militant leaders like Bishop John Hughes seemed to substantiate the worst fears of Protestants by promoting Catholic separatism and by boasting that immigrant voters would soon provide the power to convert the United States into a Catholic nation.

In 1853 and 1854 there was a sudden upsurge of anti-Catholic and anti-immigrant hysteria. Cloaked in secrecy and in some ways resembling the conspiratorial image of the Illuminati or Freemasons, the Know-Nothing party united Americans of different sections and political backgrounds in a crusade to save the country from "popish despotism." Know-Nothing candidates won landslide victories in Massachusetts, Rhode Island, Maryland, and Kentucky. At the end of 1855 the Know-Nothings in the Thirty-Fourth Congress held a decisive balance of power. Although the nativist crusade disintegrated as rapidly as it had arisen, it helped to destroy the Whig party and to create a basic political realignment geared to sectional interests and ideologies. The importance of nativism in the ante-bellum period is underscored by the fact that the emergence of the Republican party depended on a revolution in political allegiance initiated by the Know-Nothings.

In the earlier selection on "Themes of Countersubversion," we noted some of the similarities among the popular images of Freemasons, Catholics, and Mormons. One may add that throughout the literature of countersubversion there is an almost obsessive repetition of the contrast between America's political and economic well-being and the oppression and misery that dominate the rest of the world. While Americans congratulated themselves on their own unparalleled blessings, they also cast uneasy eyes on the wretched "slavery" suffered by the masses of mankind. Pride over the tangible evidence of success was mixed with spasms of fear and anxiety. Innumerable writers and orators warned that affluence breeds a false sense of security. As a result of their own good fortune, the American people had grown too complacent, too tolerant, too self-seeking. How was a self-made man or a self-made nation to preserve the golden fruits of virtue? Even in a benign and happy republic, evil forces lurked beneath a sunny exterior. And what made the American enemy so extremely dangerous was his disarming disguise. Thus the Tory opponents of Jacksonian democracy cunningly called themselves National Republicans or Whigs; Freemasons pretended to be loyal citizens; American Catholics paid lip service to religious toleration. Fortunately seceders and apostates frequently revealed the truth about these organizations and exposed the dangers which the American people faced. It is significant that the ultimate peril was always conceptualized as "slavery." Jacksonians warned that banks and monopolies were beginning to enslave the people. The Freemasons, Mormons, and Catholics had all succeeded in enslaving their adherents. This insistence on the danger of slavery, which was also a prominent theme in the anti-British propaganda of the Revolution, may have reflected a deep-seated guilt over the expansion of Negro slavery at a time of widening freedom and opportunity for white Americans.

Another characteristic of the literature is its great concern with the disintegration of a cohesive and homogeneous community. Anti-Catholic writers observed that America was peculiarly vulnerable to religious subversion because of the divisions and disunity of the numerous Protestant sects. "Divide and conquer" was a supposed Jesuit maxim, and the key to Catholic strategy, according to one writer, was to keep the diverse groups and interests of society from fusing into "a bona fide American character." The presence of a subversive enemy provided the occasion for a closing of ranks, an abandonment of ethnic and religious rivalries, and a dedication to communal solidarity. The Know-Nothing movement was consciously aimed at burying sectional conflicts over slavery and uniting the people of North, South, and West against a foreign enemy. But the failure of political nativism indicated that for many Americans, in the North as well as the South, the most dangerous conspiracy had nothing to do with Rome or the Austrian Empire. In Chapter 5, we shall turn to the conspiratorial versions of the controversy over slavery.

A Jacksonian Attack
on Monopoly (1834)

FREDERICK ROBINSON

During the early 1830's Frederick Robinson was an impassioned young leader of the left-wing Jacksonian Democrats in the Massachusetts legislature, where he championed the abolition of imprisonment for debt. In the following selection, taken from a Fourth of July speech to a Boston trades union, he interpreted the growing inequality of wealth as the product of an aristocratic conspiracy against the rights of the laboring classes. Robinson's protest against exclusiveness and special privilege focused on the "Monster" which Jacksonians portrayed as the epitome of evil, the Second Bank of the United States.

The condition of the people can never remain stationary. When not improving they are sinking deeper and deeper into slavery. Eternal vigilance alone can sustain them, and never ceasing exertion is necessary for their social and political improvement. For the interests of the thousands are always contrary to the interests of the millions. The prosperity of the one always consists in the adversity of the other. As the millions become intelligent, united, and independent, the thousands are divested of their power, importance, and wealth. The few have always understood this and seen the necessity of the closest union among themselves in 'order to maintain their ascendency, while

A fuller text may be found in Joseph L. Blau, ed., *Social Theories of Jacksonian Democracy: Representative Writings of the Period 1825–1850* (New York, 1947).

the many have not only been ignorant of this fact, but have always regarded the few as their benefactors, protectors, and friends. Hence we are doomed to never-ceasing exertion for the enjoyment of our rights and the improvement of our condition until we work out the reform of society, and by the complete enjoyment of the blessings of equality, the common good of all the people shall constitute the interest of all.

Our destiny, fellow citizens, is in our own hands, and we must rely upon ourselves alone for the improvement of our republican institutions, the reform of our laws, and the bettering of our social and political condition. And if we sink into slavery, to ourselves alone must the calamity be charged. For the governments, the constitutions, the laws, and all the institutions of the country are in our hands, and we have the power to mold them to our will. In this respect we have the advantage of all the rest of the world. . . . But our fathers have purchased for us political rights and an equality of privileges which we have not yet had the intelligence to appreciate, nor the courage to protect, nor the wisdom to enjoy. For although it cannot be denied that in this country there can be no advantages, powers, or privileges which everyone has not an equal right to enjoy, yet do we not see everywhere around us, privileges, advantages, monopolies enjoyed by the few which are denied to the many; indeed do we not see all the same machinery in operation among us which has crowded the great mass of the people of other countries down into the grossest ignorance, degradation, and slavery? While we have been comparing our condition with the miserable slavery of other nations, and boasting of our advantages, and glorying in the achievements of our fathers, ignorantly supposing that we were already in the possession of the highest degree of liberty and in the enjoyment of the most perfect equality, the enemy have been silently encroaching upon our rights. But this delusion has passed; the enchantment is broken. The people are beginning to awake. Every day brings to our ears the pleasing intelligence that the industrious classes, which always constitute the democracy of the country, are beginning to bestir themselves and are enquiring what they shall do to be saved, not from the threatened evil of another world, but from the evils which they begin to see impending over them and their children here. . . .

The aristocracy of our country are well aware that their notions of government are unsound, and in order to prevent the true appellation of aristocracy from being attached to them, they continually contrive to change their party name. It was first Tory, then Federalist, then no party, then amalgamation, then National Republican, now Whig, and the next name they assume perhaps will be republican or democrat. But by whatever name they reorganize themselves, the true democracy of the country, the producing classes, ought to be able to distinguish the enemy. Ye may know them by their fruit. Ye may know them by their deportment toward the people. Ye may know them by their disposition to club together, and constitute societies and incorporations for the enjoyment of exclusive privileges and for countenancing and protecting each other in their monopolies. They are composed in general of all those who are, or who believe themselves to be favored by some adventitious circumstances of fortune. They are those, with some honorable exceptions, who have contrived to live without labor, or who hope one day to do so, and must consequently live on the labor of others. . . .

Of all the contrivances of the aristocracy, next to the usurpation of the judiciary, and thus turning the most potent engine of the people's government against themselves, their unions in the shape of incorporate monopolies are the most subtle, and the best calculated to promote the ends of the few, the ignorance, degradation, and slavery of the many. This hydra of the adversary has within a few years grown up around us, until the monster covers the whole land, branching out annually into new heads of different shape, each devouring the substance and destroying the rights of the people. But the most potent and deadly is the bank, a monopoly which takes everything from the people and gives them nothing in return. . . . Money was designed as a measure of value, as a medium of exchange of labor, like weights and measures; and like the fair regulation of weights and measures, the coining and regulating of the value of money is one of the most important prerogatives of sovereignty. For whatever tends to derange the currency either by increasing or diminishing its quantity, has the same effect upon the community, as, without the knowledge of the people, to enlarge or to reduce the common weights and measures. Some would find themselves growing rich they know not how, and some notwithstanding every effort would sink deeper and deeper into poverty. The people would, as they now do, regard every thing as under the control of fortune, luck, chance; and a sense of the uncertainty of the result of their efforts would paralyze their exertions. Such is the effect of banking. It enlarges and contracts the value of this medium of exchange of labor, as the interests of the few require.

It now issues large quantities of paper money, and a kind of delusive prosperity succeeds. The capitalist, the merchant, the lawyer, and all who live without labor, and all who are possessed of property, find their condition improving from day to day. But what sensibly enriches the thousands, although abstracted from the millions, seems at first so small, and so indirect as not immediately to excite alarm. The producer complains not, the money market is easy, and all allow that times are good. The husbandman finds his farm gradually increasing in value; and what was formerly valued at a thousand is now worth two or three or four thousand dollars according to the increase of paper currency. The farmer wonders to find himself becoming rich. But pride and wants grow with riches. He pulls down his old house and barn and builds anew, and thus becomes in debt; his farm is now worth five thousand dollars, and his debts amount to three. He soon goes to the bank and mortgages his farm for three thousand dollars. And although he is now worth nominally twice as much as before, even if his masters suffer the currency to remain where it is, he becomes a slave for life; since the annual interest will absorb the whole profit of his farm and labor, and when he has worn himself out in their service, his portion of our mother earth, by the addition of lawyers' fees and court expenses, will pass into other hands. But if the banks withdraw the paper trash, his farm will fall immediately down to its original value, and he will be deprived of all and find himself besides in debt, thrown out of employment, his family broken up, and his children obliged to fly to the factories, "those principalities of the destitute, and palaces of the poor," for sustenance.

Thus banking, both by issuing and by withdrawing its paper, disturbs the equality of society, and only serves to make the rich richer, and the industrious portion of the people still more dependent and wretched. It is a two-edged sword in the hands of the enemy, whichever way it is wielded destroying the people. But the great monopoly has of late received a shock which it is our interest and our duty to make fatal. Now is the time to destroy the evil; and we should do it so unanimously as completely to obliterate every hope of raising another in its place. Kill the great monster, and the whole brood which are hatched and nourished over the land will fall in easy prey. But if we suffer it to escape with life, however, wounded, maimed, and mutilated, it will soon recover its wonted strength, its whole power to injure us, and all hope of its destruction must be forever renounced. The enemy are everywhere coming to the rescue and rallying to sustain it, beseeching and petitioning us to spare its life. But let us turn a deaf ear to their entreaties, and its destruction is sure.

The Address of the United States Anti-Masonic Convention (1830)

On September 11, 1830, delegates from eleven states met at Philadelphia to denounce the Freemasonic Order and to call upon their countrymen to join in a political crusade to save the nation from subversion and tyranny at the hands of Masons. In the words of Thaddeus Stevens, who represented Pennsylvania and who later led the Radicals in Congress during the Reconstruction, "though but one hundred thousand of the people of these United States are free-masons, yet almost all the offices of high profit and high honour are filled with gentlemen of that institution. Out of the number of law judges in the state of Pennsylvania, eighteen-twentieths are masons; and twenty-two out of twenty-four states of the Union, are now governed by masonic chief magistrates." William Seward, delegate from New York and later governor of that state as well as Secretary of State under Lincoln, affirmed "we will not wait for the accomplishment of this scheme of tyranny. Did our forefathers wait? Three cents tax upon a pound of tea was a small matter; but it was the entering wedge, which this community would not suffer to be applied to the fabric of her liberties." Anti Masonry was in part a vehicle for the political elevation of aspiring young men like Stevens and Seward. But as the following address indicates, it was also an instrument for defining the meaning of loyalty and openness in a free society, and of articulating new attitudes toward public opinion and popular suffrage.

To the People of the United States

FELLOW CITIZENS: It is the privilege of freemen to consult together, openly and peaceably, on all subjects interesting to their common welfare. And so long as the opinion of a majority shall prevail, enlightened and frequent consultation, among them, will furnish the most efficacious and acceptable means of expelling wrongs, and removing fears. . . .

Facts numerous and authentic, demonstrate the existence, in this community, of crimes and dangers, which, upon their first distinct

From *The Address of the United States Anti-Masonic Convention* (New York, 1830), pp. 3–6, 8–15, 18–19.

disclosure to honest inquiry, excite equal surprise and solicitude; and which cannot be reflected upon, by any mind imbued with genuine self-respect, and a just regard for human rights, without the deepest abhorrence and alarm.

Freemasonry is the source of these crimes and dangers.

In 1826, William Morgan, your free fellow citizen, was, by highly exalted members of the masonic fraternity, with unlawful violence, seized,—secretly transported through the country more than one hundred miles, to a fortress of the United States [Niagara], then in charge of freemasons, who had prepared it for his reception,—there imprisoned, several days and nights, against his utmost efforts to escape,—and after suffering the most unmanly insults, and the most inhuman abuse, he was privately murdered. Previously to his seizure, numerous meetings of freemasons, in lodges and otherwise, were held for the purpose of contriving and adopting the most certain means of carrying into effect, their unlawful objects upon him. These meetings were attended, and the designs of them approved, by several hundred of the most respectable and intelligent of the masonic brethren. They included legislators, judges, sheriffs, clergymen, generals, physicians, and lawyers. And they proceeded in discharge of, what they deemed, their masonic duties.

William Morgan was a royal arch mason. And the cause of all this unlawful violence against his liberty and life, was, his determination to publish the secrets of the order. These secrets are now published, partly from manuscripts prepared by him, but more extensively from the deliberate testimony of many worthy men, who had been initiated further into the dark mysteries of the brotherhood, than he had. The precise motive, which impelled Morgan to the determination of publishing, we do not know. As the act was one of conformity to his highest obligations, and therefore, of distinguished honour, we believe the motive to have been good. There is no room to doubt, that other members of the institution, being aware of the solemn fate, to which freemasonry had consigned him, for disobedience to its laws, felt themselves driven, by the fearful responsibility of membership, most carefully to weigh its objects, means, and tendency; and finding these, upon mature examination, to be wholly unjustifiable and dangerous, they were impelled, by good will to man, by allegiance to our government, and by the natural desire of self-approbation, to proclaim its character, and renounce its authority. . . .

In this alarming emergency, the agents of government seemed paralyzed. Our public institutions and provisions for the preservation of tranquility, and the repression of crime, seemed nugatory. And without the use of other means than the law, and its official ministers, the most daring and brutal inroads, upon our dearest rights, would have passed off, without effort to understand their origin, punish their instruments, or provide against their recurrence. No arts were left untried by freemasons to baffle the pursuit of truth, and defeat the administration of justice. The lion's grip of the order was upon our courts, and loyalty to that, displaced fealty to the state.

A large proportion of the constables, justices of the peace, lawyers, judges, sheriffs, and jurymen, of the counties where these acts were performed, were members of the society, and had taken oaths binding them, in terms, to conceal each other's crimes. The high sheriffs were all masons, and at that time, summoned as grand jurors, at their discretion, any such men as had the common qualifications. In the counties of Genesee and Niagara, where the fraternity were most afraid of criminal prosecutions, majorities of freemasons are known to have been corruptly returned as grand jurors. And these sheriffs of these counties were both indicted, subsequently, as parties to the conspiracy for the abduction of Morgan. One of them was tried and convicted; the trial of the other has not yet taken place.

Perceiving that the public functionaries, whose duty it is to initiate proceedings in criminal cases, were totally inactive, through cowardice or corruption, the people, who are both the proprietors and beneficiaries of every department of government, undertook to inquire and present for themselves, in relation to these offences. . . . They called public meetings, at which honest and intelligent committees were raised, to ascertain facts, and aid the public functionaries. And these committees entered with patriotic alacrity, upon the performance of some of the most difficult and responsible duties of freemen. Without any emolument, at great expense of time and money, in defiance of the most malignant, persevering, and ingenious counteraction of freemasons, they suspended their private concerns, and gave themselves up to all the labours of a complicated investigation. . . . They ascertained the principal facts respecting the kidnapping and murder, both as to the persons directly concerned in them, and their motives and principles of action; and thus laid a sure foundation,—not for the lawful conviction and condemnation of those who are most guilty; that has hitherto been rendered impossible, by the felon sympathies and powerful interposition of freemasonry,—but for the universal and endless execration of their crimes, and of the institution in which they originated. . . .   "·

When good men join the masonic society, and inconsiderately swear to obey its injunctions, without knowing what they are, as every mason does, they imagine there must, of course, be a reservation in favour of all civil and social duties. But this is a total mistake. The first oath, and many others in the series, fatally precludes it. It is a part of the language of the oaths, that the specific engagements contained in them, shall all be performed "without any mental reservation, equivocation, or self-evasion of mind whatever." And any brother who does not so perform them, voluntarily subjects himself to the penalty of death.

What duties do the masonic oaths impose? . . . ,

The royal arch mason swears, "I will aid and assist a companion royal arch mason, when engaged in any difficulty, and espouse his cause, so far as to extricate him from the same, if in my power, whether he be right or wrong. I will promote a companion royal arch mason's political preferment, in preference to another of equal qualifications. A companion royal arch mason's secrets, given me in charge as such, and I knowing him to be such, shall remain as secure and inviolable, in my breast as in his own, murder and treason not excepted, etc." . . .

In the degree of knights of Kadosh, the candidate swears "to follow at all times, and in all points, every matter that he is ordered, and prescribed by the illustrious knights and grand commander, without any restrictions," and especially, "to sacrifice the traitors of masonry."

Such are some of the principles expressed in their own language, which are adopted in the masonic degrees alluded to, and imposed upon the members, under circumstances most indecent, profane and frightful. . . . Revealed freemasonry is a stupendous mirror, which reflects, in all their horrors, the exact features of that vast spirit of crime, with which this nation is now wrestling, for all that makes life desirable. . . .

Can the well informed friends of freedom tolerate a society thus characterized? Is it consistent with the theory or practice of our most valued establishments, with any authority underived from itself, or any safety, but that of its adhering members? It exercises the highest powers of government, raises and appropriates money, makes and executes laws extending to life itself, which each of its subjects, in the sacred form of oaths, voluntarily abandons to its authority. It is a government of high priests, and kings, and illustrious knights, and grand commanders. And every person, who maintains connexion with it, in effect, renounces all allegiance to other governments, by swearing to perform acts entirely inconsistent with such allegiance, without any mental reservation whatever. In war, in peace, in all the business of life, every obligated mason, is bound to prefer a brother mason to other persons, and masonic duties, to other duties. . . .

To contrive the true theory of free government, is the proudest evidence of human intelligence: to institute such a government, the most glorious achievement of human wisdom: and to sustain it, with unfailing constancy, the greatest monument of human virtue. Our government is the inestimable purchase of the profound reflection, painful labours, disinterested exertions, and searching trials, of all past ages. It is free. We believe it to be the best that ever existed, because, more than any other, it corresponds with the rights, and encourages the duties of all men, over whom it is extended; and thus, more than any other, seeks and promotes the improvement and happiness of its subjects. But our government cannot be continued, without the active, strenuous, and constant, maintenance of principles directly opposed to those of freemasonry.

The first and most prominent injunction of freemasonry is secrecy. Any violation of this it punishes with infamy and death. Secrecy is the shutting up of the mind from communion with other minds. And so far as it prevails, in relation to any social good, it is selfish, sour, ignorant, and restless. Left absolutely alone, like a plant separated from the earth and the air, we should soon wither and die. . . . Our faculties are not at all adapted to it. Hermits are always the most miserable men. Ascetic and secluded associations have never been wise, or good, or happy. Neither is freemasonry, which inculcates their worst principles, not in melancholy seclusion from the world, but in the heart of it, the more successfully to prey upon it.

A virtuous mind cannot delight in secrecy. Its joy is in communion. We are made sociable by nature. Our best affections and our highest faculties equally indicate it. For they can neither be expanded into useful action, nor carry with them their appropriate rewards, without society. As social beings, if we discover useful facts, or important truths, we desire to communicate them to all, who are susceptible of benefits from their application. As all the principles of science, charity, and religion, are susceptible of beneficial application to the whole human race, good men and good governments will impose no artificial restriction, upon their universal diffusion. . . .

But secrecy is not more hostile to the spreading of useful facts and truths, than it is to their discovery. Free inquiry, free discussion, free communication, are essential requisites to the most valuable knowledge. In the arts and sciences, in ethics and theology, all liberal minds acknowledge their indispensable importance. In the political conduct of life, their importance is, if possible, still more manifest. They are the living foundations of our government, which would be speedily dissolved, in blood, without them. No man has ever yet sufficiently valued them: for they alone can safely be relied upon, to open and illuminate all the paths, in which the majestic power of public opinion displays itself. But freemasonry is opposed to free inquiry, free discussion, and free communication. Its great fear is publicity, its best virtue, silence. It professes to have inestimable treasures of social benefits, which it refuses to disclose to any but the small number of its devoted followers. . . . It first enslaves the mind by the chain of secrecy, then debases it by injurious ceremonies and vile principles, and finally insults it by mock titles and simulated virtues. It is incompetent to the support of any valuable object. There is no real duty, no honest enjoyment, no benevolent purpose, which cannot better be accomplished without it. It is a fit system for the outlaws of humanity and hope, hating the world, and making war upon it. With a misanthropic caution it excludes all the helpless and infirm from its communion, and with the stimulated ingenuity of experienced and impenitent guilt, it provides against detection and exposure. Its existence in our country is the greatest anomaly of modern times; and it is to be accounted for only, by the unsuspecting confidence in their fellow citizens, natural to men conscious of their liberty. Aware of this trait in the character of our people, designing members of the fraternity, and those who are weak enough to find pleasure in its fantastic frivolities and bloated titles, have lengthened its cords till they now probably embrace more than a hundred thousand of our countrymen. . . .

If freemasonry ought to be abolished, it should certainly be so abolished as to prevent its restoration. No means of doing this can be conceived so competent as those furnished by the ballot boxes. These means are commended to our adoption, by the most urgent considerations, by their mildness, their safety, their sufficiency, and the tested insufficiency of all others. They are the means provided, by the most venerated of our political fathers. Who shall disparage them? Whoever is opposed to freemasonry and really desires its extinction, must use them, or confess himself a slave or tyrant. To extinguish it, by violence, would be tyranny, if it were possible. To extinguish it, by the expression of honest convictions against it, would not be tyranny, but it cannot be accomplished, unless a majority unite in such expression; and whether they do or not, cannot be ascertained, without a general vote. To desire its extinction, and do nothing to effect it, must proceed from indolence, fear, or the imagined force of assumed obligations in its favour, either of which amounts to a degrading slavery. To such slavery who is willing to submit?

Debates at the Anti-Masonic Convention (1830)

At the same convention, delegates competed with one another in portraying the extreme perils the nation faced. Like the French Illuminati, the Freemasons were painted as the enemies of Christianity as well as of republican institutions. Of particular significance were the attempts to sharpen the definition of American citizenship and to see in anti-Masonry a regenerative, liberating force comparable to that of the Protestant Reformation and the American Revolution. Genuine freedom, one might conclude, depended on periodic crusades against organized despotism.

Speech of Samuel W. Dexter of Michigan

MR. PRESIDENT: I would, with other gentlemen who have preceded me, give my voice in favour of the ability and truth of the address to the people of the United States.

The strong ground taken by that address, I presume to be this: that free-masonry is an empire of itself, distinct from every government within whose limits it exists; that it has its laws paramount to all other laws, its altars and its priests exalted above the religion of the land.

Let it never be forgotten, that, in these United States, there are from one to two hundred thousand men, who have sworn allegiance

From *The Proceedings of the United States Anti-Masonic Convention* (New York, 1830), pp. 117–118, 120.

to laws not recognized by our constitution—laws in direct opposition to those of our land—laws cruel and abominable. This is not mere theory in the masonic institution; but has been reduced to practice. We have seen these unlawful oaths developed by the conduct of those who have sworn fealty to them. . . . We have, sir, the substantial testimony of about five thousand seceding masons to this effect. In addition to this, we have circumstantial evidence that is irresistible. . . .

What constitutes an American citizen? Is it that he lives within the limits of these United States—that he was born within certain boundaries, or has since submitted to certain ceremonies of naturalization? These, sir, may be necessary, but he only is at heart an American, who venerates the pure republicanism which our fathers bled to maintain—he who acknowledges no laws paramount to those of his country and his God.

When a citizen of these United States kneels at the altar of masonry, when he swears allegiance to her laws, he snaps asunder the ties that bind him to his country; he cannot at the same time be the citizen of a free republic, and the subject of a despotic empire. . . .

Free-masonry, by mingling prayers with bloody and profane oaths, by uniting the mummery of masonry with passages from holy writ, by its impious titles, such as "Most Worshipful," and "King of Heaven," by insinuations in the lower degrees, and direct declarations in the higher, stands forth as the apostle of Deism, if not of Atheism. . . .

Speech of William Slade of Vermont

Our great aim is the complete prostration of the institution of free-masonry. We would break up its lodges, its chapters, and its encampments. We would strip from its officers their gaudy trappings, and bloated titles, and mock dignities, and bring them upon a level with the plain, untitled citizens of the republic. We would convince its votaries of its pernicious character and tendency, and bring them up to *the all-essential point of absolving their allegiance to the institution,* and separating themselves from it, for ever. We would, in short, prostrate this "unhallowed temple," so that "there shall not be left one stone upon another, that shall not be thrown down." This is the direct and obvious purpose to be accomplished by our efforts.

But, sir, there are results indirectly connected with the existence of anti-masonry, which present no ordinary claims to our regard. I allude to its influence upon the general character of our country and of the age. In contemplating the subject in this light, events of other times present a parallel which is not destitute of instruction. The reformation of the 16th century, for example, though primarily a religious reformation, exerted, in various other respects, an influence of deep and lasting importance to Europe and to the world. It was not a mere emancipation from the spiritual dominion of the Papal See; but it broke the shackles which bound the human intellect. It taught men to think; it brought mind into conflict with mind; it asserted the right of free enquiry and private judgment; and it kindled the spark of that liberty which now burns upon the altars of our country. These effects naturally resulted from the character of the evil upon which the force of that reformation was brought directly to bear. And who, that is familiar with its origin and its history, can fail to see that, substantially, the same causes are now in operation, and that they are tending to the production of the same general results?

An important era in the history of our own country illustrates the same principle. Urged to the extremest point of endurance by British oppression, our fathers rose and asserted their right to independence. They put forth their strength, and were free. But, sir, there was more in that freedom than a mere emancipation from the thraldom of a foreign power. The conflicts of the revolution brought into vigorous exercise some of the noblest virtues that belong to our nature; and while the men whose souls were thus tried, were forcing their way to freedom, they were fitting themselves, in an eminent degree, for its enjoyment. A cast was given to their moral and intellectual character, which is now visible in all the institutions which they established.

Anti-masonry, sir, possesses the elements of both the revolutions to which I have adverted. I know, indeed, that there are those who affect to consider it as degrading to the moral and intellectual character of our country. I regard it, sir, in precisely the opposite light. The life and soul of anti-masonry is a spirit of free enquiry, directed to the just exposure of an institution, immoral in its tendency, and anti-republican in its whole structure. The spirit which the abduction and murder of a free citizen originally produced, was, to use the language of a high judicial functionary of your state, "a blessed spirit." It still retains that character. It was, and it is, a virtuous indignation at the perpetration of wrong, and a determination to apply every practicable corrective. It leads to a more just appreciation of the value of that liberty, so daringly invaded in the person of a free citizen, as well as of that life which was impiously sacrificed upon the altar of free-masonry. It asserts the right of the people to investigate and probe to the bottom, *every* public evil, and to apply such correctives as they may deem proper. And it invigorates the public intellect, by directing its energies to the investigation of some of the most interesting questions which can engage its attention. Masons may, indeed, deride and denounce it, and exhaust upon it all the epithets of reproach and contempt. But every intelligent, unbiased statesman will see in it the strong characteristic traits of genuine republicanism; and regard it, even in its occasional excesses, as threatening no serious danger to any thing, but the institution which it is its avowed and determined purpose, to destroy.

Masonry Proved to Be
a Work of Darkness (1830)

LEBBEUS ARMSTRONG

From 1828 to the early 1830's there was a deluge of anti-Masonic pamphlets, speeches, and reports by state conventions. The sense of acute alarm was perhaps expressed most fervently by Lebbeus Armstrong, a Presbyterian minister who sat as a delegate from New York at the Philadelphia convention of 1830 and who delivered the following address in a number of eastern cities.

Suppose the secret machinations of masonry had succeeded without molestation, until, by its mystic power of elevation, all the commanding officers of the military and maritime forces of our national defence, all officers of civil government, post masters, and directors of the various banking establishments had been masons; and all the financial sources of the nation had been brought within the compass of masonic grasp.

After all this preparation, suppose a plot had been formed to overthrow our dearbought Republican Government, to erect a throne in this western world, and place on it a Grand, Sublime, Royal, Ten Times Thrice Illustrious, and Absolutely Sovereign Masonic King. Suppose the *"Thirteenth day of the month Adar"* had been selected to

From Lebbeus Armstrong, *Masonry Proved to be a Work of Darkness, Repugnant to the Christian Religion; and Inimical to a Republican Government* (New York, 1830), p. 23.

blow the trumpet in Washington and proclaim "GOD SAVE THE MA-
SONIC KING," while all the members of the Grand and Subordinate
Lodges, Chapters, and Encampments in the Union, having been noti-
fied by posts, to prepare themselves on the day appointed, were well
harnessed, with Sword, Shield, and Buckler, and commissioned to
kill, slay, and utterly destroy all who would not respond at the sound
of the national trumpet, "GOD SAVE THE MASONIC KING." To defray the
expense of all necessary force of arms, in securing the triumph of a
Coronation, and unconditional submission to his Sovereign Masonic
Majesty, suppose the grasp had been made on the vaults of the numerous Banks, and money offered in exuberance to all who would
enter the field in support of the Revolution. Under such circumstances, what could have prevented the total overthrow of our national government, and the establishment of an absolute Masonic
Monarchy? If the government of France was revolutionized in *three*
days, might not the government of these United States have been
changed to Monarchy in *one* day by the Mystic Power of Masonic
Stratagem? Nothing could have prevented such a revolution, but the
interposition of that Divine Providence which has broken asunder the
strongly fortified enchantments of Freemasonry, and exposed its
works of darkness to the world. The God of Israel has interposed.
Glory be to his name; the Lord of Hosts has hitherto prevented our
national ruin.

An Anti-Masonic Call
for Perseverance (1834)

*By 1834 the anti-Masonic movement was threatened not only by political
pressures for compromise but by competing crusades to save the nation
from the sin of slavery, the "Monster" Bank, and the tyranny of "King Andrew" Jackson. The following excerpt from a report of the Anti-Masonic
Convention in Maine expressed a futile plea to preserve the movement from
political contamination.*

That masonry is substantially the same in all parts of the country,
and that it acts under secret laws, rites and ceremonies of a grossly

From *Proceedings of the Antimasonic Republican Convention, of the State of
Maine, Held at Hallowell, July 3d, & 4th 1834* (Hallowell, Maine, 1834), pp.
15–16.

immoral nature and tendency, have been conclusively proved in Courts of justice and elsewhere. And that instead of being, as its votaries pretend, a charitable institution, it is in fact a combination of mercenary and ambitious men, (principally, to say the least) for selfish objects—political preferment forming no small part of its views and purposes, your committee have no doubt. These are some of the reasons why Antimasons refuse to vote for the adherents of masonry. Whether they are "minor considerations," let freemen judge.

That both of the other political parties of the day are, to a considerable extent, under the dominion of masonry, is evident from the fact, that they are continually calling on Antimasons to "give up these minor considerations," and unite with them against their opponents. Masonic Jacksonmen say to us, "the United States Bank will cheat us of our liberties and ruin the country, come over and help us to destroy the *monster.*" The Masonic Whigs, alias Nationals, exclaim, "the constitution is violated, the laws are trampled upon, the country is lost—*aye, in the midst of a revolution!* Dear Anties, just lay aside your party organization and help us right the ship, or we sink."— Both parties in their blind zeal assuming as a fact that Antimasons were originally on their side, and would again act with them, but for Antimasonry. But who does not see the miserable absurdity of such a call, and its direct tendency to restore masonry to its former prosperity and splendor? It carries on its very face an insult to Antimasons. It supposes them insincere in their professions of belief that masonry is the greatest political evil of the day, and far more dangerous to our liberties than the worst dogmas of either of the other parties. It cannot be listened to by Antimasons without a total abandonment of our own principles. Our motto, "PERSEVERE," would thus be disregarded and lost, and nothing is more obvious than that a general defection of this kind in our ranks would be neither more nor less than the complete disbanding of the party. And shall we be seduced by masons and the friends of masons, under the guise of pretended patriotism, to give up our organization, and submit to be governed by the secret, irresponsible power of a blood-stained institution? No, your committee confidently believe that Antimasons will, to a man, spurn these insidious attacks, and press onward in the great cause of equal rights, until they have prostrated that secret power behind the laws, that is greater than the laws themselves.

A Plea for the West (1835)

LYMAN BEECHER

Lyman Beecher, the father of Harriet Beecher Stowe and Henry Ward Beecher, was one of New England's leading ministers and one of the nation's most outspoken opponents of dueling, intemperance, Unitarianism, Roman Catholicism, and religious indifference. Beecher's outlook and style should be sharply differentiated from that of men like Ebenezer Baldwin and Lebbeus Armstrong. Because of his profound respect for institutions and social controls, he tended to view change, either for good or ill, as a gradual process. Nevertheless, he was a vital link between the New England Federalists of the 1790's and much later alarmists like Josiah Strong. His principal themes and assumptions help illuminate the connection between fears of subversion and belief in America's mission to "emancipate the world."

Beecher's great goal in life was to help hasten the coming of a worldwide republican millennium by evangelizing the American West. To this end he left Boston to become president of Lane Theological Seminary in Cincinnati, which he envisioned as an outpost of true Christianity surrounded by a wilderness of infidelity, ignorance, and unbridled competition. Like Jonathan Edwards, whom he cites at the beginning of the present selection, Beecher was convinced that the millennium would begin in America. But unlike his Puritan and Federalist forerunners, Beecher associated the Kingdom of God with the Christianization of the American West. His sense of urgency stemmed from his appreciation of the importance of technological progress and physical expansion. If Americans could transcend individual self-interest, their technology and westward expansion would enable them to save the world. But if they were unfaithful to this stupendous mission, they would suffer appropriate retribution. Beecher was acutely sensitive to the contingency of America's great experiment, and projects an image of the nation in her "dying agonies." This mode of conceptualizing America's "either-or" destiny was to be echoed by Josiah Strong as well as by later right-wing fundamentalists like John A. Stormer and Billy James Hargis.

Insofar as Beecher limited himself to combating sin and irreligion, there is no ground for classifying him as a countersubversive. But even before

From Lyman Beecher, A Plea for the West, 2nd ed. (Cincinnati, 1835), pp. 9–12, 31–32, 36–39, 42–43, 46–47, 51–54, 56–57, 59–61, 63–64, 69–72, 114–117, 142, 146–148, 184–188.

*leaving Boston, he had become alarmed by the influx of Catholic immi-
grants and had begun to identify the Catholic Church as the most formidable obstacle to America's mission. An ardent republican nationalist, he assumed that the American example was an inspiration to the enslaved masses
of Europe and thus a constant peril to European despots. The only way
such priests and kings could avoid domestic subversion would be to subvert
the American Republic. If they could not send armies to America's shores,
they could at least send hordes of immigrants to accomplish their purpose.
The arrival of increasing numbers of Catholic immigrants provided Beecher
with an easy explanation for such shortcomings of American society as poverty, crime, and mob violence. But it is also interesting to note his argument that the civil and ecclesiastical authorities of Europe must have had a
conspiratorial design since they possessed adequate motives as well as a surplus population. Catholic policy in the past, he claimed, had always been
"to compensate for losses at home by new efforts to extend their influence
abroad." The same point can be applied to Beecher's New England clergy,
who might have intended to compensate for their steady decline from established power by diffusing New England Protestantism throughout the West.
One suspects that Beecher's picture of Catholic expansionism is in some respects a mirror image of his own aspirations for New England culture.
Moreover, the fear of an international Catholic (or Communist) conspiracy
could justify the most strenuous and dedicated efforts at cultural conquest.
It is here that we see the subtle link between countersubversion and belief
in America's mission to emancipate—or Americanize—mankind.*

It was the opinion of [Jonathan] Edwards, that the millennium
would commence in America. When I first encountered this opinion, I
thought it chimerical; but all providential developments since, and all
the existing signs of the times, lend corroboration to it. But if it is by
the march of revolution and civil liberty, that the way of the Lord is
to be prepared, where shall the central energy be found, and from
what nation shall the renovating power go forth? What nation is
blessed with such experimental knowledge of free institutions, with
such facilities and resources of communication, obstructed by so few
obstacles, as our own? There is not a nation upon earth which, in fifty
years, can by all possible reformation place itself in circumstances so
favorable as our own for the free, unembarrassed applications of
physical effort and pecuniary and moral power to evangelize the
world.

But if this nation is, in the providence of God, destined to lead the
way in the moral and political emancipation of the world, it is time
she understood her high calling, and were harnessed for the work.

For mighty causes, like floods from distant mountains, are rushing with accumulating power, to their consummation of good or evil, and soon our character and destiny will be stereotyped forever.

It is equally plain that the religious and political destiny of our nation is to be decided in the West. There is the territory, and there soon will be the population, the wealth, and the political power. The Atlantic commerce and manufactures may confer always some peculiar advantages on the East. But the West is destined to be the great central power of the nation, and under heaven, must affect powerfully the cause of free institutions and the liberty of the world.

The West is a young empire of mind, and power, and wealth, and free institutions, rushing up to a giant manhood, with a rapidity and a power never before witnessed below the sun. And if she carries with her the elements of her preservation, the experiment will be glorious—the joy of the nation—the joy of the whole earth, as she rises in the majesty of her intelligence and benevolence, and enterprise, for the emancipation of the world.

It is equally clear, that the conflict which is to decide the destiny of the West, will be a conflict of institutions for the education of her sons, for purposes of superstition, or evangelical light; of despotism, or liberty. . . .

But what will become of the West, if her prosperity rushes up to such a majesty of power, while those great institutions linger which are necessary to form the mind, and the conscience, and the heart of that vast world? It must not be permitted. And yet what is done must be done quickly; for population will not wait, and commerce will not cast anchor, and manufactures will not shut off the steam nor shut down the gate, and agriculture, pushed by millions of freemen on their fertile soil, will not withhold her corrupting abundance.

We must educate! We must educate! or we must perish by our own prosperity. If we do not, short from the cradle to the grave will be our race. If in our haste to be rich and mighty, we outrun our literary and religious institutions, they will never overtake us. . . . And let no man at the East quiet himself, and dream of liberty, whatever may become of the West. Our alliance of blood, and political institutions, and common interests, is such, that we cannot stand aloof in the hour of her calamity, should it ever come. Her destiny is our destiny; and the day that her gallant ship goes down, our little boat sinks in the vortex! . . .

This vast territory is occupied now by ten states and will soon be by twelve. Forty years since it contained only about one hundred and fifty thousand souls; while it now contains little short of five millions. At the close of this century, if no calamity intervenes, it will contain, probably, one hundred millions—a day which some of our children may live to see; and when fully peopled, may accommodate three hundred millions. It is half as large as all Europe, four times as large as the Atlantic states, and twenty times as large as New-England. Was there ever such a spectacle—such a field in which to plant the seeds of an immortal harvest!—so vast a ship, so richly laden with the world's treasures and riches, whose helm is offered to the guiding influence of early forming institutions! . . .

Such is the gravitating tendency of society, that no spontaneous effort at arms-length will hold it up. It is by the constant energy and strong attraction of powerful institutions only that the needed intellectual and moral power can be applied: and the present is the age of founding them. If this work be done, and well done, our country is safe, and the world's hope is secure. The government of force will cease, and that of intelligence and virtue will take its place; and nation after nation cheered by our example, will follow in our footsteps, till the whole earth is free. There is no danger that our agriculture and arts will not prosper: the danger is, that our intelligence and virtue will falter and fall back into a dark minded, vicious populace—a poor, uneducated reckless mass of infuriated animalism, to rush on resistless as the tornado, or to burn as if set on fire of hell.

Until Europe, by universal education, is delivered from such masses of feudal ignorance and servitude, she sits upon a volcano, and despotism and revolution will arbitrate her destiny. . . .

The great experiment is now making, and from its extent and rapid filling up is making in the West, whether the perpetuity of our republican institutions can be reconciled with universal suffrage. Without the education of the head and heart of the nation, they cannot be; and the question to be decided is, can the nation, or the vast balance power of it be so imbued with intelligence and virtue, as to bring out, in laws and their administration, a perpetual self-preserving energy? We know that the work is a vast one, and of great difficulty; and yet we believe it can be done. . . .

I would add, as a motive to immediate action, that if we do fail in our great experiment of self-government, our destruction will be as signal as the birth-right abandoned, the mercies abused and the provocation offered to beneficent Heaven. The descent of desolation will correspond with the past elevation. No punishments of Heaven are so severe as those for mercies abused; and no instrumentality employed in their infliction is so dreadful as the wrath of man. No spasms are like the spasms of expiring liberty, and no wailings such as her convulsions extort. It took Rome three hundred years to die; and our death, if we perish, will be as much more terrific as our intelligence and free institutions have given to us more bone, and sinew and vitality. May God hide me from the day when the dying agonies of my country shall begin! O, thou beloved land bound together by the ties of brotherhood and common interest, and perils, live forever—one and undivided! . . .

This danger from uneducated mind is augmenting daily by the rapid influx of foreign emigrants, the greater part unacquainted with our institutions, unaccustomed to self-government, inaccessible to education, and easily accessible to prepossession, and inveterate credulity, and intrigue, and easily embodied and wielded by sinister design. In the beginning this eruption of revolutionary Europe was not anticipated, and we opened our doors wide to the influx and naturalization of foreigners. But it is becoming a terrific inundation; it has increased upon our native population from five to thirty-seven per cent, and is every year advancing. It seeks, of course, to settle down upon the unoccupied territory of the West, and may at no distance day equal, and even outnumber the native population. What is to be done to educate the millions which in twenty years Europe will pour out upon us?

But what if this emigration, self-moved and slow in the beginning, is now rolling its broad tide at the bidding of the powers of Europe hostile to free institutions, and associated in holy alliance to arrest and put them down? Is this a vain fear? Are not the continental powers alarmed at the march of liberal opinions, and associated to put them down? and are they not, with the sickness of hope deferred, waiting for our downfall? It is the light of our republican prosperity, gleaming in upon their dark prison house, which is inspiring hope, and converting chains into arms. It is the power of mind, roused by our example from the sleep of ages and the apathy of despair, which is sending earthquakes under the foundations of their thrones; and they have no hope of rest and primeval darkness, but by the extinction of our light. By fleets and armies they cannot do it. But do they, therefore, sleep on their heaving earth and tottering thrones? Has Metternich yet to form an acquaintance with history? Does he dream that there is but one way to overturn republics, and that by the sword? Has he yet to learn how Philip, by dividing her councils, conquered Greece? and how, by intestine divisions, Rome fell?

If the potentates of Europe have no design upon our liberties, what means the paying of the passage and emptying out upon our shores such floods of pauper emigrants—the contents of the poorhouse and the sweepings of the streets?—multiplying tumults and violence, filling our prisons, and crowding our poorhouses, and quadrupling our taxation, and sending annually accumulating thousands to the polls to lay their inexperienced hand upon the helm of our power? Does Metternich imagine that there is no party spirit in our land, whose feverish urgency would facilitate their naturalization and hasten them to the ballot box?—and no demagogues, who for a little brief authority, however gained, would sell their country to an everlasting bondage? . . .

But if, upon examination, it should appear that three-fourths of the foreign emigrants whose accumulating tide is rolling in upon us, are, through the medium of their religion and priesthood, as entirely accessible to the control of the potentates of Europe as if they were an army of soldiers, enlisted and officered, and spreading over the land; then, indeed, should we have just occasion to apprehend danger to our liberties. It would be the union of church and state in the midst of us. . . .

The simple fact, that the clergy of the Catholic denomination could wield in mass the suffrage of their confiding people, could not fail, in the competition of ambition and party spirit, to occasion immediately an eager competition for their votes, placing them at once in the attitude of the most favored sect; securing the remission of duties on imported church property, and copious appropriations of land for the endowment of their institutions . . . and turning against their opponents, and in favor of Catholics, the patronage and the tremendous influence of the administration, whose ascendency and continuance might, in closely contested elections, be thought to depend on Catholic suffrage. . . .

The ministers of no Protestant sect could or would dare to attempt to regulate the votes of their people as the Catholic priests can do, who at the confessional learn all the private concerns of their people, and have almost unlimited power over the conscience as it respects the performance of every civil or social duty.

There is another point of dissimilarity of still greater importance.

The opinions of the Protestant clergy are congenial with liberty—they are chosen by the people who have been educated as freemen, and they are dependent on them for patronage and support. The Catholic system is adverse to liberty, and the clergy to a great extent are dependent on foreigners opposed to the principles of our government, for patronage and support. . . .

But before I proceed, to prevent misapprehension, I would say that I have no fear of the Catholics, considered simply as a religious denomination, and unallied to the church and state establishments of the European governments hostile to republican institutions.

Let the Catholics mingle with us as Americans and come with their children under the full action of our common schools and republican institutions, and the various powers of assimilation, and we are prepared cheerfully to abide the consequences. If in these circumstances the Protestant religion cannot stand before the Catholic, let it go down, and we will sound no alarm, and ask no aid, and make no complaint. It is no ecclesiastical quarrel to which we would call the attention of the American nation.

Nor would I consent that the civil and religious rights of the Catholics should be abridged or violated. As naturalized citizens, to all that we enjoy we bid them welcome, and would have their property and rights protected with the same impartiality and efficacy that the property and rights of every other denomination are protected. . . . Did the Catholics regard themselves only as one of many denominations of Christians, entitled only to equal rights and privileges, there would be no such cause for apprehension while they peaceably sustained themselves by their own arguments and well doing. But if Catholics are taught to believe that their church is the only church of Christ, out of whose inclosure none can be saved,—that none may read the Bible but by permission of the priesthood and no one be permitted to understand it and worship God according to the dictates of his own conscience,—that heresy is a capital offence not to be tolerated, but punished by the civil power with disfranchisement, death and confiscation of goods,—that the pope and the councils of the church are infallible, and her rights of ecclesiastical jurisdiction universal and as far as possible and expedient may be of right, and ought to be as a matter of duty, enforced by the civil power,—that to the pope belongs the right of interference with the political concerns of nations, enforced by his authority over the consciences of Catholics, and his power to corroborate or cancel their oath of allegiance, and to sway them to obedience or insurrection by the power of life or death eternal: if such, I say, are the maxims *avowed by her pontiffs, sanctioned by her councils, stereotyped on her ancient records, advocated by her most approved authors, illustrated in all ages by her history, and still* UNREPEALED and still *acted upon* in the armed prohibition of free inquiry and religious liberty, and the punishment of heresy wherever her power remains unbroken: if these things are so, is it invidious and is it superfluous to call the attention of the nation to the bearing of such a denomination upon our civil and religious institutions and equal rights? It is the *right of* SELF-PRESERVATION, and the denial of it is TREASON or the INFATUATION OF FOLLY. . . .

But, it is said, "this outcry of a conspiracy to overturn our republican institutions by immigration and ecclesiastical influence is a false alarm. There is no such design." . . .

But if the civil and ecclesiastical powers of Europe have no such design, they lack the ordinary discretion and conduct of men in their condition, annoyed and endangered, as they feel themselves to be, by our republican institutions. If they have no design to extend their influence by ecclesiastical power, they have forgotten also all the past analogies of supposed duty,—their faith authorizing and requiring them to extend the Catholic religion the world over, by persuasion if they can, and by force if they must and are able. And when or where has their executive zeal fallen in the rear of their physical ability?

If they have no design, they do not pursue the analogy of their past policy in similar circumstances, which has been always to compensate for losses at home by new efforts to extend their influence abroad. It was the boast of the Catholic church, when she lost half Europe by the Reformation, that she had more than compensated her loss by the new enterprise of her Jesuit missionaries in India and South America. But during the last half century her power in Europe has been as much curtailed by infidelity and revolution, as before it had been by the Reformation. "The spirit of the age," which Bonaparte says dethroned him, is moving on to put an end in Europe to Catholic domination, creating the necessity of making reprisals abroad for what liberty conquers at home. Their policy points them to the West, the destined centre of civilization and political power once their own, and embracing now their ancient settlements and institutions and people, and not a little wealth—bounded on the north by a Catholic population, and on the south by a continent not yet emancipated from their dominion. . . .

In all this long career of evil it is not the personal character of individuals which perverted the system and sent out the results, but the system which perverted personal character. It was the energy of an absolute spiritual dominion in corrupt alliance with political despotism—displaying their perverting power and acting out their own nature. It is the most skillful, powerful, dreadful system of corruption to those who wield it and of debasement and slavery to those who live under it, which ever spread darkness and desolation over the earth. . . .

This anti-republican tendency of clerical influence is augmented in our nation, by the fact that the control of suffrage, and secular patronage, and education, and power of conscience, is under the predominant influence of the society of Jesuits; an order of men associated at the Reformation, to stay its progress, and sustain and extend the cause of the Papacy—clothed with high privileges and devoted by oath to implicit obedience to his holiness—possessing the advantages of an efficient organization, and the energy of a despotic will, equal to the control of a commander-in-chief over every officer and private in his army, and wielding the power which belongs to talent, learning, wealth, numbers, and a deep knowledge of human nature, and the means of touching dextrously every spring of action, and securing every complexity of movement for religious and political purposes—trained as courtiers, confessors, teachers, diplomatists, saints, spies, and working men, to influence and control the destiny of nations, and guided also by a morality which permits the end to sanctify the means. An association of more moral and political power than was ever concentrated on the earth—twice suppressed as too formidable for the crowned despotism of Europe, and an overmatch for his holiness himself—and twice restored as indispensable to the waning power of the holy see. And now with the advantages of its past mistakes and experience, this order is in full organization, silent, systematized, unwatched, and unresisted action among us, to try the dexterity of its movements, and the potency of its power upon unsuspecting, charitable, credulous republicans. . . .

Education, intellectual and religious, is the point on which turns our destiny, of terrestrial glory and power, or of shame and everlasting contempt, and short is the period of our probation. . . . The education of the nation—the culture of its intellect—the formation of its conscience, and the regulation of its affection, heart, and action, is of all others the most important work. . . . It is here that we falter, and that the Catholic powers are determined to take advantage of our halting—by thrusting in professional instructors and underbidding us in the cheapness of education—calculating that for a morsel of meat we shall sell our birth-right. Americans, republicans, Christians, can you, will you, for a moment, permit your free institutions, blood bought, to be placed in jeopardy, for want of the requisite intellectual and moral culture?

A Foreign Conspiracy against the Liberties of the United States (1834)

SAMUEL F. B. MORSE

In addition to being a notable painter, inventor of the telegraph, and president of the National Academy of Design, Samuel F. B. Morse was a bitter foe of the Roman Catholic Church. Like his father Jedidiah, he was convinced that American liberty was being cunningly subverted by a foreign conspiracy. Yet instead of being alarmed by the left-wing radicalism of the French Revolution, Samuel Morse pictured America as a revolutionary force locked in an irreconcilable "war of principles" with the reactionary Europe of Count Metternich and Nicholas I of Russia. In a series of articles published in the New York Observer *in 1834 and later reprinted in pamphlet form, Morse painted a lurid picture of the Catholic Church as the Trojan Horse of European despotism. He also directed his attack on the complacency of American society—on the emerging liberal consensus which minimized religious and ideological differences and which, in the name of "tolerance," supposedly gave free play to subversive forces. (Morse charged the press, for example, with being an accomplice to subversion because of its fear of being called bigoted or prejudiced.) One gains insight into the tensions and conflicts in American values by reflecting upon Morse's interpretation of America's revolutionary heritage, his fluctuation between self-congratulation and anxiety over the nation's many successes, and his concern over the disintegration of a cohesive and homogeneous community.*

What, it will be said, is it at all probable that any nation, or combination of nations, can entertain designs against us, a people so peaceable, and at the same time so distant? Knowing the daily increas-

From Samuel F. B. Morse, *Foreign Conspiracy Against the Liberties of the United States,* 6th ed. (New York, 1844), pp. 33–40, 66–71, 99–101.

ing resources of this country in all the means of defence against foreign aggression, how absurd in the nations abroad to dream of a conquest on this soil! Let me, nevertheless, ask attention, while I humbly offer my reasons for believing that a conspiracy exists, that its plans are already in operation, and that we are attacked in a vulnerable quarter, which cannot be defended by our ships, our forts, or our armies.

Who among us is not aware that a mighty struggle of *opinion* is in our days agitating all the nations of Europe; that there is a war going on between *despotism* on one side, and *liberty* on the other. And with what deep anxiety should Americans watch the vicissitudes of the conflict! Having long since achieved our own victory in the great strife between arbitrary power and freedom; having demonstrated, by successful experiment before the world, the safety, the happiness, the superior excellence of a republican government, a government proceeding from the people as the true source of power; enjoying in overflowing abundance the rich blessings of such a government, must we not regard with more than common interest the efforts of mighty nations to break away from the prejudices and habits, and sophistical opinions of ages of darkness, and struggling to attain the same glorious privileges of rational freedom? But there are other motives than that of curiosity, or of mere sympathy with foreign trouble, that should arouse our solicitude in the fearful crisis which has at length arrived, a crisis which the prophetic tongue of a great British statesman [George Canning] long since foretold, *the war of opinion,* threatening the world with a more frightful sacrifice of human life than history in any of its blood-stained pages records. Happily separated by an ocean-barrier from the great arena where the physical action of this bloody drama is to be performed, we are secure from the immediate physical effects of the strife; but we cannot remain unaffected by the result.

Of European wars arising from the cravings of personal ambition, from thirst for national glory, from desire of territorial increase, or from other local causes, we might safely be ignorant both of cause and result. No armed bands of a conqueror flushed with victory could give us a moment's alarm. But in a war of opinions, in a war of principles, in which the very foundations of government are subverted, and the whole social fabric upturned, we cannot, if we would, be uninterested in the result. Principles are not bounded by geographical limits. Oceans present to them no barriers. All of principle that belongs to despotism throughout the world, whether in the iron systems of Russia and Austria, or the scarcely less civilized system of China, and all of principle that belongs to pure American freedom in the United States, or in the mixed systems of Britain, France, and some other European states, are in this great contest arrayed in opposition. The triumph of the one or the other principle, whether in the field of battle, or in the secret councils of the cabinet, or the congress of ministers, or the open debate, produces effects wherever society exists. The recent convulsions in Europe should not pass unheeded by Americans. . . .

No open annual message reveals frankly to all the world the true internal condition of the oppressed nations of Europe. From the well guarded walls of the secret council-chamber of the imperial power, documents seldom escape to show us the strength of the opposing *principle*. Despotism glosses over all its oppressions. The people are always happy under the paternal sway. They that plead for liberty are always enemies of public order. "Order reigns in Warsaw," was the proclamation that told the world that despotism had triumphed over Poland, and none now may know the number of her sons of freedom still at large, still unexiled to the mines of Siberia. . . .

"As long as I live," says the Emperor [Nicholas I of Russia], "I will oppose a will of iron to the progress of liberal opinions. The present generation is lost, but we must labor with zeal and earnestness to improve the spirit of that to come. It may require a hundred years; I am not unreasonable, I give you a whole age, but you must work without relaxation."

This is language without ambiguity, bold, undisguised; it is the clear and official disclosure of the determination of the Holy Alliance against liberty. It proclaims unextinguishable hatred, a *will of iron*. There is no compromise with liberty; a *hundred years* of efforts unrelaxed, if necessary, shall be put forth to crush it for ever. Its very name must be blotted from the earth. . . .

It is asked, Why should the Holy Alliance feel interested in the destruction of transtlantic liberty? I answer, the silent but powerful and increasing influence of our institutions on Europe, is reason enough. The example alone of prosperity, which we exhibit in such strong contrast to the enslaved, priest-ridden, tax-burdened despotisms of the old world, is sufficient to keep those countries in perpetual agitation. How can it be otherwise? Will a sick man, long despairing of cure, learn that there is a remedy for him, and not desire to procure it? Will one born to think a dungeon his natural home, learn through his grated bars that man may be free, and not struggle to obtain his liberty? And what do the people of Europe behold in this country? They witness the successful experiment of a free government; a government of the *people;* without rulers *de jure divino* (by divine right); having no hereditary privileged classes; a government exhibiting good order and obedience to law, without an armed police and secret tribunals; a government out of debt; a people industrious, enterprising, thriving in all their interests; without monopolies; a people religious without an establishment; moral and honest without the terrors of the confessional or the inquisition; a people not harmed by the uncontrolled liberty of the press and freedom of opinion; a people that read what they please, and think, and judge, and act for themselves; a people enjoying the most unbounded security of person and property; among whom domestic conspiracies are unknown; where the poor and rich have equal justice. . . . Every revolution that has occurred in Europe for the last half century has been, in a greater or less degree, the consequence of our own glorious revolution. The great political truths there promulgated to the world, are the seed of the disorders, and conspiracies, and revolutions of Europe, from the first French revolution down to the present time. These revolutions are the throes of the internal life, breaking the bands of darkness with which superstition and despotism have hitherto bound the nations, struggling into the light of a new age. Can despotism know all this, and not feel it necessary to do something to counteract the evil? . . .

The conspirators against our liberties, who have been admitted from abroad through the liberality of our institutions, are now *organized* in every part of the country; they are all subordinates, standing in regular steps of slave and master, from the most abject dolt that obeys the commands of his priest, up to the great master-slave Metternich, who commands and obeys his illustrious Master, the Emperor [of Austria]. They report from one to another, like the subofficers of an army, up to the commander-in-chief at Vienna (not the Pope, for he is but a subordinate of Austria). There is a similar organization among the Catholics of other countries, and the whole Catholic church is thus prepared to throw its weight of power and wealth into the hands of Austria, or any Holy Alliance of despots who may be persuaded to embark, for the safety of their dynasties, in the crusade against the liberties of a country which, by its simple existence in opposition to their theory of legitimate power, is working revolution and destruction to their thrones. . . .

This pliability of conscience, so advantageous in building up any system of oppression, religious or political, presents us with strangely contradictory alliances. In Europe, Popery supports the most *high-handed despotism,* lends its thunders to awe the people into the most abject obedience, and maintains, at the top of its creed, *the indissoluble union of church and state!* while in this country, where it is yet feeling its way . . . it has allied itself with the *democracy* of the land; it is loudest in its denunciations of tyranny, the tyranny of American patriots; it is first to scent out oppression, sees afar off the machinations of the native *American Protestants* to unite church and state, and puts itself forth the most zealous guardian of civil and religious liberty! With such sentinels, surely our liberties are safe; with such guardians of our rights, we may sleep on in peace! . . . The great body of emigrants to this country are the hard-working, mentally neglected poor of Catholic countries in Europe, who have left a land where they were enslaved, for one of freedom. However well disposed they may be to the country which protects them, and adopts them as citizens, they are not fitted to act with judgment in the political affairs of their new country, like native citizens, educated from their infancy in the principles and habits of our institutions. Most of them are too ignorant to act at all for themselves, and expect to be guided wholly by others. These others are of course their priests. Priests have ruled them at home by *divine right;* their ignorant minds cannot ordinarily be emancipated from their habitual subjection, they will not learn nor appreciate their exemption from any such usurpation of priestly power in this country, and they are implicitly at the beck of their spiritual guides. They live surrounded by freedom, yet liberty of conscience, right of private judgment, whether in religion or politics, are as effectually excluded by the priests, as if the code of Austria already ruled the land. They form a body of men whose habits of *action* (for I cannot say *thought*) are opposed to the principles of our free institutions, for, as they are not accessible to the reasonings of the press, they cannot and do not think for themselves.

Every unlettered Catholic emigrant, therefore, that comes into the country, is adding to a mass of ignorance which it will be difficult to reach by any liberal instruction; and however honest (and I have no doubt most of them are so), yet, from the nature of things, they are but obedient instruments in the hands of their more knowing leaders, to accomplish the designs of their foreign masters. Republican education, were it allowed freely to come in contact with their minds, would doubtless soon furnish a remedy for an evil for which, in the existing state of things, we have no cure. It is but to continue for a few years the sort of emigration that is now daily pouring in its thousands from Europe, and our institutions, for ought that I can see, are at the mercy of a body of foreigners, officered by foreigners, and held completely under the control of a foreign power. We may then have reason to say that we are the dupes of our own hospitality; we have sheltered in our well provided house a needy body of strangers, who, well filled with our cheer, are encouraged, by the unaccustomed familiarity with which they are treated, first to upset the regulations of the household, and then to turn their host and his family out of doors. . . .

Is not the evidence I have exhibited in my previous numbers sufficiently strong to prove to my countrymen the existence of a *foreign conspiracy* against the liberties of the country? Does the nature of the case admit of stronger evidence? or must we wait for some positive, undisguised acts of oppression, before we will believe that we are attacked and in danger? Must we wait for a formal declaration of war? The serpent has already commenced his coil about our limbs, and the lethargy of his poison is creeping over us; shall we be more sensible of the torpor when it has fastened upon our vitals? The *house is on fire;* can we not believe it till the flames have touched our flesh? Is not the enemy already organized in the land? . . . Because no foe is on the sea, no hostile armies on our plains, may we sleep securely? Shall we watch only on the outer walls, while the sappers and miners of foreign despots are at work under our feet, and steadily advancing beneath the very citadel? . . . *We* may sleep, but the enemy is awake; he is straining every nerve to possess himself of our fair land. We must awake, or we are lost. Foundations are attacked, fundamental principles are threatened, interests are put in jeopardy, which throw all the questions which now agitate the councils of the country into the shade. It is *Liberty itself* that is in danger, not the liberty of a single state, no, nor of the United States, but the *liberty of the world.* Yes it is the *world* that has its anxious eyes upon us; it is the *world* that cries to us in the agony of its struggles against despotism, THE WORLD EXPECTS AMERICA, REPUBLICAN AMERICA, TO DO HER DUTY.

Popery Compared with Mormonism (1854)

WILLIAM HOGAN

Born in Ireland and ordained a Catholic priest, William Hogan was excommunicated in Philadelphia in 1821 when he sided with lay trustees in a dispute with a bishop over control of Church property. Hogan then became the leader of a group of schismatics who attempted, with Protestant help, to strip the Catholic hierarchy of some of its economic power. In the 1830's and 1840's Hogan was apparently associated with some of the more lurid and scurrilous anti-Catholic propaganda. As an ex-priest, he assumed a prominent and authoritative role in the nativist crusade. His books, such as Synopsis of Popery *and* Auricular Confession and Popish Nunneries, *portrayed Catholicism as a "hydra-headed monster" which had not changed since the bloody days of the Inquisition.*

I lay it down as a sound principle in political as well as moral ethics, that if a government finds, within the limits of its jurisdiction, any sect or party, of whatever doctrine, creed, or denomination, professing principles incompatible with its permanency, or subversive of the unalienable right of self government, and worshipping God, according to the dictates of each and every man's conscience, that sect or party should be removed beyond its limits, or at least excluded from any participation in the formation or administration of its laws.

Would it, for instance, be wise in our government to encourage the Mormons to introduce among us, as the law of the land, the ravings and prophesies of Joe Smith? Suppose that sect maintained that Joe Smith was their *Lord God;* that the kingdoms of this world were his; that he claimed and did actually exercise the right of dethroning kings, and was endeavoring, by every means in his power, to place himself in a position to exercise, at no distant period, the right of deposing our presidents, state governors, and absolving our people from their oaths of allegiance. Should not that sect, as such, be instantly crushed? Should it not, at least, be forbidden to interfere, directly or indirectly, with our civil institutions? Let us suppose the prophet Joe

From *Popery! As It Was and As It Is* (Hartford, 1855), pp. 32–33.

Smith to hold the seat of his government in Europe, and that Europe was full to overflowing with Mormons; we may further suppose this great high priest to have thousands and millions of subordinate officers, sworn and bound together by oaths cemented in blood, to sustain him as their sovereign ruler, by every means which human ingenuity could devise, and at every sacrifice of truth and honor. Suppose, further, that this high priest was annually sending thousands of his subjects to this country, with no other view but to possess your fertile lands and overthrow your government, and substituting in its place that of this *foreign priest* and tyrant; would you permit them to land upon your shores? Would you allow them to pollute the purity of your soil? Would you allow their unclean hands to touch the altars of your liberty? Would you not first insist that they should purge themselves from the sins and slime of Mormonism, and free themselves from all further connection with this monster man, and would-be God, who impiously demanded blind obedience and unqualified homage? I could answer for you, but I will not; the history of your republic answers for you; the movements which are now going forth from one end of your country to the other, are answering for you, in tones too solemn and too loud to be drowned by the roaring of Popish bulls. But it is much to be feared that Americans do not yet fully understand the dangers to be apprehended from the existence of Popery in the United States. It is difficult to persuade a single-hearted and single-minded republican, whose lungs were first inflated by the breath of freedom, whose first thoughts were, that all men had a natural right to worship God as they pleased—that any man could be found, so lost to reason, interest, and principle, as to desire to barter those high privileges, which he may enjoy in this country, for oppression and blind submission to the dictates of a Pope.

5. The Widening Conflict
over Slavery (1835–1865)*

WE HAVE noticed how often Americans were warned that "slavery" was the inevitable fate of any people who failed to heed alarms and unite against subversive enemies. Sometimes the term "slavery" was used metaphorically; sometimes it referred to a loss of free institutions and political self-determination. But by the 1830's many northern reformers had come to see the institution of Negro slavery as the very "concentration of iniquity; the ultimate extreme of despotism; surpassing and including all other conceivable and recorded oppressions." These were the phrases adopted by an antislavery convention held in Rhode Island in 1836, at which speakers attempted to link the South's peculiar institution with all historical forms of tyranny and, significantly, with the philosophy of expediency and materialism which had led to the bloodbath of the French Revolution. The same abolitionist speakers identified their own cause with that of their Nonconformist English ancestors who had struggled against an authoritarian church and state. While the antislavery crusade was genuinely concerned with the rights and welfare of the Negro, it was increasingly directed toward purging the nation of a despotic power that threatened to subvert America's traditional liberties.

In one sense, the call to resist the "Slave Power Conspiracy" can be seen as a culmination of earlier countersubversion movements. The antislavery movement partly absorbed and replaced anti-Masonry and anti-Catholicism; for many abolitionists the Slave Power reincarnated the same unprincipled, despotic force that had tortured Protestant martyrs, persecuted English Puritans, undermined the British constitution, and corrupted the French Revolution. The American Constitution denied any priesthood official and exclusive power over their parishioners; yet slaveholders claimed government sanction for

* For a more detailed examination of the ideas presented in this introduction, see David Brion Davis, *The Slave Power Conspiracy and the Paranoid Style* (Baton Rouge: Louisiana State University Press, 1970).

their absolute control over human property. Like the Catholic or Mormon leader, the slaveholder was portrayed as monopolizing power and privilege, as violating the sanctity of marriage, and as withholding the Word of God from the people under his dominion. The nonslaveholding southern whites, as well as the Negroes, were sealed off from the cleansing currents of free inquiry and public debate. They were the victims of another "Monster Institution" that depended on systematic delusion and brutal suppression of dissent. Like earlier tyrannies, the Slave Power also depended on a policy of aggressive expansionism, since its survival required the obliteration of every free institution.

Yet the Slave Power was obviously not the product of a foreign ideology nor even the American form of an international conspiracy against liberty. Abolitionist writers had to come to terms with the knowledge that slavery in America was hardly an innovation and that the institution had been at least tolerated by the Founding Fathers and by the Constitution itself. How, then, could slavery be considered alien to the American experience? How could an irreconcilable conflict have developed between the needs of slaveholders and the continued existence of a free society?

The answers to these questions lay in a radical reinterpretation of American history. In the eyes of abolitionist historians, the Founding Fathers had assumed, rather naïvely, that Negro slavery was a dying institution. At the Constitutional Convention southern delegates had bullied the North into making "ill-considered concessions," the most fatal of which was the agreement to count three-fifths of the slave population in apportioning political representation. From that point on there had been continuing and systematic efforts by the Slave Power to weaken the free states and to increase its own domain. The Slave Power had not only betrayed the cause of the American Revolution but had cunningly plotted economic depressions, the War of 1812, the Mexican War, and every defeat or misfortune the country had suffered. Since America enjoyed God's special providence and was presumably omnipotent so long as she retained her virtue, it was obvious that every national frustration and shortcoming could be attributed to the machinations of a diabolical enemy.

Despite the paranoid qualities of this interpretation, it was not an altogether unreasonable response to perceived events. The militancy of the South during the Missouri crisis of 1820 gave substance to Benjamin Lundy's warnings in 1829 that slaveholders were conspiring to seize Texas in order to increase the number of slave states. Subsequent events seemed to confirm Lundy's charge in 1836 that the Texas Revolution was part of a deep-seated scheme to extend and strengthen the peculiar institution. This view was adopted and elaborated in the late 1830's by William Goodell, James G. Birney, and other antislavery writers. No doubt the emerging Slave Power thesis owed much to the conspiratorial imagery of the anti-Masons, the anti-Catholics, and the Jacksonian opponents of the Bank. Thus abolitionists borrowed freely from Jacksonian rhetoric when they portrayed the struggle against slavery as a struggle of the people against an aristocracy, and when they talked of a secret coalition between the Slave Oligarchy and the northern "Money Power." Yet no one could deny that northern capitalism had spun a network of ties with the slave system or that northern politicians were eager to evade or repress discussion of the slavery issue. Moreover, by the late 1830's it was clear that the South was not only determined to prevent Congress from receiving antislavery petitions, but was erecting an iron curtain around the slave states, barring controversial material from the mails and suppressing the civil liberties of any citizen who dared to question the existing social order. It was the South's own militancy that brought former southerners like Birney to conclude there could be "no middle ground" between the principles of slavery and freedom.

Sectional tensions following the annexation of Texas and the Mexican War reinforced the fear that the Slave Power, having bribed or deluded enough northern politicians, had seized control of the federal government and had progressed a long way toward executing a secret plan to spread slavery through all the states and territories. Southern radicals like Robert Toombs confidently asserted that the United States enjoyed the benefits of a proslavery government. Some southern extremists argued that slavery was the normal condition of labor and should ideally be extended to the white working class; others called for the reopening of the African slave trade and boasted that the South would expand its slave empire to include Cuba, Mexico, and Central America. By 1858, Abraham Lincoln could point out that four years earlier slavery had been excluded from more than half the states and from most of the remaining national territory. Yet the effect of the Dred Scott decision of 1857, which Lincoln thought had been long planned as the crowning piece of a master conspiracy, was to throw open all the territories to southern masters and their slaves.

Lincoln feared that a future judicial decision might even deprive the free states of power to exclude slaves. The history of the 1850's appeared to conform to a rational pattern that implied remarkable southern unity, premeditation, and control of events.

We should be careful, however, not to conflate everyone who denounced the Slave Power into a single "abolitionist" group. Many abolitionists were little concerned over the political implications of slavery, whereas the Free-Soilers and Republicans, who sought to awaken the public to the menace of Slave Power aggression, generally disavowed any interest in interfering with slavery in the existing southern states. Moreover, the Slave Power thesis was even appropriated by southern Whigs and Unionists who accepted the institution of slavery but who accused Democratic extremists of exploiting the slavery issue in order to win undisputed control of an independent South. Some southern Unionists went so far as to charge that a conspiratorial alliance had developed between northern abolitionists and southern secessionists. However absurd this notion might seem, it showed some recognition of the fact that the extremists in both sections had joined in a coordinated attack on the earlier "conspiracy of silence" over slavery. If politicians of both parties had tacitly agreed that discussions of slavery were highly imprudent, the abolitionists and southern firebrands shared the opposite conviction that the issue must be met head on.

The paranoid style seldom makes a distinction between tacit understanding and overt, premeditated conspiracy. But even among the most uncompromising exposers of Slave Power plots, there were important differences in emphasis and discrimination. The two selections by William Goodell, for example, suggest a highly suspicious and gullible mind; Goodell has no qualms about resusitating musty Federalist propaganda in order to account for the South's success in extending slavery. John Gorham Palfrey illustrates a more limited response to northern concessions on the territorial question, which he explains by the theory of a Money Power–Slave Power alliance. Carl Schurz seems to abandon the idea of individual responsibility, and sees the aggrandizements of slavery as resulting from "the irresistible power of necessity," and from the fundamental law that between freedom and slavery there can be no peaceful coexistence. George W. Julian echoes the political prejudices of the Revolutionary generation when he attacks the major parties as mere "factions" generated by self-interest. His catalogue of specific grievances is less overdrawn than the one in the Declaration of Independence, but his rhetoric also carries strong evangelical overtones, as when he writes of "the unclean spirit that must be cast out from the hearts of the people before they can be saved. We must enter the inner sanctuary of their consciences, and dispel the long gathering clouds of passion and prejudice which hold them in the slumber of unconscious guilt." For Julian a crusade against the Slave Power offered the hope of "saving" the people through a great act of moral regeneration which would begin outside the Church and other institutions.

It should be emphasized that paranoid visions were by no means confined to the antislavery camp. The great slave insurrection that devastated St. Domingue in 1791, leading to the Black republic of Haiti, sent waves of panic through the southern states and permanently traumatized the slaveholder mind. In the North as well as South, it was a widely accepted view that this bloody revolution had been instigated by radical French abolitionists, known as Friends of the Blacks. The slave plot of Denmark Vesey, which was uncovered in 1822 in Charleston, South Carolina, was attributed to foreign influences. Northern abolitionists received much of the blame for Nat Turner's stunning uprising of August 1831, which raised southern vigilance to a pitch of obsessive suspicion. Negro slaves would remain happy and content, according to the prevailing ideology, unless they were confused and inflamed by malicious outsiders. Throughout American history the alien troublemaker has been a favorite explanation for social unrest.

Leonard L. Richards' recent study of anti-abolitionism in the 1830's provides valuable insight into the sources of this important variation on countersubversion.* Richards demonstrates that the anti-abolition riots in the North were mostly the result of explicit planning and organization, and that the mobs were led or sanctioned by prominent lawyers, merchants, bankers, and even judges and Congressmen. The frequency of violent demonstrations against abolitionism mounted in 1833 and 1834, hitting a peak in the summer of 1835. Richards points to three central reasons for this volatile sensitivity to the abolitionists' challenge. First, many of the promoters of the backlash were supporters of Negro colonization who were alarmed by the decline of the American Colonization Society and by the abolitionists' concerted at-

* Leonard L. Richards, "Gentlemen of Property and Standing": Anti-Abolition Riots in Jacksonian America (New York: Oxford University Press, 1970).

tempts to discredit the idea of deportation. Second, the abolitionists not only punctured the illusion of creating a white man's society by getting rid of the Blacks, but openly worked for an interracial America. It was their attempt to educate Negroes and fight for full legal equality, far more than their doctrine of "immediate emancipation," that provoked popular outrage and mob violence. Third, the "amalgamators" and "Nigger lovers" threatened the authority of local elites by appealing directly to the people, including women and children, and by organizing a network of national auxiliary societies.

In 1834 the American Anti-Slavery Society distributed 122,000 pieces of literature; in 1835 the volume rose to 1,100,000 pieces. Although this spectacular increase was largely the result of the new steam press and other technological improvements that lowered printing costs, the sudden deluge of abolitionist publications lent credibility to the image of an enormous propaganda machine financed by British gold. Much as later Populists would blame the English for the banking and industrial consolidations of the late nineteenth century, so anti-abolitionists interpreted pressure-group journalism as part of a British plot to divide and weaken America. Not able to dispatch armies to crush the American experiment in liberty, the aristocrats of Europe cunningly relied on native front organizations, which could pose as philanthropic societies, swaying the minds of the ignorant and illiterate with propagandistic illustrations, emblems, and even chocolate wrappers. There was a shadowy vagueness, however, to the idea of British masterminds manipulating American fanatics. Abolitionism was often perceived as a radical, anarchistic force, and its proponents as a kind of Illuminati in clerical garb, mouthing platitudes about Christian love while striving to undermine church and state as well as the sanctity of marriage and private property. Their worst sin, according to William Drayton, was their willingness to tear off "the seals which our Fathers set upon the question of slavery." In Andrew Jackson's annual message of December 1835, the President himself called for "severe penalties" to suppress the abolitionists' "unconstitutional and wicked activities." Four months earlier a Philadelphia mob had seized antislavery pamphlets and dumped them in the Delaware River, in conscious imitation of the Boston Tea Party.

In the South, the arrival of shipments of abolitionist literature coincided in 1835 with the capture of a Mississippi River pirate, John A. Murrell, whose "Mystic Clan" was supposedly bent on inciting massive slave insurrections. The resulting hysteria led to a wave of lynchings and murders, some of the victims having been suspected of covert abolitionism. After decades of paranoid rumors, the South's expectations finally seemed to be fulfilled on October 16, 1859, when John Brown led his famous raid on Harpers Ferry. Brown's action stemmed from an actual conspiracy to promote slave rebellion and involved a number of highly respected and socially distinguished accomplices. Yet nothing could better underscore the distance between genuine conspiracies and paranoid fears than the discrepancy between Brown's pathetic raid and the nightmare visions which had so long haunted the southern mind. Of course one should add that the massacres of whites in St. Domingue and in Virginia, by Nat Turner's band of slaves, showed that southern fears were not entirely unfounded. The alleged Masonic murder of William Morgan hardly presented anti-Masons with a comparable danger.

Furthermore, the growth of abolitionist agitation in the North helped confirm the image of the South as a stable, orderly, and law-abiding society. If the outside world took a different view, southerners could reply, with some justice, that it was the outside world which had changed. Slavery had once been accepted everywhere. It was in the North that a group of effete, un-American radicals had seduced an army of fellow travelers, had imported alien ideas from abroad, had infiltrated institutions, and had succeeded in setting the fashions and accepted opinions of the day.

As we have already suggested, the tangible conflict over slavery in the territories, which led to an escalation in southern demands and expectations, gave increasing substance to the northern view of a Slave Power conspiracy. It is significant that a northern newspaper editor like James Watson Webb, who in the 1830's denounced abolitionism as a subversive plot to amalgamate the races, eventually became a Free-Soiler and an avowed enemy of the Slave Power. Resistance to southern expansionism, especially if the expansionism resulted from a carefully conceived plot, had far more popular appeal than did social justice or racial equality. Yet in a deeper sense, the threat of a Slave Power may have been the only way to overcome the traditional conviction that Negro slavery was an "unfortunate necessity" which would hopefully disappear some day but which could never be openly discussed or tampered with. It can at least be argued that the conspiratorial mode of thought helped counteract public inertia and focus attention on the anomaly of slavery in a democratic society. In this respect the paranoid style was at least as "realistic" as were the earlier rationalizations which disguised a fundamental conflict in values. The image of the Slave Power was a hypothetical construct that provided a way of conceptualizing and responding to a genuine problem.

There are also indications that protests against the Slave Power, like southern protests against abolitionist subversives, served social and psychological functions that had little to do with the objective issues of slavery and the sectional balance of power. In both sections an opposing body of thought was diagnosed as an ideology, in the sense of specious theorizing to support the aggressive designs of a given group. In an individualistic society, the recognition of a hostile ideology provided the means for collective identification and commitment. For northerners the discovery of Slave Power machinations gave sharper definition to the meaning of American history as the culmination of man's struggle for liberty. Much as Communism later afforded an excuse for attacking the self-seeking and the moral decay of the 1950's, so the Slave Power was linked with northern plutocracy, selfishness, materialism, and lack of noble purpose. One's stand on the slavery issue was the ultimate test of moral values. Here was a question where belief really *mattered* in a way that it never could with respect to tariffs, banks, or land policy. As Charles Sumner put it, in 1855, "Are you for Freedom or are you for Slavery? . . . Come forth, then, from the old organizations; let us range together. . . . Are you for God, or are you for the Devil?" Like the evangelical revivalists whom he so closely imitated, Sumner appealed for a cohesive community dedicated to a transcended cause.

Slavery at War with
Our Liberties (1839)

WILLIAM GOODELL

One of the originators of the Slave Power thesis, William Goodell was a leading reform journalist who helped organize the American Anti-Slavery Society in 1833. For a time he edited the Society's official organ, the Emancipator, *before taking charge of such reform newspapers as the* Friend of

From the *Anti-Slavery Lecturer* (Utica, N.Y.), September 1839.

Man *and the* Anti-Slavery Lecturer. *Goodell also lectured widely throughout the North and wrote some of the best books devoted to the antislavery
cause. He was one of the founders of the Liberty party and the foremost
critic of the argument that slavery was sanctioned by the Constitution.*

In our last Lecture we endeavored to prove that the civil and religious liberties of the country cannot be preserved unless slavery is
abolished. We cited the testimony of southern statesmen to prove that
the enslavement of *colored* laborers, if continued, would lead to the
enslavement of *white* laborers. We found the friends and the enemies
of the slave system to agree in this. We endeavored, likewise, to trace
the natural tendencies of the slave system to overturn the civil and
religious liberties of the country. We intend, in this Lecture, to exhibit those tendencies actually at work, and to note the progress of
their depredations at the south and at the north.

If slavery tends to annul law, and destroy freedom, we may expect
to see those effects strongly marked at the south. We all know what
the facts are. Lynchings, duels, murders, threats, assassinations,
among the most influential portions of the white population—these
are the every day items of news that are constantly looked for in the
southern prints. Legislative halls and courts of justice are frequently
disturbed and overawed by them. To a great and increasing extent,
mob trials, lynchings and horrid barbarities supersede the regular
courts of law. . . .

In no part of Europe, or even in Asia, are the people subjected to a
sterner despotism than are the *white* population of our own southern
States. They have no religious liberty, because they are not permitted
to declare the truth of the Bible against wickedness and oppression,
nor teach their neighbors to read the Bible. They have no civil liberty, because they dare not discuss the merits of their own institutions
and laws. To proscribe the discussion of any subject destroys liberty,
because it assumes that the government may determine what may
and what may not be discussed. Much more is liberty destroyed,
when the proscribed subject, as in the present case, is connected with
all the important principles of law, of order, of political economy, of
morals, and of religion! Nay! when the subject proscribed is the subject of *liberty and of human rights!* Very manifestly, THE PEOPLE OF
THE SOUTH ARE NOT A FREE PEOPLE!

Yet the statesmen of the south hold a controlling power over the
entire nation. Undoubtedly they think the people of the north are entitled to no more liberty than the people of the south. We are not left

to conjecture on this point. It will be illustrated as we proceed. But let us first gauge the strength of the power with which northern liberty must of course grapple in any struggle that might occur. Let us see what the slave power is capable of doing with and through the national government. . . .

Let it be borne in mind that southern statesmen (as was shown in our last Lecture) have uniformly borne testimony that the continuance of the slave system must of necessity involve the loss of liberty to the free, and result in the ultimate enslavement of the laboring white population. Connect this fact with the fact just ascertained, viz. that southern statesmen are successfully wielding the national government as the instrument of perpetuating the slave system, and what do we have? Is not the statement of the two documentary facts, a statement in other words that the slave power is successfully wielding the national government *for the enslavement of northern freemen?* What less can we make out of the known facts of the case? We speak not now of latent *tendencies:* We inquire after the *objects* and the actual *operations* of the slaveholding statesmen. They tell us in plain words, that continued slavery will destroy our liberties. But yet we find them at the same time wielding the vast power of the national government for the security and the extension of slavery! A child can put the two facts together and understand their import.

The Role of the Slave Power in American History (1852)

WILLIAM GOODELL

In his most notable book, Slavery and Anti-Slavery, *Goodell showed how southern representatives had won a succession of victories for slavery beginning with the first session of Congress in 1790. When the South had not been pressing for direct support of the slave system, Goodell discovered a systematic effort to weaken and destroy the northern economy. In short, the main events of American history, which northerners had assumed to be fortuitous and disconnected, actually formed for Goodell a coherent and consistent pattern. Like later right-wing writers who have interpreted twen-*

From William Goodell, *Slavery and Anti-Slavery; a History of the Great Struggle in Both Hemispheres* (New York, 1852), pp. 319–321, 323–334, 336–340.

*tieth-century history in terms of Communist manipulation and control,
Goodell had little difficulty in finding evidence that seemed to confirm his
thesis. He fully exploited, for example, the conspiratorial view of the War of
1812 which had been popularized much earlier by New England Federalists. But despite the speciousness of his reasoning and his fanciful efforts to
find hidden meaning beneath the surface of events, he was shrewd in sens-
ing that American politics was built on alliances and conflicts of interests,
and that the apparent national consensus was partly a myth disguising fundamental cleavages and contradictions.*

With the facts of the preceding history before us, it is very natural
to inquire on what maxims, with what aims, and for what objects, the
general policy of the Federal Government has been moulded, from
the beginning to the present time. Not a single administration of that
government have we found free from the controlling influence of slavery. Not only has slavery been steadily fostered as an important interest of the country, but as *the paramount,* the all-absorbing interest,
before whose claims every other interest and all other interests combined, have been forced to give way.

We have, thus far, considered only the *direct* action of the Federal
Government, in manifest support of slavery. But the general policy
and the political economy of the country could scarcely fail to have
had the most important bearings either for or against the slave interest. Is it credible that this has been overlooked? With the ever watch-
ful eye that we know the Slave Power has had over its own interests,
with all the successive administrations of the Government under its
control, and ready, as we have seen, to do its bidding, with slaveholding Presidents and Cabinets of their selection, forty-nine years
out of sixty-one, and while the support of slavery has been their constant care, can it be believed that the ever conflicting and totally irreconcilable interests of *free and slave labor* have never been thought
of, nor taken into consideration, in shaping our national policy? Or
can it be supposed that the always dominant Slave Power, everywhere else true to its own rapacious instincts, has, just here, where
the chess games of political economy are constantly played between
the rival interests of the country, been inattentive, or neutral, or that
it has held the balances between the slaveholding and non-slaveholding States, with an even and impartial hand? No intelligent citizen
can believe this. We might almost be certain, therefore, in advance of
all direct scrutiny of the facts of our history, that the general policy of
the country has been moulded by the Slave Power, for the benefit of

slavery, and in consequent hostility to the interests of free labor. The law of self-preservation would require this, especially as the interests of slave labor are always destined to grapple with the inherent thrift-lessness, imbecility and decline incident to the system, in striking contrast to the ever buoyant and recuperative energies of free labor. It would not be enough for the Slave Power, acting as a political economist, and mainly intent on retaining its political supremacy, to content itself with devices and expedients to prop up and encourage *slave* labor. It must do more than this. It must adroitly stab and crip-ple its rival. It must so shape and shift public measures as to disar-range, thwart, perplex, and unsettle the pursuits and the arrange-ments of free laborers, or else itself fall into inevitable eclipse, sustain certain defeat, and let go the sceptre of power. An illustration and proof of all this we have in the recent demand of the late Mr. Cal-houn, that the Constitution should be so amended as to restore to the slave States the same relative power that they had, at the first organi-zation of the government, and which we know they have lost, in despite of their political ascendancy, by the opposite tendencies of freedom and slavery. In making that desperate demand, Mr. Cal-houn laid bare his own heart, and the settled policy of the oligarchy of slaveholders. *The free North must be shorn of her own natu-ral strength, when needful, that slavery may preserve her balance of power.* With this simple key, the historian may unlock the other-wise inexplicable labyrinths of American politics, for the last sixty years. . . .

The present century opened with a remarkable state of things. Our country was at peace with all the world, and, with exception of a contest with the petty states of Barbary, we remained at peace, until the war with Britain, in 1812. Europe was embroiled in war. England, with some of the continental powers, contested the fearful strides of Napoleon. Every European nation was enlisted on one side or the other, and Europe became one vast encampment. Her agriculturists and artizans were under arms. Her commerce was swept from the sea by her own contending navies. Even Britain, "lord of the ocean," was powerful only to destroy, but could not protect her own merchant-men. America, as the only neutral and maritime nation, reaped rich harvests. She was the carrier of all christendom. She not only vended her own products at her own prices, but levied tribute at her plea-sure, upon the produce of all nations, upon those of South America, the Caribbean Islands, Eastern India, and China. . . .

But where was the sunny South at this period? Did *she* thrust in her sickle, and gather golden harvests, when the earth was reaped? Where were *her* gallant ships? Her princely merchants—*where?* . . . The spoiled sons of effeminacy, lawlessness and sloth, the heroes of the whip and the bowie-knife, are not merchants. The traffickers in women and babes excel not in lawful commerce. The land of slavery did not prosper. The curse of omnipresent justice, interwoven into the slave system itself was gnawing at her vitals. She turned her eye of anguish and envy at the free and prospering North, inquiring within herself how she could preserve her balance of power.

The Slave Power, like the power of the pit, never lacks for a stratagem. The Slave Power ruled in the Cabinet, and stood behind the Presidential Chair. I sin not against the democracy of Mr. Jefferson. His *democracy*, however correct in theory, was here, as on his plantation, held in abeyance, and cherished "in the abstract." There was nothing of Mr. Jefferson's democracy in his slaveholding; and there was nothing of it in the embargo. That measure, dictated probably against his wishes by the Slave Power, was levelled at the commercial prosperity of the free North. . . . Thus northern commerce was destroyed, to protect it from petty depredations! As a measure of retaliation or coercion against France and England, the embargo could never have been supposed to be of any value. . . . Nor can we overlook the coincidence by which this visitation was inflicted upon the North, almost simultaneously with the abolition of the African slave trade, and the explosion and defeat of the great South-Western Conspiracy under Aaron Burr, by the disclosures of a citizen of New England. The embargo was laid in December, 1807, and was continued till March, 1809, when it was exchanged for an act of non-intercourse with England and France. . . . The non-intercourse with France was terminated in 1810. That with Great Britain was continued, including a second embargo of two months, till the declaration of war by Congress against that country, in June, 1812. From the beginning of the first embargo, therefore, in Dec., 1807, until the peace of Dec., 1814 (not available to the ship-owners until the opening of navigation in the spring of 1815), the commerce of the free States was either totally prohibited, or rendered of little pecuniary value. . . .

In 1811, the charter of the old National Bank expired, and was not permitted by the dominant Slave Power to be renewed, on the alleged ground that a national bank was unconstitutional, a consideration not discovered when it was chartered. The real reason was that the South had become bankrupt, as it periodically does, as often generally as once in ten or fifteen years, throwing off the greater part of its indebtedness upon its creditors in some other community. No country cultivated by slave labor does otherwise. . . . In old colonial times, the creditors of the South were chiefly in England, and the South went into the Revolution of 1776 (in despite of her inherent and prevalent toryism) for the purpose, mainly, of wiping out the old score. But since the revolution, the northern cities of New York, Philadelphia and Boston have shared largely in the honors and emoluments of southern custom. The result came upon them in company with other calamities, in 1811. But along with the embargo and non-intercourse, it greatly assisted the South to regain, in a pecuniary view, her endangered balance of power. Almost the sum total of her indebtedness to the North was now to be dexterously shifted from one scale to the other, with the double effect of relieving the South of the same weight that was to be thrown upon the North. In many ways the demise of the National Bank was exceedingly opportune to them at this juncture. The South had got out of the Bank in the shape of loans, all it could, and southern securities were now in bad odor with the directors, while northern paper was discounted freely, and the Bank was a financial assistant of the northern merchants. More than this. The Bank was the agent employed by the North to collect her debts at the South. What could the South now want of the Bank? A national bank was unconstitutional of course, and had leave to be interred. In mourning over the loss of their Bank, and the depredations of the non-intercourse and embargo, the attention of the northern merchants would be diverted, in a measure, from the direct losses they sustained from the indebtedness of the South. The greater the smoke and the more scattered the fires, the better chance for pillage, and the less fear of detection.

Calamities seldom come singly, and crime is the precursor of crime. The Slave Power now demanded a war. Unhappily a pretext was at hand. . . . The South undertook, very kindly, the protection of the North. "Free trade and sailors' rights" was now the southern watchword:—that same "free trade" that had been so long denounced by the South as the bane of the republic, a national curse, and proscribed by non-intercourse and embargo! . . .

The war party was led on by John C. Calhoun, of South Carolina, who claimed the paternity of the measure, and drove it furiously through both houses of Congress. . . . At one stage of the proceed-

ings, early in June, 1812, a motion was made in the Senate to postpone the declaration of war till the opening of the next session of
Congress in December, when the policy of the British Government
would be developed. On this question the Senate was understood to
be nearly equally divided, and Mr. Calhoun, whose influence was potential in both Houses, exerted himself to defeat the motion. . . . Mr.
Calhoun was inexorable, and by extraordinary appliances, one or two
members were gained over to his party, and *the postponement was
defeated in the Senate by a majority of one vote.* This decided the
question of war, which was declared by a vote of 79 to 49 in the
House of Representatives, and of 19 to 13 in the Senate. In a few
weeks, news arrived, as was expected, of the repeal of the British Orders in Council, thus removing the chief cause of the war. But the object of the Calhoun party was gained. The nation was plunged into a
war, in the midst of the pecuniary embarrassments arising from a
general southern bankruptcy (the North being the creditor), and from
the sudden demise of the National Bank. New England, at such a crisis, more than Old England, would be the sufferer by the war, and
the North would be burdened with the chief expense of the infliction.

The result of the measure, and especially the manner in which the
war was conducted and terminated, were such as to justify, fully, this
account of its object and its origin. Two commanders, in sympathy
with the administration, Generals Hull and Smythe, the latter a Virginian, were sent, successively, on expeditions of pretended invasion
of Canada, but in both instances, the enterprise was abandoned when
the Canadas were apparently in their power. General Hull surrendered to the British, to their great astonishment. The whole country
accused him of treason, a court-martial sentenced him to death, but he
was pardoned by the President. General Smythe "suddenly retreated,
to the great surprise of his troops." These facts, together with the systematic and even skillful withholding of supplies from the forces
under other commanders, afterwards, made it perfectly evident that
the administration not only never intended the conquest of Canada,
but took special care that no such acquisition of territory should add
to the number of non-slaveholding States. Had Canada been adjacent
to the slave States, and adapted to slave culture, there can be no reasonable doubt that it could have been conquered as expeditiously as
were California and New Mexico. . . .

When the war had accomplished its grand objects, when the bankrupt slave States had regained and more than regained their balance

of power with the North by despoiling it of half its remaining wealth, after the previous inflictions of non-intercourse and embargo, when Old England had been successfully employed to chastise and humble New England, when insult had been added to injury, and the loss of honor and reputation conjoined with the loss of wealth and political influence, the Slave Power was ready to restore peace. And this was done without a single lisp of "free trade and sailors' rights." Neither the treaty, nor the negotiations, nor the instructions from the Cabinet under which they were conducted, contained the slightest allusion to the ostensible grounds of the war, or provided or sought the least semblance of any security against similar aggressions in future. Thus ended a war of nearly three years, conducted at an expense of nearly thirty millions per annum, chiefly paid by the free States, the price of their own subjugation and disgrace—a war whose "glory" has given us two Presidents, one of them a slaveholder, the other a native Virginian, and a steady supporter of the Slave Power—a war that virtually enthroned, from 1812 to 1850, the bitter enemy of northern as well as southern liberty, JOHN C. CALHOUN. . . .

The same memorable era, 1816, was marked by the establishment of a second national bank, and by the same Slave Power that had dictated the two embargoes, the non-intercourse, the war, and the tariff. It was dictated by the same policy and to subserve the same end— the preservation of the balance of power between free and slave labor, or rather, the ascendency of the latter over the former. A national bank was deemed unconstitutional in 1811, but it became constitutional in 1816, for the South, after all her depredations upon the North, now condescended to become a borrower of northern capital! Mr. Madison, in particular, whose constitutional scruples were insuperable, in 1811, overcame them in 1816, and not long afterwards became, it was said, a borrower from the National Bank of a large sum. Other slaveholding statesmen conferred upon the Bank the same honor. But it cost the northern banks and the northern capitalists and merchants a severe money pressure of three or four years to spare sufficient specie to get the new National Bank under way. So that the pecuniary embarrassment of 1819–20, arising from a reaction of the high tariff policy, was increased by the process of re-establishing a national bank, and both burthens fell at the same time upon the free laboring North. The general southern bankruptcy of 1824, renewed and aggravated by the southern cotton speculation of 1826, (an infamous process of gambling) trode rapidly upon the heels of the former inflictions of the Slave Power. An extensive, not to say general, bankruptcy visited Boston in 1824, and New York in 1826, from these joint causes, but chiefly from the accumulation of southern debts to the estimated amount of upwards of one hundred millions of dollars, of which (as afterwards, in 1837) scarcely five cents on the dollar were ever realized.

Precisely at what date the second United States Bank was effectually pillaged and reduced to bankruptcy by its slaveholding customers, is not certainly known, but it must have been at a very early period, probably in 1823, soon after its specie capital had been supplied, and chiefly by the over-confiding North. Its condition was for many years concealed, perhaps in the vain hope of retrieving its fortunes. . . . The Bank was in the hands of demagogues, a tool of political corruption, and chiefly for the pecuniary and political emolument of the South at the expense and for the management and subjugation of the North, purchasing editors if not Senators by its loans. Like its predecessors, it was first robbed and then buried, and all through the action of the Federal Government, at the dictation of the Slave Power. . . .

Thus Slavery controls all the leading measures of the nation and moulds its political economy,—quite as remarkable for its real and inflexible CONSTANCY as for its apparently capricious CHANGE. A comparison of dates, as before hinted, will show how exactly all these changes have corresponded and chimed in with the more direct and palpable action of the Federal Government in support of slavery. Whenever such *direct* action, by the Government or by combinations, has been suspended, a more active control and a more rapid change of general measures has supplied the deficiency. And when the *general* policy of the country has been for any length of time undisturbed, it has been because more *direct* measures in support of slavery have been in progress. Thus, from 1807, on the explosion of the Southern and Western Conspiracy, till the first armed invasion of Texas, in 1819, the slave interest was sufficiently promoted by embargoes, nonintercourse, war, tariff, the destruction of the first National Bank, and the establishment of the second. So, likewise, from 1836 to 1850, while so much direct action in favor of slavery has been witnessed, the questions of tariffs and banks have been left comparatively undisturbed.

With equal skill and tact has the Slave Power contrived to keep up two political parties, extending through the North and the South, on the most fallacious and deceptive issues, or upon scarcely any issue at all. By this means she diverts attention from the real to the merely nominal issues before the country, while by controlling both parties, she secures her ends through the ascendency of either, makes the one a check upon the other, and manages them through fear or through hope.

The Alarming Progress
of the Slave Power (1851)

JOHN GORHAM PALFREY

When John Gorham Palfrey inherited some Louisiana slaves, he emancipated them without hesitation. Palfrey was a New England Unitarian minister, a Harvard professor, a distinguished authority on the Hebrew Scriptures, and an editor of and frequent contributor to the North American Review. *In addition to writing scholarly tomes of history, he worked actively with Horace Mann in the cause of public education. Palfrey, as a member of the Boston intellectual and social elite, had nothing but scorn for the nouveaux riches of the North who courted southern planters in order to enhance their social status. He also attacked the political and economic alliances between northern capitalists and southern slaveholders. Alarmed by the concessions made to slavery in the Compromise of 1850, he wrote a series of articles in the Boston* Commonwealth *in the summer of 1851. The following excerpts develop Palfrey's view of the growing peril of the Slave Power.*

We have seen that 30 votes out of 62 in the Senate of the United States, 90 votes out of 230 in the House of Representatives, and 120 out of 290 in the Electoral Colleges, directly represent the Slave Power, which power in its elementary condition resides in less than one hundred thousand voting citizens out of the more than three millions of voters of the United States. We have seen how this power, holding the property and education of fifteen States, represents those States in the national councils; and how, by means of controlling the patronage, it dictates the policy of the country. And we have recalled

From John Gorham Palfrey, *Five Years' Progress of the Slave Power* (Boston, 1852), pp. 19–20, 25–26, 29.

attention to some facts connected with the extremely bold and dexterous blow which it struck for its perpetuity and enlargement in the partition of Mexico, first, by the annexation of Texas, and then by the magnificent extortions of the war which followed.

That the war must result in acquisition of territory was obvious, from its commencement. Mr. President Polk—the treaty-making power, without whom no peace was to be had—said that what he wanted was "indemnity for the past and security for the future." "Security for the future" any one might interpret as might please him. It was a phrase not ill-conceived to favor the idea that Mexico was a powerful and arrogant bully, that had cruelly assailed her peaceable and unoffending neighbor. But "indemnity for the past" could signify nothing more nor less than broad lands, for Mexico had no money.

The material question of the time, therefore, was that which was brought to view in Mr. Wilmot's Proviso, viz. whether slavery was to be allowed to establish itself in the territory that might be conquered or ceded. And this did seem to be a question impossible to be settled except in one way, if considerations of right, of enlightened policy, or of national honor, should have any weight. It was not even the Missouri question over again, sadly as Freedom had been cheated then. Far, far from it. Missouri was part of Louisiana, in which territory slavery existed at the time of the purchase; and herein was a sort of pretence for the claim of the Slave Power to strengthen itself with votes from Missouri in Congress. But every foot of territory held by Mexico was free soil. Her half-civilized people (often so called) had put their boastful neighbors to the blush, by sweeping the odious institution from their borders. And it did seem too bad to be feared, that men or communities, with any character to keep or lose, would entertain the thought of establishing it anew. . . . The question as to Mexico is, whether the happy progress of things shall be arrested and rolled back, to afflict her with what has been everywhere the shame of the white man, and the curse of both white and black; and whether the model republic of the nineteenth century shall carry on a bloody war for an end so horrible.

. . . To secure the Money Power of the North on its side is an immense object for the Slave Power of the South. It is the old policy by which Sparta and Athens successively governed Greece by having a party of their own within its cities.

How is this power in the midst of ourselves secured to the service of an interest foreign and hostile to us? By what means is it that the wealth of the Free States is made an instrument in the conspiracy against their freedom?

Some of the least definite and perhaps the least considerable of the causes of this alliance are a mere natural development of our very feeble and foolish human nature. Wealth sets the fashion, and wealth must be in the fashion; and where the fashions of a large portion of the affluent connect themselves with an institution,—slavery or any other,—attractive associations come to attach to it in the minds of others of the affluent class. Again, wealth is power, and to power it belongs more or less to be unfeeling, arrogant, tyrannical. To many people the privilege of oppressing the weak, and next to that, the privilege of being indifferent to their oppressions, is one of the most comfortable luxuries of a condition of ease. The cry of Mr. Pickwick's assailants, "Hit him again, he's got no friends," is apt to be the cry alike of the rich and of the rowdy vulgar. . . .

Again, there are plenty of merchants, and those sometimes rich and talkative merchants, who have trained themselves to sacrifice any and every thing that interferes with the success of their business, and who at the same time understand so little of the principles of their own business as to suppose that it is in the power of a combination of Southern customers to reduce them to the alternative of dishonoring their Northern manhood, on the one hand, or of bankruptcy and ruin, on the other. . . .

The great stroke which the Slave Power strikes for the control of the Money Power is through the dependence of the latter on that federal legislation which the former conducts. No part of our history is more dishonorable than that of the successive bargains, or attempts at bargains, by which great interests of humanity and freedom have been sacrificed to the Slave Power for pecuniary advantages which its help was wanted to secure.

This wretched course of policy had its beginning as far back as the origin of the Federal Constitution. In the Convention, the power of passing navigation laws for the benefit of Northern commerce was the great consideration for the concessions made to Slavery by the Northern States. Let us not judge our ancestors too severely. They made a capital mistake, and did a great wrong. But they had this excuse. They believed, and they had the best reason for believing, that Slavery was near its last gasp in the country. "I found the Eastern States," said Luther Martin, "notwithstanding their aversion to Slavery, were very willing to indulge the Southern States at least with a temporary liberty to prosecute the Slave-trade, provided the Southern States would in their turn gratify them by laying no restriction on navigation acts." "Tobacco," said Patrick Henry in the Virginia Convention, —for as yet there was no cotton,—"tobacco will always make our peace with them." He meant that with the business advantages they could give us, then consisting mainly in the carrying trade, the Southern statesmen could always make their own terms as to other measures. He said what was but too true; what has since developed itself into a permanent policy, to an extent far exceeding what he could have imagined; and what the Southern statesmen have counted upon more and more confidently, from his day to the present.

The Strength and Weakness
of the Slave Power (1852)

GEORGE W. JULIAN

An Indianan by birth and a lawyer by profession, George W. Julian began attacking slavery in newspaper articles in the 1840's. In 1848 he was elected to Congress on the Free-Soil ticket and soon joined a small group of antislavery Representatives who bitterly opposed the Compromise of 1850. This experience is reflected in a speech he delivered in Cincinnati in 1852, from which the following selection is taken. Julian's conviction that the existing parties had become obsolete and that reform must begin outside the established political system led him to participate actively in the organization of the Republican party. Elected to Congress as a Radical Republican in 1860, he was influential in pressing the government to move toward direct emancipation.

The slaveholders, as we have seen, numbering only one twenty-fifth of their white brethren of the South, one fortieth of the entire popu-

From Lydia Maria Child, ed., *Speeches on Political Questions* (New York, 1872), pp. 70–77, 79–80, 82.

lation of the South, and one hundredth part of that of the Union, are yet the real sovereigns in this Republic. The powers of the government are in their keeping, and they determine all things according to the counsels of their own will. They say to the politician of the North "Go," and he goeth; to the Northern priest, "Do this," and he doeth it. They lay their mesmeric hands upon the moral pulse of the nation, and it ceases to beat. Nothing that is earthly can stand before the dread authority of these men. They are the reigning lords and *masters* of the people, white and black. Look at the facts. They hold in the most galling bondage three millions of their fellow-creatures, being more than twelve times their own number. They keep in subjection and comparative slavery more than six millions of their own race in the South, who dare not even murmur at their lot. They lord it over fourteen millions of people in the free States, subsidizing their leaders in Church and State, debauching the public sentiment of the country, and pragmatically announcing and then enforcing, the conditions upon which the Union shall be preserved. They determine who shall be our Presidents and Vice-Presidents; who shall be the Speakers of the House of Representatives, and the presiding officers of the Senate; who shall stand at the head of the important committees of both houses, and how those committees shall be constituted, all with spe-cial reference to the slave interest. They secure to themselves or to their Northern slaves the monopoly of all the important offices of the government, of the judiciary, the army, the navy, and our foreign di-plomacy, hoisting their black flag in distant nations of the earth. They rifle the mails of the United States, and decide what shall and what shall not be conveyed by them under the impudent surveillance which they thus set up with impunity. They imprison hundreds of our colored freemen from the North and sell them into perpetual slavery, by a law *lower* than the Constitution, for the crime of being found in Southern ports in the prosecution of their lawful business; and with a mob at their heels they defy the Federal Government to bring the constitutionality of their misdeeds before the courts of the country. They nationalize slavery by compelling us to support it in the District of Columbia, to aid in carrying on the coastwise slave-trade, and to conform our policy in all things to the principle that slavery is to be protected "wherever our flag floats." . . . They send their minions into Texas while yet a province of Mexico, who establish slavery there in violation of Mexican law to which they had become subject; and then, in violation of their allegiance to the United States, raise the

standard of revolt, and assert their independence by what Dr. Chan-
ning justly styles "the robbery of a realm"; and when their work has
been consummated by the help or connivance of the United States,
Texas, a whole empire of slavery, is annexed to this country through
the machinery of the Whig and Democratic parties.

Instigated by a still growing lust for slave domination they drive
the government into a war with Mexico for the avowed purpose of ac-
quiring more slave territory; and when the war terminates, at a cost
of many thousands of lives, and hundreds of millions of money, they
assert their own will and pleasure in the disposition of the spoils of
conquest. By threats to dissolve the Union, and to use the pistol and
the bowie-knife, they induce Northern members of Congress to unite
with them in dismembering New Mexico, while begging for admission
as a free State, thus cursing with the blight of slavery eighty thousand
square miles of soil that was free. They force these Northern members
to give Texan slaveholders ten millions of dollars besides, to which
they have not even the semblance of a title. They exact from them a
law of Congress by which slavery may be extended over all our Territories, stipulating in advance that as many slave States as may be
carved out of them shall be admitted into the Union whenever they
shall make application. They exact another law by which the people
of the free States are made their constables and slave-catchers, bound
as "good citizens" to engage in a business at which their humanity
must revolt; . . . which tramples upon the writ of *habeas corpus*, and
denies a trial by jury in a case involving a man's liberty, dearer than
life; which taxes us all to pay the expense of sending men into slavery
by its summary process, and bribes men to carry out its diabolical
purpose; and which punishes, by fine and imprisonment, the holiest
duties of religion to our fellow-men. . . .

Would that I could draw an adequate picture of the slave power,
and show you how it subordinates every other power in the nation to
its lawless rule. It pervades and governs every interest. In the language of John Quincy Adams, "the propagation, preservation, and
perpetuation of slavery is the vital and animating spirit of the National Government." We cannot escape its presence without forsaking
the country. We inhale it at every breath, and imbibe it at every
pore. We "live, and move, and have our being" in the midst of this
frightful moral pestilence, which is hovering like a dark cloud over
the land, and menacing the very life of the Republic.

And now, does any one ask how we shall successfully wage war against this monster power? I answer, that American politics and American religion are the bulwarks which support it, and that we must attack them. If we do this wisely and perseveringly, we shall succeed. We need no new weapons, but only a faithful use of those we already possess, in more direct assaults upon these strongholds of the enemy. And first allow me to refer to the political organizations of the country.

There was once a time when the Whig and Democratic parties were arrayed against each other upon certain tolerably well defined political issues. That time is past. These issues are obsolete. Who now thinks it worth while to talk about a Bank of the United States? Why a Whig who would publicly advocate, or a Democrat who would oppose such an institution, would run no small hazard of being set down as crazy by all parties. It has passed away, and with it one of the standards of party orthodoxy. And is not the same perfectly true of the old question of Land Distribution? . . . And can any man define the difference between these parties at this time on the question of River and Harbor Improvements? . . .

I respectfully ask then if these parties have not outlived the questions which called them into being, and organized their forces under their early champions? They are the surviving effects of causes now no longer operative, and have therefore no apology for their existence, thus lengthened out beyond its time, save the traditionary reverence of their votaries for names under which they once did battle. They are at this time pitted against each other in a mere scramble for place and power, however anxious their leaders may be to hide the fact from the eyes of the masses.

But if I am right in this, then I have been wrong in dignifying these organizations as *parties*. They are *factions*, the great bane of republics, and every lover of his country should labor for their overthrow. . . . I have already briefly recited some of the achievements of the slave power. I have shown you, by actual facts, that it is the supreme power in the nation; and it has maintained its supremacy for years past through the agency of these heartless factions. Submission to its behests in all things is the appointed means of obtaining power, the sole and openly avowed condition upon which their existence can be continued. Who will dare deny this? Who is there so blind as not to see that existing party associations can only be maintained by an unqualified surrender of the interests of freedom? . . .

Northern Whigs and Democrats always pay the drafts of the slaveholders at sight, whatever the amount may be. Of course, I would not speak disparagingly here of the great body of the people. I refer to regular politicians, and that strange devil-worship of party by which well-meaning men are induced to throw their whole weight on the wrong side of this great question. The mass of the people in the North, of all parties, dislike slavery. Their consciences condemn it; . . . but, anchored in the toils of their leaders, they complacently say, "We believe the government will be better administered by our party than by our opponents; we have confidence in our public men; and if we divide on the slavery question it will only insure the triumph of our foes, who are at least as pro-slavery as ourselves. We therefore think it wisest to keep up our party, and postpone, for the time, if not indefinitely, all action on the question."

Here, Mr. President, is our foe. Here is the unclean spirit that must be cast out from the hearts of the people before they can be saved. We must enter the inner sanctuary of their consciences, and dispel the long gathering clouds of passion and prejudice which hold them in the slumber of unconscious guilt. We must sound it incessantly in their ears, and in trumpet tones, that by remaining in the service of these factions they are guilty of the untold wrongs of slavery. . . .

But leaving this topic, permit me, in conclusion, to notice briefly the other main bulwark of slavery,—the religious organizations of the country. . . . What are our churches doing for the anti-slavery reform? Alas! the popular religion of the country lies imbedded in the politics and trade of the country. It has sunk down to a dead level with the ruling secular influences of the age. It has ceased, I fear, to be a divine power, practically capable of saving the world from its sins. It has formed a wicked compact with the wealth and fashion of society, and become their servant, instead of bringing them into subjection to its supreme law. . . . Even our tract, and missionary, and Sunday-school associations, those mighty agencies for the diffusion of Christian truth, are under slaveholding espionage. The scissors of the peculiar institution must be applied to their publications, which must be so carved and mangled as not to send forth even an intimation that freedom is a blessing, or slavery a curse. The meek and lamb-like clergy and churches of the North submit to this cold-blooded priestly havoc in uncomplaining silence, lest the ire of the slaveholder should be kindled, and the *harmony* of the Church be endangered. In all the late publications of the American Tract Society, I am informed that not a syllable can be found against slavery. Such sins as Sabbath-breaking, dancing, fine dressing, etc., are abundantly noticed and condemned, but not even a whisper must go forth against the "sum of all villainies." The great denominations of the North are thus made to uphold American slavery, and, like our great political organizations, necessarily involve their supporters in the guilt of slaveholding. . . .

Our reliance, indeed, must be on Christianity as a divine message to man. It is the light and hope of the world, the inspirer of every good work, the only power "given among men whereby we must be saved." The Church, I fully believe, is to redeem the race. But as in ancient days, so now, the work of reform must begin outside of existing systems, beyond the shadow of our ruling church judicatories, among the great body of the people. We must not commence with the chief priests and rulers, who are always ready to crucify Reform, but like Fox and Wesley take our stand in the midst of the multitude, who have no other interest than to find and embrace the truth.

Thoughts on the New Assault upon Freedom in America (1854)

THEODORE PARKER

Sometimes described as the most erudite man in ante-bellum America, the self-educated Theodore Parker was both a Unitarian minister and a transcendentalist reformer. He was closely associated with the Boston and Concord literary world, and won fame for his speeches and sermons attacking a variety of social injustices. Parker took pride in the fact that his grandfather had led the Minute Men at Lexington on April 19, 1775. On May 24, 1854, Parker delivered a speech at Boston's Faneuil Hall inciting his supporters to attack the courthouse in a futile attempt to free Anthony Burns, a fugitive slave who had been captured under the law which was part of the Compromise of 1850. Though Parker was arrested, the indictment was soon dismissed. Three months earlier, Parker had given an address, part of which is reprinted below, responding to the implications of the Kansas-Nebraska Bill. The sectional crises beginning with the Mexican War convinced him that the South had always been a separate civilization,

From Theodore Parker, *Some Thoughts on the New Assault Upon Freedom in America and the General State of the Country* (Boston, 1854), pp. 26–29, 70–72.

morally and culturally retarded by the institution of slavery. But while Parker emphasized the sectional cleavage and even predicted the Civil War, he often directed his harshest criticisms toward the northern capitalists who profited from slavery. As this selection indicates, he was ambivalent toward the blessings and corruptions of wealth; yet he hoped that the crusade against the Slave Power might become a high and ennobling cause, similar to the American Revolution, which would restore moral commitment and righteousness among the people and prepare the nation for its high mission of spreading liberty around the globe.

Materialism shows itself in the swift growth of covetousness, in the concentration of the talent and genius of the nation upon the acquisition of riches. The power to organize things and men comes out in the machines, ships, and mills, in little and great confederations, from a lyceum to the Federal Union of thirty-one States. The natural exclusiveness appears in the extermination of the red man, in the enslavement of the black man, in the contempt with which he is treated—turned out of the tavern, the church, and the graveyard. The lack of high qualities of mind is shown in the poverty of American literature, the meanness of American religion, in the neglect and continual violation of the idea set forth in our national programme of Principles and Purpose. Since the Revolution, the immediate aim of America appears to have changed.

At first, during the period of America's colonization and her controversy with England, and her affirmation and establishment of her programme of political principles,—the great national work of the disunited provinces was a struggle for local self-government against despotic centralization beyond the sea. It was an effort against the vicarious rule of the middle ages, which allowed the people no power in the State, the laity none in the Church, the servant none in the family. . . . This forced men to look inward at the natural rights of man; outward at the general development thereof in history. It led to the attempt to establish a Democracy, which, so far as Measures are concerned, is the government of all, for all, by all; so far as moral Principle is concerned, it is the enactment of God's Justice into human laws. There was a struggle of the many against the few; for man's nature, with its instinct of progressive and perpetual development, against the accidents of man's history. It was an effort to establish the eternal law of God against the provisional caprice of tyrants, . . .

From 1620 to 1788 there was a rapid development of ideas. But since that time the outward pressure has been withdrawn. The nation is no longer called to protest against a foreign foe; no despot forces us to fall back on the great principles of human nature, and declare great universal truths. Even the Anglo Saxon people are always metaphysical in revolution. We have ceased to be such, and have become material. We have let the programme of political principles and purposes slip out of the nation's consciousness, and have betaken ourselves, body and soul to the creation of riches. Wealth is the great object of American desire. Covetousness is the American passion. . . .

Slavery is one great enemy of America, but there is one other foe—corrupt politicians filibustering for the Presidency, defending Slavery out of the New Testament, volunteering to shoulder their musket and shoot down men claiming their unalienable rights; politicians who deny God's Higher Law, who call upon us to conquer our prejudices against wickedness, inaugurating Atheism as the first principle of Government. In 1788, they put Slavery into the Constitution; in 1850, they enacted iniquity into Law; and in 1854, they are about their old work "saving the Union." Shall such men always prevail! . . .

As soon as the North awakes to its ideas, and uses its vast strength of money, its vast strength of numbers, and its still more gigantic strength of educated intellect, we shall tread this monster underneath our feet. See how Spain has fallen—how poor and miserable is Spanish America. She stands there a perpetual warning to us. One day the North will rise in her majesty, and put Slavery under our feet, and then we shall extend the area of freedom. The blessing of Almighty God will come down upon the noblest people the world ever saw—who have triumphed over Theocracy, Monarchy, Aristocracy, Despotocracy, and have got a Democracy—a government of all, for all, and by all—a Church without a Bishop, a State without a King, a Community without a Lord, and a Family without a Slave.

The Irrepressible Conflict (1860)

CARL SCHURZ

Although the following speech was delivered in St. Louis in the heat of the presidential campaign of 1860, it develops implications contained in the selections by Palfrey, Julian, and Parker. According to Carl Schurz, the Slave Power was governed less by willful intent than by inherent necessity. Like some malignant growth, slavery could perpetuate itself only by aggressive expansion. Schurz, who was born in Germany and who fled to America after participating in the abortive Revolution of 1848, never doubted that history was on the side of liberty. He saw the American Civil War as a decisive episode in the emancipation and progress of the human race. A celebrated orator and dedicated Republican, he served as the American minister to Spain during the early war years and then returned to the United States to play an important role as a general in the Union army. In his later career he held the posts of Secretary of Interior and United States Senator from Missouri.

The slave power is impelled by the irresistible power of necessity. It cannot exist unless it rules, and it cannot rule unless it keeps down its opponents. All its demands and acts are in strict harmony with its interests and attributes; they are the natural growth of its existence. I repeat, I am willing to acquit it of the charge of wilful aggression; I am willing to concede that it struggles for self-preservation. But now the momentous question arises: How do the means which seem indispensable to the self-preservation of slavery agree with the existence and interests of free labor society? . . .

Cast your eyes over that great beehive called the free States. See by the railroad and the telegraphic wire every village, almost every backwoods cottage, drawn within the immediate reach of progressive civilization. Look over our grain fields, but lately a lonesome wilderness, where machinery is almost superseding the labor of the human hand; over our workshops, whose aspect is almost daily changed by the magic touch of inventive genius; over our fleets of merchant ves-

From Frederic Bancroft, ed., *Speeches, Correspondence, and Political Papers of Carl Schurz*, I (New York: G. P. Putnam's Sons, 1913), 130–134. Copyright, 1913, by Schurz Memorial Committee.

sels, numerous enough to make the whole world tributary to our prosperity; look upon our society, where by popular education and the continual change of condition the dividing lines between ranks and classes are almost obliterated; look upon our system of public instruction, which places even the lowliest child of the people upon the high road of progressive advancement. . . .

To what do we owe all this? First and foremost, to that perfect freedom of inquiry, which acknowledges no rules but those of logic, no limits but those that bound the faculties of the human mind. Its magic consists in its universality. To it we owe the harmony of our progressive movement in all its endless ramifications. . . . Let the slave power or any other political or economic interest tell us that we must think and say and invent and discover nothing which is against its demands, and we must interrupt and give up the harmony of our progressive development, or fight the tyrannical pretension, whatever shape it may assume. . . .

Slaveholders, look at this picture and at this. Can the difference escape your observation? You may say, as many have said, that there is, indeed, a difference of principle, but not necessarily an antagonism of interests. Look again.

Your social system is founded upon forced labor, ours upon free labor. Slave labor cannot exist together with freedom of inquiry, and so you demand the restriction of that freedom; free labor cannot exist without it, and so we maintain its inviolability. Slave labor demands the setting aside of the safeguards of individual liberty, for the purpose of upholding subordination and protecting slave property; free labor demands their preservation as essential and indispensable to its existence and progressive development. Slavery demands extension by an aggressive foreign policy; free labor demands an honorable peace and friendly intercourse with the world abroad for its commerce, and a peaceable and undisturbed development of our resources at home for its agriculture and industry. Slavery demands extension over national territories for the purpose of gaining political power. Free labor demands the national domain for workingmen, for the purpose of spreading the blessings of liberty and civilization. Slavery, therefore, opposes all measures tending to secure the soil to the actual laborer; free labor, therefore, recognizes the right of the settler to the soil, and demands measures protecting him against the pressure of speculation. Slavery demands the absolute ascendency of the planting interest in our economic policy; free labor demands legislation tending to develop all the resources of the land, and to harmonize the agricultural, commercial and industrial interests. Slavery demands the control of the general government for its special protection and the promotion of its peculiar interests; free labor demands that the general government be administered for the purpose of securing to all the blessings of liberty, and for the promotion of the general welfare. Slavery demands the recognition of its divine right; free labor recognizes no divine right but that of the liberty of all men.

With one word, slavery demands, for its protection and perpetuation, a system of policy which is utterly incompatible with the principles upon which the organization of free-labor society rests. There is the antagonism. That is the essence of the "irrepressible conflict."

A Republican Appeal for Unity (1855)

CHARLES SUMNER

Sent to the United States Senate in 1851, Charles Sumner, a native of Massachusetts, soon became one of the most hated enemies of the South. From his opposition to the Kansas-Nebraska Bill to his vital role in Radical Reconstruction, Sumner bitterly fought what he called the "Slave Oligarchy," even though it nearly cost him his life when he was attacked on the Senate floor. The following selection, which is part of a speech delivered at Faneuil Hall in 1855, makes a clear bid for immigrant support in its emphatic repudiation of the Know-Nothing movement. Sumner's overture to Irish Catholic voters gives a new dimension to his appeal for unity, which echoes so much of the earlier literature of countersubversion. Since the southern enemy was supposedly united in purpose, Sumner called upon all northerners to forget their minor disputes and differences and close ranks, as the patriots had done in the American Revolution.

A party, which, beginning in secrecy, interferes with religious belief, and founds a discrimination on the accident of birth, is not the party for us.

It was the sentiment of that great apostle of Freedom, Benjamin Franklin, uttered during the trials of the Revolution, that, "Where Liberty is, there is my country." In similar strain, I would say,

From Charles Sumner, *Speech of the Hon. Charles Sumner, November 2, 1855,* in Faneuil Hall (Washington, n.d.), pp. 13–14, 16.

"Where Liberty is, there is my party." Such an organization is now happily constituted here in Massachusetts, and in all the free States, under the name of the Republican party. . . .

The object to which, as a party, we are pledged, is all contained in the acceptance of the issue which the Slave Oligarchy tenders. To its repeal of the Missouri Compromise, and its imperious demand that Kansas shall be surrendered to Slavery, we reply, that Freedom shall be made the universal law of all the national domain, without compromise, and that hereafter no slave State shall be admitted into the Union. To its tyrannical assumption of supremacy in the National Government, we reply, that the Slave Oligarchy shall be overthrown. Such is the practical purpose of the Republican party.

It is to uphold and advance this cause, that we have come together, leaving the parties to which we have been respectively attached. Now, in the course of human events, it becomes our duty to dissolve the political bands which bound us to the old organizations and to assume a separate existence. Our Declaration of Independence has been made. Let us, in the spirit of our Fathers, pledge ourselves to sustain it with our lives, our fortunes, and our sacred honor. In thus associating and harmonizing from opposite quarters, in order to promote a common cause, we have learned to forget former differences, and to appreciate the motives of each other. We have learned how trivial are the matters on which we may disagree, compared with the Great Issue on which we all agree. Old prejudices have vanished. . . .

It only remains that I should press the question with which I began —"Are you for Freedom, or are you for Slavery?" As it is right to be taught by the enemy, let us derive instruction from the Oligarchy we oppose. The 347,000 slave-masters are always united. Hence their strength. Like arrows in a quiver, they cannot be broken. The friends of Freedom have thus far been divided. They, too, must be united. In the crisis before us, it becomes you all to forget ancient feuds, and those names which have been the signal of strife. There is no occasion to remember anything but our duties. When the fire-bell rings at midnight, we do not ask if it be Whigs or Democrats, Protestants or Catholics, natives or foreigners, who join our efforts to extinguish the flames; nor do we ask any such question in selecting our leader, then. Men of all parties, Whigs and Democrats, or however named, let me call upon you to come forward, and join in a common cause. Do not hesitate. When Freedom is in danger, all who are not for her are against her. The penalty of indifference, in such a cause, is akin to the penalty of opposition; as is well pictured by the great Italian poet [Dante], when, among the saddest on the banks of Acheron—rending the air with outcries of torment, shrieks of anger, and smiting of hands—he finds the troop of dreary souls who had been cyphers only in the great conflicts of life:

> Mingled with whom, of their disgrace the proof,
> Are the vile angels, who did not rebel,
> Nor kept their faith to God, *but stood aloof.*

Come forth, then, from the old organizations; let us range together. Come forth, all who have stood aloof from parties. Here is an opportunity for action. You who place principles above men, come forward! All who feel in any way the wrong of Slavery, take your stand!

The Great Conspiracy to Overthrow Liberty in America (1866)

JOHN SMITH DYE

When we consider how often Americans have believed that imaginary conspiracies had won control of their destiny, there is a certain irony in the fact that the Civil War era was marked by two genuine conspiracies, in 1859 and 1865, which were the products of two gifted but highly disordered minds. It is also ironic that John Wilkes Booth, the distinguished actor and author of the second conspiracy, was a member of the Virginia militia that arrested and executed the leader of the first conspiracy, John Brown. While Booth and his followers acted without the knowledge or sanction of Confederate officials, their plot to kill the President, the Vice President, and the Secretary of State was inevitably attributed to the defeated and embittered leaders of the South. Writing soon after Lincoln's assassination, John Smith Dye offered evidence to "prove" that even Presidents Harrison and Taylor had not died from natural causes but had been secretly murdered by the Slave Power. He was further convinced that President Buchanan had been nearly killed by poisoning when he had resisted southern demands. Though such charges seem ridiculous when read literally, they may also be interpreted as a more personal dramatization of the thesis that the Slave Power was secretly "poisoning" the political and economic life of the nation.

From John Smith Dye, *History of the Plots and Crimes of the Great Conspiracy to Overthrow Liberty in America* (New York, 1866), pp. iii–iv.

It is the object of the author to give, in a small compass, a complete history of the political crimes originating with African Slavery, and perpetrated by its friends, during the last century, in America.

We think it necessary, for the good of future generations, to show how these men resorted to the most atrocious means to defeat the nation's will, and control the Government; and all these failing, how they rose in open rebellion, determined to destroy the power they could no longer control. We deem it useless to speak here of the assassination of three of our most illustrious Presidents, all of whom were swept aside like cobwebs when they stood in the way of the conspirator's unholy designs.

Thus all the chief magistrates elected, since the foundation of the Government, in opposition to the slave interests, in some form or other, became victims of assassination.

We have given the history of these foul deeds in detail; and the evidence furnished will enable the reader to judge understandingly, and correctly. . . .

The slaves, by the *logic of events*, should now become as free as their masters. But as the latter sought to destroy the Federal Government when they ceased to control it, so they now seek by various devices to bring about a condition of things calculated to produce a war of races. They want the civilized world to justify them in their mischievous designs in defying the General Government behind their old fortification, *the rights of the States*, where they are now enacting unequal laws, determined to retain all the *substance*, while they acknowledge that the *form* of slavery has become extinct.

Abolitionism Is the Product
of a Foreign Plot (1836)

JAMES KIRKE PAULDING

Many of the most eloquent defenders of slavery were northerners who had little direct experience with the South's peculiar institution. James Kirke Paulding, a native of Putnam County, New York, was one of the northern novelists who helped create the romantic myth of southern leisure,

From James Kirke Paulding, *Slavery in the United States* (New York, 1836), pp. 110, 134–136, 284, 302–303.

gracious living, and benevolent paternalism as an antidote to the competi-
tive and pecuniary culture of the North. An ardent nationalist who cele-
brated America's virtues in essays, poems, and novels, Paulding held a life-
long grudge against the English and was particularly sensitive to the
criticisms of English travelers who visited the United States. When William
Loyd Garrison went abroad to seek the support of British antislavery lead-
ers and to expose the American Colonization Society as an enemy of the
American Negro, Paulding denounced him as a traitor to his country. The
ties between American and foreign abolitionists made it possible for writers
like Paulding to portray the antislavery movement as an un-American force.
According to Paulding, American abolitionists were simply the tools of a
foreign conspiracy to weaken and divide the United States; they were thus
public enemies who had forfeited their rights to speak or be heard.

It cannot have escaped the notice of our countrymen, who mingle in the society of foreigners, that the most devoted adherents of aristocracy, those who deride the miseries of the people of Ireland, and oppose with obstinate pertinacity the progress of free principles throughout the world, are the most tender in their sympathies in behalf of the negro slaves of the United States, the most loud in their declamations on the subject. There is not a despotic monarch in Europe who does not mourn over the wrongs of Africa; and even the Emperor Nicholas himself, it is said, expresses a strong sympathy in favour of universal emancipation, with the exception of all white men. In fact, it cannot be denied that the enemies of liberty in Europe are the great and leading advocates of the natives of Africa. They seem to be playing on the credulity of the world, by affecting a marvellous regard to the rights of one colour, while resolutely withholding their rights from another; and apparently strive to make some amends for their oppression at home, by crusading in behalf of human rights in the distant regions of the world; thus gaining the credit of humanity without any sacrifice of interest. . . .

That the late intemperate proceedings of the abolitionists have been stimulated by an impulse derived from abroad, is evident from the whole history of their newborn zeal. It will be remembered that the denunciation of the Colonization Society, which was the first step in their proceedings, was at a meeting in the city of London, at which very distinguished statesmen of all parties attended, and in which the two great liberators, Garrison and O'Connell, equally distinguished themselves by their abuse of the people of the United States. From that meeting the emissaries of the English abolitionists came, red hot with furious zeal, to light the fires of contention, insurrection, disunion, and massacre. We feel no hesitation in declaring our belief that they are not only stimulated by foreign influence, but by foreign money; because it is otherwise incomprehensible how they obtain the means of gratuitously distributing so many papers, pamphlets, and pictures, or of supporting such a number of brawling incendiaries who are every day disturbing the peace of communities by their disgusting and inflammatory harangues. . . .

If we combine with these circumstances, the tone and language of the British press—reviews, magazines, and newspapers; the public declarations of her statesmen and orators; the voice of the pulpit; the resolutions of public meetings; and the officious intermeddling of a host of travellers . . . it would seem sufficiently evident that a great concentrated effort is making against the good name and well being of the United States. . . .

Of all the forms under which fanaticism has appeared, that assumed by the abolitionists is the most dangerous to the existence of civil government and the principles of liberty, in their enlarged and liberal construction. . . . The conduct and sentiments of the abolitionists are marked by an utter disregard, a ferocious hostility to those laws and institutions which stand in the way of their mad schemes, and under whose salutary influence the people of the United States exhibit a spectacle of happiness and prosperity without a parallel. In the pretended pursuit of the rights of human beings, they trample on all the feelings of humanity, and immolate the laws of their country on the altar of a wilful misrepresentation of the law of God. Some of their defenders have denied the language that has come forth under the auspices of their own acknowledged organs, and the inferences which have been drawn from their own declarations. But it will not do: we impeach them as enemies of the law of the land, the constitution of the government, the union of the states, the common courtesies of life, the precepts of religion, and the rights and lives of millions of our countrymen. We charge them with using every exertion, straining every nerve, and resorting to every device, open and underhand, to produce, to foster, and to inflame feelings between the master and the slave, the South and the North, that cannot but be productive of consequences as fatal to the happiness of the former, as to the friendly relations and salutary union of the latter. The proofs are their own declarations, their words and their actions; and to these we appeal.

Abolitionism Is Equivalent to Revolution (1835)

HARRISON GRAY OTIS

*Northern conservatives were particularly alarmed by the abolitionists'
methods and tactics. In a speech at Faneuil Hall in 1835, the aged and
aristocratic Harrison Gray Otis expressed indignation over the populist character of the antislavery movement. Instead of deferring to recognized leaders and established authorities, the abolitionists were organizing branch societies in hundreds of communities and, even worse, were appealing to the
emotions and untutored minds of women and children. Otis was a proud
survivor of New England Federalism. He had helped suppress Shays' Rebellion, had supported the Alien and Sedition Acts, and had promoted the
secessionist movement that led to the Hartford Convention. He had served
in both the House of Representatives and the United States Senate, and had
three times been elected mayor of Boston. Despite his devotion to New
England sectionalism, he had developed intimate ties with South Carolina
Federalists and remained a firm defender of the Constitution. He was relatively unconcerned with the slavery issue until 1835, when the sudden out-
pouring of abolitionist literature convinced him that the Union was imperiled by a revolutionary movement which had already gone far toward
subverting the established order.*

It has of late become certain, though not yet perhaps generally
known, that an association has been formed in a neighboring state
[New York] for the avowed purpose of effecting the *immediate abolition of slavery*. Their number is at present comparatively small and
insignificant, but as they boast, augmented within the last year. Their
printed constitution and proceedings, seen by me only within a few
days, frankly develop their desire to establish auxiliary societies in
every state and municipality, and to enlist in the service of the cause
man, woman and child. This simple statement shows it to be a dangerous association. A very rapid exposition of the tendency of their
principles will prove them to be not only imminently dangerous, but
hostile to the spirit and letter of the constitution of the union. I will,

---

From the speech of Harrison Gray Otis, Faneuil Hall, Boston, August 22, 1835,
in *Niles' Register*, September 5, 1835, pp. 10–11.

in order to make this apparent, call the recollection of my fellow citizens to the history of the constitution and to the constitution itself—and compare the doctrines of the constitution with the canons of the anti-slavery association, and demonstrate that if the latter be not yet an unlawful association (which some sound jurists think it is), it is in a fair way to become so, by its design to trench upon the provisions of the constitution by overt acts, and its tendency to break down the sacred palladium. . . .

The first step adopted by them is to erect themselves into a *revolutionary society*—combined and affiliated with auxiliary and ancillary societies, in every state and community, large or small, in the eastern and western states. All men are invited to join in this holy crusade. The ladies are invoked to turn their sewing parties into abolition clubs, and the little children when they meet to eat sugar plumbs [sic] or at the Sunday schools are to be taught that A B stands for abolition:—Sir, I do not exaggerate—there is the book—[an anti-slavery pamphlet which lay on the table]—all I assert is in substance; men, women and children are stimulated, flattered and frightened in order to swell their numbers. . . .

Now I deny that any body of men can lawfully associate for the purpose of undermining, more than for overthrowing, the government of our sister states. There may be no statute to make such combinations penal, because the offence is of a new complexion. But they are not the less intrinsically wrong. This will be evident if the express intention of the association was to operate upon the government of Cuba or of Russia, or even of Turkey. The sovereigns of those countries might and rightfully would demand the suppression of such combinations. . . .

The next means resorted to for effecting their object is the printing and publishing and circulating immense numbers of books, pamphlets, tracts and newspapers of the most inflammatory character, and raising funds for the purpose of circulating them far and wide throughout the southern country. These documents, they gravely say, are for the master and not for the slave. This excuse, by the by, is an admission that it would be wrong to put them into the hands of the slave. But such a pretext is an insult to common sense. . . . They may as well believe that they can set all the bells in Richmond ringing so as to arouse and alarm the white inhabitants, and affect the slaves only as a tinkling lullaby to soothe them to repose.

From the Sinks of Europe
a Plotter Has Come (1835)
JOHN TYLER

On the same day that Otis denounced the abolitionists in Boston, John Tyler delivered an even more inflammatory and threatening speech at Gloucester Courthouse, Virginia. A Jeffersonian who had first been sent to Congress in 1816, Tyler was on record as wishing "to see slavery pass away." But like most southern politicians, he supported the "conspiracy of silence" which had kept the slavery issue out of national politics. He was shocked and outraged when northern abolitionists began petitioning Congress for the exclusion of slavery from the District of Columbia, and was even more incensed by the sudden flood of antislavery newspapers and pamphlets which arrived in the South in the summer of 1835. In the Gloucester speech Tyler emphasizes the wealth and power of the American Anti-slavery Society—which he erroneously infers from the quantity and cheapness of their publications. In a section of the speech not reprinted here, he expresses the common indignation over the abolitionists' organizing of women "to rejoice over the conflagration of our dwellings and the murder of our people," and over the wickedness of appealing to the impressionable minds of children. He observes that northern agitators had become so morally degraded and forgetful of patriotism that they had actually welcomed a British abolitionist, George Thompson, to instruct Americans on the rights of humanity. Tyler demands that the northern states enact criminal laws to suppress and punish fanaticism. The fact that abolitionists could hardly think of telling the southern states to suppress and punish the organizers of the Slave Power was indicative of continuing sectional differences.

At the time of the Gloucester speech Tyler was a United States Senator from Virginia; he later succeeded William Henry Harrison as President. The record of his speech was originally taken from a newspaper account which mixed direct quotation with third-person description.

After the lapse of more than half a century, during which time all had acquiesced in the undisturbed condition of things as they were, and the most unexampled prosperity had blessed us and the land be-

---

From Gardiner Tyler (ed.), *Letters and Times of the Tylers* (3 vols., Richmond, Va., 1884–1894), I, 575–578.

queathed to us as an inheritance by our forefathers, a new sect has arisen, possessed pretendedly of nicer sensibilities, a more refined moral sense, and greater love of the human race, than those who had gone before them: who were disposed to manifest their superiority in all these particulars, by setting the people of these States by the ears, and threatening the overthrow of political institutions which have been the source of unmeasured happiness, and which we had fondly hoped to hand over to our posterity as the richest legacy we could leave them. Nor are their pretensions and their movements confined to native born citizens of the several States, who may have been misled into the belief that it was sufficient for a mere majority to will in order to enforce, but a foreign emissary [George Thompson] had dared to venture across the broad Atlantic to aid in this work.

I confess, Mr. Chairman, that I regard it as not among the least portentous signs of the times, that native born citizens should gather themselves together to listen to anathemas uttered against their own brethren, by a feed and paid emissary, who comes here to teach *them* the principles of civil liberty and the rights of humanity. When was it before that this would have been tolerated? The day has been when every man's hand would have fallen in weight to crush a reptile who had crawled from some of the sinks of Europe, with the reward of an emissary in his hand, to sow the seeds of discord among us. For my own part, I cannot think of this with patience. Are the sons of revolutionary sires so much degenerated as to be dependent on foreigners to teach them lessons of political ethics?—or is it come to this, that every plotter of mischief from abroad is to be received into our households, to instruct us in our duties as citizens? Mr. Tyler expressed the fear that the toleration which had been practised towards Thompson manifested a condition of feeling at war with the perpetuity of our institutions. . . .

He had never, until lately, believed that any serious head could be made in the United States upon the subject—much less had he feared that the spirit of incendiarism would be permitted by the States to walk abroad in the face of the day, unrestrained and unchecked. These feelings and sentiments had been forced to give place to others. The unexpected evil is now upon us; it has invaded our firesides, and under our own roofs is sharpening the dagger for midnight assassination, and exciting cruelty and bloodshed. The post-office department, which was established for the purpose of commercial interchange, or to transport from remote places the friendly greetings of those of kindred blood, has been converted into a vehicle for distributing incendiary pamphlets, with which our land is at this moment deluged.

A society has sprung up whose avowed object it is to despoil us of our property at the hazard of all and every consequence. It had been his [Tyler's] duty, occupying as he did a public station which devolved on him the obligations of a sentinel to watch over the rights and interests of Virginia, to make himself acquainted as far as practicable with the rise and progress of that society, and with its means to do mischief; and his opinion was, that it was now powerful, and if not speedily checked in its mad career, was destined to attain much greater power. He had seen it in its origin, some two years ago, consisting of a mere handful of obscure persons, who were the subjects of ridicule from one end of the Union to the other. That small association, thus despised and thus contemned, had already established two hundred and fifty auxiliaries, and at a single meeting contributed $30,000 towards the furtherance of its scheme,—some half of which was paid down promptly. It has established numerous presses, four of which circulated from the city of New York, with copies of three of which they had been so *extremely kind* as to favor me through the mail. These papers were circulated gratuitously among us, and at mere nominal prices to actual subscribers. He [Tyler] had then in his possession one of those publications, and he would exhibit it for the inspection of those present. (He here drew from his pocket the *Anti-Slavery Record.*) Here, said he, is a picture upon the external covering, designed to represent each of you, gentlemen. A scourge is in your hand, and three victims bound and kneeling at your feet. You are represented as demons in the shape of men; and by way of contrast, here stands Arthur Tappan, Mr. Somebody Garrison, or Mr. Foreigner Thompson, patting the greasy little fellows on their cheeks and giving them most lovely kisses. *They* are the exclusive philanthropists—the only lovers of the human race—the only legitimate defenders of the religion of Christ. But I propose to show you the cheap rate at which these papers are delivered out to actual subscribers. (He read from the external sheet: "*Human Rights,* twenty-five cents per annum; *Anti-Slavery Record,* one dollar-and-a-half *per hundred; Emancipator* [a paper larger than the *Whig* or *Enquirer*], fifty-cents per annum; *Slave's Friend,* single number, one cent.) He had not seen the *Slave's Friend;* judging, however, from the other papers, he concluded it to be a misnomer. It should rather be called the *slave's enemy,* since its circulation among us, in company with its three adjuncts, had produced a curtailment of privileges heretofore willingly, nay, gladly granted by the master to his slaves, and which, before these fanatical teachers had arisen in the land, were gradually and daily becoming greater and greater. In addition to these, there was a numerous tribe of tracts, and he believed, prints, designed to make impression on the minds of children. Here, then, Mr. Chairman, are the evidences of a powerful combination; here some of the means relied upon. Look into the contents of this little pamphlet; you will find it full of stories of the white man's cruelty and the negro's suffering; garbled statements are herein contained to stir up the feelings of the Northern brethren against us. . . .

How are they [the abolitionists] to be met and overthrown? I believe that they can only be met successfully by a firm and decided course on our part. Timid counsels but too frequently betray. The attention of the whole people of the North must be awakened to a knowledge of the true state of things, and I am pleased to see that the good old town of Boston is already in motion. A meeting has been called by means of her most distinguished citizens. It behooved her to take the lead. It is to be hoped that she will give back from Faneuil Hall, as in former times, the voice which has reached her from Virginia. Her example, I trust, will be followed in quick succession by other towns and cities. These proceedings would do much towards allaying the excited feeling of the day.

But mere declarations of public meetings in the North will not suffice. We have a right to call for measures of coercion on the part of our sister States; Virginia and the other Southern States should make a demand for legislation. Her peace is daily threatened through the actions of the fanatics; the lives of her people are placed in jeopardy; nothing short of penal enactments will do. For when did fanaticism ever listen to reason? The curse of the world, it is possessed of its own vain imaginings, to the exclusion of everything else. It hath no eyes to see, no ears to hear. It drives onward, reckless of consequences, and its efforts at reform terminate only with the destruction of human hopes. We have a right to ask that it shall be restrained by laws. If there existed a combination in our State to affect the lives and property of the people of any other State, should we hesitate to restrain and punish all who might be concerned? I answer, unhesitatingly, in the negative. Unless there be immediate and active co-operation on the part of our co-States, I know not what is to be done.

A Northern Party Is Seeking to Convert the Government into an Instrument of Warfare upon Slavery (1850)

ROBERT MERCER HUNTER

Robert Mercer Hunter was a Virginia lawyer who served as Speaker of the House of Representatives before being elected to the Senate. A disciple of John C. Calhoun, he became so alarmed by the northern stand on the territorial question in 1850 that he attended the disunionist Nashville Convention and would have accepted secession if the majority had decided on such a move. From the time of the Missouri crisis in 1820 Hunter detected an accelerating series of encroachments on southern rights by the antislavery faction, which was attempting to mobilize northern public opinion and seize control of the federal government.

Live together, sir, we cannot, unless something is done to settle these differences and compose this strife which seems to be growing daily in intensity and bitterness. The cords which bind this Union together, will fret asunder from the mere force of agitation, unless something can be done to quiet it.

The evil, Mr. President, of which the South complains, arises out of the fact that a party in the North, by no means contemptible in point of numbers, is seeking to convert this Government, through its direct legislation, into an instrument of warfare upon the institution of slavery in the States, and from the fear that a majority of those in the free States, who are hereafter to control and manage this Government, will use, if not its positive legislation, at least its moral influence, for that purpose. Government is designed to protect persons and property, but with what feelings will it be regarded if, instead of performing those functions, it should become either directly or indirectly the source of constant assaults, not only upon twelve or fifteen hundred millions of property in the South, but upon the very safety of those

From the speech of Senator Robert Mercer Hunter, March 25, 1850, in the *Appendix to the Congressional Globe, for the First Session, Thirty-First Congress* (Washington, 1850), pp. 375–376.

whose peace depends upon preserving the existing relations between master and slave in those States. . . .

In reviewing this history, I shall pass over the early and better days of the Republic, when the recollections of common sufferings and a common struggle were yet fresh in the minds of men, when all felt the necessity of union and common exertions for future security, and a fraternal spirit animated the people of all the States. I know that the northwestern ordinance was then adopted, but the fruit of the seed which was then sown did not mature until long after. The warfare really commenced, as has been said before, at the time of the agitation of the Missouri question—a contest into which the North entered to prevent the addition of any more slave States, and which ended in depriving the South of the right to settle and colonize the larger portion of the territory acquired by the Louisiana cession. . . . Associations were formed for the abolition of slavery, presses were established, tracts were disseminated, and a system of agitation was commenced, whose object was to make the institution odious, unprofitable, and even dangerous, and thus lead to its destruction. To alarm the slaveholder for his property, was one of the purposes of their agitation; but they looked beyond this; they sought not only to convert the halls of national legislation into the arena for anti-slavery agitation, but also to commit the Government of the United States, through a series of measures, to the proposition that there can be no *property* in *man*. In this purpose they have not only been persevering but consistent; it is to this end that all of their efforts through Federal legislation have been directed. They got up what has been denominated a "run of petitions" upon every subject upon which the passions or prejudices of northern members could be plausibly invoked, so as to induce them to commit themselves and the Government to this proposition. If there was a rivet loose in all the armor, or the smallest breach in the constitutional defences of slavery, some treacherous shaft was sure to find it. They petitioned Congress to withdraw the protection of law from slavery wherever it was given by the National Government. . . . They petitioned Congress to abolish slavery in the forts, arsenals, and dock-yards of the United States, even in the slave States. Their object was, to exhibit to the master and to the slave in those States, the example and influence of the General Government operating in their very midst, and in opposition to slavery. They had probably other things in view, which were even better calculated for use in this war upon slavery. These places were thus to be fitted as the arenas for anti-slavery agitation in those States, and to be opened as a sort of free-negro Alsatia, where he might hold his perpetual saturnalia of license and of crime. Thus the forts, designed for our military protection, were to be converted into abolition strongholds in the slave States themselves. . . .

But it may be said that these persons, whose efforts are so dangerous to our peace and our property, constitute but a small portion of the people of the free States. But, Mr. President, when we look to the effects they have had upon the legislation in the free States, and even here, we cannot suppose that they are contemptible in point of numbers, or to be despised in regard to ability.

A Southern Response to John Brown and Black Republicanism (1859)

SYDENHAM MOORE

Sydenham Moore was an Alabama lawyer and judge who served as a captain in the Mexican War and as a colonel in the Confederate army. He was killed in battle in the Civil War. On the eve of the conflict he spent a brief term in Congress, where he denounced the northerners who had expressed support for John Brown and for Hinton R. Helper's book, The Impending Crisis of the South, *which pictured a fundamental conflict between Negro slavery and the true interests of the nonslaveholding southern whites. In the eyes of Moore and many of his colleagues, the North had become so completely subverted by antislavery radicals that the remaining patriots and conservative men of goodwill could no longer be heard. He described as a fatal weakness of the American political system the fact that a "sectional, fanatical party" like the Republicans could gain unchecked power by deluding and manipulating a majority of voters.*

The gentleman from Pennsylvania [Mr. Morris] says it is unfair to charge against the whole North complicity with, or even sympathy for, John Brown and his cause. I have heard no such charge made, and I should be sorry to hear it made. I believe there are men at the North as true to the Constitution as any in the South. . . . We make

From the speech of the Hon. Sydenham Moore, December 8, 1859, in *The Congressional Globe: Containing the Debates and Proceedings of the First Session of the Thirty-Sixth Congress* (Washington, 1860), pp. 38–39.

no such indiscriminate charge upon the people of the North; but when gentlemen endeavor to persuade us that there are no sympathizers with that old felon, or only a few, in that quarter, they do but attempt to practice most shamefully upon our supposed credulity. We are advised that in most of the towns and cities of the North, demonstrations of sympathy were exhibited; and newspapers come to us draped in mourning for his death. The editor of the leading organ of the Republican party (Mr. Greeley) eulogized him, and said that his name would be handed down to after times as that of a glorious martyr.

When gentlemen tell us of the conservative spirit of the northern people, and of their loyalty to the Constitution, with a view to quiet our apprehensions, we point them to the startling fact, here disclosed, that sixty-eight members of the American Congress, including one of the candidates for the Speakership, have signed and recommended for circulation this vile, incendiary publication of [Hinton R.] Helper, intended to excite our slaves to insurrection, and the non-slaveholders to wage war against the slaveholders of the South; and to the significant circumstance, that three only, of all that number, have as yet, though called upon, disavowed and repudiated the sentiments and recommendations of that book. We point them, too, to the additional fact, that from all the New England States there is not a single Representative who is not a member of the Republican party; and, besides, that over one hundred and thirteen members of the present Congress belong to that political association, organized, as it is, upon grounds sectional in their character, unconstitutional, and offensive to us beyond all endurance.

What are the aims and objects of that organization? They are, in my conception, first to seize the reins of Government, and then, by indirect, if not direct means, to destroy the institution of African slavery—a destruction which would involve the South in a loss of property exceeding in value two thousand million dollars; to be followed, perhaps, by all the horrors of another St. Domingo or South Hampton [Nat Turner] insurrection. . . .

I know that the Republican party is composed of men of various shades of opinion, that it embraces, with Abolitionists of the deepest dye, others less openly and violently hostile to our rights. Yet I know that hatred for slavery and slaveholders animates the whole party. This is the common bond which holds it together. This it is which has caused its members, no matter to what political party they formerly belonged, to lay aside, for a time, their differences of opinion respecting all other questions, and unite under a common flag. Even the few men at the North who are now conservative and true to the Constitution, will soon, I fear, be compelled to bend before the storm of fanaticism which has there been raised, or be driven into retirement, as Daniel Webster was when the doors of Faneuil Hall were closed against him because he sanctioned the fugitive slave law. . . .

Not contented with equal privileges, equal benefits, and equal burdens of a common Government, the northern people, or at least a large majority of them, would deprive us, as they have sought to do again and again, of all share in the common territories; would build up their manufactures by imposing upon us onerous protective tariff laws; would squander the public money for local internal improvements, and, in a thousand other ways, enrich themselves by impoverishing us. What a bright prospect would be presented to the southern people, to see their liberties, their property, and their all, at the disposal and mercy of a mere numerical majority in this Union, and that majority composed of their bitter enemies! Think you, sir, that when this sectional, fanatical party gets the control, if it ever shall, of this Government, that the Union, which the wisdom of our fathers framed, would survive? The form might remain, the name might still be preserved, but the spirit of the Constitution would have departed forever. No troops of armed men; no secession of sovereign and independent States; no bloody revolution, though these might follow, will have caused the knell of the Union to be sounded. Base, reckless men, by their unhallowed party associations, will have accomplished at the polls its final overthrow. The verdict of impartial history would be, that a sectional party, envenomed by hate, and impelled by lust of power and dominion, had, through the forms of the Constitution, usurped the power and control of the Government.

6. Enemies Old and New in the Gilded Age and Beyond (1865–1908)

INSOFAR AS the Slave Power had become a symbol of universal evil which could be blamed for most of America's frustrations and shortcomings, the South's decisive defeat gave the appearance of purging the nation of all dangerous subversion and opening a new era of self-confident freedom. When compared with the stormy antebellum decades, the period from 1865 to 1890 exhibits a façade of stability, moderation, and pragmatic balance. Prior to the depression and social unrest of the 1890's, it would have been difficult to convince any sizable segment of the population that American institutions were in imminent danger of being overthrown by a vast conspiratorial organization. The American people have probably never felt such self-assurance and security as when they turned from sectional conflict to the great enterprises of industrializing and urbanizing the continent.

Nevertheless, the idea of conspiracy acquired new force and vividness from actual events. Only months after Lincoln's assassination, a group of former Confederate officers founded the Ku Klux Klan at Pulaski, Tennessee. Dedicated to "chivalry," "humanity," "patriotism," and above all, to the maintenance of white supremacy, the Klan incorporated the secret signs, acrostic passwords, and fearful oaths that had always characterized imagined "invisible empires" like the Illuminati. But though the Klan practiced murder and terrorism in resisting Radical Reconstruction, it raised no threat of subverting the national government or of penetrating the North and West.

Few Americans of that time were genuinely concerned over the rights of Negroes. But by the early 1870's there was a greater sense of danger from conspiracy of a different kind. The scandals of Grant's first administration; the machinations of Jay Gould, Jim Fisk, and Daniel Drew; the corruption of municipal government by such groups as the Tweed Ring of New York, showed that conspiracy for private profit permeated all levels of American public life. In the 1870's repeated exposures of wholesale fraud and corruption gave substance to the "paranoid" conviction that things are never what they seem to be, that innocent appearances often conceal the most sinister plots. Nevertheless, the "gold conspiracy" of Fisk and Gould and the conniving of the St. Louis Whisky Ring presented no direct challenge to American ideology. The cheats and scoundrels of the Gilded Age followed the dictates of unrestrained self-interest, and were thus merely carrying to an extreme a way of life fully sanctioned by the business community.

The dominant values of capitalism were more sharply challenged in the early 1870's, however, by the murders and arson of the Molly Maguires in the coalfields of eastern Pennsylvania. Based on an Irish secret society, the Molly Maguires were an organization of immigrant workers who sought to gain control over their working conditions by terroristic methods. Although the society was infiltrated by a Pinkerton detective and soon broken up, journalists greatly exaggerated its strength and helped to popularize the idea of subversive labor organizations imported from abroad. When the nation was paralyzed by violent railroad strikes in the summer of 1877, there was virtual panic over the spectre of "alien agitators" instigating class warfare. Following the tradition of anti-Illuminism and anti-abolitionism, conservatives blamed social unrest on foreign plots to subvert the Republic.

Prior to the labor conflicts of the late 1870's and 1880's, American images of conspiracy generally involved the values and concerns of the ante-bellum years. In 1868, for example, Pittsburgh hosted a National Christian Convention Opposed to Secret Societies, which was largely aimed at resurrecting the anti-Masonic movement. Many of the delegates were veterans of the older crusade who now recalled that nothing had ever been done about the evils of Freemasonry, which had long been eclipsed by the iniquities of the rising Slave Power. The participants in this and subsequent antisecret-society conventions were searching for ways to make the symbols of the reform past relevant to the new, postwar era. Unlike the earlier anti-Masonic movement, the new protests against secret societies were seldom preoccupied with dark criminality or nefarious plots. The reformers pointed to Freemasonry as only one of various "artificial" fraternal societies which weakened the bonds of "natural" organizations like the family, church, and community. Reflecting the tensions of an increasingly competitive society, the attacks on secret fraternal organizations emphasized the corruption of social relationships which occurred when certain groups enjoyed a hidden and unfair advantage. Thus it was alleged that in the Civil War and in new communities of the West, Freemasons had won arbitrary privileges and preferences. When artificial circumstances were placed above "real trustworthiness and genuine worth," suspicion and mistrust inevitably undermined the moral basis of the competitive system. While Freemasonry could still be used as a meaningful symbol, at least for the older generation, the dread of imminent subversion gave way to the fear that artificial associations were preventing the creation of a truly open society in which even the most rootless men could confidently assume a perfect equality of opportunity.

It is interesting to note that speakers at the Pittsburgh Convention of 1868 drew explicit parallels between Freemasonry, Mormonism, and Roman Catholicism. In 1885 a young Congregationalist minister named Josiah Strong won national fame with a remarkable book, *Our Country*, which argued that the American West, and thus the destiny of the nation and the world, was imperiled by Mormonism, Catholicism, and socialism. Strong's book was a significant link between the clerical outlook of ante-bellum reformers like Lyman Beecher and the mentality of later nativists and anti-Communists. Trained at Lane Theological Seminary in Cincinnati, where Beecher had once presided as president, Strong was steeped in the values and assumptions of Beecher's *Plea for the West*. Strong echoed the themes of ante-bellum evangelism in his fervent appeal to "save the West" from the subversive forces of intemperance, Catholicism, Mormonism, and atheism. He also helped inaugurate a new and revitalized phase of anti-Catholicism by drawing attention to the rising tide of Catholic immigration. Indeed, for Strong, unrestricted immigration was the force that fed and unified the diverse threats to American freedom. He thus anticipated the arguments of the American Protective Association, which was founded two years after the publication of *Our Country* and which made the early 1890's a high-water mark in the history of nativism. Strong was also a harbinger of the future in his warnings against the conspiracies of anarchists and socialists. In the year following the publication of *Our Country*, his worst fears seemed to be confirmed by the Haymarket bomb episode in Chicago, which triggered the first genuine "Red Scare" among the general public.

While Strong seemed to anticipate immigration restriction and domestic repression, and can thus be linked with some of the more reactionary groups of the late nineteenth and early twentieth centuries, he was also groping for a new understanding of openness and opportunity. His attack on socialism allowed him to expose the gross inequalities in American life that served as a breeding ground for revolution. His concern for the dispossessed and his radical critique of plutocracy anticipated the major themes of Populist and Progressive writing. There was a curious but significant contradiction between Strong's assumption that America would be free and pure if only she could be purged of such extraneous forces as Mormonism and Catholicism, and his partial realization that the worst injustices in America had resulted from the operation of unrestrained self-interest. There was a parallel discrepancy between Strong's desire to liberate individuals from the restraints of corporate bodies like the Mormon and Catholic Churches, and his eagerness to enforce public obedience and uniformity through state coercion and indoctrination. It was one of the supreme paradoxes of the paranoid style that assaults on concrete symbols of subversion often led to a growing conviction that the entire society was out of joint and must thus be "subverted" in order to be cured.

With this paradox in mind, we can better understand why the American Protective Association proposed to combat the secret power of Catholicism with a secret, quasiconspiratorial organization, complete with awesome initiations and mysterious rituals. Like the earlier Know-Nothings and radical abolitionists, the A.P.A. sought to regenerate a sick society, and directed its angriest attacks against the existing party system and the compromises of expediency-minded politicians. It was not without reason that in 1891 the future Populist leader, Ignatius Donnelly, published an influential fantasy of violence and class warfare, entitled *Caesar's Column: A Story of the Twentieth Century*, in which America's plutocratic rulers are attacked by a secret Brotherhood of Destruction.

During the late nineteenth and early twentieth centuries the fear of subversion often reflected new anxieties over the seemingly irreversible trends toward national consolidation and specialization. The threat of exclusive privilege shifted from old-fashioned fraternal societies like the Freemasons to a bewildering collection of new bureaucracies, professional associations, and managerial groups. Local elites and self-taught professionals increasingly found themselves displaced or superseded by national agencies, corporate powers, and standardized procedures. For the many Americans who still clung to the Jacksonian ideal of "boundlessness," to use John Higham's term, equal opportunity was becoming dangerously circumscribed by a shadowy "they"—who might be the vested interests attacked by Henry Demorest Lloyd, or the professional economists whose claims to expert knowledge outraged the self-educated Henry George. In view of the traditional American beliefs in laissez-faire and individual opportunity, it was only natural that consolidation and professionalization should raise suspicions of conspiracy. Nor were such suspicions entirely unjustified. Any corporate or professional group must adopt a public stance which conceals, or at least greatly simplifies, its interests, standards, and procedures for making decisions. Neither size nor power is any guarantee that these interests, standards, and procedures promote the general welfare. No doubt Progressive critics had a strong case when they accused the great banking syndicates of conspiring against the public interest. And we cannot easily dismiss recent attacks on private foundations and on the "military-industrial complex" for their lack of public accountability. But we should distinguish the merit of specific accusations from the more generalized tendency to interpret consolidation and professionalization as the products of nefarious conspiracy. This is particularly true of the Populist movement in the 1890's.

In one sense Populism was a realistic response to acute economic problems. In the 1890's commercial farmers around the world were suffering from the effects of overexpansion and improved technology; in America falling commodity prices were aggravated by monetary deflation, tight credit, and discriminatory storage and transportation rates. Many Populist leaders understood the dangers of unrestrained capitalism and advocated reforms that would control industrialization for the public interest. But Populism was also a crusade, based in the rural South and West, which was aimed at cleansing the nation of recent corruptions and restoring the supposed purity and harmony of the past. Much as abolitionists had rewritten American history in terms of the Slave Power's encroachments, Populist writers reinterpreted the post-Civil War period as a series of victories over the unsuspecting people by an international Money Power supported by leading American politicians and business interests. If Populism was a fountainhead for later democratic reforms, it was also a frantic outcry against the emerging modern world, and thus anticipated many of the hysterical themes of right-wing fundamentalism.

A Voice from the Past (1870)

GERRIT SMITH

When the New York State Anti-Secret Society Convention met at Syracuse in November 1870, the star speaker was the aged Gerrit Smith, a famous New York philanthropist who had played an active role in the movements promoting Sunday school and Sabbath observance, temperance, vegetarianism, feminism, prison reform, and antislavery. Smith's presence was a visible reminder of the earlier reform tradition which had struggled to liberate individuals from the coercions of power, from ignorance and arbitrary custom, and from the corruptions of the material world. Ironically, though Smith was dedicated to the ideals of peace and openness, he had given approval and financial support to John Brown's conspiracy of 1859.

I am here not to take an active or prominent part in your Convention. At the age of 73 I find myself too old to do so. . . . I am here simply to add my testimony to yours against secret societies. One of the habits of my life has been free utterances against great public wrongs. Hence, nearly the whole of my adult years have been a standing testimony against such wrongs as imprisonment for debt, slavery, dram-selling, land-monopoly, war, secret societies, and the injustice done to woman. I hardly need add that, consequently, my life has been a-toiling-uphill with minorities, which very rarely became majorities, and which, indeed, very rarely, outgrew derision, contempt and hatred.

My chief objection to secret societies is that their feature of secrecy gives them an undue and fearful advantage over outsiders. They can see what outsiders are designing and doing;—but outsiders cannot see what they are designing and doing. The genius of our American institutions calls for equal rights—in other words, for equality all around. But to have equality all around, there must, necessarily, be openness all around. When men find themselves in the hands of a despot, it may be entirely proper for them to plot in secret against him. But, here, in this land of liberty and equal rights, there can be no justification for any plotting against each other. Is it said that

From the speech of Gerrit Smith, *New York State Anti-Secret Society Convention* (n.p., 1870), pp. 1–2.

those who join our secret societies are too virtuous and just to avail themselves of the opportunity afforded by their secret tie to wrong outsiders? If they are so, then, indeed, how painful the evidence that a secret fraternity has the power to transform virtuous and just persons who join it, into criminals, ay even into murderers! Masons murdered Morgan. Alas, that horrid murder! Although it is between 44 and 45 years since it was perpetrated, it seems as fresh in my memory, as if it had taken place but a year ago. . . .

We who, at the time of the murder of Morgan, had reached manhood, are much to be blamed for having suffered the agitation against masonry to subside and pass away. It is true that, ere we did so, the masonic lodges had generally surrendered their charters and the people generally become sick of the nonsensical and wicked ceremonies, the horrid and blasphemous oaths and imprecations, of masonry. Just here, let me say that it is quite idle to pretend that the people were ignorant of the secrets of masonry. There is no such thing as evidence and no such thing as certainty, if, after the concurrent revelations made by thousands of seceding masons, it is not evident to the public, nay an absolute certainty, what are the secrets of masonry. We should have kept up the agitation against masonry as long as a single lodge remained to imperil life, to control the ballot-boxes, and to override the laws and the courts. . . .

We who wronged you by this unfaithfulness, will, probably, not live to see the end of masonry and of other secret societies. But you, who are young and you who are middle aged, will, if you do your duty and work "arm and soul" for the overthrow of these abominations, witness the end of them. By the way, woman, who is soon to be a greater power in our land than she has been will come to your help and will work with you for the extinction of these secret societies, which by excluding her, insult her. Greatly does woman suffer from these societies. Greatly, too, does she suffer from those somewhat kindred associations called clubs, which, like secret societies, are composed exclusively of men. The excitements of these clubs make tame and insipid the sweet and healthful enjoyments of the family fireside; and thus do they wean from their wives and children thousands of husbands and fathers. . . .

We cannot deny, nor do we wish to deny, that there are many good men in [secret societies], and that very frequent are the instances of their benevolence. Their benevolence, however, is chiefly to their own members: and they are rather Mutual Insurance Companies than Benevolent Societies. The boastful argument that masonry is, sometimes, known to make friends of foes, rising above even national enmities, and, by force of its mystic tie, bringing into friendship with each other soldiers of contending armies, is, after all, an argument against masonry. The benevolence, which interferes with what is due to country, is unprincipled and spurious. The natural claims of the human brotherhood are disparaged by setting above them the conventional claims of an oath-bound portion of it. The good we do each other we should do as members of the whole human family.

I close with saying that we have reached an age of the world to which these secret and exclusive societies are emphatically unsuited, and from which they should rapidly pass away. These societies are composed of men, who forsake the human brotherhood, and, to a remarkable extent, confine their sympathies and fellowship to one another. Now, the age, in which it is our happiness to live, is one which calls for the solidarity and oneness—the cordially recognized solidarity and oneness—of all human beings. . . . But these secret societies go to part them from each other, and to build impassable barriers across the human brotherhood. In this religion there is neither male nor female, but all are one in Christ Jesus. Masonry, on the contrary, shuts out woman—and well it may shut her out from witnessing its horrid oaths and indecent and blasphemous ceremonies. Which, my hearers, shall we choose for our portion? I say *which?*—for we cannot choose both. We cannot choose both, for they are opposites. The one excludes the other. May God help us to make a wise choice!

A New Plea for the West (1885)

JOSIAH STRONG

Although Josiah Strong came from a Massachusetts family, he was ordained and began his ministry in Cheyenne, Wyoming, in 1871. He was active in the home missionary movement, devoting his early life to Lyman Beecher's ideal of extending the morals and civilization of New England into the West. An early exponent of American imperialism, he had little tolerance for cultural diversity and was convinced that the future emancipation of the world depended on the progress of American democracy and

From Josiah Strong, *Our Country: Its Possible Future and Its Present Crisis* (New York, 1885), pp. 30, 39, 43, 53–56, 59–63, 65–66.

Protestant Christianity. On the other hand, Strong became increasingly dis-
turbed by the excesses of industrial capitalism and preached a brand of so-
cial Christianity that was designed to awaken a sense of collective responsi-
bility for economic and social injustice. Believing that a vital religion must
have practical consequences in society, he labored above all for a united
community dedicated to a higher purpose than the accumulation of wealth.
It was this higher purpose which Strong saw as critically threatened by the
1880's. The unity provided by the Civil War had given way to brutal self-
interest and communal disintegration. In Strong's eyes, man had arrived at
a crucial turning point in history and the fate of the world hung in the bal-
ance.

Political optimism is one of the vices of the American people.
There is a popular faith that "God takes care of children, fools, and
the United States." We deem ourselves a chosen people, and incline
to the belief that the Almighty stands pledged to our prosperity.
Probably not one in a hundred of our population has ever questioned
the security of our future. Such optimism is as senseless as pessimism
is faithless. The one is as foolish as the other is wicked.

Thoughtful men see perils on our national horizon. Let us glance at
those only which peculiarly threaten the West. America, as the land
of promise to all the world, is the destination of the most remarkable
migration of which we have any record. During the last four years we
have suffered a peaceful invasion by an army more than twice as vast
as the estimated number of Goths and Vandals that swept over Southern Europe and overwhelmed Rome. . . .

In view of the fact that Europe is able to send us nearly nine times
as many immigrants during the next thirty years as during the thirty
years past, without any diminution of her population, and in view of
all the powerful influences co-operating to simulate the movement, is
it not reasonable to conclude that we have seen only the advance
guard of the mighty army which is moving upon us? . . .

We can only glance at the political aspects of immgration. As we
have already seen, it is immigration which has fed fat the liquor
power; and there is a liquor vote. Immigration furnishes most of the
victims of Mormonism; and there is a Mormon vote. Immigration is
the strength of the Catholic church; and there is a Catholic vote. Immigration is the mother and nurse of American socialism; and there is
to be a socialist vote. Immigration tends strongly to the cities, and
gives to them their political complexion. And there is no more serious
menace to our civilization than our rabble-ruled cities. . . .

Manifestly there is an irreconcilable difference between papal principles and the fundamental principles of our free institutions. Popular government is self-government. A nation is capable of self-government only so far as the individuals who compose it are capable of self-government. To place one's conscience, therefore, in the keeping of another, and to disavow all personal responsibility in obeying the dictation of another, is as far as possible from *self*-control, and, therefore, wholly inconsistent with republican institutions, and, if common, dangerous to their stability. It is the theory of absolutism in the state, that man exists for the state. It is the theory of absolutism in the church, that man exists for the church. . . .

Many who are well acquainted with the true character of Romanism are indifferent to it, because not aware of the rapid growth of the Catholic church in the United States. They tell us, and truly, that Rome loses great numbers of adherents here through the influence of our free schools, free institutions, and the strong pervasive spirit of independence which is so hostile to priestly authority. But let us not congratulate ourselves too soon. The losses of Romanism in the United States are not, to any extent, the gains of Protestantism. When a man, born in the Catholic church, loses confidence in the only faith of which he has any knowledge, he does not examine Protestantism, but sinks into skepticism. Romanism is chiefly responsible for German and French infidelity. For, when a mind to which thought and free inquiry have been forbidden as a crime attains its intellectual majority, the largeness of liberty is not enough; it reacts into license and excess. Skepticism and infidelity are the legitimate children of unreasoning and superstitious credulity, and the grandchildren of Rome. Apostate Catholics are swelling our most dangerous classes. Unaccustomed to think for themselves, and having thrown off authority, they become the easy victims of socialists or nihilists, or any other wild and dangerous propagandists. . . .

The people of the United States are more sensible of the disgrace of Mormonism than of its danger. The civilized world wonders that such a hideous caricature of the Christian religion should have appeared in this most enlightened land; that such an anachronism should have been produced by the most progressive civilization; that the people who most honor womankind should be the ones to inflict on her this

deep humiliation and outrageous wrong. Polygamy, as the most striking feature of the Mormon monster, attracts the public eye. It is this
which at the same time arouses interest and indignation; and it is because of this that Europe points at us the finger of shame. Polygamy
is the issue between the Mormons and the United States government.
It is this which prevents Utah's being admitted as a state. It is this
against which congress has legislated. And yet, polygamy is not an
essential part of Mormonism; it was an after-thought; not a root, but
a graft. . . .

What, then, is the real strength of Mormonism? It is ecclesiastical
despotism which holds it together, unifies it, and makes it strong. The
Mormon church is probably the most complete organization in the
world. To look after a Mormon population of 108,000, there are
28,838 officials, or more than one to every five persons. And, so highly
centralized is the power, that all of these threads of authority are
gathered into one hand, that of President Taylor. The priesthood, of
which he is the head, claim the right to control in all things religious,
social, industrial and political. Brigham Young asserted his right to
manage in every particular, "from the setting up of a stocking to the
ribbons on a woman's bonnet." Here is a claim to absolute and universal rule, which is cheerfully conceded by every orthodox "saint."
Mormonism, therefore, is not simply a church, but a state, an "*impe-
rium in imperio*" ruled by a man who is prophet, priest, king and
pope, all in one—a pope, too, who is not one whit less infallible than
he who wears the tiara. And, as one would naturally expect of an
American pope, and especially of an enterprising western pope, he
outpopes the Roman by holding familiar conversation with the Almighty, and getting, to order, new revelations direct from heaven;
and, another advantage which is more material, he keeps a firm hold
of his temporal power. Indeed, it looks as if the spiritual were being
subordinated to the temporal. Rev. W. M. Barrows, D.D., after a residence at the Mormon capital of nearly eight years, said: "There is no
doubt that it is becoming less and less a religious power, and more
and more a political power. The first Mormon preachers were ignorant fanatics; but most of them were honest, and their words carried
weight that sincerity always carries, even in a bad cause. The preachers now have the ravings of the Sibyl, but lack the inspiration. Their
talk sounds hollow; the ring of sincerity is gone. But their eyes are
dazzled now with the vision of an earthly empire. They have gone
back to the old Jewish idea of a temporal kingdom, and they are en-

deavoring to set up such a kingdom in the valleys of Utah and Idaho and Montana, Wyoming, Colorado and New Mexico, Arizona and Nevada."

If there be any doubt as to the designs of the Mormons, let the testimony of Bishop Lunt be conclusive on that point. He said, a few years ago: "Like a grain of mustard-seed was the truth planted in Zion; and it is destined to spread through all the world. Our church has been organized only fifty years, and yet behold its wealth and power. This is our year of jubilee. We look forward with perfect confidence to the day when we will hold the reins of the United States government. That is our present temporal aim; after that, we expect to control the continent." When told that such a scheme seemed rather visionary, in view of the fact that Utah cannot gain recognition as a state, the Bishop replied: "Do not be deceived; we are looking after that. We do not care for these territorial officials sent out to govern us. They are nobodies here. We do not recognize them, neither do we fear any practical interference by congress. We intend to have Utah recognized as a state. To-day we hold the balance of political power in Idaho, we rule Utah absolutely, and in a very short time we will hold the balance of power in Arizona and Wyoming. . . .

"In the past six months we have sent more than 3,000 of our people down through the Sevier valley to settle in Arizona, and the movement still progresses. All this will build up for us a political power, which will, in time, compel the homage of the demagogues of the country. Our vote is solid, and will remain so. It will be thrown where the most good will be accomplished for the church. Then, in some great political crisis, the two present political parties will bid for our support. Utah will then be admitted as a polygamous state, and the other territories we have peacefully subjugated will be admitted also. We will then hold the balance of power, and will dictate to the country. In time, our principles, which are of sacred origin, will spread throughout the United States. We possess the ability to turn the political scale in any particular community we desire. Our people are obedient. When they are called by the church, they promptly obey." . . .

Bishop Lunt is not altogether alone in the anticipations quoted above. Hon. Schuyler Colfax says: "With Utah overwhelmingly dominated by the Mormon Theocracy of their established church, and wielding, also, as they already claim, the balance of power in the adjoining territories, this Turkish barbarism may control the half-dozen new states of our Interior, and, by the power of their Senators and Representatives, in both branches of our Congress, may even dictate to the nation itself." Those best acquainted with Mormonism seem most sensible of the danger which it threatens. The pastors of churches and principals of schools in Salt Lake City, in an address to American citizens, say: "We recognize the fact that the so-called Mormon Church, in its exercise of political power, is antagonistical to American institutions, and that there is an irrepressible conflict between Utah Mormonism and American republicanism; so much so that they can never abide together in harmony. We also believe that the growth of this anti-republican power is such that, if not checked speedily, it will cause serious trouble in the near future. We fear that the nature and extent of this danger are not fully comprehended by the nation at large."

If the Mormon power had its seat in an established commonwealth like Ohio, such an ignorant and fanatical population, rapidly increasing, and under the absolute control of unscrupulous leaders, who openly avowed their hostility to the state, and lived in contemptuous violation of its laws, would be a disturbing element which would certainly endanger the peace of society. Indeed, the Mormons, when much less powerful than they are to-day, could not be tolerated in Missouri or Illinois. And Mormonism is ten-fold more dangerous in the new West, where its power is greater, because the "Gentile" population is less; where it has abundant room to expand; where, in a new and unorganized society, its complete organization is the more easily master of the situation; and where state constitutions and laws, yet unformed, and the institutions of society, yet plastic, are subject to its molding influence.

The Identification of
America's True Enemy (1884)

RICHARD ELY

A study of American fears of subversion, from the fantasies of the Illuminati to the more substantial image of the Slave Power, suggests a certain

From Richard T. Ely, "Recent Phases of Socialism in the United States," *The Christian Union*, XXIX (April 24, 1884), 389–391, 393–394.

groping for an ideal enemy, a force that would stand in unequivocal opposition to the emergent ideals and aspirations of American democracy. If such a perfect enemy had been fabricated from the historical remnants of earlier conspiracies, real and imaginary, it would surely have been grounded on the European continent and would have operated through immigrants and native-born renegades; it would have combined the reactionary despotism of Catholic Austria with the atheistic radicalism of Jacobin France; it would have threatened the American laborer and farmer as well as the Wall Street banker; it would have opposed America's mission to save the world with the equally ambitious mission of enslaving the world; it would have challenged American permissiveness and disunity with hard discipline and efficient organization; it would have confronted American idealism with the terrifying doctrine that a noble end justifies any means. One might conclude then that revolutionary socialism was simply the invention of the American paranoid mind. But the issues and tensions which produced these American fears of subversion were grounded in historical facts. For example, the despotism of nineteenth-century Europe had produced the violent anarchism of Mikhail Bakunin; and it was partly to escape the influence of Bakuninism that the headquarters of the Marxist International was moved in 1872 to New York. When revolutionary socialism sought temporary refuge in the New World, it confronted a rival ideology which had long promised to emancipate mankind.

One of the first Americans to give systematic attention to the menace of European socialism was Richard Ely, a German-trained economist who in the 1880's was a professor at the Johns Hopkins University. Although Ely was to be remembered as one of the Progressive social theorists who advocated a form of welfare capitalism, his familiarity with contemporary German writing enabled him to win an early reputation as an expert critic of dangerous new currents from abroad.

Henry George's work, *Progress and Poverty*, was published in 1879. In 1884, not five years later, it is possible to affirm, without hesitation, that the appearance of that one book formed a noteworthy epoch in the history of economic thought in England and America. The march of industrial forces had opened a way for the operation of ideas new and strange to the great masses. A period of unparalleled prosperity had in one generation transformed the face of the earth, and its beneficent fruits made optimists of men. A severe crisis in 1873, with all its train of varied disasters, checked economic progress and brought the crushing weight of poverty upon tens of thousands. Bright visions gave place to gloomy forebodings, and six years later the ground was ripe for the seed sown by Henry George. . . . Ten years ago English-speaking laborers were considered too practical to listen to dreamers of dreams and heralds of coming Utopias. The sturdy common sense of English and American workingmen was thought an all-sufficient shield against the speculations of Continental philosophers and the allurements of French and German agitators. Now all that is changed. The models of order threaten to form the vanguard of a rebellious army. . . .

Henry George has rendered two distinct services to the cause of socialism. First, in the no-rent theory . . . he has furnished a rallying-point for all discontented laborers; second, his book has served as an entering wedge for other still more radical and far-reaching measures. It is written in an easily understood and even brilliant style, is published in cheap form both in England and America, and in each country has attained a circulation which for an economic work is without parallel. Tens of thousands of laborers have read *Progress and Poverty* who never before looked between the two covers of an economic book, and its conclusions are widely accepted articles in the workingman's creed. . . .

Socialists very generally accept the no-rent theory as a chief article in their creed and one of the first to be realized. If they often reject Henry George's statement of his propositions, it is to their form rather than to their substantial purport they object. A New York organ of the Socialistic Labor Party published not long ago a "Declaration of Principles," of which the first sentence reads as follows: "The land of every country is the common inheritance of the people in that country, and hence all should have free and equal access to its settlement." And the San Francisco *Truth*, a rabid socialistic paper, published this economic law in a recent issue: "Warning! Landowners, look out! There are breakers ahead! This is the new law governing the price of land in both city and country: The price of land is determined by the sale of Henry George's *Progress and Poverty*, falling as it rises and rising as it falls. It is now past its hundredth edition, and it is going faster than ever. In ten years from now town lots will not be worth more than the taxes! Private property in land is doomed!" . . .

Several questions naturally suggest themselves: What are the ultimate aims of American socialists? How do they expect or desire to attain their purposes? What is the precise character of their agitation?

Is any danger to be apprehended from this agitation? If so, what is its extent, and what measures should be adopted to ward off these dangers? . . .

There are in the United States two distinct parties of socialists, both of which aim at an overthrow of existing economic and social institutions, and the substitution therefor of totally new forms. This programme includes primarily the substitution of some form of cooperation in production and exchange for the capitalistic method of production and exchange, and the abolition of private property to make place for common property. A division of productive property (capital) is not desired, nor has it ever been advocated by any body of professed socialists. Products, save such as serve the purposes of further production, however, are to be divided in such manner as to satisfy the legitimate needs of all.

Perhaps these general statements include as much as can safely be pronounced common to all the members of the two parties, which it is most convenient to consider separately. It may, however, be stated that in general the teachings of Carl Marx are accepted by both parties, and his work on capital (*Das Kapital*) is still the Bible of the socialists. This work has not as yet been translated into English, but extracts from it have been turned into our tongue and published, and brochures, pamphlets, newspapers, and verbal expositions have extended his doctrines, while H. M. Ryndman has recently expounded the views of the great teacher in his *Historical Basis of Socialism in England*.

The two parties are known as the "Socialistic Labor Party" and the "International Workingmen's Association," designated usually by their respective initials, S.L.P. and I.W.A., which one sees continually in their publications, and upon which incessant repetition seems to have conferred, in the minds of socialists, a peculiar cabalistic quality. In treating of the present character of socialists in this country, it is perhaps desirable to consider first the views of the extremists, and then discuss the modifications introduced in the programme of the comparatively moderate reformers. It is not difficult to do this. Both parties have recently published declarations of principles, or manifestoes; both are sufficiently represented by newspapers and other publications; both distribute tracts far and near to disseminate their views, and both send missionaries hither and thither to make propaganda for the new moral and economic world. Party quarrels lead to heated discussions which expose clearly such differences as exist, and which would bring to light any dark secrets were there any to be disclosed.

The extremists, constituting the International Workingmen's Association, held a Congress October last in Pittsburg, and published a manifesto, unanimously adopted, in which they describe their ultimate goal in these words:

Establishment of a free society based upon co-operative organization of production.

Free exchange of equivalent products between the productive organizations without commerce and profitmongery.

Organization of education on a secular, scientific, and equal basis for both sexes.

Equal rights for all without distinction to sex and race.

Regulation of all public affairs by free contracts between autonomous (independent) communes and associations existing on a federalistic basis.

This is the dream of the Anarchists, as these Internationals call themselves. To use words borrowed from Mr. Ryndman, it is "individualism gone mad." Each member of society is to be absolutely uncontrolled. The whole world is to be made up of independent, self-governing communes or townships, grouped loosely into federations which have no authority. Each commune is at liberty to sever its connection with the common body at pleasure; but it is thought the social nature of man will be a sufficient adhesive force to hold them together. All regulation and control centers in free and voluntary and self-enforced contract. Rent falls away, as there is no authority to enforce its payment, and laborers lay hold and use freely the means of production (capital), as Anarchism recognizes no power to prevent this. Possession takes the place of property, and possession lasts only so long as the means of production possessed are actually used by the possessor. Their own ideas in these respects are too vague to admit of more precise description. It is to be noticed that in their own organization they practice what they preach. The International is composed of independent "groups," with no central authority or executive, both of which expressions many of them detest. The only bond of union between them is found in their common ideas, in their press, their congresses and local organizations, and a Bureau of Information formed by the Chicago groups, which bureau appears to be the nearest approach to a center of life and activity. . . .

The Internationalists attack both religion and the family, and that with what may be considered practical unanimity. While it is not right to connect this attitude with socialism *per se*, the fairest-minded person cannot blame a writer for holding up to condemnation any concrete, actually existing party which wages war against all that we hold most sacred, and which seeks to abolish those institutions which we hold to be of inestimable value both to the individual and to society.

Religion and the family are not only attacked by the extremists, but the onslaught on them is made in language of unparalleled coarseness and shocking impiety. Here are two quotations from *Truth*, which are indications of the general tone of the paper: "Heaven is a dream invented by robbers to distract the attention of the victims of their brigandage." "When the laboring men understand that the heaven which they are promised hereafter is but a mirage, they will knock at the door of the wealthy robber with a musket in hand, and demand their share of the goods of this life now." *Freiheit*, the most blasphemous of all the socialistic papers, concludes an article on the "Fruits of the Belief in God" with the exclamation: "Religion, authority, and State are all carved out of the same piece of wood—to the devil with them all!" The *Vorbote* speaks of religion as destructive poison. The Pittsburg Manifesto—unanimously adopted, be it remembered—contains this sentence: "The Church finally seeks to make complete idiots out of the mass, and to make them forego the paradise on earth by promising them a fictitious heaven."

There appears to be scarcely the same unanimity concerning the family. It was not directly condemned in the Pittsburg Manifesto, nor does *Truth* say much about it. But there is no doubt about the general policy of these journals. They sneer incessantly at the "sacredness of the family," and swell with pleasure on every dirty scandal which is noticed by the "capitalistic press." Especial attention is given to divorces, to show that the family institution is already undermined, and they are thorough-going skeptics regarding the morality of the relations between the sexes in bourgeois society. The *Vorbote* for May 12, 1883, contains an article on the "Sacredness of the Family," from which these sentences are extracted: "In capitalistic society marriage has long become a pure financial operation, and the possessing classes long ago established community of wives, and, indeed, the nastiest which is conceivable. . . . They take a special pleasure in seducing one another's wives. . . . A marriage is only so long moral as it rests upon the free inclination of man and wife."

A poem which appeared in *Truth*, January 26, 1884, is in the same spirit. It is entitled:

MARRIAGE

UNDER THE COMPETITIVE SYSTEM.

"Oh, wilt thou take this form so spare,
This powdered face and frizzled hair,
  To be thy wedded wife;
And keep her free from labor vile,
  Lest she her dainty fingers soil,
And dress her up in gayest style,
  As long as thou hast life?"
    "I will."

"And wilt thou take these stocks and bonds,
This brown-stone front, these diamonds,
  To be thy husband dear?
And wilt thou in his carriage ride,
And o'er his lordly home preside—
And be divorced while yet a bride,
  Or ere a single year?"
    "I will."

"Then I pronounce you man and wife;
  And with what I've together joined,
The next best man may run away
  Whenever he a chance can find."

Our attention must now be devoted to an inquiry into the means by which these ends are to be attained.

Their method is violence and revolution, as they have lost all faith in the ballot. The following from their Manifesto makes this sufficiently plain: "Agitation for the purpose of organization; organization for the purpose of rebellion. In these few words the ways are marked which the workers must take if they want to be rid of their chains, as the condition of things is the same in all countries of so-called civilization. . . . We could show by scores of illustrations that all attempts in the past to reform this monstrous system by peaceable means, such as the ballot, have been futile, and all such efforts in the future must necessarily be so for the following reasons: the political institutions of the time are the agency of the property class; their mission is the upholding of the privileges of their masters; any reform in your own behalf would curtail these privileges. To this they will not and cannot consent, for it would be suicidal to themselves. . . . There remains but one recourse—force! Our forefathers have not only told us that against despots force is justifiable, because it is the only means, but they themselves have set the immemorial example." . . .

The newspapers of the Internationalists proclaim a similar doctrine, of which the following specimen quotation from *Truth* may serve as an example: "It is beyond doubt that if universal suffrage had been a weapon capable of emancipating our people, our tyrants would have suppressed it long ago. Here in America it is proved to be but the instrument used by our masters to prevent any reforms ever being accomplished. The Republican party is run by robbers and in the interest of robbery. The Democratic party is run by thieves and in the interest of thievery. Therefore, vote no more." . . .

But we have not yet come to the worst; for there is no conceivable crime or form of violence against individuals or classes which the Internationalists as a party do not indorse, provided their crimes and acts of violence aid them to accomplish their ends. Hypocrisy, fraud, deceit, adultery, robbery, and murder are held sacred when beneficial to the revolution. Not every individual member, certainly, maintains this view, but it is upheld unreservedly by the extremists, and more or less explicitly by their leaders and journals. . . .

A position has now been attained from which it is possible to estimate the precise nature of the danger to be apprehended. While it is extremely unpleasant to be called an alarmist, it is foolish to underrate the possible disasters in store for us; and it is precisely what people from time immemorial have been wont to do. Again and again have leaders of social forces behaved with the wisdom of the ostrich which buries its head in the sand and believes there is no danger because it can see none. . . .

Truth, in its number for December 15, 1883, published an article entitled "Street Fighting; How to meet the Military Forces of Capital when it is Necessary. Military Tactics for the Lower Classes." It purports to be written by an officer in the United States Army, but it is said to have been proved that this cannot be true. However, that makes little difference. It suggests new methods of building barricades and improved methods of meeting attacking troops. Numerous and apparently reasonable diagrams are given, though the writer will not attempt to form an opinion of their value from a military standpoint. "Military knowledge," says the "officer in the Army of the United States," "has become popularized a little even since [the national strikes of] 1877, and it would not be hard to find in every large city of the world to-day upon the side of the people some fair leaders capable of meeting the enemy in some such way as this:"—Then follows one of the diagrams. The *Vorbote* has recently published a series of articles on the arming of the people. . . .

Now, can there be any doubt about the seriousness of the situation? If it were known that one thousand men like the notorious train robbers, the James boys, were in small groups scattered over the United States, would not every conservative and peace-loving householder be filled with alarm, and reasonably so? Yet here we have more than ten times that number educated to think robbery, arson, and murder are justifiable—nay, even righteous; taught to believe the slaughter of the ruling classes a holy work, and prepared to follow it with all the fanaticism of religious devotion; ready to die, if need be, and prepared to stifle all feelings of gratitude and natural affection, and to kill with their own hands every opponent of the sacred cause.

Why America Is Particularly
Vulnerable to Socialism (1885)

JOSIAH STRONG

In his highly influential treatment of socialism in Our Country, *Josiah Strong drew heavily on the scholarly revelations of Richard Ely. Since the Marxist International had died shortly after being transplanted to America, and since socialism had failed to make significant gains in the trades unions, Strong had a formidable task in persuading his readers that the nation faced a genuine danger. The most common objection to his thesis was that anarchism and socialism were the fruits of European tyranny and could not possibly survive in the free air of America. But like his Puritan forebears, Strong was convinced that America was uniquely vulnerable to the devil's stratagems precisely because of her people's liberty and high mission. This line of reasoning led him into a trenchant critique of social injustice and laissez-faire ideology. But to less reform-minded alarmists, Strong's emphasis*

From Josiah Strong, *Our Country: Its Possible Future and Its Present Crisis* (New York, 1885), pp. 85–86, 91–99, 102–103, 106–112.

on the vulnerability of American institutions engendered a mood of panic,
suspiciousness, and repression.

Socialism attempts to solve the problem of suffering without elimi-
nating the factor of sin. It says: "From each according to his abilities;
to each according to his wants." But this dictum of Louis Blanc could
be realized only in a perfect society. Forgetting that "there is no political alchemy by which you can get golden conduct out of leaden
instincts," socialism thinks to regenerate society without regenerating
the individual. . . .

The despotism of the few and the wretchedness of the many have
produced European socialism. It has been supposed that its doctrines
could never obtain in this land of freedom and plenty; but there may
be a despotism which is not political, and a discontent which does
not spring from hunger. We have discovered that German socialism
has been largely imported, has taken root, and is making a vigorous
growth. Let us look at it as it appears in this country. . . .

A writer in *The New Englander* for January, 1884, says there are in
this country "200,000 members of labor organizations who are more
or less familiar with the doctrines of socialism." This is apparently a
very mild statement, as the leading papers of New York City claimed,
as long ago as the summer of 1881, that "The Knights of Labor" alone
numbered 800,000, besides many smaller organizations, which are
more or less socialistic in their sympathies and ideas, though not
avowedly connected with either of the socialistic parties. The *Vorbote*
of Chicago says: "You might as well suppose the military organizations of Europe were for play and parade, as to suppose labor organizations were for mere insurance and pacific helpfulness. They are organized to protect interests, for which, if the time comes, they would
fight." But the present strength of socialistic organizations in the
United States concerns us less than their prospective numbers. Let us
look at the conditions favorable to the growth of socialism. The reception given to the books of Mr. Henry George is one of the signs of
the times. *Progress and Poverty* has been read by tens of thousands of
workingmen. And the fact that the demand for an economic work
should exhaust more than a hundred editions, and still continue unsatisfied, indicates a great deal of popular sympathy with its doctrines. . . .

Most of the Internationals, the anarchic socialists, in this country
are Germans, whose numbers are constantly being recruited by immi-

gration. And not only is immigration to increase, but socialism is spreading rapidly in Germany, which will influence its growth here. . . .

The prevalence of skepticism, also, is significant in this connection. A wide-spread infidelity preceded the French Revolution, and helped to prepare the way for it. A criminal in a prison on the Rhine left, not long since, on the walls of his cell, the following message for his successors: "I will say a word to you. There is no heaven or hell. When once you are dead there is an end of everything. Therefore, ye scoundrels, grab whatever you can; only do not let yourselves be grabbed. Amen."

Not only does irreligion remove all salutary fear of retribution hereafter, and thus give over low-minded men to violence and excess; but, when a man has lost all portion in another life, he is the more determined to have his proportion in this. There are, doubtless, Christian socialists; but the Internationalists are gross materialists. . . .

Before the age of machinery, master, journeymen, and apprentices worked together on familiar terms. The apprentice looked forward to the time when he should receive a journeyman's wages, and the journeyman might reasonably hope some day to have a shop of his own. Under this system there was little opportunity to develop class distinctions and jealousies. Moreover, there was a great variety of work. A blacksmith, for instance, was not master of his trade until he could make a thousand things, from a nail to an iron fence. There was relief from monotony, and scope for ingenuity and taste. But machinery is introduced, and with it important changes. It is discovered that the subdivision of labor both improves and cheapens the product. And this double advantage has stimulated the tendency in that direction until a single article that was once made by one workman now passes through perhaps threescore pairs of hands, each doing a certain part of the work on every piece. Manchester workmen, complaining of the monotony of their work, said to Mr. Cook: "It is the same thing day by day, sir; it's the same little thing; one little, little thing, over and over and over." Think of making pin-heads, ten hours a day, every working day in the week, for a year—twenty, forty, fifty years! . . .

Under the low wages of the present industrial system, there is a strong tendency among operatives to form an hereditary class, and thus degenerate the more. In Massachusetts, where statistics of labor are the most elaborate published, the average working man is unable to support the average working man's family. In 1883 the average expenses of working men's families, in that state, were $754.42, while the earnings of workmen who were heads of families averaged $558.68. This means that the average working man had to call on his wife and children to assist in earning their support. We accordingly find that, in the manufactures and mechanical industries of the state, in 1883, there were engaged 28,714 children under sixteen years of age. Of the average working man's family 32.44 per cent of the support fell upon the children and mother. I am not aware that the condition of the working man is at all exceptional in Massachusetts. . . . In 1880, of persons engaged in all occupations in the United States, 1,118,356 were children fifteen years of age or under. Their number, in ten years, increased 21 per cent more rapidly than the population. These children ought to be in the school instead of the mill or the mine. How much longer will the operatives of the United States be distinguished for their intelligence if our children under sixteen are pressed into the factory? In many cases the body is stunted, the mind cramped, and the morals corrupted. A writer in the *North American Review,* for June, 1884, says that in Pennsylvania there are "herds of little children of all ages, from six years upward, at work in the coal breakers, toiling in dirt, and air thick with carbon dust, from dawn to dark, of every day in the week except Sunday. These coal breakers are the only schools they know. A letter from the coal regions, in the Philadelphia *Press,* declares that 'there are no schools in the world where more evil is learned, or more innocence destroyed, than in the breakers. It is shocking to watch the vile practices indulged in by these children, to hear the frightful oaths they use, to see their total disregard for religion and humanity.'" In the upper part of Luzerne County there are three thousand children, between six and fifteen years of age, at work in this way. . . . Moreover, our labor system, together with mechanical invention, is steadily developing an unemployed class, which furnishes ready recruits to the criminal, intemperate, socialistic and revolutionary classes. Mr. Gladstone estimates that manufacturing power, by the aid of machinery, doubles for the world once in seven years. Invention is liable, any day, to render a given tool antiquated, and this or that technical skill useless. Every great labor-saving invention, though it eventually increases the demand for labor, temporarily throws great numbers out of employment. The operative, who for years has confined himself to one thing, has, thereby, largely lost the power of adaption. He cannot turn his hand to this or that; he is very likely too old to learn a new trade, or acquire new technical skill; he has no alternative; and, unless anchored by a family, probably turns tramp. Competition produces over-production, which results in closing mills and mines for long periods, thus swelling the floating population. . . .

There is much dissatisfaction among the masses of Europe. There would be more if there were greater popular intelligence. Place Americans in the circumstances under which the peasant of Continental Europe lives, and there would be a revolution in twenty-four hours. Hopeless poverty, therefore, in the United States, where there is greater intelligence, will be more restless, and more easily become desperate than in Europe. Many of our working men are beginning to feel that, under the existing industrial system, they are condemned to hopeless poverty. We have already seen that the average working man in Massachusetts and Illinois is unable to support his family. At that rate, how long will it take him to become the owner of a home? Of males engaged in the industries of Massachusetts in 1875, only one in one hundred owned a house. When a working man is unable to earn a home, or to lay by something for old age, when sickness or the closing of the factory for a few weeks, means debt, is it strange that he becomes discontented?

And how are such items as the following, which appeared in the papers of January, 1880, likely to strike discontented laborers? "The profits of the Wall Street Kings the past year were enormous. It is estimated that Vanderbilt made $30,000,000; Jay Gould, $15,000,000; Russell Sage, $10,000,000; Sidney Dillon, $10,000,000; James R. Keene, $8,000,000; and three or four others from one to two millions each; making a grand total for ten or twelve estates of about eighty millions of dollars." Is it strange if the working man thinks he is not getting his due share of the wonderful increase of national wealth? . . .

This is modern and republican feudalism. These American barons and lords of labor have probably more power and less responsibility than many an olden feudal lord. They close the factory or the mine, and thousands of workmen are forced into unwilling idleness. The capitalist can arbitrarily raise the price of necessaries, can prevent men's working, but has no responsibility, meanwhile, as to their starving. Here is "taxation without representation" with a vengeance. We have developed a despotism vastly more oppressive and more exasperating than that against which the thirteen colonies rebelled. . . .

We have glanced at the causes which are ministering to the growth of socialism among us: a wide-spread discontent on the part of our wage-working population, the development of classes and class antipathies, and the appearance of an unemployed class of professional beggars, popular skepticism, a powerful individualism, and immigration. If these conditions should remain constant, socialism would continue to grow; but it should be remembered that all of these causes, with the possible exception of skepticism, are becoming more active. Within the life-time of many now living, population will be four times as dense in the United States as it is to-day. Wage-workers, now one-half of all our workers, will multiply more rapidly than the population. After our agricultural land is all occupied, as it will be a few years hence, our agricultural population, which is one of the great sheet-anchors of society against the socialistic current, will increase but little, while great manufacturing and mining towns will go on multiplying. In the development of our manufacturing industries and our mining resources we have made, as yet, hardly more than a beginning. When these industries have been multiplied ten-fold, the evils which now attend them will be correspondingly multiplied.

It must not be forgotten that, side by side with this deep discontent of intelligent and unsatisfied wants, has been developed, in modern times, a tremendous enginery of destruction, which offers itself to every man. Since the French Revolution nitro-glycerine, illuminating gas, petroleum, dynamite, the revolver, the repeating rifle and the Gatling gun have all come into use. Science has placed in man's hand superhuman powers. Society, also, is become more highly organized, much more complex, and is therefore much more susceptible of injury. There never was a time in the history of the world when an enemy of society could work such mighty mischief as to-day. The more highly developed a civilization is, the more vulnerable does it become. This is pre-eminently true of a material civilization. Learning, statesmanship, character, respect for law, love of justice, cannot be blown up with dynamite; palaces, factories, railways, Brooklyn bridges, Hoosac tunnels, and all the long inventory of our material wonders are destructible by material means. "The explosion of a little nitro-glycerine under a few water mains would make a great city uninhabitable; the blowing up of a few railroad bridges and tunnels would bring famine quicker than the wall of circumvallation that Titus drew around Jerusalem; the pumping of atmospheric air into the gas-mains, and the application of a match would tear up every street and level every house." * We are preparing conditions which make possible a Reign of Terror that would beggar the scenes of the French Revolution.

Conditions at the West are peculiarly favorable to the growth of socialism. The much larger proportion of foreigners there, and the strong tendency of immigration thither, will have great influence. There is a stronger individuality in the West. The people are less conservative; there is less regard for established usage and opinion. The greater relative strength of Romanism there is significant; for apostate Catholics furnish the very soil to which socialism is indigenous. Mormonism also is doing a like preparatory work. It is gathering together great numbers of ill-balanced men, who are duped for a time by Mormon mummery; but many of them, becoming disgusted, leave the church and with it all faith in religion of any sort. Skeptical, soured, cranky, they are excellent socialistic material. Irreligion abounds much more than at the East; the proportion of Christian men is much smaller. "Into these Western communities the international societies and secret labor leagues and Jacobian clubs, and atheistic, infidel, rationalistic organizations of every name in the Old World, are continually emptying themselves. They are the natural reservoirs of whatever is uneasy, turbulent, antagonistic to either God or man among the populations across the sea. They are also the natural places of refuge for all in our own country who are soured by misfortune, misanthropic, seekers of radical reforms, renegades, moral pariahs. They are hence, in the nature of things, a soil of hot-beds where every form of pestilent error is sure to be found and to come to quick fruitage. You can hardly find a group of ranch-men or miners from Colorado to the Pacific who will not have on their tongue's end the labor slang of Denis Kearney, the infidel ribaldry of Robert Ingersoll, the socialistic theories of Karl Marx." † . . .

We need not quiet misgiving with the thought that popular government is our safety from revolution. It is *because* of our free institutions that the great conflict of socialism with society as now organized is likely to occur in the United States. There is a strong disposition among men to charge most of the ills of their lot to bad government, and to seek a political remedy for those ills. They expect in the popu-

---

* Quotation is from Henry George, *Social Problems.*—Ed.
† Rev. E. P. Goodwin, D.D., Home Missionary Sermon, p. 16.

larization of power to find relief. Constitutional government, a free press and free speech would probably quiet popular agitation in Russia for a generation. The new Franchise Bill will allay restlessness in England for a time. If Germany should become a republic, we should hear little of German socialism for a season. But all our salve of this sort is spent; there are no more political rights to bestow; the people are in full possession. Here then, where there is the fullest exercise of political rights, will the people first discover that the ballot is not a panacea. Here, where the ultimate evolution of government has taken place, will restless men first attempt to live without government.

There is nothing beyond republicanism but anarchism.

The Haymarket Riot (1886)

MICHAEL J. SCHAACK

It would be a mistake to think of revolutionary anarchism merely as a harmless nightmare that haunted the minds of late nineteenth-century conservatives. In 1881 Russian terrorists, members of a "Party of the People's Will," assassinated Czar Alexander II. From 1894 to 1914 six heads of state, including President McKinley, were slain by anarchist fanatics. The event in America which first dramatized the violent message of anarchism was the explosion of a dynamite bomb in Chicago's Haymarket Square.

In the 1880's American anarchism and revolutionary socialism were largely confined to a few immigrants, mostly of German origin. In Chicago they had sufficient strength to publish a radical German-language daily and to mobilize vocal demonstrations; but in general they were completely overshadowed by the more conservative labor organizations that were agitating for an eight-hour day. Nevertheless, the stubbornness of employers and the brutality of police against strikers gave the radicals an opportunity to call a public demonstration at Haymarket Square on May 4, 1886, the day after a striker had been killed by police. Before the demonstration could begin, a sizable body of police arrived and ordered the assembly to disperse. Someone threw a bomb at the police, who then opened fire on the crowd. Eight policemen and many spectators ultimately died from the conflict. Although there was no evidence as to who carried or threw the bomb, eight anarchists were arrested as accessories to murder. They were accused, in effect,

From Michael J. Schaack, *Anarchy and Anarchists: A History of the Red Terror and the Social Revolution in America and Europe* (Chicago, 1889), pp. 74, 103, 104, 156, 256, 334, 390, 393, 457, 658–660, 662–663.

of having advocated doctrines which made the crime possible, since there was no proof that any one of them had been involved in the bomb-throwing. Before he was hanged, August Spies, the editor of Die Arbeiter-Zeitung, *said, "Let the world know that in 1886 in the state of Illinois eight men were sentenced to death because they believed in a better future!" Four of the men were actually executed, and a fifth committed suicide before being taken to the gallows. Michael J. Schaack, captain of the East Chicago Avenue Police Station, was widely credited with having uncovered the anarchist conspiracy.*

The Constitution of the United States guarantees the right of free speech, free discussion and free assemblage. These are the cardinal doctrines of our free institutions. But when liberty is trenched upon to the extent of advocacy of revolutionary methods, subversion of law and order and the displacement of existing society, Socialism places itself beyond the pale of moral forces and arrays itself on the side of the freebooter, the bandit, the cut-throat and the traitor. . . .

In their declarations of principles and encouragements to violence, these agitators have proved themselves traitors to their country or the country of their adoption, and ingrates to society. They have sought, and are seeking, to establish "Anarchy in the midst of the state, war in times of peace, and conspiracy in open day." They are the "Huns and Vandals of modern civilization."

While Socialists are bent on a revolution in the economic condition of the working class, or, as they choose to term it, the proletariat, they have conclusively shown that they do not desire to further that movement by pacific means. Imbued with the doctrines of violence and intent on the complete destruction of government, they do not seek their end by orderly, legitimate methods. This fact has been most thoroughly established by the extracts from their public declarations which I have already given. . . .

It was not difficult to locate the moral responsibility for the bold and bloody attack on law and authority [the Haymarket bomb]. The seditious utterances of such men as Spies, Parsons, Fielden, Schwab and other leaders at public gatherings for weeks and months preceding the eight-hour strike, and the defiant declarations of such papers as the *Arbeiter-Zeitung* and the *Alarm*, clearly pointed to the sources from which came the inspiration for the crowning crime of Anarchy. It was likewise a strongly settled conviction that the thrower of the bomb was not simply a Guiteau-like crank, but that there must have been a deliberate, organized conspiracy, of which he was a duly constituted agent. In the work, therefore, of getting at the inside facts, the points sought were: What was the exact nature of that conspiracy, and who constituted the chief conspirators? The possession of every detail in connection with these two points was absolutely necessary in order to fix the criminal responsibility, and to the solution of this problem the officers bent all their energies. . . .

With the information already obtained we had managed to secure a pretty clear insight into the diabolical plots of the "revolutionary groups." It was apparent that Chicago had been regarded by Anarchists everywhere as the head center of Socialism in America, and that it had been decided that here should be the first test of strength in the establishment of the new social order. Any reasoning, sentient being ought to have seen the utter folly of such an undertaking in the very midst of millions of liberty-loving, law-abiding citizens, but these Anarchists, hypnotized as they were by the plausible sophisms and the inflammatory writings of unscrupulous men bent on notoriety, could view it in no other light than as a grand stride towards their goal. As boys are led astray by yellow-covered literature, these poor fools were crazed by Anarchistic vaporings. Day or night, sleeping or waking, the beauties of the new social order to be inaugurated by the revolution were continually before their minds.

It was clear that such people were capable of desperate deeds, and that it was not only necessary to bring to justice the instigators of the massacre, but to show their deluded followers the inevitable result of carrying out ideas repugnant to our free institutions and inconsistent with common sense and right. . . .

The work of ferreting out and arresting the conspirators might have stopped with the number already gathered in, so far as the necessity for procuring evidence to be used in court was concerned, but it was continued to the end that every conspicuous or minor character in the murderous plot might be made to feel the power of the law, which each had so persistently defied. . . . Anarchist localities were overhauled, unfrequented places visited, and convenient hiding-places inspected. Every one wanted was finally brought from under cover. . . . Anarchistic sympathizers did everything in their power to conceal their friends, but the police proved equal to the emergency. . . .

It was on Thursday, the 15th of July, that the preliminary work was finally ended and the court was ready for a formal statement of the case. This statement was made by State's Attorney Grinnell, and his arraignment of the defendants was such a clear, convincing and masterful argument—giving, as it did, the whole history of the Anarchist conspiracy, and foreshadowing eloquently and in detail all the proof which was to be got before the jury—that I will print here a verbatim copy of his speech. . . .

Mr. Grinnell said [in part]:

Gentlemen:—For the first time in the history of our country are people on trial for their lives for endeavoring to make Anarchy the rule, and in that attempt for ruthlessly and awfully destroying life. I hope that while the youngest of us lives this in his memory will be the last and only time in our country when such a trial shall take place. It will or will not take place as this case is determined. . . .

I want to suggest to you now, gentlemen, this is a vastly more important case than perhaps any of you have a conception of. Perhaps I have been with it so long, have investigated it so much, come in contact with such fearful and terrible things so often, that my notions may be somewhat exaggerated; but I think not. I think they are worse even than my conception has pictured. The firing upon Fort Sumter was a terrible thing to our country, but it was open warfare. I think it was nothing compared with this insidious, infamous plot to ruin our laws and our country secretly and in this cowardly way; the strength of our institutions may depend upon this case, because there is only one step beyond republicanism—that is Anarchy. See that we never take that step, and let us stand to-day as we have stood for years, firmly planted on the laws of our country. . . .

When the public began to see the character of the evidence against the Anarchists, sentiment crystalized into a feeling that no fair-minded juror could be led astray by specious pleas or sophistical arguments into voting for an acquittal of any one of the defendants. The facts of the conspiracy had been brought out with startling boldness, and with every witness the points against the prisoners were fortified with added effect. . . .

I come now to the present status of Anarchy. The authorities have recognized the constant menace which the existence of this conspiracy conveyed to the cause of law and order, and consequently the malcontents have been watched with unceasing vigilance. Their meetings, their plottings, their purposes, their plan of organization and their system of propaganda we know nearly as well as they know it themselves.

The Socialists themselves estimate their numbers in Chicago at 75,000 men, women and children. As Socialism is the parent of Anarchy—the two are identical in their ultimate aims, differing only in tactics—these figures are significant.

The number of Anarchists in Chicago to-day is not far from 7,300 men and women. Of these there are thirty-five known to us to be desperate men, ready to commit murder, arson or any other crime to revenge themselves upon the officers and the magistrates who were concerned in bringing about the hanging of their leaders. . . .

Of all this more will be said hereafter, but first I will call attention to the fact that the organizations named are only what appear on the surface. Underlying and controlling all these is the secret organization, which in Chicago consists of an "invisible committee." It must be understood that the movement toward the object to which the Internationale looks forward—the social revolution—is local, national, and international, and it is probable that the committee for Chicago was appointed from the headquarters of the Internationale in New York, at the suggestion of that arch-conspirator and mischief-maker, Johann Most. The "invisible committee," although they have full direction of the movement in Chicago, are supposed to be unknown to the mass of the order. They work individually, and not as a body, and always quietly. Their identity they hold sacredly secret. It is only when open revolutionary work has actually begun that they are to come to the front. In the meantime, the open workers and agitators report to the individual "invisibles," and act under their advice. The "invisibles" themselves make it a point to practice moderation in their public utterances to divert suspicion. The old-time centralized organization, the reds believe, led to the detection and conviction of their leaders, after the failure of the Haymarket plot, and this it was that made the new plan not only advisable but necessary. Decentralization is now the ruling principle.

The Aims and Methods of the A.P.A. (1894–1896)

W. J. H. TRAYNOR

By the late 1880's many Anglo-Saxon Protestants were becoming alarmed by the growing political power of the Irish Catholics in the eastern cities

From W. J. H. Traynor, "The Aims and Methods of the 'A.P.A.'," *North American Review* (July, 1894), pp. 67–73; and Traynor, "Policy and Power of the A.P.A.," *North American Review* (June, 1896), pp. 658–659, 661–664, 666.

and by the mounting influx of immigrants from the Catholic countries of southern and eastern Europe. To oppose such alien influences, various secret societies appeared, such as the Patriotic League of the Revolution and the Minute Men in New York City. The American Protective Association was simply one among many "patriotic," nativist groups until the early 1890's, when it suddenly made impressive gains in national membership and political power. Founded in 1887 in Clinton, Iowa, the A.P.A. absorbed other anti-Catholic groups and gave national direction to the nativist movement. As a secret, ritualistic society the A.P.A. probably had no more than one hundred thousand members, but as a political federation of anti-Catholics it claimed the support of some two and a half million Americans. In 1893 the A.P.A. disseminated a false encyclical in which the pope supposedly ordered American Catholics to kill all heretics on a certain date. A.P.A speakers also portrayed the depression and industrial violence of 1893 and 1894 as part of a papal plot to weaken and undermine the United States. The organization's president was William Traynor, a Canadian by birth who went into the livestock and lumber business in Detroit. A Freemason and inveterate joiner, he brought a flair for salesmanship and organization to the post. But despite his confident assertions, the A.P.A. began to decline rapidly after 1895.

We have now to determine by evidence whether the assumptions of the Papal church are consistent with good citizenship. There is no obscurity in the position taken by the United States in the matter of allegiance; the state requires most perfect and complete fidelity and obedience to the Republic. The voice of the Papacy is no less uncertain; it demands the unqualified obedience of its adherents to the Pontiff. Thus Cardinal Manning, speaking in the name of the Pope has said:

I acknowledge no civil power; I am the subject of no civil power; I am the subject of no prince, and I claim to be more than this. I claim to be the supreme judge and director of the consciences of men, of the peasants that till the fields, and of the prince that sits upon the throne; of the household that sits in the shade of privacy, and the legislature that makes laws for kingdoms. I am sole, last, supreme judge of what is right and wrong. Moreover, we declare, affirm, define, and pronounce it to be necessary to salvation to every human creature to be subject to the Roman Pontiff.

All of which may be found in Quirinus . . . and the *Tablet* of October 9, 1864. . . .

The Revised Statutes of the United States declare:

The alien seeking citizenship must make oath to renounce forever all allegiance and fidelity to any foreign prince, potentate, state, or sovereignty, in particular that to which he has been subject.

The obligation of the oath of allegiance to the United States, from the point of view of a Papist, may be measured by the following:

No oaths are to be kept if they are against the interests of the Church of Rome.—*Corpus Juris Canonici,* Leipsig ed., 1839, p. 1159.

Again:

Oaths which are against the Church of Rome are not to be called oaths, but perjuries.—*Ibid,* p. 358.

Again, Pius IX asserted to himself the right to annul the constitutions and laws of certain countries, viz., New Grenada, in 1852; of Mexico, in 1856; of Spain, in 1855; and of Austria in 1868. . . .

Thus we can see that the Papal hierarchy declares its complete sovereignty over the state, and, in utter disregard of the Constitution and the laws of the land, decrees that the Papal fiat is superior to the voice of the people; and that the Papists of the United States yield acquiescence and obedience to this assumption of authority is shown in the following:

We glory that we are, and, with God's blessing, shall continue to be, not the American church, nor the church in the United States, nor a church in any other sense, exclusive or limited, but an integral part of the one holy Catholic and Apostolic Church of Jesus Christ.—*Acta et Decreta Concilii Plenarii Baltimorensis Tertii,* p. LXXVI. (Baltimore, 1886.)

Nor are there in the world more devoted adherents of the Catholic Church, the See of Peter, and the Vicar of Christ than the Catholics of the United States.—*Ibid.*

The position taken by the Papacy regarding matters of state as illustrated by the authorities quoted, and a hundred others equally as pertinent, form the fundamental reasons for the existence of the American Protective Association, although it is doubtful whether, if these conditions had existed as a theory only, the organization would ever have been anything more than a mere name. It was the active and aggressive application of the temporal claims of the Papacy by its subjects in this country that made the perfection of the "A.P.A." not only possible, but an actual necessity, our legislators, for the greater part, being either unwilling or too corrupt to deal with an issue in which their personal interests had become inextricably involved. . . .

"Arms in Catholic churches" or rumors thereof, is a matter that needs neither confirmation nor refutation. It is sufficient that Papist societies, from which non-Papists are religiously excluded, armed with rifles and bayonets, may be seen upon the public streets at any important Roman Catholic celebration. . . . It is enough for me that both men and arms are actual and visible auxiliaries to the Papal church. . . .

The assumption of the Papacy to control in politics was illustrated most fully during the recent debate upon the civil-marriage bill in Hungary. The moment the state claimed the right to legalize civil marriage, the church created almost a revolution to defeat the claim, acting upon the self-asserted right of *defining its own jurisdiction.* Even so with our public schools; the state declares that they shall be non-sectarian, yet in defiance of the state the church sends its nuns and priests into the public schools of Pennsylvania and elsewhere to teach Papal dogmas.

The Constitution declares that no appropriation shall be made for sectarian purposes; the church, *defining its own jurisdiction,* demands a portion of the public money for the support of Romish parochial schools. The state declares the right of free speech; the church permits its subjects to reject this principle, and they attack and attempt to murder public lecturers at Lafayette, Ind.; Kansas City; St. Louis; and scores of other places.

Closely allied to the principle that underlies the liberty of conscience is *freedom of speech and of the press.*

The First Amendment to the Constitution reads:

Congress shall make no law . . . abridging the freedom of speech or the press.

Yet, in the light of this, Leo XIII, in a letter, June 17, 1885, says:

Such a duty (obedience), while incumbent upon all without exception, *is most strictly so on journalists* who, if they were not animated with the *spirit of docility and submission* so necessary to every Catholic, would help to extend and greatly aggravate the evils we deplore.

A writer of the *Catholic World,* in an article published July, 1870, entitled "The Catholics of the Nineteenth Century," explains the position of the Papists on the question of free speech and of free press. He says:

The supremacy asserted for the Church in matters of education implies the additional and cognate function of the censorship of ideas, and the right to examine and approve or disapprove all books, publications, writing, and utterances intended for public instruction, enlightenment, or entertainment, and supervision of places of amusement. This is the principle upon which the Church has acted in holding over to the civil authorities for punishment criminals in the world of ideas.

Yes, Galileo was a splendid example of the Papal "censorship of ideas." Wycliff, Huss, Bruno, and many thousand victims of the Spanish Inquisition are a few other early instances; and the attempted assassination of public speakers within a few months in the United States may be taken as illustrating the later days of Rome's censorship. . . .

The American Protective Association, or as it is more generally known, the A.P.A., is now in the tenth year of its existence. No organization in the history of the American Republic ever had so spontaneous a birth, so remarkable a career, so radical an effect upon American politics, or has been the subject of such general interest and friendly and adverse comment as this association, while no institution has been so widely misrepresented or misunderstood.

The American Protective Association is neither a religious body nor an institution adverse to the religion, *per se*, of any person, sect, or faith. . . . The reasons advanced by the founders of the order for its institution were based, practically, upon the following grounds:

I. That the spirit of the National Constitution was being violated in various ways by certain persons and bodies in the United States.

II. That certain members and sections of the national government were in connivance with the said violators.

III. That the conditions governing our national immigration were such as to weaken our democratic institutions and form of government and to substitute therefor a system of government not in harmony therewith.

IV. That the immigrant vote, under the direction of certain ecclesiastical institutions, had become so dominant a factor in politics as to virtually control it.

V. That this domination had resulted in political prostitution, corruption, and favoritism of the worst kind.

VI. That the great majority of the American people, while painfully cognizant of the sinister and debasing results of these conditions, and desirous of amending them, were either ignorant of any efficient means of counter-organization, or fearful of the injury to their personal interests at the hands of their powerful and organized opponents. . . .

For the first two or three years the growth of the order was practically spontaneous, indicating that the movement was neither a craze nor the conception of cranks, but the spark of consequences which fired a train of circumstances laid by corrupt legislators and self-seeking ecclesiasts and their adherents through a course of many years. It is not surprising that a sect so tenacious of its principles, the assumed rights of its head and the antiquity of its institutions, as the Papists of the United States, were in no mood to brook any abridgment of the privileges which the perfection of their political organization had secured to them, more particularly as they (the Irish Papists especially) had been the dominant and courted element in the politics and government of the nation for many years. Their reprisals for the political opposition of the A.P.A. took the form of the deadly boycott, politically, personally, socially, and in business. This boycott was prosecuted all the more harshly from the fact that the boycotters were composed for the greater part of the most illiterate elements of the nation. Nearly every member of the A.P.A. who made himself prominent in the movement retired absolutely ruined in politics and purse, and while hundreds of thousands sympathized and accorded to the order their passive support, only a small percentage dared brave the storm of disaster that inevitably followed membership in the order. These conditions led to the enforcement of absolute secrecy both as to membership and place of meeting, but to no purpose. The daily press, which was almost unanimously adverse to the movement, took special pains to hold the order up to public odium, and to publish its membership, while the two dominant parties used every effort to crush an organization which it soon became palpable to both they could not use without seriously disarranging their own political machinery. This was the period of guerrilla warfare, when the order was too weak to meet the forces of their opponents openly in the field of politics without the certainty of defeat. It was also the period when the acts of the order were almost entirely defensive and absolutely negative. . . .

Although between the years 1890 and 1893, the initiated membership of the order never exceeded 70,000, and was scattered but sparsely through less than twenty states, it was a period of undoubted health and usefulness from the fact that affiliation with the order was rather a disadvantage than an advantage, as it attracted to its ranks the disinterested almost exclusively. The year 1893, however, showed such remarkable success for the order in the political field that the conditions changed and the ambitious politician suddenly awoke to the realization that baptism in A.P.A. water was attended with pleasant and profitable political consequences. Of these the earnest were, for the greater part, accepted; the unworthy were rejected to a large extent, but many found their way into the order through the carelessness of investigating committees.

In the two years that followed, the order planted itself firmly in every state and territory in the Union and was instrumental in overturning the entire political machinery in New York, Massachusetts, Michigan, Missouri, Tennessee, Kentucky, Ohio, and Iowa, and of California, Minnesota, Pennsylvania, Wisconsin, Washington, and Oregon, in part. With these victories commenced a general policy of active aggression and the negative tactics of the organization were practically abandoned. This, in my opinion, was a departure fraught with much danger, involving, as it necessarily must, entangling alliances with parties and political rings, and tending to destroy that political independence, without which the order must inevitably gravitate into the arms of one or other of the old parties and become absorbed. Fortunately the change brought its own rebuke. . . . Party candidates, elected almost entirely through the efforts of the order, in many cases either repudiated their pledges or evaded them, and the experience, although bitter, was a most salutary one to the organization, which has wisely learned to distrust the pledges of those who do not possess the moral courage to make them openly or before the altars of the order.

The opening of the Fifty-fourth Congress demonstrated the power of the organization in the political field as no event had previously done. Nearly one hundred members of the House of Representatives were elected to office, pledged to support the platform of the order, either as a whole or in part, while several members of the Senate were elected under similar conditions. It would be as unfair as it is untrue to assert that the great majority of these were honestly the friends of the American Protective Association or imbued with the principles of the organization. . . . While it is eminently to the credit of those who have maintained their obligations to the order entire, it must be confessed that the laxity of some of the political committees of the order, and the strong spirit of partyism which has prevailed in some sections, are to blame that all our representatives in the national Legislature are not primarily and entirely members of our order both nominally and practically. The aphorism that half a loaf is better than no bread has exercised a most pernicious and enervating influence upon the organization in many sections, pernicious because it has paved the way for compromises with those acts of the old parties which the order was organized most strenuously to resist; and enervating because it leads to the suggestion that the least of two evils is in itself good. . . .

The American Protective Association is the strongest and purest political force that the Western world ever knew. It grew from the parent stem of pure motives and patriotism. I have taken pains to point out its weaknesses and have dwelt but briefly upon its many merits. . . . It holds the political balance of power in the United States with its membership of nearly 2,500,000 persons, who influence at least 4,000,000 votes.

The Conspiracy against Silver (1886)

E. J. FARMER

The selections in this chapter are not intended to give a rounded or balanced picture of Populism and the movement for free silver. Populism, though largely rooted in the desire of entrepreneurial farmers to restore lost profits, was a complex upsurge of social protest which included intellectual reformers and certain leaders of organized labor. The movement for free silver was directed against a small creditor class which profited from the growing discrepancy between a restricted supply of currency and the credit needs of an expanding population and economy. Public protest against the inelasticity and continuing deflation of money ran from the Greenbacker movement of the 1870's to the Silver Crusade of 1896, and formed only an incidental part of the Populist reform programs of 1892 and 1894.

What unifies these movements and makes them relevant to the present study is their widespead conviction that America's economic ills could all

From E. J. Farmer, *The Conspiracy Against Silver in the United States* (Cleveland, 1886), pp. 5–8.

be traced to dark international intrigue. Thus in the Populist and Silverite imaginations, an international clique of bankers and financiers had bribed the American government into demonetizing silver (the "Crime of 1873") and had subsequently manipulated the business cycle in order to enrich creditors and rob the people of their hard-earned wealth. In light of previous American mythology, it is significant that this grandiose conspiracy was ultimately attributed to the British. In light of later fulminations against an "international Jewish conspiracy," it is significant that the British bankers were commonly associated with "Shylock" and the Rothschilds. While Richard Hofstadter has contended that the Populists were at most guilty of a "rhetorical anti-Semitism," he has also pointed out that Henry Ford and other later anti-Semites were much influenced by Populist imagery.

No nation under the shining sun has a fairer future than these United States of America, whose shores are bathed by two mighty oceans, whose climate has every varying change, from the tropics to the poles; whose mountains are teeming with gold and silver; whose rivers flow through fertile valleys, and whose plains are outstretched to the rains of heaven, yielding each year their increase in a golden harvest, sufficient to feed the world. Here is a land so fair that to its hospitable shores are coming in unnumbered thousands of the oppressed of other lands. Here, under the ample folds of the American banner of Liberty, shall flourish the most prosperous nation that the sun has ever shone upon in its circuit of the globe. Free and independent —before us lie the grandest opportunities that ever came to any people in the history of time. We threw off the shackles of England in the war of the American revolution. We have cleared our shores of the tyranny of Spain. We have by peaceful purchase absorbed an empire from our old friends and allies, the French. We have encroached upon ancient Mexico and conquered a kingdom from her. We have blotted out the conspiracy of a great rebellion, and though still in our youth, we are the richest nation upon the earth.

While these things are so we find old England envious and still grappling with us for our wealth. She has grown rich upon the $1,300,000,000 of gold we have sent her since 1849 from our gold mines. She has grown impudent toward us since we have opened our treasure vaults of silver, of which she has none. She has conspired with the Tory capitalists of our Eastern States to rob us of our possessions as surely as she conspired with Benedict Arnold to betray to her our armies in the days of the Revolution. This England has never yet given up the idea of victory over the material resources of America. She tampers with our Congress, in our finances and our tariffs. She reaches forth her golden arm to destroy the value of our silver, and she finds her dupes and her co-conspirators amid the bankers of New York and Boston. Having lost the American market for her iron, for her coal, and largely for her manufactured goods, she seeks now, by destroying the value of our silver product, to filch from us that metal by enhancing the value of her gold. . . . . While gold is the money of England, silver is the money of her Indian Empire, and into India goes the silver that England obtains, not only from the European nations, but also fifteen millions which she annually secures from the United States. This silver is necessary to England—she must have it. She has no silver mines of her own, and therefore delights to filch it from surrounding nations. Cut off America's supply of silver to England and instantly the price of silver will advance in the English market. One-half of all that goes from England to India comes from the United States. As long as we are fools enough to melt our silver into bullion, and sell it to England at any price she chooses to give us for it, so long will she depreciate the value of this precious metal. . . . England knows that she cannot get one of these silver dollars for less than a gold dollar, and therefore has she conspired with a certain class in America to stop the coinage of silver, and, if possible, to demonetize it.

Through treachery silver was demonetized in the United States by the law of February 12, 1873; but so secretly was this done, that General Grant, who signed the law, did not know it; nor did he seem to be aware of its contents as late as January 14, 1875, for, at that date we find him recommending one or two new mints to be established at Chicago, St. Louis or Omaha. . . . The parties who concocted that law understood its purpose, however, and no doubt received their reward, whether it was in 30 pieces of gold, or more. They as completely sold out the nation, as Judas sold out Christ, and yet we have apologists for that transaction all over the country to-day. When the people became aware of how their interests had been sacrificed to the "golden calf," they demanded the re-instatement of silver, and with great difficulty procured it, in an emasculated form, in the Bland Bill passed February 28, 1878. Then it was that the enemies of silver began to pour out the vials of their wrath, and to predict the direst evils that ever befell a nation. These conspirators have kept up their Cataline assemblages ever since, and, backed by England, have their daggers every ready to strike down the silver dollar.

A Fervent Appeal for
Free Silver (1889)

THOMAS FITCH

*After practicing law in California, Thomas Fitch helped frame the consti-
tution of Nevada and then represented that mining state in Congress from
1869 to 1871. His speech at the first National Silver Convention at St.
Louis in November 1889, expanded on the Greenbacker myth of the
"Crime of '73" and played upon the traditional American suspicions of British intrigue.*

MR. PRESIDENT AND GENTLEMEN OF THE CONVENTION—It is now sixteen years since the demonetization of silver was interpolated into the
national laws. During all these years the grip of the monometalist has
been tightening around the throat of the laborer. During all these
years the vampire bats of finance have been increasing both their
power of suction and their capacity for deglutition. During all these
years the rich have been growing richer and the poor poorer. During
all these years Congress has dallied and dawdled and dawdled and
dallied until we are led to question whether the interests of the people
or the interests of Wall Street are more potent at Washington. If we
expect to accomplish the restoration of silver to its former value we
must carry our purpose into the domain of practical politics. [Ap-
plause.] . . . Separate political action would be to abandon the great
parties of the country to the gold monometalists. It is, I think, better
policy for the friends of silver to capture both the Republican and
Democratic parties first locally, and afterwards nationally. [Ap-
plause.]

Free coinage would, as you know, not only restore silver to its
former value, but it would, as has been shown here, add 35 per cent
to the present prices of wheat, of cotton, and of farm produce, and it
would increase the wages of the laborer and add to his opportunities
for obtaining employment. . . .

Neither miner, nor farmer, nor planter need seek far nor long for a

From *Proceedings of the First National Silver Convention* (St. Louis, 1889),
pp. 221, 223, 227, 230.

cause of their distress. They will find it in the offices of the Bank of England; in the Chancellor's palace at Berlin; in the counting-rooms of Wall Street. They will find it in the phrases demonetizing silver, which, whether fraudulently or inadvertently inserted in the national laws, have ever since been kept there by the efforts of a cruel and rapacious cabal. The clandestine law of 1873 ought to be ejected from the national statutes immediately and unconditionally. [Applause.] Any lesser measure of relief will be paltry and ineffectual. It is idle for the monometalists to tell us that the prices have been reduced because of the increased production of wheat and cotton in India. This may be the proximate cause, but the cause of the cause will be found in silver demonetization alone. The production of both wheat and cotton in India has been stimulated artificially, and it has been made possible for English millers and spinners to bring the grain of the Punjab and the cotton of Bengal to Liverpool at such reduced cost as enables them to beat down by 35 per cent the prices of American products, simply because of the existence and working of the act of 1873. England purchases silver in the United States where it is demonetized, at 90 to 95 cents per ounce, and by stamping it into Indian rupees, disposes of it in India—in exchange for wheat and cotton—at $1.29 per ounce. The Northern farmer loses 30 cents per bushel on his wheat, and the Southern planter loses 3 cents per pound on his cotton, because the rupee which passes for 32 cents in Bombay is composed of 23 cents worth of British gold and 9 cents worth of British diplomacy and power, or rather because England can buy 32 cents worth of American silver with 23 cents worth of British gold and 9 cents worth of British gall. . . .

How much longer will our miners, planters and farmers consent that Republican and Democratic Senators and Representatives at Washington shall continue to subordinate the interests of American firesides to the exigencies of European finance and the cupidity of New York bankers? Is it not time for the American eagle to rise and shake the Liverpool salt from his tail. [Applause.]

The British Plot to Enslave
the World (1892)

A. J. WARNER AND H. C. BALDWIN

A second National Silver Convention met in Washington in May 1892. Its organizer and guiding spirit was A. J. Warner, who had been a brigadier general in the Civil War, a railroad promoter, and a Congressman for three terms. In the late 1870's and early 1880's Warner had led the fight for the free coinage of silver; after being elected in 1892 as president of the American Bimetallic League, he was a powerful force in preparing the way for William J. Bryan's Silver Crusade of 1896.

One of the most far-fetched and interesting speeches at the 1892 convention was that of H. C. Baldwin, of Naugatuck, Connecticut, who charged that emancipation of Negro slaves, initiated by Great Britain, had been part of a scheme to subject the world to the dominion of British capitalism. His theory was a curious resurrection of the proslavery argument of many antebellum southerners.

General A. J. Warner

For twenty years the money power has held us in its grasp. By an act imposed upon the people in 1873, without their knowledge, they were deprived of the ancient and Constitutional right to have gold and silver coined into money without restriction. By the subtle device of limiting the money supply to one metal the value of the money unit has been increased, and with it the burden of all debts and taxes, by at least 40 per cent. And the end is not yet, but the increase goes on, and must go on as the use of gold is extended over the world and becomes scarcer and dearer.

The change in the money standard from gold and silver to gold alone after two of the greatest wars of modern times, and when the world was weighted down with mountain loads of debt, created, in large part, in depreciated paper, stands unparalleled for iniquity in the history of mankind.

That this movement had its origin in a conspiracy of foreign capi-

From speeches by A. J. Warner and H. C. Baldwin, *Proceedings of the Second National Silver Convention* (Washington, 1892), pp. 5–6, 70–71, 75.

talists who controlled, to a large extent, the world's debts, can no longer be rationally doubted. It took Satanic genius to devise it, and it could be carried out only by veiling from the people the real purpose of the act. The people of the United States knew nothing of it till long after the deed was done. It has been conclusively shown that not a half dozen members of the House knew that the mint act of 1873 contained the provision by which the money unit of the Constitution and of the law of 1792 was changed. If more than one member of the Senate knew it he has never admitted it.

Take the situation as it existed in this country in 1873, with public debts amounting to nearly $3,000,000,000, largely owned abroad, with no steps yet taken looking to a return to coin values, what reason could be offered at such a time for changing the old metallic standard of money? There was none—there is none—it was purely an act of spoliation. Cyrus, Alexander or Caesar never more deliberately planned the conquest and plunder of a country than was planned this scheme to plunder the world by changing the money standard in the interest of creditors and against debtors and producers. Such an opportunity never before presented itself, if there were ever before money pirates audacious enough to have attempted such a scheme of plunder. [Applause.] . . .

Mr. H. C. Baldwin

I was down in a meeting house in Florida last fall and I heard a hymn sung I never heard before; and as its strains went out on the air I thought it was a suitable song for the people of the United States to work up and learn, and sing to John Sherman, Benjamin Harrison, Grover Cleveland, and the whole gang of British conspirators that conspire against silver. Let me tell you how that song began; no, how it ended:

> De road am wide, and hell is deep
> Oh, man, your days is numbered.

That is a song the American people want to learn and sing. I want to say to those of you here, and especially to my silver friends, that you don't comprehend the depth, the power, the means and capacity of the enemy you are fighting. This financial condition is not the result of a day, it is not the result of the conspiracy hatched in Lombard street a few years ago; it reaches back of that. Gentlemen, the money power is as relentless as steel, as cruel as the hell of John Calvin, and as unprincipled and unscrupulous as the father of lies. This thing began, gentlemen, away back in 1820, when Great Britain did that philanthropic act that poets and orators have lauded to the skies, when she liberated the African slave within her borders.

Then it was that a contest began between two systems of spoliation. One may be denominated as the British system, the other as the Spanish system. The Spanish system contemplated the spoliation of labor simply by owning the slaves and assuming the responsibility of their care. The British system inaugurated then in connection with the fiscal policy of Great Britain (perpetual debt and gold standard), contemplated the establishment of contract relations, in other words the wage system with all that it implies. There was no more philanthropy about Great Britain in emancipating her slaves than there was when they shot down Chinamen to make them buy her opium. Then again, the contest between these two systems began in the United States, promoted by the greed of the dollar worshippers of New England on the one hand, where a factory system similar to that of Great Britain had been established; and the Spanish system on the other. And that contest went on; the British idea gradually gaining force and strength, until 1861, when the contest began which was to end in landing the entire christian civilization of the world under the English system of spoliation instead of the Spanish.

I want you to-day, as you are prepared to go into this fight, to go back to that contest. Think of the noble fellows in their garments of blue, listening to the strains of "John Brown's Body," as we marched to the heights of Fredericksburg and onwards to Appomattox. We thought we were fighting for human freedom. We were made to think that, but that contest, gentlemen, was nothing but a contest between two rival systems, each one of which had for its object the spoliation of labor. And when that conflict was at its height, in London it was seen conclusively that the British system was to go to the front and the Spanish system go to the wall. England had learned that the British policy of hiring labor and then controlling prices by controlling the volume of money, was cheaper and more profitable to capital; that it was cheaper to hire labor than it was to own it. Then it was that that Hazard Circular was sent to appeal to the greed of the manufacturers who had become bankers in New England and New York and Pennsylvania. Then it was that that unholy conspiracy to establish a system of finance which is fast reducing the whole people to the condition of debt slaves was started. . . .

What has a Silver Convention to do? What measures do you propose? I tell you that there will be no change in the fiscal policy of this Government, as dictated by the directors of the bank of England, until there is such an uprising as we have never seen. In that uprising party lines will have to be obliterated; old prejudice, old theories will have to be swept away. Men must overcome, in the higher aspirations for a better civilization, for the abolition of poverty, for the increase and the increased distribution of wealth, their prejudice. Remember, that the money power knows no geography; it knows no religion; it knows no politics; it knows no boundaries except to fix its tentacles wherever the foot of industry treads or the hand of industry toils. There it puts its blood-sucking tentacles, and is putting them the world over. [Applause.] . . .

Where will it end? What must be the result? Slavery, absolute and complete; something worse than tenant farmers. It means a condition of poverty for the great masses; of luxuriant wealth for an idle few. Let not the American people in their treatment of the money power who are controlling the two political party organizations, allow themselves to be fooled with promises which are only made to be broken.

Shylock as Banker
and Conspirator (1894)

GORDON CLARK

Like the abolitionist who portrayed the Founding Fathers as naïve regarding the evils of slavery, Gordon Clark, who wrote for the Bimetallic League, pictured Lincoln as an innocent with respect to high finance. It was this fatal but forgivable weakness that had permitted the beginnings of a vast bankers' conspiracy against the people. In this selection Clark draws a striking parallel between the Tories in the Revolution and the later American bankers who were collaborating with the British "gold-plot against the plain people of the United States." Fortunately, he felt that national salvation could be achieved through the science of money, which would unlock the mysteries of political economy for the common man.

From Gordon Clark, *Shylock: As Banker, Bondholder, Corruptionist, Conspirator* (Washington, 1894), pp. 3–4, 7–8.

Soon after the first inauguration of Abraham Lincoln as President of the United States, he was met, one morning, by an old acquaintance, a banker, who happened to be in Washington. "Mr. President," said he, "how are you going to raise funds to carry on the war?" "It must be done," replied Mr. Lincoln, "but I don't know *how:* I don't know anything about money, and, to tell the truth, I never had much respect for anybody who did." Our great and good President had no time and no heart, just then, to consider the banker's question, and, quite as he said, he had never informed himself in the principles of money. It was a great pity. For had he been familiar with those principles, we may be sure that he would have insisted on saving the productive toilers of his country about one half of their interest-bearing war-debt, which, in 1865, amounted to some twenty-four hundred millions of dollars. Putting the figures at the lowest point of such experts as have dared to be honest in their statements, a thousand millions, with the interest added, might possibly reach the part of that debt which the money-class, as such, filched from the rest of us—soldiers, workers, widows and orphans. Those greedy and remorseless "sharks" did not exactly *steal* this vast property belonging to their fellow-citizens: they only wheedled and coerced a few of our public servants to procure the passage of certain laws for them, by which they could commit virtual larceny without going to jail. So they were not "thieves." They were "highly respectable gentlemen," as the world now goes, because their "manipulations" were large; but, compared with their *legalized crimes,* the technical and punishable crimes against property of all other classes of our people, from that day to this, have been like the moral lapses of infants at the breast.

THOSE MONSTROUS SHYLOCKS, however, were *successful,* and they lived unwhipped of justice. Emboldened by this result, the same band—partly the old generation and partly new recruits of two continents—have since combined, with their headquarters in England, to despoil, for what they can make out of it, the honest, industrious, common people of *the whole world.* This is the short of that much more than tragic affair, commonly dubbed *"the demonetization of silver."* . . .

In 1848 gold was discovered in California, and at about the same time in Australia. This new wealth filled the whole family of Shylock with horror. As gold increased in quantity, they feared it would *decrease* in the power of buying and controlling other things. They had enjoyed the advantage of its *scarcity* for thousands of years; but now the bread and meat of the people stood for a fifth more of "the precious metals" than when mankind were going about half-fed and half-clothed. So Shylock *declared war on* GOLD, and filled the heads of writers, economists and journalists with his sorrows. . . .

While that conspiracy lasts, *England is our deadly foe*—quite as much our enemy as she was in 1776 or in 1812; though now, as then, many friends of ours might be counted, even in a British Parliament. And that *Americans* are participants in the British attack on their country, makes no difference. So were the richest aristocrats and money-sharks, in the days of the Revolution. Those despicable "Tories" were not more dangerous, then, to American liberty and prosperity, than the shareholders, vassels and attorneys of the English gold-pot are to-day. This, of course, does not mean that everybody, either in Europe or America, who favors a single gold-standard of money, is essentially and deliberately a villain. It means only that he is such, *if he understands the principles of economics as applied to currency.* Bank-men, perhaps, as a *class*, demand the gold-basis. Are they all dishonest and unpatriotic? Certainly not. But because a man can count a pile of coin or paper, or decide on discounting a neighbor's note, it is no sign he knows anything about the science of money. A grocer can sell a dozen eggs without comprehending biology, and a tape-merchant may get rich, yet never have heard of the reason for the length of his yard-stick. . . .

THE AMERICAN PEOPLE MUST LEARN THE LESSON OF MONEY, or they are LOST! For every man, woman and child in the land—as indeed in the world—it is the most vital question of practical welfare that can now engage the human mind. And it is *not* difficult. Journalistic attorneys and ostensible teachers of political economy are often suborned to *pretend* difficulty, and do it in proportion to the fee received; for the poor wretches must eat and drink, and harlotry of the pen is in great demand.

The Problem of Civilization Solved (1895)

MARY ELIZABETH LEASE

The daughter of an Irish political exile, Mary Elizabeth Lease was brought up and educated as a Catholic, but then rebelled against all orthodox religion, going on to become a lawyer and political agitator in Kansas. She was an ardent and colorful speaker for the Populist cause, and was chiefly remembered for advising Kansas farmers to "raise less corn and more hell." Mrs. Lease was also ambitious. She aspired to be a United States senator and even President; and she proposed to solve the "problem of civilization" by opening new frontiers in Africa and South America, where white planters would cultivate the wilderness with the aid of Negro and Oriental workers. Her paternalism toward the non-Caucasian races was combined with an appeal for a more positive, paternalistic state which would take over the railroads and telegraph and actively combat the causes of poverty.

Mr. Carnegie is a Briton. He claims residence in America, a province which he occasionally visits for revenue only. But he resides in Scotland.

He is as much a Briton as was Cornwallis, Lord Howe or Tarleton.

Our forefathers bled and died at Bunker Hill, Saratoga and Yorktown that America might be free from Britons and Hessians, yet here is a man, who after making fifty millions in America, retires to his baronial castle among the hills of Scotland and from his stronghold of British royalty he may wreck three-fourths of the iron mills in America by under-bidding all competitors, through his electrical devices and labor-saving machinery, and at the same time turn adrift ninety-seven per cent of his operatives to compete with their brethren, *or starve!*

Paternal government should grapple with and overcome such dangers.

Labor-saving devices when applied in shop and factory, should not be used wholly to enrich either native or foreign millionaires; but the

From Mary Elizabeth Lease, *The Problem of Civilization Solved* (Chicago, 1895), pp. 259–260, 279–280, 317–320.

unearned increment therefrom should accrue equally to the capitalist controlling them, the public, or consumer, and the operative. . . .

A band of railway janizaries have arisen in our midst who hold the key to our commerce. A few men in New York may meet at a wine supper and decree a reduction of wages for a million men, thus inviting a strike that might paralyze the industries of the whole nation, precipitating riots that might give a pretext for calling out national troops through the specious and elastic law of Interstate Commerce. A great civil war might any day be launched upon us by the avaricious folly of a band of half-drunken, wine-bibing railroad magnates, who, intent only on self-aggrandizement, might plunge the nation into a gulf of woe and misery by one act of supreme selfishness.

In the estimation of these janizaries the plundered public has become valuable only as a dividend-paying institution, which, like the Turkish peasant, may be bastinadoed by the tax collector out of his last piaster. . . .

Let us, therefore, transpose a good old maxim and decide that *what can't be endured must be cured*. Let us, too, train the cannon of public opinion upon the railway janizary and annihilate him and his system with a volley of free American ballots. The sovereignty of the American people must be invoked, and by the law of eminent domain the railroads can be acquired by the nation. . . .

In the economy of God there is no room for a *usurer or a landlord*.

Reclaim and restore by congressional action the unearned lands given with lavish prodigality to the railroads.

Limit landholdings to naturalized citizens, and repurchase—or confiscate—the homes of the people upon which the vampire of English landlordism, rack-rent tenantry and eviction, now fatten. Accessability to the land, with government aid to the dependent classes until they become self-supporting, and enforcement of that sensible maxim: "If a man shall not work neither shall he eat."

The French revolution that wrote the declaration of human rights in fire and blood and thundered it to the world with flame and smoke, resulted at least in one particular in great benefit to the people. Previous to this uprising the lands were held by the few. The priests held the greater part of it and rented it to the people. Women and babies might starve, but these rents must be paid to support the worthless, idle dignitaries of church and court; but the pendulum of time swung the hour of justice. Priests and nobles were driven from the country. Their lands were confiscated, assignats issued and made redeemable in lands. The peasantry invested their assignats in land —securing themselves small farms which no government has since dared to take from them. . . .

We are not only a debtor nation, but a nation, as gleaned from the eleventh census report, of tenant serfs, and our illustrious President —Grover the First—a marvel of profundity and rotundity, the agent of Jewish bankers and British gold, recommends in his recent message the "formation of regimental battalions," the increase of armed force, that capital may put the knife to the throat of a brother, forgetting that the people, whom they would oppress and slay, placed the angel of immortality on the fields of Bunker Hill . . . that the majesty of human right, liberty of conscience and justice might be evolved.

Then, as now, the great common people had faith in the right and saw the issue, as the old prophet saw the Messiah; for the one lesson gleaned from the history of right and wrong since the world began proves that however much wrong may triumph for a time, right in the end prevails.

A Small Group of Men Hold in Their Hands the Business of This Country (1908)

ROBERT M. LA FOLLETTE

Although agitation for currency reform and denunciations of Wall Street subsided with the return of prosperity after 1896, the so-called "bankers' panic" of October 1907 brought widespread demands for public investigations and reform. The Aldrich-Vreeland Act of 1908 provided for an emergency currency system and a National Monetary Commission to study and report on banking reforms. Since the Aldrich bill was part of a growing impulse among conservatives for a privately controlled central banking system, it was attacked by Progressives like Senator La Follette as a means of perpetuating Wall Street's control of national credit. La Follette, who as governor of Wisconsin had won popular acclaim as a champion of the public interest, was particularly alarmed by the growing power of financiers and investment bankers. In this speech, delivered before the Senate on March

From the *Congressional Record: Containing the Proceedings and Debates of the Sixtieth Congress, First Session*, XLII (Washington, 1908), 3434–3436, 3450–3451.

17, 1908, he offered solid evidence concerning the role of banking interests, such as those of J. P. Morgan, in the recent consolidation and integration of the economy. While it would be unfair to classify La Follette's speech as simply another specimen of the "paranoid style," his exposure of the lack of public accountability of such powerful men was coupled with an exaggerated view of fiscal conspiracy and manipulation. Like so many other speakers and writers represented in this book, he assumed that evidence of power and self-interested motives "proved" a hidden control over seemingly fortuitous events.

The Aldrich bill in my view . . . can not be fairly judged without considering the changes which have been wrought in the industrial and commercial life of this country within a decade, and the consequent changes that have taken place in banking within a few years. . . .

Eighteen hundred and ninety-eight was the beginning of great industrial reorganization. Men directly engaged in production brought about in the first instance an association of the independent concerns which they had built up. These reorganizations were at the outset limited to those turning out finished products similar in kind. Within a period of three years following, 149 such reorganizations were effected with a total stock and bond capitalization of $3,784,000,000. In making these reorganizations the opportunity for a larger paper capitalization offered too great a temptation to be resisted. This was but the first stage in the creation of fictitious wealth. The success of these organizations led quickly on to a consolidation of combined industries, until a mere handful of men controlled the industrial production of the country.

The opportunity to associate the reorganization of the industrial institutions of the country with banking capital presented itself. Such connections were a powerful aid to reorganization, and reorganization offered an unlimited field for speculation. It was a tremendous temptation.

It contributes nothing of value to this discussion to denounce individuals on the one hand or laud them on the other. I have compiled a list of about one hundred men with their directorships in the great corporate business enterprises of the United States. It furnishes indisputable proof of the community of interest that controls the industrial life of the country.

I shall ask, Mr. President, to have incorporated in the Record this list of about 100 men with their directorships. It discloses their connections with the transportation, the industrial, and the commercial life of the American people. This exhibit will make it clear to any-one that a small group of men hold in their hands the business of this country.

No student of the economic changes in recent years can escape the conclusion that the railroads, telegraph, shipping, cable, telephone, traction, express, mining, iron, steel, coal, oil, gas, electric light, cotton, copper, sugar, tobacco, agricultural implements, and the food products are completely controlled and mainly owned by these hundred men; that they have through reorganization multiplied their wealth almost beyond their own ability to know its amount with accuracy. It is not necessary to examine in detail the related events that have led to this marvelous concentration of business. The facts are well understood and generally recognized.

But the country seems not to understand how completely great banking institutions in the principal money centers have become bound up with the control of industrial institutions, nor the logical connection of this relationship to the financial depression which we have so recently suffered, nor the dangers which threaten us from this source in the future.

That there was a tendency on the part of the great banking associations to merge and combine could not be overlooked; and while financial and economic writers had directed public attention to the fact, and had even pointed out the opportunity and temptation for the use of this augmented power in connection with the promotion of the speculative side of business organization, they have been slow to believe that banking institutions could be so prostituted. . . .

As early as in 1903 the *Wall Street Journal,* in an editorial entitled "Evolution of a strong financial oligarchy," thus strongly set forth the dangerous tendencies in banking:

In the New York money market there are now seven great groups or chains of banks, trust companies, and insurance companies. These groups in some cases represent common ownership, and in others such an alliance of interests that the very institutions are controlled practically under a common policy. The tendency is for the large banks to control by ownership several smaller banks, and to be in close alliance with one or more trust companies.

. . . Under the title "Perils of the money trust," the *Wall Street Journal* again pointed out these dangers in the following language:

What is taking place is a concentration of banking that is not merely a normal growth, but a concentration that comes from combination, consolidation, and other methods employed to secure monopolistic power. Not only this, but this concentration has not been along the lines of commercial banking. The great banks of concentration are in close alliance with financial interests intimately connected with promotion of immense enterprises, many of them being largely speculative. The bank credits of the country are being rapidly concentrated in the hands of a few bankers who are more interested in banking on its financial (watered stock) side than in banking on its commercial side.

Such concentration as this is dangerous in a political sense. The people have already been greatly disturbed by the concentration that has taken place in the industrial world. ° ° ° But concentration in the industrial world is a far less menacing condition than concentration in banking. The men or set of men who control the credits of the country control the country. . . .

Mr. President, the bare names of the directors of two great bank groups—the Standard Oil group and the Morgan group—given in connection with their other business associations is all the evidence that need be offered of the absolute community of interest between banks, railroads, and all the great industries.

There are twenty-three directors of the National City Bank (Standard Oil). There are thirty-nine directors of the National Bank of Commerce (Morgan). Examination of these directorates shows that the two groups are being knit together in business associations, suggesting their ultimate unification. . . .

This subversion of banking by alliance with promotion and stock speculation is easily traced.

There was every inducement for those who controlled transportation and a few great basic industries to achieve control of money in the financial center of the country.

The centralization of the banking power in New York City would not only open the way for financing the reorganization and consolidation of industrial enterprises and of public utilities throughout the country, but would place those in authority where they could control the markets on stocks and bonds almost at will.

With this enormous concentration of business it is possible to create, artificially, periods of prosperity and periods of panic. Prices can be lowered or advanced at the will of the "System." When the farmer must move his crops a scarcity of money may be created and prices lowered. When the crop passes into the control of the speculator the artificial stringency may be relieved and prices advanced, and the illegitimate profit raked off the agricultural industry may be pocketed in Wall Street.

If an effort is made to compel any one of these great "Interests" to obey the law, it is easy for them to enter into a conspiracy to destroy whoever may be responsible for the undertaking.

Story of the Panic

I have placed before you the record evidence that less than one hundred men own and control railroads, traction, shipping, cable, telegraph, telephone, express, mining, coal, oil, gas, electric light, copper, cotton, sugar, tobacco, agricultural implements, and the food products, as well as banking and insurance. Does anyone question the overcapitalization of these consolidated corporations which cover the business of the country? Does anyone doubt the community of interest that binds these men together? Does anyone question their vital interest in maintaining their overcapitalization and protecting their stocks and bonds? Does anyone doubt their hostility to the declared policies of President Roosevelt, and the progressive movement throughout the country, and their readiness, nay, their determination, to make an end of it at any cost? Was this not made abundantly manifest during the summer of 1907? The White House was not far wrong when it gave out the information that a great fund had been pledged to block any third-term possibility. . . .

There were no commercial reasons for a panic. There were speculative, legislative, and political reasons why a panic might serve special interests. There were business scores to settle. There was legislation to be blocked and a currency measure suited to the system to be secured. There was a third term to be disposed of and policies to be discredited.

A panic came. I believe that it needs only to be followed step by step to show that it was planned and executed, in so far as such a proceeding is subject to control, after once in motion. Such a statement without support in facts warranting it would deserve condemnation. To withhold such a statement, to shrink from plain speech setting forth the facts in so far as they can be uncovered in the discussion of this legislation would be to shirk a plain public duty.

7. Responses to International Involvement and Ethnic Pluralism (1918–1948)

DESPITE THE turmoil of the 1890's, despite the rhetoric of Populists and the occasional outbursts of hysteria over anarchists, Catholics, and unassimilated immigrants, Americans enjoyed a period of relative stability and self-confidence from the end of Reconstruction to the First World War. Seldom has the world experienced such a prolonged era of peace and social progress as between the 1870's and 1914. It appeared that Americans were free to exploit the wealth of a continent without external interference or the risk of foreign involvements. The open-mindedness of this era can be quickly indicated by noting two significant facts: the failure of proposals for discriminatory restrictions on immigration, and the willingness of Progressive reformers with diverse interests and backgrounds to join with socialists in agitating for fundamental changes in the American economic and social structure.

The issue of America's entry into the First World War not only shattered the Progressive–socialist coalition but revealed a growing polarization between "modernists" and "fundamentalists" over basic values and ways of life. Although these terms were originally limited to religious philosophies, "modernism" was soon extended to imply a hospitality to new approaches in art, psychology, sex, political science, and literature. Fundamentalists fought to preserve the norms of the isolated, rural, Protestant society that had only recently begun to discover its inextricable involvement in the twentieth century. The emotional shock of a world war, incomprehensible in terms of traditional American idealism, led fundamentalists to blame the Hun, and then the Russian Bolshevik, for all the disturbing conflicts and innovations of the modern era.

The years from 1917 to 1921 are probably unmatched in American history for popular hysteria, xenophobia, and paranoid suspicion. The psychological impact of becoming involved in a major European war was aggravated by the stunning news that Marxist revolutionaries had overthrown the government of America's most populous ally. The belief that the Germans had instigated the Russian Revolution served to link rabid anti-German sentiment with anti-Communism. The older image of bomb-throwing anarchists was easily merged with new fears of German sabotage and subversion. Thus the Industrial Workers of the World were denounced on the Senate floor in 1918 as a "criminal and treasonable organization," secretly supported by Germany for the purpose of undermining the American people's belief in God, morality, the sanctity of marriage, and the legitimacy of private property.

While there was a continuity of symbols and themes with earlier movements of countersubversion, traditional suspicions and enmities acquired new meaning in the light of an appallingly destructive war which had obviously failed to make the world safe for democracy. For example, the Populist and Progressive image of Wall Street conspirators could be used to explain America's entry into a war that turned out to subordinate idealistic goals to selfish interests. Yet, if international bankers and munitions makers could push the American government into acts of belligerency and manipulate public opinion with fabricated tales of German atrocities, what hope was there for popular democracy? This "leftist" interpretation of a capitalist conspiracy was not so far removed as one might think from the "right-wing" hysteria over German and Bolshevik intrigue. Both were the products of disillusion—of a loss of faith in the correspondence of appearance and reality. The desire for a single, comprehensive explanation of bewildering events encouraged the merging of formerly discrete symbols of hidden enemies. This tendency became evident soon after the war in a sudden upsurge of anti-Semitism. The "International Jew" was accused of being the secret force responsible for the entire course of recent history.

Americans did not originate the belief that cunning Jews were simultaneously responsible for the growing power of both capitalist bankers and Communist revolutionaries. Like the Order of Illuminati, the notion of an international Jewish cabal was the fabrication of European conservatives whose bitter hostility toward social change was peculiarly relevant to the mood of disillusioned Americans in search of simple answers. In Russia, prior to the Revolution, a forged document had appeared which was advertised as the Jewish master plan for world conquest. These *Protocols of the Elders of Zion* provided a specious explanation for Russia's growing internal difficulties and were intended to vindicate the most extreme anti-Semitic measures. Their full impact was delayed, however, until 1918 and 1919 when they were translated into western European languages and circulated, mostly by Czarist emigrés, as the secret key explaining the Revolution. Even before the end of the war, Czarist army officers had introduced the *Protocols* to the United States. Although they failed to impress government officials, they were soon being printed and distributed by a wealthy and well-connected organization of superpatriots who called themselves the American Defense Society.

As John Higham has pointed out in his valuable study of nativism, *Strangers in the Land,* anti-Semitism outlived its early alliance with the Red Scare of 1919–1920. As the base of nativism broadened in the early 1920's, Jews were blamed not only for Marxism and revolution but for modern finance, the stock market, liberal or "nondenominational" religion, the strange ideas being taught in American universities, and the indecent and shocking tone of modern art and literature. The great prophet of this anti-Semitic brand of fundamentalism was Henry Ford, whose *Dearborn Independent* introduced millions of Americans to the startling revelations of the *Protocols of the Elders of Zion,* which had already been proved to be a forgery, the contents having been plagiarized from a work that had nothing to do with Jews. An ardent idealist who had hoped to stop a senseless world war in 1915 by sailing on a "Peace Ship" to Europe, and who had then run for the Senate in 1918 supporting Wilson's fight for the League of Nations, Ford typified the disillusioned American liberal. He was shaken by the discovery of power relationships that were unaffected by individual achievement and goodwill, by the promise of higher wages and more automobiles. The *Protocols* showed that even a Peace Ship had no chance of overcoming the influence of Jewish bankers who plotted wars for their own profit. Long a champion of rugged individualism, Ford shared the western Populist suspicion of eastern bankers and Wall Street manipulators. The *Protocols* pointed to the Jewish origins of the international Money Power that exploited American enterprise; they also helped explain the financial difficulties Ford was suffering by 1920. (In 1927, Ford said that after studying the subject and learning that the *Protocols* was a "gross forgery," he was "deeply mortified" over the *Dearborn Independent's* contributions to anti-Semitism. This public apology followed a particularly vicious series of anti-Semitic articles in 1924–1925 which brought a million-dollar suit for defamation of character by a prominent Jewish attorney. It is clear that the apology and the suit, which was finally settled out of court, were closely related.)

In an important sense, the fundamentalist mind of 1920 was a culmination of the entire history of American countersubversion. Whether anti-Semitic, anti-Catholic, or antiradical, the new-style nativist was above all preoccupied with the threat of social and intellectual diversity. Clearly the idealistic visions and expectations of the past had been unfulfilled. America had not escaped the class and industrial conflict of the Old World; immigrants had not been converted by the eager missionaries of Anglo-Saxon Protestant culture; the world had not followed America toward universal peace and democracy. Wherever one looked there was disunity, change, and uncertainty. According to the *Dearborn Independent*, "the Jewish nation is the only nation that possess the secrets of all the rest." In short, the Jews (or the Catholics or the Marxists) not only enjoyed the unity and self-confidence which Americans lacked, but were the secret authors of America's disunity and confusion as well as of the corruption and decline of Europe. It is evident that the image of a subversive enemy served many psychological needs that were heightened by the frustrating experiences of the war and postwar periods. Progressive reformers could use Communism or the International Jew as an excuse for their own failures. The *Dearborn Independent* could assure self-made manufacturers that *they* were not evil capitalists, since they were dependent for funds on the international Jewish bankers, who were the only true capitalists.

One of the most disturbing revelations of the war had been the effect of propaganda on public opinion. The concept of propaganda also accounted for the supposed success of subversives in transforming American thought and behavior. The *Protocols* bluntly proclaimed that Gentiles were like sheep who could be led in any direction. Hence conformism and other disturbing phenomena of mass society could be attributed to Jewish machinations. If the American weaknesses for changing fashions and conspicuous consumption seemed to contradict older Puritan values, it was because American consumers had been cunningly seduced by Jewish businessmen and advertisers. The existence of a diabolical enemy explained why Americans behaved the way they did.

Moreover, as in the past, the belief in conspiracy provided an excuse for closing ranks and for renewed dedication to a selfless cause. During the war, the American Defense Society modernized the Biblical rhetoric of early Protestant missionaries and exhorted patriots to "come out" from unclean foreign influences and fight for "one hundred percent Americanism." Over two hundred thousand citizens enlisted in the American Protective League, described by its official historian as "a vast, silent, volunteer army organized with the approval and operated under the direction of the United States Department of Justice, Bureau of Investigation." This meant that anyone who was deprived of shooting Huns in France could at least defend his country by taking secret oaths and becoming a member of a local vigilante society; he could then spy on his neighbors, report "disloyal utterances," and perhaps help send an I.W.W. sympathizer to a concentration camp.

After the war, the quest for unity and one hundred percent Americanism took a variety of forms. The fear that Bolshevik revolution would spread through Europe coincided in 1919 with nationwide strikes in America, which were further aggravated by a financial panic, growing unemployment, and ruinous inflation. The fanatical nativism of 1919 and 1920 probably gave many Americans a sense of security in the midst of these disturbances. It was no doubt reassuring to read that Attorney General A. Mitchell Palmer, who hoped soon to be President, had ordered the arrest and detention of thousands of suspicious aliens, over two hundred of whom were subsequently deported to an unannounced destination (Finland). Since the public mind associated all varieties of subversion with recent immigrants, imagining that before their arrival the nation had enjoyed idyllic harmony, there was mounting pressure to go beyond deportations and end the influx of dangerous elements. There were other motives behind the immigration restriction acts of 1921 and 1924; but the provisions discriminating against the countries of southern and eastern Europe reflected a belief that one hundred percent Americanism required a continuing majority of Anglo-Saxon Protestants.

No group championed this proposition more fervently than the Ku Klux Klan, which was dedicated, in its second incarnation, to the restoration of an older and happier America. There was little connection between the Klan of Reconstruction times and the nativist organization founded in Atlanta in 1915 by William J. Simmons. While the new Klan's prestige was greatly enhanced by the 1915 film, "Birth of a Nation," which gave a romanticized picture of hooded horsemen defending white supremacy during Reconstruction, the new Klan was primarily directed against Catholics, immigrants, and radicals. Like the superpatriot organizations of the First World War era, the Klan was a highly moralistic group devoted to its own definition of one hundred percent Americanism. It defended prohibition and immigration restriction and combated sexual freedom, "modernist" religion, racial equality, and alien ideas. After a period of phenomenal growth in the early 1920's, it hit a peak membership in 1924 of some four and a half million. A dominant political force in such states as Oregon, California, Texas, Indiana, and Ohio, the Klan controlled the votes of governors and Senators. It played a critical role in the Democratic National Convention of 1924, where it fought a resolution condemning secret societies, and helped prevent the Catholic Al Smith from being nominated for President. There is no clearer illustration of a movement of countersubversion becoming in itself a secret and genuinely subversive force.

The fear of conspiracy subsided abruptly in the second half of the 1920's, although the Red Scare years had established patterns of thought that would become revitalized in later times of crisis. If a paranoid hostility to the New Deal marked the initial stage of a new phase of antiradicalism, it was also a continuation of earlier movements against "un-American" ideas. The rise of totalitarian regimes in Europe brought a new fear of creeping dictatorship and insidious propaganda. The New Deal's modest and somewhat amateurish efforts at public relations raised the specter of manipulated opinion. This fear was particularly pronounced among the isolationists who claimed that Jews and left-wing New Dealers controlled the mass media and were pushing America into a disastrous war against Hitler. The issue of intervention to aid the Allies rekindled a vicious, if largely underground, form of anti-Semitism. And while the Japanese attack on Pearl Harbor created a national unity which contrasted sharply with the divisions of the opinion over the First World War, President Roosevelt's actions of 1940 and 1941 raised suspicions that lingered in many minds. Thus this period ended debating questions similar to those with which it began. Had Americans been deceived by an international plot? Had a wily President betrayed the people in order to save England and the Jews? Was there not a simple explanation for the nation's involvement in the complexities of a power-hungry world?

Shall It Be Again? (1922)

JOHN KENNETH TURNER

During the war the American public was bombarded with the official anti-German propaganda of the Creel Committee, which greatly exaggerated German barbarism and the altruism of the Allies. Rejecting the official view of the war as a great crusade against evil, writers like John Kenneth Turner reasoned that American foreign policy had been in conformity with the interests of Wall Street and the Money Trust, and that these had in fact favored war for their own private profit. By 1922 this explanation, which simply repeated what socialists had been saying all along, fit the mood of many disenchanted Americans, who pictured themselves as dupes and who vowed "never to let it happen again."

Patriotism of the Profitmakers

To what extent was America's war a war for business?

Did Woodrow Wilson lead America into war in order to serve the selfish interests of the few?

The answer is determined by looking into the essential facts. In the first place, *Wall Street wanted war.*

Not a single recognized spokesman of our greatest financial and industrial interests, anywhere in public life, expressed opposition to the war during the critical weeks of February and March, 1917. On the contrary, our leading financiers themselves, who up to that period had seldom been quoted on political questions, personally endorsed the proposition of belligerency.

April 4, the New York *Times* said: "Not since Woodrow Wilson became President has any utterance of his met with such instant and hearty approval by leaders in the financial district as his war address to Congress." This conclusion was backed by a column of quotations. "It [the war message] was . . . exactly right," said Judge Gary, head of the U.S. Steel Corporation. "It was 100 percent American," said Frank Vanderlip, moving genius of the American International Corporation and head of the National City Bank. "The President's ad-

---

From John Kenneth Turner, *Shall It Be Again?* (New York, 1922), pp. 256–257, 261.

dress was magnificent," said James Wallace, head of the Guaranty Trust Company. "It was well worth waiting for," said A. Barton Hepburn, another of our leading bankers. "The speech breathes the true spirit of the American people," said Martin Carey, of the Standard Oil Company. These opinions of the President's address, said the *Times,* "were echoed in one form or another by bankers, brokers, and executives in large number." . . .

March 26, at the solicitation of the Chamber of Commerce of the United States, J. P. Morgan and Co. loaned the government $1,000,000 without interest and without security, for the purchase of supplies immediately desired in anticipation of war.

During March, J. P. Morgan, Mrs. E. H. Harriman, George Baker, Jr., Vincent Astor, and others of their class offered their private yachts for service as submarine chasers in the event of war. At the same time, Wall Street was giving the President the fullest assurances that it was ready to cooperate also in the matter of loans. March 23, we find Thomas W. Lamont delivering a patriotic address entitled "America Financially Prepared," in which he promised: "If the Treasurer should decide to issue a government obligation tomorrow for a billion dollars, the whole sum would be waiting for it."

One of the most effective things that big business did, in those critical weeks, in working its will for war, was to demand naval guns and crews for its ships and to tie up transportation and commerce until that demand was satisfied.

Immediately after the breaking of diplomatic relations, the International Mercantile Marine Company—a British-controlled corporation, in which, however, America's most powerful financiers are interested—began holding its ships in port. February 12 its president made formal application for naval guns and crews. At the same time the railroads, which are under the control of the same American financiers who are interested in the International Mercantile Marine Company, began to refuse shipments because of alleged congestion due to the ships' being held in port. This tying up of American domestic commerce "by Germany" was played upon with great effect by the press. When, on February 26, President Wilson appeared before Congress asking for authority to arm merchant ships, he was able to offer the argument that "our own commerce has suffered, is suffering . . . rather because so many of our ships are timidly keeping to their home ports than because American ships have been sunk."

Had there been any good reason to believe that the means of "protection," which the International Mercantile Marine demanded, would in fact protect, its demand for such means might be taken as sincere. But for many months, ships flying the British flag had been trying precisely the same means of "protection," and it had been proven that these means did not protect. Five weeks later, the President himself admitted that such protective measures were futile, *although meanwhile no new incidents had happened to render that truth any clearer than before.*

We may well take the President's word for this, especially as no one—much less the officials of the International Mercantile Marine—disputed it. Since this truth was as clear on February 26 as on April 2, the tying up of American shipping by big business in February and March cannot be explained in any other way except as a conspiracy to promote war sentiment. . . .

In February, 1917, Representative Calloway, on the floor of Congress, charged the Morgan interests with having, in March, 1915, organized and financed a huge propaganda machine embracing twelve influential publishers and 179 selected newspapers, for the purpose of manufacturing sentiment favorable to American participation in the war. These charges were renewed in May, 1921, by Representative Michelson of Illinois. The latter called attention to the fact that, in his history of the war, Gabriel Hanotaux tells of a conference with the late Robert Bacon, then a member of the Morgan firm, in 1914, in which he and Bacon drew up plans and specifications for a great scare campaign in this country. Hanotaux also suggests that France was ready to make peace in 1914, but was dissuaded by Bacon and other American politicians, who gave assurances that they could ultimately bring America into the war on the side of France.

These charges are worth recording, but they are important only when taken in connection with other evidence. As a means to establishing the wish of our great financial interests for war, at least for some time before it was declared, they do not need to be proven. For, aside from the circumstantial evidence here given, any one who has read the Pujo Committee report on the Money Trust, showing the concentration of credit in the hands of three great banks, and the control of small banks by the big ones—and any one who appreciates the dependence of the more powerful organs of the press upon the dominant business interests of the communities which they serve, and especially upon the banks—will understand that the propaganda storm of the months preceding our entrance into the war would have been impossible without the approval and instigation of Wall Street.

The Hun within Our Gates (1917)

THEODORE ROOSEVELT

Theodore Roosevelt was an incredibly complex and multi-faceted figure who was by no means at his best during the First World War. Exasperated by Woodrow Wilson's early expressions of neutrality, he became a passionate advocate of intervention and a bitter foe of anyone less committed to the war than he.

The Hun within our gates is the worst of the foes of our own household, whether he is the paid or the unpaid agent of Germany. Whether he is pro-German or poses as a pacifist, or a peace-at-any-price man, matters little. He is the enemy of the United States. Senators and Congressmen like Messrs. Stone, La Follette and Maclemore belong in Germany and it is a pity they cannot be sent there. . . . Such men are among the worst of the foes of our own household; and so are the sham philanthropists and sinister agitators and the wealthy creatures without patriotism who support and abet them. Our Government has seemed afraid to grapple with these people. It is permitting thousands of allies of Berlin to sow the seeds of treason and sedition in this country. The I.W.W. boasts its defiance of all law, and many of its members exultingly proclaim that in their war against industry in the United States they are endeavoring to give the Government so much to do that it will have no troops to spare for Europe. Every district where the I.W.W. starts rioting should be placed under martial law, and cleaned up by military methods. The German-language papers carry on a consistent campaign in favor of Germany against England. They should be put out of existence for the period of this war. The Hearst papers, more ably edited than the German sheets, play the Kaiser's game in a similar way. When they keep

From Theodore Roosevelt, *The Foes of Our Own Household* (New York, 1917), pp. 293–295. Reprinted by permission of the Theodore Roosevelt Association.

within the law they should at least be made to feel the scorn felt for them by every honest American. Wherever any editor can be shown to be purveying treason in violation of law he should be jailed until the conflict is over. Every disloyal German-born citizen should have his naturalization papers recalled and should be interned during the term of the war. Action of this kind is especially necessary in order to pick out the disloyal but vociferous minority of citizens of German descent from the vast but silent majority of entirely loyal citizens of German descent who otherwise will suffer from a public anger that will condemn all alike. Every disloyal native-born American should be disfranchised and interned. It is time to strike our enemies at home heavily and quickly. Every copperhead in this country is an enemy to the Government, to the people, to the army and to the flag, and should be treated as such.

This pro-German, anti-American propaganda has been carried on for years prior to the war, and its treasonable activities are performed systematically to-day. . . . These men support and direct the pro-German societies. They incite disloyal activities among the Russian Jews. They finance the small groups of Irish-Americans whose hatred for England makes them traitors to the United States. They foment seditious operations among the German–American socialists and the I.W.W.'s. They support the German-language periodicals. Their campaigns range from peace movements and anti-draft schemings to open efforts in favor of sedition and civil war.

These traitors are following out the vicious teachings of Prussian philosophers; there is no cause for surprise at their treasonable course. Unfortunately there is cause for surprise at the license which the Administration extends to their detestable activities. In this attitude the Administration is repeating its course of indifference to world-threatening aggression, and of submission to studied acts of murderous violence, which resulted, after two and a half years of injury and humiliation, in our being dragged unprepared into war.

If during those two and a half years a policy of courage, and of consistent and far-sighted Americanism, had been followed, either the brutal invasion of our national rights would have been checked without war or else if we had been forced into war we would have brought it instantly to a victorious end. Our failure to prepare is responsible for our failure now efficiently to act in the war. In exactly the same fashion it may be set down as certain that continuance of the present craven policy of ignoring sedition and paltering with treason will encourage and aid German autocracy, and will be translated either into terrible lists of Americans slain and crippled on the battlefield or else into an ignoble peace which will leave Germany free at some future time to resume its campaign against America and against liberty-loving mankind.

Awake! America (1918)

WILLIAM T. HORNADAY

William Hornaday's book was one of many publications sponsored by the American Defense Society, which moved from supporting military preparedness in 1915 to virulent attacks on Germans, radicals, immigrants, and Jews.

For forty years and more the Huns of Germany went masquerading under cloaks and dominos of "kultur" that deceived the whole world. They diligently exploited camouflages of "German art," "science," "music" and "literature," successfully distracted attention from the gross and the material side of German character, and everywhere set up idols made in Germany with feet of clay. . . .

And the new Hun of Germany,—what of him?

With his mask and his cloak now contemptuously thrown aside, his misshapen and ugly form now nakedly stands forth, a horrible surprise to the civilized world. His former friends and admirers, and many of his relatives, also, now regard this new gorilla with horror and aversion. His mentality and his moral principles are even more warped and twisted than his physique,—a combination of big body, small head, and reptilian heart. Of moral principles, of bed-rock honor and gentlemanly ethics he has none. He even enjoys jabbing and pin-pricking the weak and the helpless, morning, noon and night; just as a cruel brute of a boy loves to torture kittens. If you doubt this, read about the German occupation of Belgium and northern France. On the coldest day it will make your blood boil. . . .

After twenty years of snoring, about one-tenth of one per cent of the American people have aroused sufficiently to realize that for

From William T. Hornaday, *Awake! America: Object Lessons and Warnings* (New York, 1918), pp. 71–72, 80, 82, 106, 108, 110, 112, 118.

twenty years the greedy Huns have been thrusting and driving and worming the German language into American public schools; and along with it there have been jammed into the hands of American school pupils hundreds of thousands of German readers which openly and brazenly extol the Kaiser and the military power of Germany, and pan-Germanism generally. . . .

This situation was first exposed in New York City in the six weeks between December 1, 1917, and the middle of January, 1918. It was brought about chiefly by the movement of the American Defense Society against disloyal teachers in the public schools, coupled with a demand for the expulsion of the German language from all the schools of New York. . . .

The question is, how long will it take to convince ignorant, weak-kneed and pro-German boards of education in the United States that it is folly, and an utter waste of good money and time, to teach to American youth the language of our deadliest enemy,—the enemy that would tear the very heart out of America if it could? How long, oh Lord! how long will it take the American people to WAKE UP? . . .

Germany has made herself the tremendous power that she is partly by welding together and maintaining her Germanic stock, and by as far as possible preventing mixtures with the Slavic race. That is one reason why millions of Germany to-day are a unit, working like one vast machine, to serve the one purpose of expanding, domineering, grasping, and selling "Germany over all." . . .

Here in America, ever since the United States began housekeeping, we have pursued an exactly opposite course. Not only have we permitted the continuous inflow of alien races from all quarters of the globe, but we have fostered and encouraged it. Under the fatal spell of our perfectly idiotic eagerness for quantity in immigration, we have flung aside nearly all considerations making for quality! Along with desirable accessions, which have done much to build up this country, America has become the dumping-ground for the ashes and the cinders of all nations. . . .

Meanwhile we have to reckon with alien socialism, which day by day is becoming more bold, more clamorous, and in the large cities more ugly and dangerous. We must be prepared for a clash with that element, for the socialists themselves predict that it surely is coming. . . .

I have before me now a letter on the stationery of the Intercollegiate Socialist Society (70 Fifth Avenue), and I think it will give the reader a shock. It bears the names of sixty American universities and colleges, great and small, and it shows how thoroughly honeycombed and tunneled are our higher institutions of learning by socialism. . . .

"Come out from among them, my people!" saith the prophet. The name of your party has been irretrievably disgraced. The odium of continued associations with the Bolsheviki and the I.W.W. gang is not for you. You and the students of your institutions are not disloyal; you do not oppose the war for liberty; you do not discourage enlistments or curse the draft; and you do not refuse to subscribe to the Liberty bonds which represent a part of the price we have to pay for the liberty of mankind.

It is time for all the American socialists to make a sweeping change in the name of their party, and cast out from their ranks all the American Bolsheviki. . . .

And how is it about the radical socialists of America,—those who are throwing out of their party all the moderates, all the American socialists?

In the first place, they are of exotic birth and growth. The leaders who have not been driven out of that party are Russian Jews who mentally are no more fit to lead "the people" than are the Russian "soldiers" who gave up Galicia to the Germans without firing a shot, and even stole the artillery horses from their field guns in order to ride them in that shameful retreat. And after all the Jew-baiting in Russia, and our government's championship of the Russian Jews, think of the Russian Jews in America who now refuse to buy Liberty bonds, and do everything in their power to promote the peace that Germany wants! What shall we do with such people?

Their influence among the ignorant Jews of New York is very deadly. They tend to discredit all loyal Jews. Really the patriotic Jews of New York should do something to protect their race from the parasites who live by preying upon it, and at times disgrace it.

The teaching and advocacy of this foreign radical socialism should not be permitted in any institution of learning in America. American socialism now is dead; and in the name of common sense, why spread the doctrines of cobras and rattlesnakes?

The Web (1919)

EMERSON HOUGH

Emerson Hough's The Web *was publicized as the "authorized history" of the American Protective League. During the war the League was a major force in widening the attack on "German influences" to include everything from prolabor sentiment to lack of zeal in purchasing Liberty bonds. The following selection illustrates the remarkable logic that lay behind such fanaticism: effective propaganda made people "nervous, uneasy, or discontented"; the American people were obviously nervous, uneasy, and discontented; therefore, German propaganda was the source of domestic difficulties.*

Although there was great pressure within the League to continue its crusade against un-Americanism into the postwar period, the Attorney General made it clear that the Department of Justice could no longer sanction citizen spies and underground vigilantes. The American Legion and other groups soon took over many of its activities in defense of "one hundred percent Americanism."

Let no one undervalue the work of propaganda. No army is better than its morale, and no army's morale is better than that of the people which send it to the front. The entire purpose of enemy propaganda is to lessen the morale either of an army or a people; and that precisely was Germany's purpose with us.

Anything is good propaganda which makes a people nervous, uneasy or discontented. Many of the stories which Germany spread in America seemed clumsy at first, they were so easily detected. Yet they did their work, even though sometimes it would have seemed that the rumors put out were against Germany and not for her. These rumors, repeated and varied, did serve a great purpose in America—they made us restless and uneasy. That certainly is true.

One of the favorite objects of the German propaganda was the Red Cross work. Hardly any American but has heard one or other story about the Red Cross. The result has been a very considerable lessening of the public confidence in that great organization. The average

---

From Emerson Hough, *The Web* (Chicago: The Reilly and Lee Co., 1919), pp. 62–63, 65–67, 71–73, 79, 133–134, 140.

man never runs down any rumor of this sort. At first he does not believe what he hears. At the fourth or fifth story of different sorts, all aiming at one object, he begins to hesitate, to doubt. Without any question, the Red Cross has suffered much from German propaganda. . . .

The report of Polish pogroms, general Jew killing expeditions by the Poles, were magnified and distorted, all with the purpose of making both the Poles and Jews dissatisfied with the conduct of the war. Continually these anti-Ally stories got out, and always they were hard to trace.

This form of propaganda, spread by word of mouth, was the most insidious and most widely spread of all forms. It was, of course, made the more easy by the excited state of mind of the people during war times. . . .

There was no way, shape nor manner in which Germany did not endeavor to embarrass us. She had, besides her carefully trained public speakers, her secret workers who had assigned to them definite objectives. For instance, it was known that the negro race would furnish a considerable number of soldiers for our army. A very wide German propaganda existed among the negroes in Georgia and Carolina, and in such northern cities as Indianapolis, where large numbers of that race were located. A certain German was indicted under seven counts for this manner of activity. It was proved that he had told a great many negro privates in the army that they would be mutilated if captured, and that they were going to starve to death in France if they ever got across. The horrors of war with the American forces were pointed out to these simple people; but, on the other hand it was explained to them that if they would work for the German interests, they would be allowed to set up a government of their own in America if Germany won the war! They were told Germany loved the negroes and believed in their equality with the white race in every way, and would support their government when once her war was won! . . .

It is known that in many towns the German element undertook to sow seeds of discontent in the minds of savings bank depositors. Rumors got out—no one could tell where they started—to the effect that the United States Government was going to confiscate all the savings of the people; that the bonds would never be paid off. Of course, all this was absurd, but it had its effect upon servant girls and others who were loyally putting their savings into the securities of the government. It cost a great deal of time and expense to run down such rumors.

The pulpit was a recognized part of the German system of spy work in America, as has elsewhere been noted. It is not just to accuse all Lutheran ministers of desecrating the cloth they wore. There are good Lutheran ministers who are loyal Americans without question. At the same time it is true that more charges have been brought against pastors of the Lutheran church, and charges of more specific nature, than against any other class or profession in our country. There are scores and hundreds of such reports which came into the National Headquarters of the A.P.L. from all parts of the country, more especially those parts which have heavy German settlements. These are so numerous that one cannot avoid calling the Lutheran pulpit in America one of the most active and poisonous influences which existed in America during the war. . . .

It has always been charged against the Germans in America that they were the most clannish of all the foreigners coming to settle in this country. They, longer than any other people, retain their own institutions, their own language, their own customs. In parts of the country there are schools which teach the German language more than they do the English—a practice which, in all likelihood, will be discontinued when the troops come back from France and Germany. Without any doubt or question, pro-German school teachers were German propagandists, usually of the indiscreet and hotheaded sort. . . .

Champaign, Illinois, is the home of the University of Illinois, and for some reason university towns seem to act as chutes for all sorts of independent thought. There are two strong German settlements in Champaign County, and a very strong German settlement in the city, where many residents have shown very pro-German tendencies. These German settlements have their own German schools, taught by their German Lutheran ministers under the pretense of teaching religion. Sentiment became so intense that the local A.P.L. Chief was requested by the Government to close these schools if possible. Some of them have reopened since the armistice. In such localities the Germans have been very independent and often quite outspoken, so that it was necessary in many cases for the A.P.L. to use influence to prevent violence to them. There were only one or two cases where the citizens got out of control, although many citizens of German descent refused to buy bonds and made disparaging remarks regarding the war.

The A.P.L. Chief says: "We were confronted with the problem of ousting five alien enemies at the University of Illinois, two of them regarded as dangerous. We also had to handle a cook at the aviation barracks, an alien enemy who was deliberately wasting food. We convicted the wife of a German minister in the Federal Court for making disloyal remarks. We had some difficulty with Russellites, Mennonites, and radical Socialists, but all have been kept in hand. . . ."

The greatest trial with which the American Protective League was identified was the genuine *cause célèbre* known all over the world as the I.W.W. trial. It began in the Federal Court for Chicago . . . and ended with ninety-seven convictions and sentences in one lot. The case was concluded at two in the afternoon of August 30, 1918. . . .

With this great case, the American Protective League had been connected practically all the time from the date of its own inception. It had men shadowing the suspects, men intercepting their mail, men ingratiating themselves into their good graces, men watching all their comings and goings, men transcribing and indexing the reports, men looking into the law in all its phases as bearing on these cases. No one knows how many A.P.L. operatives, in all the states from Michigan westward, worked on this case for months before an arrest was made. . . .

For months and years before the arrests, the Industrial Workers of the World, as they call themselves, had been notorious for their anarchy and violence. Countless acts of ruthlessness had marked their career; millions and perhaps billions in property had been destroyed by them; their leader had been tried for the murder of a governor of a Western state, though acquitted. Nothing lacked in their record of lawlessness and terror, and they were inspired by a Hun-like frightfulness as well as a Hun-like cunning which for a time both excited and baffled the agents of the law in a dozen Western states. . . .

Their literature was a continuous blasphemy. Cursing the name of the Savior was nothing to their writers. They put lime in men's shoes and burned their feet to the bone. They had a special sort of club they used in attacking "scabs." It had short, sharp nails driven along it, painted the color of the club so they could not easily be seen. The victim would catch at the club to wrest it from his assailant. It was then jerked through his hands, often tearing out the sinews, always scarring and often maiming him forever. Always they were cowards. To injure and not destroy was part of their religion. "Strike while you work" meant to disable a machine for a while and so to stop work for the crew or for the whole plant. "Feed the kitty more cream" meant to use more emery on bearings, to do more dirt in factories, to wreck and mar and mutilate more cunningly and covertly—and to escape by feigning the innocent laboring man. If they were not all Huns, they had the foul Hun imagination, and also the methods of the Hun.

By December of 1918, the trial of a half hundred more alleged I.W.W. men was progressing at Sacramento, California. The attempt of the prosecution there was to show a nation-wide plot against the Government of the United States. And again, A.P.L. had the evidence ready, ticketed and tabulated, for A.P.L. covers all of the United States and not merely one part. On January 16, 1919, forty-six of the defendants were convicted.

If we have 100,000 I.W.W. members such as these yet among us, and internment camps full of Germans and pro-Germans, would there not seem need for a house cleaning? It is time now for a new American point of view. We are not going to allow America to be used as it has been by these men. *Fear* at least they shall understand.

A Program for Counteracting Seditious Activities (1920)

CLAYTON R. LUSK

In 1919 and 1920 the New York State legislature went on the offensive against all local manifestations of international radicalism. Five socialists who had been legally elected to the legislature were refused their seats and publicly denounced. Clayton R. Lusk, a fervent antiradical, assumed leadership of a legislative committee charged with investigating all seditious activities in the state. His committee's report reviewed the history and aims of revolutionary radicalism and recommended a sweeping program of state indoctrination to protect young minds from the ideas of Karl Marx.

Seeing the situation as we do, as something transcending not only the State but the nation, and as reaching down to the fundamentals of man's nature and of the organization of society, the Committee feels that it must appeal in the strongest way to every member of the Legislature, to every man who holds any position of authority or of influence, to take every possible step, not only to understand the cardinal

From *Revolutionary Radicalism: Its History, Purpose and Tactics . . . Being the Report of the Joint Legislative Committee Investigating Seditious Activities* (Albany, 1920), pp. 14–18.

facts of the situation but to devote his thoughts and his acts to a crusade in support of every agency, every policy, that will counteract and defeat this movement. Only complete knowledge will give us the leadership that is absolutely necessary, a leadership that will be based on clear conviction and a feeling for the necessity of action: a leadership that will understand that there must be a revival of religious and moral standards as the basis of any political and economic program. The community must be appealed to, must be given the facts, must be made to see the causes and the remedies, must be made to band itself together as a civic force in every center of the State in action that shall not be the action of individuals, the sporadic, ineffectual duplicating action that will lead us nowhere. If American ideals of individual freedom and initiative are to be maintained, every citizen must be militant in their defense.

But the very fact of organizing for social defense and for social offense against those who are attacking our life is in itself dangerous, because unless we are keen of insight, these very organizations are going to be, as they have been in the past, taken possession of by astute, hardworking, clearheaded revolutionists, and turned from the purposes of reconstruction to purposes of contamination.

As much energy and organized thought and action must be put by our leading men into the solution of economic and sociological problems as they have given to the solution of their own business problems. They must show as much altruistic energy in the defense as the radical leaders have been showing in the attack. The disjointed, unprincipled, unpractical or sentimental altruism which is doing so much harm as practiced in university, in church, in philanthropic and in social circles must be shown up or made to understand the realities and dangers of its efforts, and be led, by this new insight, to shift to the camp of constructive action.

The re-education of the educators and of the ecucated class must go hand in hand with the reorganization and extension of our educational system. We cannot give the right point of view to our foreign population and to our children unless it is clearly and firmly ingrained in all of us. . . .

Recommendations for Educational Legislation

. . . It must be observed that no matter how imposing are the school buildings, how elaborate the curricula, how sound the text books, the success of the school system depends in the last analysis upon the character and viewpoint of the teachers and instructors who carry out the program, and who influence the pupils with whom they come in contact. It is apparent that these teachers must be acquainted with the forces at play upon public opinion. They must recognize the influences which seek to undermine the confidence and respect which their pupils or students should have for the government and laws of this commonwealth. They should be trained and eager to combat those influences, and, in order that they may do this, it is essential that they themselves shall be in full accord and sympathy with our form of government and the system of society under which we live. There is a further element which has been overlooked in the selection of teachers, and that is character. In the main, the teachers in our public schools and private and philanthropic institutions have been chosen because of their academic and pedagogical attainments. . . .

Having these considerations in mind, the Committee has recommended that a law be placed upon the statute books of this State which shall require the teachers in public schools to secure, before the first of January, 1921, a special certificate certifying that they are persons of good character and that they are loyal to the institutions of the State and Nation.

In another portion of this report descriptions are given of various so-called schools of social reform, masquerading under different names and being carried on by various subversive organizations. An examination of their curricula shows that the fundamental purpose of these schools is to destroy the respect of the students for the institutions of the United States. Many of them advocate the overthrow of the governments of this State and of the United States by force, violence or unlawful means. In many schools and courses of lectures and classes, class hatred and contempt for government are being preached, and all those fundamentals which make for good citizenship are either ignored or ridiculed. It is the fundamental purpose of these institutions to develop agitators to enter the labor fields, to preach the doctrine of revolt, and to divide the people of the United States into contending classes so that they may be instrumental in hastening the social revolution. . . .

To meet this situation the Committee recommends to the Legislature the passage of a law requiring all schools, courses and classes that are not now under the supervision or control of the Department of Education, or are not created and maintained by well-recognized religious denominations or sects, to procure a license from the Board of Regents of this State.

The Case against the Reds (1920)

A. MITCHELL PALMER

Forum *magazine, which printed Palmer's justifications for arresting and deporting aliens, stated that the Attorney General had in his files detailed plans for a nationwide revolution. In the face of such a threat, no "nice distinctions" could be drawn between beliefs and theories advanced by radicals and their actual violation of laws.*

In this brief review of the work which the Department of Justice has undertaken, to tear out the radical seeds that have entangled American ideas in their poisonous theories, I desire not merely to explain what the real menace of communism is, but also to tell how we have been compelled to clean up the country almost unaided by any virile legislation. Though I have not been embarrassed by political opposition, I have been materially delayed because the present sweeping processes of arrests and deportation of seditious aliens should have been vigorously pushed by Congress last spring. . . .

The anxiety of that period in our responsibility when Congress, ignoring the seriousness of these vast organizations that were plotting to overthrow the Government, failed to act, has passed. The time came when it was obviously hopeless to expect the hearty co-operation of Congress, in the only way to stamp out these seditious societies in their open defiance of law by various forms of propaganda.

Like a prairie-fire, the blaze of revolution was sweeping over every American institution of law and order a year ago. It was eating its way into the homes of the American workman, its sharp tongues of revolutionary heat were licking the altars of the churches, leaping into the belfry of the school bell, crawling into the sacred corners of American homes, seeking to replace marriage vows with libertine laws, burning up the foundations of society.

Robbery, not war, is the ideal of communism. This has been dem-

From A. Mitchell Palmer, "The Case Against the 'Reds,' " Forum (February 1920, pp. 173–176.

onstrated in Russia, Germany, and in America. As a foe, the anarchist is fearless of his own life, for his creed is a fanaticism that admits no respect of any other creed. Obviously it is the creed of any criminal mind, which reasons always from motives impossible to clean thought. Crime is the degenerate factor in society.

Upon these two basic certainties, first that the "Reds" were criminal aliens, and secondly that the American Government must prevent crime, it was decided that there could be no nice distinctions drawn between the theoretical ideals of the radicals and their actual violations of our national laws. . . .

It has always been plain to me that when American citizens unite upon any national issue, they are generally right, but it is sometimes difficult to make the issue clear to them. If the Department of Justice could succeed in attracting the attention of our optimistic citizens to the issue of internal revolution in this country, we felt sure there would be no revolution. The Government was in jeopardy. My private information of what was being done by the organization known as the Communist Party of America, with headquarters in Chicago, of what was being done by the Communist Internationale under their manifesto planned at Moscow last March by Trotzky, Lenine, and others, addressed "To the Proletariats of All Countries," of what strides the Communist Labor Party was making, removed all doubt. In this conclusion we did not ignore the definite standards of personal liberty, of free speech, which is the very temperament and heart of the people. The evidence was examined with the utmost care, with a personal leaning toward freedom of thought and word on all questions. . . .

My information showed that communism in this country was an organization of thousands of aliens, who were direct allies of Trotzky. Aliens of the same misshapen caste of mind and indecencies of character, and it showed that they were making the same glittering promises of lawlessness, of criminal autocracy to Americans, that they had made to the Russian peasants. How the Department of Justice discovered upwards of 60,000 of these organized agitators of the Trotzky doctrine in the United States, is the confidential information upon which the Government is now sweeping the nation clean of such alien filth.

The International Jew: The World's Foremost Problem (1920)

THE DEARBORN INDEPENDENT

There was nothing peculiarly American about the outburst of anti-Semitic hysteria which followed the First World War. The Protocols of the Elders of Zion *aroused considerable excitement in England, where newspapers like the* Morning Post *anticipated many of the themes and arguments that would later appear in Henry Ford's* Dearborn Independent. *But the* Independent, *whose circulation included Ford dealers across the country, was able to graft European anti-Semitic fabrications on native antiurban and anti-intellectual traditions. At a time when Americans were painfully conscious of disrupting change, it was illuminating to discover that social disintegration had long been the prime method of Jewish conspirators aspiring toward world domination.*

Who it was that first entitled these documents with the name of the "Elders of Zion" is not known. It would be possible without serious mutilation of the documents to remove all hint of Jewish authorship, and yet retain all the main points of the most comprehensive program for world subjugation that has ever come to public knowledge.

Yet it must be said that thus to eliminate all hint of Jewish authorship would be to bring out a number of contradictions which do not exist in the Protocols in their present form. The purpose of the plan revealed in the Protocols is to undermine all authority in order that a new authority in the form of autocracy may be set up. Such a plan could not emanate from a ruling class which already possessed authority, although it might emanate from anarchists. But anarchists do not avow autocracy as the ultimate condition they seek. The authors might be conceived as a company of French Subversives such as existed at the time of the French Revolution and had the infamous Duc d'Orleans as their leader, but this would involve a contradiction between the fact that those Subversives have passed away, and the fact

From *The International Jew: The World's Foremost Problem, Being a Reprint of a Series of Articles Appearing in "The Dearborn Independent" from May 22 to October 2, 1920* (n.p., 1920), pp. 109–112, 114–116, 118–128, 137–140.

that the program announced in these Protocols is being steadily carried out, not only in France, but throughout Europe, and very noticeably in the United States.

In their present form, which bears evidence of being their original form, there is no contradiction. The allegation of Jewish authorship seems essential to the consistency of the plan.

If these documents were the forgeries which Jewish apologists claim them to be, the forgers would probably have taken pains to make Jewish authorship so clear that their anti-Semitic purpose could easily have been detected. But only twice is the term "Jew" used in them. After one has read much further than the average reader usually cares to go into such matters, one comes upon the plans for the establishment of the World Autocrat, and only then it is made clear of what lineage he is to be. . . .

These quotations will illustrate the style of the Protocols in making reference to the parties involved. It is "we" for the writers, and "Gentiles" for those who are being written about. This is brought out very clearly in the Fourteenth Protocol:

In this divergence between the Gentiles and ourselves in ability to think and reason is to be seen clearly the seal of our election as the chosen people, as higher human beings, in contrast with the Gentiles who have merely instinctive and animal minds. They observe, but they do not foresee, and they invent nothing (except perhaps material things). It is clear from this that nature herself predestined us to rule and guide the world.

This, of course, has been the Jewish method of dividing humanity from the earliest times. The world was only Jew and Gentile; all that was not Jew was Gentile.

The use of the word Jew in the Protocol may be illustrated by this passage in the eighth section:

For the time being, until it will be safe to give responsible government positions to our brother Jews, we shall entrust them to people whose past and whose characters are such that there is an abyss between them and the people.

This is the practice known as using "Gentile fronts" which is extensively practiced in the financial world today in order to cover up the evidences of Jewish control. How much progress has been made since these words were written is indicated by the occurrence at the San Francisco convention when the name of Judge Brandeis was proposed for President. It is reasonably to be expected that the public mind will be made more and more familiar with the idea of Jewish occupancy—which will be really a short step from the present degree of influence which the Jews exercise—of the highest office in the government. There is no function of the American Presidency in which the Jews have not already secretly assisted in a very important degree. Actual occupancy of the office is not necessary to enhance their power, but to promote certain things which parallel very closely the plans outlined in the Protocols now before us. . . .

Moreover, taking the Protocols at their face value, it is evident that the program outlined in these lecture notes was not a new one at the time the lectures were given. There is no evidence of its being of recent arrangement. There is almost the tone of a tradition, or a religion, in it all, as if it had been handed down from generation to generation through the medium of specially trusted and initiated men. There is no note of new discovery or fresh enthusiasm in it, but the certitude and calmness of facts long known and policies long confirmed by experiment. . . .

The criticisms which these Protocols pass upon the Gentiles for their stupidity are just. It is impossible to disagree with a single item in the Protocols' description of Gentile mentality and veniality. Even the most astute of the Gentile thinkers have been fooled into receiving as the motions of progress what has only been insinuated into the common human mind by the most insidious systems of propaganda. . . .

It is true that occasionally a keen observer has asserted that the recent debauch of luxury and extravagance was not due to the natural impulses of the people at all, but was systematically stimulated, foisted upon them by design. It is true that a few have discerned that more than half of what passes for "public opinion" is mere hired applause and booing and has never impressed the public mind.

But even with these clues here and there, for the most part disregarded, there has never been enough continuity and collaboration between those who were awake, to follow all the clues to their source. The chief explanation of the hold which the Protocols have had on many of the leading statesmen of the world for several decades is that they explain whence all these false influences come and what their purpose is. They give a clue to the modern maze. It is now time for the people to know. And whether the Protocols are judged as proving anything concerning the Jews or not, they constitute an education in the way the masses are turned about like sheep by influences which they do not understand. It is almost certain that once the principles of the Protocols are known widely and understood by the people, the criticism which they now rightly make of the Gentile mind will no longer hold good. . . .

Just to run through the Protocols and select the salient passages in which this view is expressed is to find a pretty complete philosophy of the motives and qualities of human beings.

Take these words from the First Protocol:

It should be noted that people with evil instincts are more numerous than those with good ones; therefore, the best results in governing them are attained by intimidation and violence, and not by academic argument. Every man aims for power; everyone desires to be a dictator, if possible; moreover, few would not sacrifice the good of others to attain their own ends.

People in masses and people of the masses are guided by exceptionally shallow passions, beliefs, customs, traditions and sentimental theories and are inclined toward party divisions, a fact which prevents any form of agreement, even when this is founded on a thoroughly logical basis. Every decision of the mob depends upon an accidental or prearranged majority, which, owing to its ignorance of the mysteries of political secrets, gives expression to absurd decisions that introduce anarchy into government.

In working out an expedient plan of action, it is necessary to take into consideration the meanness, the vacillation, the changeability of the crowd. ° ° ° It is necessary to realize that the force of the masses is blind, unreasoning and unintelligent, prone to listen now to the right, and now to the left. ° ° °

Our triumph has also been made easier because, in our relations with the people necessary to us, we have always played upon the most sensitive strings of the human mind—on calculation, greed, and the insatiable material desires of men. Each of these human weaknesses, taken separately, is capable of paralyzing initiative and placing the will of the people at the disposal of the purchaser of their activities.

In the Fifth Protocol, this shrewd observation on human nature is to be found:

In all times, nations as well as individuals, accepted words for acts. They have been satisfied by what is shown them, rarely noticing whether the promise has been followed by fulfillment. For this reason we will organize "show" institutions which will conspicuously display their devotion to progress.

And this from the Eleventh Protocol:

The Gentiles are like a flock of sheep. ° ° ° They will close their eyes to everything because we will promise them to return all the liberties taken away, after the enemies of peace have been subjugated and all the parties pacified. Is it worth while to speak of how long they will have to wait? For what have we conceived all this program and instilled its measures into the minds of the Gentiles without giving them the possibility of examining its underside, if it is not for the purpose of attaining by circuitous methods that which is unattainable to our scattered race by a direct route?

Notice also this very shrewd observation upon the "joiners" of secret societies—this estimate being made by the Protocols to indicate how easily these societies may be used to further the plan:

Usually it is the climbers, careerists and people, generally speaking, who are not serious, who most readily join secret societies, and we shall find them easy to handle and through them operate the mechanism of our projected machine.

. . . The method is one of disintegration. Break up the people into parties and sects. Sow abroad the most promising and utopian of ideas and you will do two things: you will always find a group to cling to each idea you throw out; and you will find this partisanship dividing and estranging the various groups. The authors of the Protocols show in detail how this is to be done. Not one idea, but a mass of ideas are to be thrown out, and there is to be no unity among them. The purpose is *not* to get the people thinking one thing, but to think so diversely about so many different things that there will be no unity among them. The result of this will be vast disunity, vast unrest —and that is the result aimed for.

When once the solidarity of Gentile society is broken up—and the name "Gentile society" is perfectly correct, for human society is overwhelmingly Gentile—then this solid wedge of another idea which is not at all affected by the prevailing confusion can make its way unsuspectedly to the place of control. It is well enough known that a body of 20 trained police or soldiers can accomplish more than a disordered mob of a thousand persons. So the minority initiated into the plan can do more with a nation or a world broken into a thousand antagonistic parties, than any of the parties could do. "Divide and rule" is the motto of the Protocols. . . .

In this manner, theory after theory has been exploited among the masses, theory after theory has been found to be impracticable and has been discarded, but the result is precisely that which the program of the Protocols aims for—with the discarding of each theory, society is a little more broken than it was before. It is a little more helpless before its exploiters. It is a little more confused as to where to look for leadership. As a consequence society falls an easy victim again to a theory which promises it the good it seeks, and the failure of this theory leaves it still more broken. There is no longer any such thing as public opinion. Distrust and division are everywhere. And in the midst of the confusion everyone is dimly aware that there is a higher group that is not divided at all, but is getting exactly what it wants by means of the confusion that obtains all around. It will be shown, as claimed by the Protocols, that most of the disruptive theories abroad in the world today are of Jewish origin; it will also be shown that the one solid unbroken group in the world today, the group that knows where it wants to go and is going there regardless of the condition of society, is the Jewish group. . . .

The modern theory of "ferment," that out of all the unrest and change and transvaluation of values a new and better mankind is to be evolved is not borne out by any fact on the horizon. It is palpably a theory whose purpose is to make a seeming good out of that which is undeniable evil. The theories which *cause the disruption* and the theory which *explains the disruption as good,* come from the same source. The whole science of economics, conservative and radical, capitalistic and anarchistic, is of Jewish origin. This is another of the announcements of the Protocols which the facts confirm.

Now, all this is accomplished, not by acts, but by words. The *word-brokers* of the world, those who wish words to do duty for things, in their dealings with the world outside their class, are undoubtedly the Jewish group—the international Jews with which these articles deal—and their philosophy and practice are precisely set forth in the Protocols. . . .

(It is to be hoped that the reader, as his eye passes over these details of the Program, is also permitting his mind to pass over the trend of events, to see if he may detect for himself these very developments in the life and thought of the past few years.)

To prevent them from really thinking out anything themselves, we shall deflect their attention to amusements, games, pastimes, excitements and people's palaces. Such interests will distract their minds completely from questions on which we might be obliged to struggle with them. Becoming less and less accustomed to independent thinking, people will express themselves in unison with us because we alone offer new lines of thought—of course through persons whom they do not consider as in any way connected with us.

In this same Protocol it is plainly stated what is the purpose of the output of "liberal" theories, of which Jewish writers, poets, rabbis, societies and influences are the most prolific sources:

The role of the liberal Utopians will be completely played out when our government is recognized. Until that time they will perform good service. For that reason *we will continue to direct thought into all the intricacies of fantastic theories, new and supposedly progressive.* Surely we have been completely successful in turning the witless heads of the Gentiles by the word "progress."

Here is the whole program of confusing, enervating and trivializing the mind of the world. And it would be a most outlandish thought to put into words, were it not possible to show that this is just what has been done, and is still being done, by agencies which are highly lauded and easy to be identified among us.

A recent writer in a prominent magazine has pointed out what he calls the impossibility of the Jewish ruling group being allied in one common World Program because, as he showed, there were Jews acting as the leading minds in all the divisions of present-day opinion. There were Jews at the head of the capitalists, Jews at the head of the labor unions, and Jews at the head of those more radical organizations which find even the labor unions too tame. There is a Jew at the head of the judiciary of England and a Jew at the head of Sovietism in Russia. How can you say, he asked, that they are united, when they represent so many points of view?

The common unity, the possible common purpose of it all, is thus expressed in the Ninth Protocol:

People of all opinions and of all doctrines are at our service, restorers of monarchy, demagogues, Socialists, communists and other Utopians. We have put them all to work. Every one of them from his point of view is undermining the last remnant of authority, is trying to overthrow all existing order. All the governments have been tormented by these actions. But we will not give them peace until they recognize our super-government.

The function of the *idea* is referred to in the Tenth Protocol also:

When we introduced *the poison of liberalism* into the government organism, its entire political complexion changed.

The whole outlook of these Protocols upon the world is that the *idea* may be made a most potent poison. The authors of these documents do not believe in liberalism, they do not believe in democracy, but they lay plans for the constant preaching of these ideas because of their power to break up society, to divide it into groups, to destroy the power of collective opinion through a variety of convictions. The poison of an idea is their most relied-on weapon.

The plan of thus using ideas extends to education:

We have misled, stupefied and demoralized the youth of the Gentiles by means of education in principles and theories, patently false to us, but which we have inspired.—Protocol 9.

It extends also to family life:

Having in this way inspired everybody with the thought of his own importance, we will break down the influence of family life among the Gentiles, and its educational importance.—Protocol 10.

And in a passage which might well provide the material for long examination and contemplation by the thoughtful reader, this is said:

Until the time is ripe, let them amuse themselves. ° ° ° Let *those theories of life which we have induced them to regard as the dictates of science* play the most important role for them. To this end we shall endeavor to inspire blind confidence in these theories by means of our Press. ° ° °
Note the successes we have arranged in *Darwinism, Marxism,* and *Nietzscheism.* The demoralizing effect of these doctrines upon the minds of the Gentiles should be evident at least to us.—Protocol 2.

That this disintegration and division of Gentile society was proceeding at a favorable rate when the Protocols were uttered is evident from every line of them. For it must be remembered that the Protocols are not bidding for support for a proposed program, but are announcing progress on a program which has been in process of fulfillment for "centuries" and "from ancient times." They contain a series of statements regarding things accomplished, as well as a forelook at things yet to be accomplished. The split of Gentile society was very satisfactorily proceeding in 1896, or thereabouts, when these oracles were uttered. . . .

But a deeper division is aimed for, and there are signs of even this coming to pass. Indeed, in Russia it has already come to pass, *the spectacle of a Gentile lower class led by Jewish leaders against a Gentile upper class!* In the First Protocol, describing the effects of a speculative industrial system upon the people, it is said that this sort of economic folly—

° ° ° has already created and will continue to create a society which is disillusioned, cold and heartless. Such a society is completely estranged from politics and religion. Lust of gold will be the only guide of the people. ° ° ° THEN, not for the sake of good, nor even for the sake of riches, but solely on account of their hatred of the privileged classes, the lower classes of the Gentiles will follow us in the struggle against our rivals for power, the Gentiles of the intellectual classes.

. . . If that struggle were to occur today, the leaders of the Gentile insurgents against Gentile society would be Jewish leaders. They are in the leader's place now—not only in Russia, but also in the United States.

❖

. . . Many a father and mother, many a sound-minded, uncorrupted young person, and thousands of teachers and publicists have cried out against *luxury*. Many a financier, observing the manner in which the people earned and flung away their money, has warned against *luxury*. Many an economist, knowing that the nonessential industries were consuming men and materials that were necessary to the stabilizing of essential industries; knowing that men are making knick-knacks who should be making steel; knowing that men are engaged in making gew-gaws who should be working on the farm; that materials are going into articles that are made only to *sell* and never to *use*, and that materials are thus diverted from the industries that support the people's life—every observer knowing this crazy insistence on luxurious nonessentials has lifted up a strong voice against it.

But, according to these Protocols, we have been starting at the wrong end. The people, it is true, buy these senseless *nonessentials* which are called *luxuries*. But the people do not devise them. And the people grow tired of them one by one. But the stream of varieties continues—always something else being thrust at the people, dangled before their eyes, set bobbing down the avenue on enough manikins to give the impression that it is "style"; newspaper print and newspaper pictures; movie pictures; stage costumes enough to force the new thing into "fashion" with a kind of force and compulsion which no really worthy essential thing can command.

Where does it come from? What power exists whose long experience and deliberate intent enable it to frivolize the people's minds and tastes and compel them to pay most of their money for it too? Why this spasm of luxury and extravagance through which we have just passed? How did it occur that before luxury and extravagance were apparent, all the material to provoke and inflame them had been prepared beforehand and shipped beforehand, ready for the stampede which also had been prepared?

If the people of the United States would stop to consider, when the useless and expensive thing is offered them—if they would trace its origin, trace the course of the enormous profits made out of it, trace the whole movement to flood the market with uselessness and extravagance and thus demoralize the Gentile public financially, intellectually and socially—if, in short, it could be made clear to them that Jewish financial interests are not only pandering to the loosest elements in human nature, but actually engaged in a calculated effort to render them loose in the first place and keep them loose—it would do more than anything else to stop this sixfold waste—the waste of material, the waste of labor, the waste of Gentile money, the waste of Gentile mind, the waste of Jewish talent, and the worse than waste of Israel's real usefulness to the world.

We say the *Gentile public* is the victim of this stimulated trade in useless luxuries. Did you ever see Jewish people so victimized? They might wear very noticeable clothing, but its price and its quality agree. They might wear rather large diamonds, but they are diamonds. The Jew is not the victim of the Jew, the craze for luxuries is just like the "coney island" crowd to him; he knows what attracts them and the worthlessness of it.

And it is not so much the financial loss that is to be mourned, nor yet the atrocities committed upon good taste, but the fact that the silly Gentile crowds walk into the net willingly, even gaily, supposing the change of the fashion to be as inevitable as the coming of spring, supposing the new demand on their earnings to be as necessary and as natural as taxes. The crowds think that somehow they have part in it, when their only part is to pay, and then pay again for the new extravagance when the present one palls. There are men in this country who know two years ahead what the frivolities and extravagances of the people will be, because they decree what they shall be. These things are all strictly business, demoralizing to the Gentile majority, enriching to the Jewish minority.

Look at the Sixth Protocol for a sidelight on all this:

This is an excerpt from a longer passage dealing with the plans by which the people's interest could be swung from political to industrial questions, how industry could be made insecure and unfair by the introduction of speculation into its management, and finally how against this condition the people could be rendered restless and helpless. Luxury was to be the instrument:

To destroy Gentile industry, we shall, as an incentive to this speculation, *encourage among the Gentiles a strong demand for luxuries—all enticing luxuries.*

And in the First Protocol:

Surely we cannot allow our own people to come to this. The people of the Gentiles are stupefied with spirituous liquors. ° ° °

—incidentally, the profits of spirituous liquors flow in large amounts to Jewish pockets. The history of the whiskey ring in this country will show this. Historically, *the whole prohibition movement may be described as a contest between Gentile and Jewish capital,* and in this instance, thanks to the Gentile majority, the Gentiles won.

The amusement, gambling, jazz song, scarlet fiction, side show, cheap-dear fashions, flashy jewelry, and every other activity that lived by reason of an invisible pressure upon the people, and that exchanged the most useless of commodities for the prices that would just exhaust the people's money surplus and no more—every such activity has been under the mastery of Jews.

They may not be conscious of their participation in any wholesale demoralization of the people. They may only be conscious of "easy money." They may sometimes yield to surprise as they contrast the silly Gentiles with their own money-wise and fabric-wise and metal-wise Jews. But however this may be, there is the conception of a program by which a people may be deliberately devastated materially and spiritually, and yet kept pleasant all the time—and there also is the same program translated into terms of daily transactions and for the most part, perhaps altogether under control of the members of one race.

Jewish Activities in
the United States (1921)

THE DEARBORN INDEPENDENT

By assimilating Jews into the older negative images of Wall Street and the Money Power, the Independent *was able to suggest a continuing history of Jewish threats to American liberty that went back to the War of Independence, when the Rothschilds had supported the British crown! Many of the anti-Semitic ideas that were published in the* Dearborn Independent *reappeared in some of the anti-New Deal writing of the 1930's.*

Jewish high finance first touched the United States through the Rothschilds. Indeed it may be said that the United States founded the Rothschild fortune. And, as so often occurs in the tale of Jewish riches, the fortune was founded in war. The first twenty million dollars the Rothschilds ever had to speculate with was money paid for Hessian troops to fight against the American colonies.

Since that first indirect connection with American affairs, the Rothschilds have often invaded the money affairs of the country, though always by agents. None of the Rothschild sons thought it necessary to establish himself in the United States. . . .

The first Jewish agent of the Rothschilds in the United States was August Belmont, who came to the United States in 1837, and was made chairman of the Democratic National Committee at the outbreak of the Civil War. The Belmonts professed Christianity and there is today a Belmont memorial, called the Oriental Chapel, in the new Cathedral of St. John the Divine on Morningside Heights.

Rothschild power, as it was once known, has been so broadened by the entry of other banking families into governmental finance, that it must now be known not by the name of one family of Jews, but by the name of the race. Thus it is spoken of as International Jewish Finance, and its principal figures are described as International Jewish Financiers. Much of the veil of secrecy which contributed so greatly

From *Jewish Activities in the United States: Being a Reprint of a Second Selection from Articles Appearing in The Dearborn Independent from October 9, 1920 to March 19, 1921* (n.p., n.d.), pp. 43–44.

to the Rothschild power has been stripped away; war finance has been labeled for all time as "blood money"; and the mysterious magic surrounding large transactions between governments and individuals, by which individual controllers of large wealth were made the real rulers of the people, has been largely stripped away and the plain facts disclosed.

The Rothschild method still holds good, however, in that Jewish institutions are affiliated with their racial institutions in all foreign countries. There are Jewish banking firms in New York whose connections with firms in Frankfort, Hamburg and Dresden, as well as in London and Paris, can be traced by the mere matter of the signs over the doors. They are one.

As a leading student of financial affairs puts it, the world of high finance is largely a Jewish world because of the Jewish financier's "absence from national or patriotic illusions."

To the International Jewish Financier the ups and downs of war and peace between nations are but the changes of the world's financial market; and, as frequently the movement of stocks is manipulated for purposes of market strategy, so sometimes international relations are affected for mere financial gain.

It is known that the recent Great War was postponed several times at the behest of international financiers. If it broke out too soon, it would not involve the states which the international financiers wished to involve. Therefore, the masters of gold, that is, the international masters, were compelled several times to check the martial enthusiasm which their own propaganda had aroused. It is probably quite true, as the Jewish press alleges, that there has been discovered a Rothschild letter dated 1911 and urging the kaiser against war. The year 1911 was too early. There was no such insistence in 1914.

What Price Tolerance? (1928)

PAUL M. WINTER

Paul M. Winter's defense of the Ku Klux Klan is an excellent specimen of American fundamentalism. Prior to the First World War, in Winter's view,

From Paul M. Winter, *What Price Tolerance?* (Hewlett, Long Island, 1928), pp. 1–2, 4–6, 8–9, 11–16, 255–258, 270–273.

America had been a peaceful and happy republic, undisturbed by subversive immigrants and radical new ideas imported from Europe. Winter draws an arresting parallel between immigration and the African slave trade—seeing both as dangerous threats to American liberty which had been encouraged by a few selfish men willing to put immediate profit above the national interest. By making this analogy, Winter borrowed moral sanction from the American reform tradition. But by the 1920's the reform tradition had gone sour. The Ku Klux Klan was hardly a worthy descendant of the antislavery societies.

National Distrust

Arrayed against each other, each clan facing clan; neighbor facing neighbor; church facing church, and the air filled with the acrimonious verbiage of mightly forces shifting for strategic positions, America is threatened with the greatest political conflict she has ever been forced to encounter. It is the inevitable conflict between the forces of traditional Americanism and the thoroughly organized legions of modernism and alienism. The ultimate climax will mean the sacrifice of liberty and fundamental Americanism for the devastating institutions of medieval autocracy and religious dogma, or a greater, more spiritual nation.

Some generations ago the people of America were of one species. For long periods these Americans lived as a united people, separated from the religious and political intrigue of Europe and dependent wholly upon Almighty God for guidance. Americans have been a homogeneous people in the main, thinking and acting alike in the common welfare of all; and with this satisfaction of safety came the dangerous and devitalizing sleep from which she was rudely awakened during the great World War.

During the slumbering years in American history, the forces of alienism were boring into the heart-fibres of our national life, sucking from America the very blood of patriotism. At the outbreak of the World War the patriotic citizenry realized for the first time that a spirit of pacifism and indifference was the direct result of a dangerous mind created by the unassimilated hordes of Europe, who had sought shelter under our flag during the years of peace and plenty. The widespread spirit of pacifism and disloyalty was the child born of this apparent foreign group-mind, and created among this liberty-loving people the first feelings of distrust.

Following the World War the consciousness of the American people was partially aroused and awaited some medium through which it might vent its pent-up feelings. Crime waves spread over the country. Accompanying the steady advance of alienism came the rapid encroachments of the Roman Catholic Hierarchy, and the patriotic people who had held the breastworks of American nationalism during the World War now turned their forces to the defense of the free institutions, which were being swept aside by the dual legions of Romanism and alienism. . . .

Among the many steps which augmented this national distrust was the construction of thousands of parochial schools in open competition to the Public Schools, which have constituted a traditional corner-stone of Americanism. Not satisfied with establishing these Roman Catholic inspired institutions, priests and higher dignitaries of the Hierarchy entered upon a series of vitriolic attacks on the public schools, which have increased in volume and severity. To the lover of the free institutions of America this was a direct attack on the established institutions of the nation. . . .

Then came the injection of Romanism into the commercial and social life of the nation by the formation of The Catholic Press Association, The Catholic Actors' Guild, The Roman Catholic Library Association, The Catholic Writers' Guild, Bureau of Immigration, etc., etc. In large cities The League of the Sacred Heart was instituted for Roman Catholic police and firemen. The Protestant American Nationalist saw in the formation of these organizations the cause for degrading slurs directed at the Protestant clergy in the theatrical playhouses, and similar attacks emanating from the movies. These aroused Americans point to the fun-producer, Charlie Chaplin, in "The Pilgrim" as one of the most glaring examples. They also direct attention to the great amount of Roman Catholic propaganda being disseminated through the medium of Press, the stage, and the movies. Many of the large manufacturing plants have their Roman Catholic clubs and associations. . . .

Through an un-natural alignment the Roman Hierarchy in America drew to itself many powerful allies. The Jews, seeing in the Hierarchy a powerful international power, have lent great prestige to their hereditary enemies in the large cities. The political supremacy of Romanism in New York City and State can be largely accredited to a coalition of these two forces. It is also to be noted that both of these blocs are opposed to restricted immigration. . . .

There is little doubt today regarding the lines of demarkation between the forces engaged in the great struggle. On one side we find the militant champions of Protestantism, who have assumed the responsibility of maintaining traditional American nationalism and its fundamental free institutions. They have lifted the sword and declared themselves as the enemy of political Romanism, alienism, Bolshevism, internationalism, political debauchery and lawlessness. . . . Various compromises have been submitted and various reasons have been projected, but no one has ventured a sincere solution. To the forces of Protestantism and American Nationalism there is no compromise or solution other than the complete victory of American ideals and institutions.

The White Giant

There are clans and clans, but only one Ku Klux Klan.

Rising like a mighty ghost from the mists of distrust which enveloped the continent and clouded the minds of the American people at the close of the World War, the Ku Klux Klan entered the political arena of the United States as a spectre of long forgotten fears and dangers. The great mass of American people received immediate visions of re-enactment of the night-riding days of the Reconstruction, which had been indelibly impressed on their minds through the prejudiced propaganda of political highbinders during times when the white manhood of the South employed the most adaptable weapon to save their blood-drenched land from moral and political ruin. Visions of night riders, lynchings, and secret tribunals dealing out justice from hidden mountain caves, filled the imaginations of the sensitive public. Seizing upon these nightmares of a people suffering from an after-war attack of "Nerves," the enemies of the white-robed crusade quickly set about to establish these fears through a series of hectic exposés, which, despite their great publicity value to the Klan, created antipathy among a great portion of the American citizenry.

With the characteristic rapidity of a mushroom the Knights of the Ku Klux Klan grew by leaps and bounds. Rekindled through the patriotic inspiration of a small group of men who ascended the granite sides of Stone Mountain on Thanksgiving, 1915, and there built an altar under the glowing rays of a fiery cross, the reborn Klan started the long journey, which was to be marked with tribulations and astounding victories. Klan tradition relative to the birth of the organization relates how this small group of sturdy Americans, each carrying a stone, climbed the sides of the rocky Gibraltar of the Southland that they might rededicate themselves to the principles of unqualified Americanism, and might reincarnate a crusade which would save America from the invading hordes of alienism. . . .

With thousands of organizers operating in every section of the United States, fiery crosses soon gleamed forth on the mountainsides from Maine to California and from Canada to the Gulf of Mexico. Realizing the strength of their enemies the Klan leaders placed their hopes in rapid organization. . . .

While it is admitted that here and there Klansmen have been guilty of acts which have reflected discredit upon the organization, still the writer does not believe that any fair-minded citizen would attempt to exact judgment or restitution from the entire membership. Even the Christian Church, with its religious atmosphere of sanctity, does not escape its share of human miscreants, neither could any group of individuals who are heirs to human frailties. Conrol of the action of individual members by the Klan leaders was an absolute impossibility. Reliable sources have estimated that at one time the Klan membership was more than eight million native-born American citizens, which to partially control would be a stupendous task. Comparing this membership with the actual boiled-down instances of individual malconduct one must admit that the Klan can rightfully boast of an unusual and even remarkable record. . . .

Klan Principles

It is estimated that more than twenty-million cards have been circulated in the United States bearing the principles of Klancraft. Under the caption "Non Silba Sed Anthar," or "Not for Self But for Others," this indomitable force of American patriots have enumerated the principles in defense of which they have invited the whirlwind of public opinion. It is the following basic principles of the Klan that have created the storm-center in American politics, incited riots and bloodshed, and even prompted the common prevalent charge of intolerance:

The Tenets of the Christian Religion.
White Supremacy.
Protection of our pure womanhood.
Just Laws and Liberty.
Closer relationship of Pure Americanism.
The upholding of the Constitution of these United States.
The Sovereignty of our State Rights.

The Separation of Church and State.

Freedom of Speech and Press.

Closer relationship between Capital and American Labor.

Preventing the causes of mob violence and lynchings.

Preventing unwarranted strikes by foreign labor agitators.

Prevention of fires and destruction of property by lawless elements.

The limitation of foreign immigration.

The much-needed local reforms.

Law and Order.

. . . Opposition to the organization sponsoring these principles would indicate that its opponents are opposed to these principles and therefore place themselves open to charges of un-Americanism, dual allegiance, and even alien conspiracy. It is logical to assume that if the enemies of the Klan are opposed to these principles, which was recently expressed in an open letter from Governor Alfred E. Smith of New York, who in denouncing the Klan said: "I regard the purposes of the Klan with abhorrence," then they become a revolting voice against the predominant group-mind of these United States and in open conflict with the great majority of American citizens.

Foreign Dangers

What has become of the American? Is he vanishing from the earth? Must America accept a new type in the future?

These questions have arisen from the fact that America today is not the America of twenty-five years ago, but stands mongrelized, alienized and demoralized in the eyes of her own citizens. Volumes might be written regarding the pot that failed to melt. Loose morals, labor troubles, hyphenated organizations, foreign language newspapers, propagandized press, foreign flags, dual allegiances, pacifism, Bolshevism, Fascism, and the spread of foreign customs and institutions, are the prices paid by Americans for the costly theoretical experiment known as "The Melting Pot."

Twenty-five years ago London, Paris, Berlin, Rome, and in fact the entire world stood in awe before the American. He was the hero of history and fiction. They idolized and respected the chivalric, courageous and conscientious stalwart of the American soil who chanced to tour the world in search of adventure and conquest. He had none of the sheik or flapper-loving characteristics, but was the product of a rugged Nordic ancestry, who cleared the New World wilderness, proclaimed liberty and freedom, established a new national civilization, and stood the test in the crucible of hardship and adventure on a new hemisphere. His clear eyes and strength of character were evidences of untarnished environment. He was America's best advertisement; her best ambassador—the Lindbergh of days gone by.

Except in rare instances, this is not true today. Our modern sojourners in Europe have renounced traditional American ideals in an effort to be cosmopolitan, sporty, European, and collectors of medals and titles, thereby making themselves ridiculous in the eyes of foreign citizens, and also in the eyes of their brother Americans, who still retain the God-given instincts of traditional Americanism. Most of these new sojourners have been poor advertisements; the sorry products of the alien centers of America; the inmates of our polyglot boarding houses. . . .

An initial feeling of distrust among the American people came during the World War, when they were rudely awakened by the traitorous activities of certain hyphenated monsters within our borders. Monsters which preached pacifism, anarchy and sedition. It was the unquestionable product of an alien mind, which had been boring into the heart fibres of our national life. From this awakening came the distant rumbling of the mobilizing forces of American Nationalism.

"The Melting Pot" and "Tolerance" have been the implements employed to camouflage the activities of alienism within the United States. These hypothetical expressions have been the literal anaesthetics employed to stupify the American people, rendering them unfit for active aggressive defense. They have been the smoke-screens thrown out to hide the establishing of foreign institutions, behind which alienism in all its forms might advance its lines in quest of power. . . .

Mass-immigration was, like slavery, introduced or permitted in our Republic for economic reasons. Both were misfits in the framework, ideals, and principles of American democracy. In slavery we find violence, sin, and Godlessness, while in the heterogeneous mass-immigration we find a national sagging under the strain of the mass of cultural and spiritual alienage. It has created a modern Tower of Babel. . . .

Bolshevism and Fascism are apparently the two militant ideals of European political turmoil, which America has inherited from the alien invasion. . . . Communist forces have reached their tentacles into every phase of America's national life; not only the economic and labor circles, but also into the more vital phases. Their work among the negroes has brought considerable recruits into their ranks, while their press has worked havoc among the conservative labor bodies.

While the adult members have not caused deep concern among Americans generally, there is one underlying danger which should be faced by every true American. This deals with the radical education of the youth. In many of the large cities Communists have organized the children into groups in order to feed them on the propaganda of the Soviet Government. . . .

When Americans will demand that strict justice be administered by the courts of the land; when political demagogues will be shorn of their power, and when justice will not be swayed by political "pull," then all America can rest assured that Bolshevism will fail, and the principles and ideals of the Fathers of this Republic shall rebound to the glory of their makers.

The Conspiracy against Labor (1922)

SAMUEL GOMPERS

Even in the 1920's the fear of conspiracy was not monopolized by conservatives. The massive right-wing reaction against social reform gave labor leaders like Samuel Gompers good reason to suspect a national conspiracy to destroy the power of organized labor. If there was no "tremendous interlocking arrangement," as Gompers thought, American businessmen did cooperate in breaking strikes and promoting the open shop. One should note that Gompers saw no irreconcilable conflict between labor and management. Both would benefit, he believed, from cooperation and economic progress.

Labor has repeatedly made the charge that there exists a conspiracy to destroy the trade union movement—that there is under way a concerted movement on the part of employers to restore and maintain absolute autocratic control of American industry. This charge has been challenged by various persons, principally representatives of employers or employers' associations.

It has been suggested that the production of evidence might settle the question of whether there is or is not such a concerted effort.

Those who are engaged in a conspiracy or in a concerted effort to

From Samuel Gompers, "The Conspiracy Against Labor," *American Federationist*, XXIX (October 1922), 721, 723, 739.

bring about the destruction of an antagonist do not customarily send broadcast the full evidence of their intentions or of their plans. Most prima facie evidence which would prove the charge that labor has made and that labor repeats would necessarily have to be found in the confidential records of such organizations as the National Association of Manufacturers, The National Erectors' Association, The National Industrial Conference Board, The United States Steel Corporation, The Bethlehem Steel Corporation, The National Open Shop Association, various chambers of commerce throughout the United States . . . and a considerable number of other organizations of employers, bankers and commercial interests. . . .

While the struggle to prevent the organization of workers has from the beginning engaged the attention of employers, there has been since the conclusion of the World War such a manifestation of united effort toward that end as to force upon any careful observer the conclusion that unusual forces have been at work and that unusual plans have been laid.

The fact is, as labor sees it, that while prior to the war there was what might be termed a normal opposition to the organizations of workers, *there has been since the conclusion of the war an abnormal or stimulated opposition inspired and in all probability more or less actively directed from a central point.*

The basic industries of our country are steel, coal and railroads. Of these three steel is the undisputed leader. And the three exercise a combined leadership which is felt down to the very bottom of our industrial structure.

Before the war was ended, and while, under the pressure of war necessity the dominating industrial combinations were compelled to deal with some fairness in their relations with labor, the threat was commonly made, "wait until the war is over!". . .

We have witnessed the mightiest onslaught of reaction through which our nation ever passed. We have witnessed the most brilliant and effective resistance ever offered by Labor in defense of rights and standards and principles.

Our hope is that the time is near when full attention and thought may be given to constructive, cooperative effort. Labor's innermost thought always is the improvement of the processes of production, the perfection of service, the elevation of the standards of life for all. If we can presently emerge finally from the contest against autocratic domination of industry into which we were plunged by the deliberate

planning of powerful combinations of high finance and great industries after the war, we shall enter upon a period of development and
progress such as we have never known. The arts of the producer are
the arts that thrill our souls. They send to us the call to which our natures and our training vibrate and respond. It is not of our choice
that we resist injustice; it is because injustice bars our path.

The Menace of the World Court (1935)

CHARLES E. COUGHLIN

*Franklin D. Roosevelt was frequently accused of using the New Deal as a
Trojan Horse for introducing Communism or Fascism into the United
States. The 1930's also witnessed the growth of a new brand of isolationism
that merged earlier traditions of hostility toward bankers, socialists, Jews,
and the British. Father Coughlin, the demagogic "radio priest" of Detroit,
initially responded to the Depression with echoes of Populist and Silverite
rhetoric. He never tired of denouncing "Tory bankers"—the J. P. Morgans,
the Rothschilds, the Kuhn-Loebs; he advocated extreme inflationary measures and backed a new silver movement in 1934. In his attack on the Senate's impending approval of the World Court, he pictured the League of
Nations as the creation of bankers and international businessmen who were
primarily afraid of Communism. But for all such apparent links with the liberal and Populistic past, Father Coughlin also referred to silver as the "Gentile metal" and spoke of mobilizing all Christianity against the "god of
gold." After breaking with President Roosevelt when the latter failed to nationalize the currency, Coughlin went on to become an apologist for the
Nazis and a leading anti-Semite. Convinced by 1938 that the Jews were responsible for both the Depression and the growing international tension, he
reprinted the* Protocols of the Elders of Zion *in his official organ, which was
entitled, without intended irony,* Social Justice.*

Permit me to be more definite in explaining why the National
Union for Social Justice is opposed to the League of Nations and to
its World Court. In 1917 came the red revolution of Russia. For centuries the citizens of that nation had been manacled by the chains of

From Charles E. Coughlin, "The Menace of the World Court," radio address
of January 27, 1935, in *A Series of Lectures on Social Justice Published by the
Radio League of the Little Flower* (Royal Oak, Mich., 1935), pp. 124–125.

serfdom. While wealth was concentrated in the hands of a few the Russian laborer and farmer had been exploited. Seldom if ever had a voice been raised in their defense. Behind the shameful cloak of silence the state-controlled Church hid its head.

No wonder that Karl Marx found fertile soil upon which he sowed his seed of atheism! No wonder that communism grew! Carried on the wings of poverty, it began to take root in France, in Germany, in England and in America—wherever oppression reigned, wherever, even in a modified form, the principles of Czarism were practiced.

Communism is a social disease which is bred in the lurid ulcers of unjust poverty.

International communism was the irrational revolt against the irrational plutocracy of the international banker.

To offset the rapid development of communism, there was organized this League of Nations where, at its secret sessions never published to the world at large, it was planned to build up a counter internationalism whose main purpose was the protection of the international banker, the international plutocrat.

Fellow countrymen, I am opposed to communism as much as I am opposed to a plague. But, thanks be to God, I have sufficient sagacity to realize that if I suffer stinking carcasses to rot on my doorstep, I can rant and rail in vain against the plague until doomsday.

So it is with communism. I can set up my League of Nations to oppose it and my World Court to condemn it. But all this is futile unless the causes which created communism—the unnecessary poverty, the exploitation—are eradicated and removed from our midst.

Thus, the international bankers and those in league with them—they who have guided the destinies of England, of Germany, of France, of Italy and who still hold sway over the destinies of the United States of America have unfurled their colorless flag, have organized their own secretive government and established their own international court to dominate the armies and navies of the world hoping thus to oppose communism and protect plutocracy.

Between the forceps of these mighty forces the innocent people of the world and you, the people of America, await to be crushed by the certain conflict which will ensue.

I realize that this thought has not been expressed hitherto in any publicized document, nor is it commonly known among the Senators of the United States. But this was taught to me by men who sat in at the secret sessions when the abortion of the League of Nations was cradled by those who were determined to protect injustice, to bandage the cancer of exploitation, to keep the carcasses on their doorsteps and to deceive the guileless citizen and the innocent Senator with their program of peace.

Thus, on Tuesday next, America, instead of rescuing from the hands of the international bankers the right to coin and regulate the value of money, instead of limiting the accumulation of wealth by the favored few, instead of bending her efforts to rescue the impoverished farmer, instead of guaranteeing a just and living wage to every laborer who is willing to contribute his honest work—America is ready to join hands with the Rothschilds and Lazerre Frères, with the Warburgs and Morgans and Kuhn-Loebs to keep the world safe for the inevitable slaughter.

America in Danger! (1940–1941)

CHARLES B. HUDSON

By the late 1930's bigoted nativism had virtually disappeared from the regular news media. Ideas that had once been tolerated by respectable magazines and newspapers were increasingly confined to crude, semiliterate hate sheets, such as the newsletter published in Omaha, Nebraska, from which the following selections are taken. Charles B. Hudson, the editor, repeated the common fundamentalist charge that a leftist Jewish conspiracy had taken over the government, the news media, and the film and publishing industries. In opposing any intervention to aid the victims of Naziism, Hudson advanced the remarkable argument that the Second World War was itself the product of a Jewish conspiracy.

Reminds that THE JEWISH PRESS 11-15-40 gloats under caption: "GEN. JOHNSON APOLOGIZES—Retracts Statement That Jews Seek War . . . ," referring to *Hugh S. Johnson's* pre-election address in which he was charged with "implying" that "American Jews were pushing USA into war against Hitler." *Bernard Baruch's* "hired man" also got a personal reprimand from that Prince of Jewry whom Jewish press calls

From Charles B. Hudson, ed., *American in Danger! Weekly Exposé of Un-Americanism in Education, Finance, Labor, Politics, and Religion* (Omaha, Nebraska) (November 18, 1940), pp. 1–3; (April 7, 1941), pp. 1–2; (April 28, 1941), p. 4.

"Asst. Pres. of USA." Significantly THE JEWISH PRESS 10-25-40 editorially "burned up" over Johnson's speech, prophecying: ". . . If Hugh Johnson *is forced to eat his column*, as he has threatened to do in case Pres. Roosevelt is re-elected, we can assure him a good case of indigestion. We (the Jews) get sick merely from reading the trash."

Further reminding that *Phineas J. Biron,* Jewish columnist in THE JEWISH PRESS 11-15-40, gives Jewry's attitudes at same time illustrating "control" over, and tactics of "kept" authors and lecturers. . . .

Further illustrating above, *Biron* praises with: ". . . We have Hitler to thank for the presence in this country of the royal family of literature the *Mann* family, with *Thomas, Heinrich, Klaus* and *Erika Mann* all being very *much in demand by publishers.* . . . Klaus Mann, son of Thomas, is going to edit a monthly magazine called THE NEW WORLD. . . ." *Biron* failed to say that while Thomas as sort of "Christian Socialist" (impossible—see definitions) attempts to remain aloof from Communist company, yet brother Heinrich and notorious daughter and son are active in Red camps. Significantly, it was largest Jew publishing firm in Berlin that published all of *Thos. Mann's* writings from his youth up, and "made" him a great author à la movie stars, for dual purpose of making money and using him to "front" for Jewry. These Red "refugees" with "control's" ballyhoo collect lots of dough from dumb Gentiles who read their voluminous poison or attend their high-priced lectures. And 11-17-40 Omaha World-Herald gives war-monger "refugee" *Thos. Mann* 2-column-wide spread to his warning against Hitler, while builder-of-America, *Henry Ford* rates only 1-column-wide item advocating peace instead of prolonged war that Organized Jewry-Intl. Finance seeks thru its own and "stooge" spokesmen like "refugee" *Thos. Mann!* . . .

This recently consolidated "allied relief societies" into said *British War Relief Society, Inc.* which, having 470 active groups thruout USA, now putting on special drive as evidenced here, *is sponsored by same internationalists who got us into World War I!!!* Here's brief data on just one of its Bd. of Directors:

Sir William Wiseman, now partner of Kuhn-Loeb & Co. (who control almost 11 billion dollars of industry in USA, ranking next to Rothschild agent J. P. Morgan & Co.), was head of *British Secret Service*—propaganda in USA during and before World War I. Said that he so skillfully camouflaged his movements prior to our entry into that war that even our State Dept., where he went in and out, did not know his official position until he later chose to disclose himself. He had absolute authority in America. . . .

HOME GUARDS. As AID! predicted upon mobilization of *Natl. Guards*, that, among reasons Organized Jewry-Intl. Finance desirous of denuding industrial states of local defense units, was fact that Nu-DEAL-countenanced-strikes would force cities and states to call for Federal aid—just another link in the dictatorship chain. That move facilitates, in name of "national defense," the "take-over" of both unions and industries.

AID! also pointed out that the NUDEAL was loath to authorize Christian Americans to organize *Home Guards* to take place of Natl. Guards, yet, with NUDEAL's blessing, at least 2 Jewish Armies, composed of "tough Jews," many being Red "refugees," were permitted to drill, armed and in uniforms, particularly in New York State.

The "hatchet-men" guilty of terrorism and unwarranted brutality at the scene of current strikes, are same breed that in Europe the past 23 years—in "revolutions" in Russia, Central Europe, and Spain—have, when even temporarily in power, slaughtered, many with unspeakable tortures, over 11,000,000 (mostly Christians), besides starving to death, another 30,000,000.

Leading Jewish weekly, THE AMERICAN HEBREW, in 1938, bragged that 35,000 or one-third of the Intl. Brigades guilty of above in Spain, were "Jews from all over the world." Jewish organizations been bringing these gangsters to USA ever since Mch. '39. . . .

REFUGEES. Something fishy in fact that in Jewish NY TIMES 3-28-41 you find the *Dept. of Justice* has "gotten round" our immigration laws by ruling that "refugees" from Hungary, Rumania, Poland, Czecho-Slovakia and *France* (mostly Jews), now in USA, can make a round-trip to Canada, re-entering then as immigrants under their national quota, thus making it easy for "refugees" to change their status from that of visitor to that of an immigrant. Under the old procedure they would have had to return to Europe and then obtain the necessary documents.

Yet on same page you read that NUDEALER *Sen. Wagner* of New York heads just organized *Amn. Palestine Committee* of over 300 Govt officials, legislators, Governors, educators, churchmen and civic leaders—to support the movement for developing Palestine as "an outpost of freedom and social justice," and to prepare for large-scale colonization of Jewish "refugees." He claims that by treaty and Congressional enactment our Govt has recognized and approved the establishment of a Jewish national home in Palestine, being endorsed by Presidents Wilson, Harding, Coolidge, Hoover and Roosevelt. Joined in this "unholy" united front are NUDEALERS: Jackson, Ickes, Wickard, Dykstra, McNutt, Carmody, Barkley, George, Rayburn, McCormack, King, Msgr. John A. Ryan; and so-called Republicans: Willkie, McNary, Vandenberg, Lodge, Martin, Wm. Allen White, Al Smith.

Why isn't the public informed that the real reason Organized Jewry–Intl. Finance wants Palestine is so that Anti-Christ Power may control the mineral wealth there estimated at from 3 to 10 times total wealth of USA? . . .

Now you understand why *Chaim Weizmann*, who got American Jewry to bring USA into World War I on side of Britain (fruits of Balfour Agreement which was to give Palestine to Jewry), and who now as Pres. of *Jewish Agency* (holding company of Warburg-Kuhn-Loeb and Rothschild groups) for Palestine, and as Pres. of *World Zionist Organization*, is in USA (NY TIMES 3-27-41) pleading that Britain permit Palestine Jews (most of them Reds) to organize an army of more than 40,000. *Dr. Weizmann* had an interview with part-Jew *Churchill* just before he left England on this trip. Churchill always Jewry's tool. . . .

THE PATRIOT (London), 4-3-41, leading editorial "VICTORY IN THE AIR" credits the Royal Air Force with having defeated Germany so far, and quoting official publication "THE BATTLE OF BRITAIN," covering the worst blitzkreig months Aug., Sept., Oct. '40 (significantly *before* our Nov. 2 election—creating justification for all aid to Britain platforms in both Republican and Democratic parties), confirms what AID! been giving you piecemeal. Accounts for only 1,700 persons killed with 3,360 seriously injured by German daylight raids, and only 12,581 killed and 16,965 injured by night attacks—*"nearly all civilians."* Only *"some"* aerodromes and factories and docks hit, but *"thousands"* of houses. Railroads and bridges hardly touched.

Considering that the whole United Kingdom is smaller than Florida, and yet has 44,000,000 population, and with hundreds of thousands of troops in camps, it is obvious that with practically no soldiers killed (when the same bombs that blasted hospitals, churches, etc. could have wiped out whole armies), the whole war is being staged by Organized Jewry–Intl. Finance solely, at this stage, to force military-economic dictatorships on all countries of the world. Just as in World War I, the military take orders from OJ-IF, and properties —"military objectives" necessary to produce planes, ships, munitions, guns, etc., owned or controlled by OJ-IF—are hardly touched, otherwise the war would have been over with when British fled from France-Belgium-Holland.

The Ruling Oligarchy Wants to Engage in a Foreign War (1941)

CARL H. MOTE

In the summer of 1941 the Senate Committee on Military Affairs held hearings on a bill to authorize the President to requisition certain property in the interest of national defense. The testimony of Carl H. Mote, president of Northern Indiana Telephone Company, expressed the conservative business opinion that pro-Ally sentiment was linked with pro-Communism, and that President Roosevelt's recent acts of intervention were part of a plot to create excuses for an American dictatorship.

Just why is it believed in 1941 by anybody in America that the confiscation of privately owned property is necessary or proper? Is it because the ruling oligarchy wants to engage in a foreign war that is known to be unpopular and that this ruling oligarchy believes it necessary first to strip our citizens of all their property in order to crush their resistance and eliminate their opposition? Or, is it because the prospect of a foreign war offers the ruling oligarchy a mask behind which this oligarchy can accomplish the collectivization of all privately owned property and introduce America to the Marxian state?

I suspect both these reasons are motivating our bureaucrats in Washington. I have been told that bureaucrats already have told your committee that this measure is necessary for defense and necessary to obtain the proper response from labor. These are reasons stated in such general terms that they are difficult to analyze or answer, and it ought to be obvious that they are quite insincere and hypocritical, else there would be more particularity, more revealing facts given to the members of this committee.

From *Hearings Before the Committee on Military Affairs, United States Senate, Seventy-Seventh Congress, First Session* (Washington, 1941), pp. 158–161.

I don't believe the confiscation of any privately owned property is necessary for the defense of the country, and I do not believe labor demands any such un-American measure. I don't believe labor is wholly without knowledge of what happens finally to labor when the state undertakes to stamp out the rights of private property. At the beginning of the French Revolution there were new dealers who wanted to confiscate all privately owned property and change everything, including human nature. The French trade-unionists who cheered such proposals lived to see their unions dissolved, after which they were compelled to walk the streets without work and in deep despair. . . .

A week ago I spent 2 hours in New York City with the president of the National Industrial Conference Board, Dr. Virgil Jordan. I consider him not only the foremost American economist but, above all, a citizen of great patriotism and courage. . . . This is what Dr. Jordan wrote on September 1, 1940:

To many men of insight and integrity in the American community it seems that after 7 years of persistent dissipation and demoralization of its resources by a subtle, comprehensive, and carefully planned political conspiracy, the American Republic, like the French, has been destroyed and replaced by military dictatorship, and after little more than five generations the great American experiment in free, creative community life has been ended for an indefinite period.

To many such men, however, hopeful that they may prove mistaken, the application of "emergency" legislation of conscription and confiscation of the community resources by the State immediately preceding a national election sounds ominously like the death rattle of the American Republic. They must see in it the symptoms of advanced political degeneration and social disintegration, signifying the collapse of personal independence, self-discipline, and capacity for voluntary cooperation in the American community.

. . . I cannot improve upon the language Dr. Jordan has used, "comprehensive and carefully planned political conspiracy." This language explains what I think and explains why I am opposed to such legislation as S. 1579, both the original bill and the substitute. What I ask has become of security? What has become of the "due process of law" in America? . . .

I am against a foreign war, of course, but I am in favor of reasonable appropriations for defense. I am opposed to any hoax inflicted on a long-suffering people in the name of and behind the cruel mask of "defense." As an American, I renounce any share in the "comprehensive and carefully planned political conspiracy" which is preparing America for a bloody revolution. As an American, I denounce the conspirators—all of them—and wherever they are—in the White House, in the Congress of the United States or in any of the departments and bureaus of the Federal Government.

In the *New York Times Magazine* of Sunday, June 22, Mr. Morgenthau who was called "Treasurer to the democracies" was quoted regarding American objectives in the immediate future.

"There is just one job that faces the world today. That job is to lick Hitler," he said. To this I say, as a realist, if Hitler smashes Stalin and his cutthroats of Red Russia, the job of licking Hitler is going to be rather difficult.

After Hitler is licked, according to Mr. Morgenthau, we are going to have "complete disarmament," an "international police force" and "redistribute our gold ° ° ° to help rebuild the world."

If these are our peacetime objectives, after we have licked Hitler, then I say candidly, I am without enthusiasm for licking Hitler. I did not like the treaty Hitler made with Stalin, just before Hitler invaded Poland, though I was realist enough to recognize the military purpose of the treaty from Hitler's standpoint. I am glad that treaty has been scrapped and I hope Germany will be able to destroy the last vestige of Communism in Europe. I have always mistrusted the coddling of Communists and communism here in America and I still do. . . .

Of course, this bill is not lacking in timeliness. In the past 2 years, the administration in Washington has made this country the virtual ally of England which has lately committed itself, and so has Mr. Roosevelt, to aid Red Russia. It is certainly significant that Congress is asked to provide for the confiscation of private property in America at a time when the President is promising to aid Stalinism in Russia.

A Study in Appearances and Realities (1948)

CHARLES A. BEARD

A *bitter critic of Franklin D. Roosevelt's foreign policy, the famous historian Charles A. Beard raised serious questions about the economic sources of American "internationalism" and the erosion of limitations on executive power. Unlike less responsible critics, Beard did not point to a vast international conspiracy of Communists, Englishmen, or Jews. He blamed Roosevelt personally for deceiving the people and subverting constitutional government; and also attacked academicians for giving theoretical justification for increasing executive power. Beard's constitutional arguments carried overtones of right-wing isolationism and the defense of property rights; yet he curiously anticipated the New Left of the 1960's in his mistrust of a strong executive, his suspicion that official American altruism concealed economic imperialism, and his rejection of America's mission to liberate the world.*

The discrepancies between official representations and official realities in the conduct of foreign affairs during the year 1941, until the coming of war, stand out starkly in documents already available. Other documents that bear on the subject, running into the thousands, are known to exist, but they are still under the seal of secrecy. What they will reveal, if all of them are ever unsealed, can only be a matter of conjecture for the general public and students of history. But in any event several primary discrepancies are established beyond question by the documents now published. . . .

For these discrepancies a favorable interpretation has been and is still being offered by many American publicists in the following form. The great end which President Roosevelt discerned and chose justified the means which he employed. As a farsighted statesman he early discovered that unless the United States entered the war raging in Europe, Hitler would be victorious; and the United States, facing

From Charles A. Beard, *President Roosevelt and the Coming of the War 1941* (New Haven, Conn.: Yale University Press, 1948), pp. 573–575, 577, 581–584, 589–590, 594–595, 598. Copyright © 1948 by Yale University Press.

alone this monstrous totalitarian power, would become a victim of its merciless ideology and its despotic militarism. According to this interpretation, it was a question of democracy, the Four Freedoms, the noble principles of the Atlantic Charter, and world security on the one side; of totalitarianism, consummate despotism, and military subjugation on the other side. Since the American people were so smug in their conceit, so ignorant of foreign affairs, and so isolationist in sentiment that they could not themselves see the reality of this terrible threat to their own safety and a necessity to meet it by a resort to war, President Roosevelt had to dissemble in order to be re-elected in 1940 as against Wendell Willkie, then the antiwar candidate of the Republicans on an antiwar platform. Furthermore, as members of Congress, Democrats and Republicans alike, continued throughout the year, until December 7, their vigorous opposition to involvement in war, President Roosevelt, in conducting foreign affairs, had to maintain the appearance of a defensive policy until the Japanese attack on Pearl Harbor. But the means which President Roosevelt actually employed in the conduct of foreign affairs were justified by the great end which he, with peculiar clairvoyance, had early discerned and chosen for himself and his country. . . .

The interpretation that the end justified the means, like all other interpretations, depends upon the point of view of those who make or accept it; and though it be proclaimed as the settled truth, its validity is nonetheless open to tests of knowledge. Even a cursory examination of the thesis raises questions of time and consequences, foreign and domestic. . . .

Since, as a consequence of the war called "necessary" to overthrow Hitler's despotism, another despotism [Soviet Russia] was raised to a higher pitch of power, how can it be argued conclusively with reference to inescapable facts that the "end" justified the means employed to involve the United States in that war? If the very idea of neutrality with regard to Hitler was shameful in 1941, what is to be said of commitments made in the name of peace and international amity at Teheran and Yalta, where the avowed and endorsed principles of the Atlantic Charter for world affairs were shattered—in commitments which were subsequently misrepresented by President Roosevelt, publicly and privately? . . .

It is true that the Constitution is flexible in many respects, but as to the division and limitation of power its language is explicit. Certainly it does not vest in the Congress or the President illimitable power secretly to determine the ends of the government in foreign or domestic affairs and secretly to choose and employ any means deemed desirable by either branch of the government to achieve those ends. . . .

Yet, if the precedents set by President Roosevelt in conducting foreign affairs, as reported in the records of the Congressional Committee on Pearl Harbor and other documents, are to stand unimpeached and be accepted henceforth as valid in law and morals then:

The President of the United States in a campaign for re-election may publicly promise the people to keep the country out of war and, after victory at the polls, may set out secretly on a course designed or practically certain to bring war upon the country.

He may, to secure legislation in furtherance of his secret designs, misrepresent to Congress and the people both its purport and the policy he intends to pursue under its terms if and when such legislation is enacted.

He may, by employing legal casuists, secretly frame and, using the powers and patronage of his office, obtain from Congress a law conferring upon him in elusive language authority which Congress has no constitutional power to delegate to him.

He may, after securing such legislation, publicly announce that he will pursue, as previously professed, a policy contrary to war and yet at the same time secretly prepare plans for waging an undeclared "shooting war" that are in flat contradiction to his public professions.

He may hold secret conferences with the Premier of a foreign government and publicly declare that no new commitments have been made when, in fact, he has committed the United States to occupying, by the use of American armed forces, the territory of a third country and joining the Premier in parallel threats to another government.

He may make a secret agreement with a foreign power far more fateful in consequences to the United States than any alliance ever incorporated in a treaty to be submitted to the Senate for approval. . . .

He may, after publicly announcing one foreign policy, secretly pursue the opposite and so conduct foreign and military affairs as to maneuver a designated foreign power into firing the first shot in an attack upon the United States and thus avoid the necessity of calling upon Congress in advance to exercise its constitutional power to deliberate upon a declaration of war.

He may, as a crowning act in the arrogation of authority to himself, without the consent of the Senate, make a commitment to the head of a foreign government which binds the United States to "police the world," at least for a given time, that is, in the eyes of other governments and peoples policed, to dominate the world; and the American people are thereby in honor bound to provide the military, naval, and economic forces necessary to pursue, with no assurance of success, this exacting business.

In short, if these precedents are to stand unimpeached and to provide sanctions for the continued conduct of American foreign affairs, the Constitution may be nullified by the President, officials, and officers who have taken the oath, and are under moral obligation, to uphold it. For limited government under supreme law they may substitute personal and arbitrary government—the first principle of the totalitarian system against which, it has been alleged, World War II was waged—while giving lip service to the principle of constitutional government. . . .

The theory of unlimited power in the Executive over international relations is by no means confined to Army and Navy circles. Close students of international law and foreign affairs who follow the literature of the subject, including articles in law journals, are aware that numerous defenders of President Roosevelt's methods have been for years engaged in stretching political precedents and obiter dicta of Supreme Court justices in an effort to establish two propositions in particular: (1) the President's power in the management of foreign affairs is practically sovereign; and (2) the President may incorporate in an executive agreement with a foreign government—even a secret executive agreement—any commitment he wishes to make in the name of the United States, despite the constitutional provision for the ratification of treaties by the Senate.

Subsidized and powerful private agencies engaged nominally in propaganda for "peace" are among the chief promoters of presidential omnipotence in foreign affairs. They look to the President rather than Congress for assistance in advancing their ideas of America's obligation to join other "peace-loving" nations in ordering and reordering the world. Moreover, as these agencies in turn subsidize professors and "students of international relations" by the hundreds, they thereby help to exalt presidential "leadership" and, correspondingly, degrade the Senate or the House of Representatives or both with regard to their responsibilities in foreign affairs. Consequently, American education from the universities down to the grade schools is permeated with, if not dominated by, the theory of presidential supremacy in foreign affairs. Coupled with flagrant neglect of instruction in constitutional government, this propaganda in universities, colleges, and schools has deeply implanted in the minds of rising generations the doctrine that the power of the President over international relations is, for all practical purposes, illimitable. . . .

Closely associated with the idea that the President is serving the United States and mankind when he emits grand programs for imposing international morality on recalcitrant nations by American power, alone or in conjunction with that of allies or associates, is another doctrine which helps to build up public support for Executive supremacy in foreign affairs and to make enemies abroad. This doctrine proudly announces that it is the duty of the United States to assume and maintain "the moral leadership of the world" in the interest of realizing American programs of world reform. Apart from the feasibility of establishing such moral leadership in fact, the assertion of it adds to the discord rather than the comity of nations.

To sensibility, the very idea is repulsive. As ladies and gentlemen who publicly proclaim their own virtues are suspected and resented by self-respecting persons, so the Government and people of the United States, by loudly proclaiming their moral leadership of the world, awaken suspicion and resentment in Great Britain, France, Russia, China, and other countries of the world; and, what may be worse in the long run, contemptuous laughter. Nor, in truth, can American democracy, culture, or ways of life be "sold" to the world over the radio or by any other means of communication. . . .

At this point in its history the American Republic has arrived under the theory that the President of the United States possesses limitless authority publicly to misrepresent and secretly to control foreign policy, foreign affairs, and the war power.

More than a hundred years ago, James Madison, Father of the Constitution, prophesied that the supreme test of American statesmanship would come about 1930.

Although not exactly in the form that Madison foresaw, the test is here, now—with no divinity hedging our Republic against Caesar.

8. Toward the End of
Consensus? (1936–1968)

AFTER THE dismal spectacle of the 1968 Democratic National Convention, defenders of Mayor Richard J. Daley charged that Communist-inspired agitators had converged on Chicago with the secret intention of disrupting the Convention, of provoking city police into violence by verbal and physical assault, and even of assassinating leading officials and dignitaries. Thousands of college students and many newsmen took a different view: the mayor and his police had pitched temper tantrums and had ruthlessly beaten innocent demonstrators and spectators; this violent punishment had been planned in advance, out of an eagerness to teach a lesson to a younger generations of hippies and protesters who flouted all the symbols of middle-class decency and respectability (including haircuts) and who had the audacity to enter politics and challenge authoritarian procedures of decision. Moreover, in the eyes of many radicals and disillusioned liberals, both national conventions had been carefully rigged by conservatives; both major parties were equally impervious to change, to serious dissent, or to democratization. But if a small but influential group of intellectuals and reformers had become increasingly alienated from the sources and centers of power, concluding that the American political system had been totally captured by reactionary forces, a third independent candidate for President was arousing astonishing support in all parts of the nation by attacking the "liberal establishment" and by appealing for a return to the simpler, purer America that had been subverted and corrupted over the past generation.

The strained, anxious mood of the 1968 political campaign suggested a qualitative change in the American fear of conspiracy, a change that reflected the increasing uncertainties and complexities of the interdependent world of the mid-twentieth century. Even in the critical and hysteria-ridden years of 1919 and 1920, the main threat to security had been associated with a small group of radicals and alien immigrants who could easily be classed as "outsiders." But by the 1960's a growing number of Americans had begun to lose trust in the integrity of major institutions and in the legitimacy and motives of the governing classes of society.

As we have already suggested, the myth of a Great Betrayal had its origins in the 1930's when conservatives perceived the experimental programs of the New Deal as an insidious plot to undermine the traditional American system. One of the distinctive characteristics of the decade was a sense of unprecedented conditions, of a wholly new era. Never before had the federal government impinged so directly on the lives of so many citizens; when Franklin D. Roosevelt tried to alter the composition of the Supreme Court and then broke all precedent by seeking a third term as President, conservatives screamed that constitutional government had given way to incipient dictatorship. Yet the economic depression was so extensive and persistent that radical solutions, both from the extreme right and the extreme left, won dedicated supporters. A diverse group of leftists, for example, agreed that the palliatives of the New Deal could not touch the heart of the nation's problem while a small class of "economic royalists" hoarded capital and plotted to prolong the Depression until workers would accept starvation wages and company-controlled unions. Meanwhile, the rise of totalitarian regimes in Europe suggested that entire populations could be drugged by skillful propaganda, that dictators and "fifth columns" could subvert constitutional government and reverse the supposedly inevitable progress of liberty and democracy in world history. More than at any time in the past, Americans could reasonably conclude that there were dark forces, inexplicably powerful, at loose in the world.

But the era of the Second World War also witnessed a re-enactment and fulfillment of older American ideas and expectations. Once again, Europe proved to be a place where an imperfect liberty was lost, where satanic forces triumphed. The successes of totalitarianism were interpreted as an almost providential warning of what *could* happen in the United States if Americans failed to be vigilant and faithful to their traditional mission. Though faith in America's mission had dimmed during years of depression, it was rejuvenated by involvement in a war against enemies who seemed to be evil incarnate. In no previous war had the American people been so united in purpose or so confident in the righteousness of their cause. And precisely because the foe was so easily identified and so obviously external to American society, the war years were relatively free from crusades against internal enemies. Aside from a superficial fright over saboteurs and the inexcusable detention of Japanese-Americans on the Pacific Coast, there was nothing comparable to the xenophobia, the antiradicalism, and the persecution of German-Americans during the First World War.

Unfortunately, the sense of national unity and national self-confidence hardly survived the war. A succession of shattered expectations, coupled with a new set of conflicts of interest, revived and intensified the suspicions of earlier decades. The defeat of the Axis Powers did not usher in a sunny, peaceful world under the benevolent dominion of the United States. Rather, the world in which Americans had taken a new interest and for which they assumed a new and self-appointed responsibility exploded into anticolonial wars and revolutions, coups d'état, and Communist-led insurrections. Regardless of the much disputed origins of the cold war, it soon became a genuine and dangerous conflict that gave new meaning to the old fears of conspiracy and espionage. If a few scientists could transmit atomic secrets to the Soviet Union, it seemed plausible that some future espionage might tip the scales in the "balance of terror" and enable Russia to annihilate the United States without costly retaliation. The fears and suspicions generated by the cold war easily led to a wild exaggeration of the extent and danger of Communist subversion. Writers and politicians who labored under what Denis Brogan termed "the illusion of American omnipotence" found it easier to blame Communist conspirators for every conflict in the world than to study the origins and complexities of civil wars or to accept the inevitable limitations of American power. Thus it became an article of right-wing faith that the fall of China to the Communists had been plotted by American traitors and had nothing to do with the corruption and incompetence of the Chinese Nationalist government, with that government's lack of popular support, or with its failure to inaugurate meaningful reforms.

Further suspicions of duplicity were nourished by rapid changes in the domestic scene. The Second World War brought spectacular increases in the productivity of the American economy; instead of plunging into a much dreaded postwar depression, the nation entered a period of phenomenal economic expansion, of rising personal incomes and living standards. But despite the self-congratulatory sermons on how America had solved the age-old problems of poverty and inequality, there was relatively little change in the *distribution* of income or in social stratification. In other words, while there was improvement in the standard of living for the poor, they were still in no better position when compared with the wealthy, whose standard of living was also rising. We have no proof of a causal relation between this enduring inequality and the growing tendency to believe that the authentic America, the America of unlimited promise, had been betrayed. It seems likely, however, that many Americans were frustrated and disillusioned when they discovered a conflict between the *appearance* of infinite affluence and opportunity and the resistant barriers of the social structure. For Negroes, who as a group had been hardest hit by the Depression and who had then achieved an economic breakthrough during the war, it was particularly intolerable to witness a continuing denial of equal opportunity and a growing racial disparity in income, education, and housing. Some Afro-Americans concluded that the "white power structure" had been deliberately and systematically contrived to exploit the nonwhite races. On the other hand, upward-mobile whites often feared that Negro competitors would deprive them of their newly-won security or undermine the "respectability" of an aspiring middle-class neighborhood. If Negroes were discontent over their "place" in society and hungered after the white man's job and home (and even women), this could readily be attributed to Communist instigation.

We can hardly touch on the remarkable public alarms over crime waves and moral corruption except to note that these postwar spasms of indignation helped to undermine faith in the existing social system and in the legitimacy of constituted authority. Regardless of the party in office, the late 1940's and the 1950's seemed to be the age of the "expense-account rich," of lavish government contracts, and of "wheeler-dealers" who peddled political influence for "gifts" of deep freezers and vicuña coats. Moreover, as the newly created television audience watched the hearings of Senator Estes Kefauver's investigations into organized crime, it became apparent that political machines were closely allied with crime syndicates and with the immense "invisible empire" of the Mafia. Alger Hiss, who epitomized the privileged Ivy League elite of the Northeast, could be convicted of perjury and branded, in the public eye, as a spy for the Soviet Union; there were also supposedly respectable businessmen and politicians, many of them self-made men and the children of immigrants, who were shown to have intimate ties with the most sinister and powerful figures of the underworld. When the mass media responded to foreign, and especially to Communist, criticism of this American decadence, they portrayed an idyllic, Norman Rockwell America of town-meeting democracy, business honesty, and responsible citizenship; yet in an oddly contrasting succession of revelations and exposures, the same mass media projected endless images of syndicated crime, political corruption, student cheating and drug addiction, sexual immorality, the bribery of athletes, and an all-pervasive deception and swindling of the general public.

Of course there is a considerable difference between public outrage over the growth of organized crime and the belief that gangsters, progressive educators, abstract painters, and novelists who use four-letter words are all engaged in a master plot to demoralize and destroy the nation. Yet many minds, both trained and untrained, seem predisposed to seek underlying patterns and connecting ligaments in what at first appear to be unrelated configurations of evil. Surely it is more than coincidence, they say, that the triumphs of Communism in the external world have been accompanied by so many signs of disintegration and moral weakness at home. This tendency became especially pronounced in the 1960's, when, as in the 1850's, an increasing number of Americans repudiated the political consensus of the center, including its capacity for pragmatic compromise and its relative lack of moral commitment. What seems to be a growing polarization of left and right may be related, as Michael Harrington has suggested, to a diminishing importance of local identity and regional solidarity. Thus when spokesmen for the extreme left and the extreme right keep telling the public who America's "real enemies" are, they are clearly competing for new *national* blocs unified by common fears and shared indignation.

But even if political polarization is part of a nationalizing trend away from older regional divisions and alliances, the newer crusades of countersubversion have echoed traditional themes that we have already encountered in this book. The cultural conflict between modernists and fundamentalists has sharpened as fundamentalism has moved into the cities and has been confronted, even in rural areas, with the shocking knowledge that the major religious denominations have become increasingly heterodox and socially oriented; that public education has become more permissive and experimental; and that books, movies, and magazines have been virtually freed from censorship and have consequently become vehicles for irreverence, skepticism, and frank sensuality. Writing in the tones of a nineteenth-century revivalist, John A. Stormer has attracted an immense following by blaming Communist conspirators for everything from teen-age drinking to premarital pregnancies, and by warning that America cannot turn back to God and be "saved" until the people are brought "face-to-face with the treachery and wickedness in the White House, the Court, the Congress and the Church."

On the other side, the Communist leader William Z. Foster often sounded like a Jacksonian Democrat denouncing the Money Power for its infamous conspiracies against the common people, even when he was following a shifting party line dictated from Moscow. Similarly, the sensational exposés of ex-Communists have been strikingly reminiscent of the mid-nineteenth century confessions of apostate Catholic priests and "liberated" Mormon wives. Phyllis Schlafly's popular tract written for Barry Goldwater in 1964, which attacked the eastern Republican "kingmakers" who had supposedly dominated the party since 1936, contained curious echoes of Populist rhetoric. Her right-wing diatribe was far less concerned with Communists than with New York bankers and rich, Sybaritic Republicans who read *The New Yorker* magazine. More recently, Populist prejudices and suspicions have re-emerged in the literature of the "Constitution party," based in Houston, Texas, which asserts that Communism itself is merely a "myth" invented, nurtured, and financed by four "One World Establishments" or "Dens of Thieves"—the Federal Reserve Bank, the Council on Foreign Relations, the United Nations, and the Public Administration Service of Chicago. This remarkable fantasy is founded on the belief that a group of powerful international bankers, including Jacob Schiff, the Guggenheims, Kuhn, Loeb & Company, and others (mostly Jewish), conspired to establish the Federal Reserve system, financed both sides in the First World War, backed the Russian Revolution, and ultimately created the United Nations. Similar logic has led a writer in *Common Sense*, a news sheet that advertises itself as the "Leader in the Nation's Fight Against Communism," to brand Abe Fortas, Arthur Goldberg, and Walt Whitman Rostow as the architects of President Lyndon Johnson's "anti-Christian" Great Society, to assert that Goldberg has been groomed "to be the first Jewish American president," and to warn that by 1970 "Zionists, Negroes and Sodomites, will have complete control of the nation."

These suggestions of continuity in themes and prejudices should not blind us to fundamental changes. It seems probable that fears of national conspiracy have never been so diverse or widespread as in the 1960's. Even in the early 1950's, when right-wing extremists screamed over the betrayal at Yalta and the wicked abandonment of Nationalist China, few Americans doubted the integrity of the country's leaders or the soundness of its institutions. Perhaps there had been a laxness in detecting the machinations of an Alger Hiss or in ferreting out Soviet spies, but the nation as a whole seemed relatively united and secure. While one must be tentative in generalizing about recent history, it now appears that the response to President Kennedy's assassination marked a critical turning point. Opinion polls indicated that a majority of Americans suspected that the crime was not the work of a lone fanatic. And whether one accepted the reasoning of Mark Lane, or Jim Garrison, or of innumerable right-wing writers who pictured Oswald as the appointed agent of Communist governments, there remained the haunting question of the possible duplicity of the Warren Commission. If the Commission was wrong, many Americans asked, was it trying to shield something from the public? Given the conflicting and confusing evidence, what was the role of the Dallas police? of the FBI and the CIA? It was probably no accident that the controversy over Kennedy's assassination was followed by a presidential campaign in which a major party (the Republican) frankly advanced a conspiratorial view of recent American history; or that in the succeeding years, the general public was prepared to believe there was a "credibility gap" between official pronouncements and the truth.

Of course many other factors contributed to growing suspicions that various groups, in and out of the government, were plotting to undermine traditional liberties. A series of shocking civil rights murders in the South revealed the existence of genuine conspiracies to thwart new laws and to intimidate militant Negroes and their friends. The deepening racial crisis, coupled with the persisting Vietnam War, convinced an increasing number of radicals that the American "power structure" was beyond reform and should be destroyed by acts of real or symbolic violence. The urban riots of 1967, followed by the assassinations of Martin Luther King and Robert Kennedy, led more and more people to conclude that American society was either "sick" or permeated with lethal conspiracies.

To some extent, the belief in the existence of conspiracies has been self-fulfilling. The conviction that America has fallen into the hands of a Power Elite or of Communist infiltrators leads easily to a mood of desperation, to a rejection of both the existing social order and of peaceful or legal means to promote change. By the late 1960's the nation contained a disturbing number of secret or semisecret organizations, ranging from leftist revolutionaries to the Minutemen and the Ku Klux Klan, all of whom justified violence in the name of overthrowing the "usurpers" who controlled American society. And if the number of such extremists remained very small, only the future could tell whether millions of other disillusioned Americans could re-establish a unifying consensus, regain faith in the integrity of public officials, and come to see intellectual and cultural diversity as a mark of strength instead of evidence of disunity and corruption engineered by malicious subversives.

Democratic Despotism (1936)

RAOUL E. DESVERNINE

One of the leaders of the right-wing Liberty League, Raoul E. Desvernine was a New York attorney and the president of Crucible Steel Company. He was a bitter foe of the New Deal, which he compared to European totalitarianism. Like the earlier opponents of Jeffersonian "Illuminati," and "Tory" Whigs, Desvernine charged that New Dealers were masking revolutionary designs with deceptive party labels. The conflicts of interest between the Roosevelt administration and the conservative business community gave rise to a theory of political conspiracy that also anticipated many of the themes of McCarthyism and the later radical right. Thus Desvernine pictured the New Deal as gradually subverting the Constitution and brainwashing the American people into submission.

We have seen that our traditional democratic ideas have been violently distorted, and our constitutional concepts manhandled, by a coterie of visionaries, appointed to non-elective key positions, and that the President himself has progressed under their tutelage to a practical acceptance of their "professed objectives." We have seen that the New Deal was not included in the Democratic platform of 1932. It was rather evolved from the motives and ideals of those who sprang out of the unknown after the election. We are now confronted with a universal belief in the philosophy of the "New Order" by all those composing the directive force of the New Deal. There is every

From Raoul E. Desvernine, *Democratic Despotism* (New York: Dodd, Mead & Company, 1936), pp. 158–162.

reason, therefore, why the alert and the inquiring should endeavor to determine the direction that the New Deal is giving to our political thinking, and to understand the professed ideals of individual freedom, and of the political institutions of the new social and political order, which its votaries visualize and strive to achieve. Surely, it has been "blue-printed" sufficiently clearly, and with enough detail, to give us an acquaintance with it adequate to predicate a reasoned opinion thereon as to whether or not it is the system of society which we would prefer to our present system. Beyond any question of doubt, we are, at least, convinced that it is basically different from our American system of constitutional democracy and is absolutely incompatible therewith. It has a striking resemblance in its fundamental thoughts with certain European philosophies which we have called "The New Despotisms." . . .

To gain power by a cunning misuse of democratic methods is the most generally adopted technique of all astute politicians, who are planning to destroy, for their own self-seeking purposes, cherished governmental theories and institutions, and history proves it to be more efficacious, and certainly less perilous, than violence. Revolution is the exceptional, and the last-recourse, method. But once having democratically assumed power, the beginnings of an early transition to despotism become noticeable. The party names, platforms, and principles, which were utilized as a means to gain power are remolded to fit the real motives and ideals of the incipient usurpers.

The New Dealers followed this historic pattern. They rode into power on the political machine of the Democratic Party. They paraded, and still parade, as Democrats though their "professed objectives," as we have observed them, are far removed from anything that traditional Democrats ever professed. . . .

Henry Wallace most clearly explains the situation:

So enlisted, men may rightfully feel they are serving a function as high as that of any minister of the Gospel. They will not be Socialists, Communists or Fascists, but plain men trying to gain *by democratic methods the professed objectives of the Communists, Socialists and Fascists;* . . . (Italics Ours.)

That accurately describes the technique which they have adopted. They "will not be Socialists, Communists or Fascists" by openly and officially aligning themselves with those parties, or identifying themselves with their organized activities, "even though they are trying to gain the professed objectives of the Communists, Socialists and Fascists," so long as they are hopefully seeking to attain these "professed objectives" "by democratic methods."

They purpose deceitfully to use party labels and machinery, to manipulate democratic processes, to maneuver democratic forces, and finally, as we will soon see, to convert, improperly, constitutional machinery to the furtherance of their designs.

Let us, therefore, briefly pursue the record of the use of this technique!

Wallace says: "The experimental method of democracy may be slow, but it has the advantage of being sure. When you change people's minds you change the course of a nation." To divert the nation's course, we are naively told, we must first "change people's minds." We must free them from their intellectual bondage to outworn and obsolete ideals. We must demonstrate that their traditional institutions, their constitutional processes and limitations, are outmoded and inadequate under new conditions, arrest progress, and prevent man from achieving his new destiny, from realizing his new promise. We must, therefore, give a new direction to political thought.

The "scientific" approach, however, requires that we must not directly and openly attack the efficacy of the existing systems, as this might shock the people's susceptibilities and thereby make them hesitant to change, but we should rather step by step prepare the people's minds for a gradual and unconscious acceptance of the new ideas. We have already seen the subtle maneuvers made to impregnate our political thinking with new economic and social concepts, by demonstrating that our economic and social advances demand the expansion of political agencies into economic controls, by guiding our reason and imagination through our present constitutional confines across "New Frontiers" into "social discipline," "planned economy," and the "Third Economy." But teaching must be pursued by action!

The Roosevelt Red Record
and Its Background (1936)

ELIZABETH DILLING

A rabid antiradical and anti-Semite, Mrs. Elizabeth Kirkpatrick Dilling accused the New Deal of implementing a Communist plot to stir up Negro discontent and promote racial intermixture. She was particularly outraged by the willingness of Franklin D. Roosevelt and especially his wife to be photographed with prominent Negroes; she also singled out Harold Ickes, the Secretary of the Interior, for his supposedly criminal efforts to mingle the races in federal housing projects. During the Second World War, Mrs. Dilling was indicted for trying to incite mutiny in the American armed forces and for attempting to establish a Nazi regime in the United States. The charges were dropped at the end of the war.

Some twelve years ago the patriotic expert, R. M. Whitney, cited in his booklet, *Back to Barbarism*, published by the American Defense Society, the various resolutions, identical in theme, passed by the I.W.W., the Socialist Party and the Communist International for the purpose of roping the Negroes into the Red "class struggle." . . .

Back in 1919 the Socialist Party put out a book entitled *Socialism Imperiled or—the Negro—A Potential Menace to Radicalism* (a menace unless he were radicalized). This laid out a program which has been followed to the letter. Its Socialist advice contained this:

It should paint the advantages of the cooperative commonwealth and point out the inevitable destruction, if any of its component groups is exploited and discriminated against.

It should expose the sham democracy today existing in America, with special reference to negroes.

It should point out that Christ, William Lloyd Garrison, Horace Greeley, John Brown and Abraham Lincoln were abused as radicals in their day, and that today they are esteemed as among the world's great benefactors.

IN SHORT, IT SHOULD AIM TO CHANGE THE RACE-CONSCIOUS WORKER.

From Elizabeth Dilling, *The Roosevelt Red Record and Its Background* (n.p., 1936), pp. 218, 220–222, 226, 236.

In supporting radical negro publications FINANCIALLY, white radicals will be making their best investment.

Whitney's comment was: "From the present outflow of negro radical writing it would seem that not a little 'white radical money' has been 'invested.'" . . .

Whitney continues:

Negro newspapers and magazines, some of which were formerly conservative publications, devoted to the best interests of the negro, and, in the case of the newspapers, giving him the straight, uncolored news, are now poisoning the minds of their colored readers with communistic doctrines, and dishing out all the news with Marxian dressing. That such publications are financed by some branch of the communist party, if not directly from Moscow, seems unmistakable.

Radical white speakers appear before negro audiences wherever and whenever they can. They visit negro schools and colleges and talk about a race equality they feel no more than the negro does. They paint a terrible picture of the oppression of negro workers, a picture that is false, but which they manage to impress upon some of the less balanced negro minds as true. . . .

The Jews are accounted, by radicals, the best organizers of negroes for radical work. Up to the time of the Russian revolution it was said that no negroes were radicals except a few foreign born or reared black men, and one or two who had come under the influence of Jewish radicals.

Just as Socialism proposes to enforce sex equality and rob mankind of its natural birthright of an individual mother and father and home, of belief in God and His commandments, so it proposes to obliterate racial lines everywhere by enforcing social equality and social intermingling and promoting inter-breeding.

The inter-racial idea is one of the strongest dogmas of Socialism-Communism. Wholesome, self-respecting, honest friendship between the separate races is not what is sought at all. This is bitterly derided as mere "bourgeois" race "chauvinism" or pride. There must be a complete surrender of individuality, blending and inter-marriage to satisfy Communist objectives. Social intermingling is the opening wedge, coupled with Red agitations among the Negroes. . . .

It remained for Karl Marx to insist that agitation must not cease until the races and sexes be poured into one melting pot to be moulded into one mass, as planned by Marx, not by God.

The regrettable fact is that it is the Marxians, not the sound Americans, who have long been spending great amounts of money and energy to spread their doctrines among the Negroes with the expectation that this will bear fruit.

Wherever one goes in Red circles, whenever one reads Red literature, one sees the relentless and artificial efforts being made to break down racial lines. . . .

I have never attended a Communist Party mass meeting without observing the public petting of Negroes and whites. This is a deliberate and staged policy. At one meeting three burly Negroes were pawing their white girl companion, a college-type blonde wearing a squirrel coat. At the huge American League Against War and Fascism Congress in Chicago, a Negro in front of me sat with one arm around his white girl companion; with his other hand he stroked her leg. . . .

The *New Republic,* "advocate of revolutionary Socialism," admiringly says (6/10/36): "President Roosevelt and his wife have opposed social discrimination against the Negro, and partly because of this fact it is reported that in the election he will receive the support of many thousands of Negroes in Northern states who have always heretofore voted the Republican ticket."

Omitting the disgraceful carpet bagging era, the Republican Party has stood for political and economic opportunity and freedom for the Negro people but has not stood for racial inter-marriage and social intermixture, nor have the best Negroes.

Well-meaning Negroes are often surprised when shown that the National Association for the Advancement of Colored People and the National Urban League are steered by Communistic whites and have received thousands of dollars from the Communist Garland Fund because they serve specific Red purposes. They break down racial lines, agitate Negro social equality, in fact continually file law suits demanding it, and feed the Negroes with continuous radical propaganda under the guise of friendship to the race.

Mrs. Roosevelt's picture appears in the 4/20/35 issue of the Washington *Afro-American* addressing a meeting of the National Association for the Advancement of Colored People in the Metropolitan African M.E. Church. The huge caption at the head of the page is, "FIRST LADY HELPS NAACP GET 600 NEW MEMBERS." Beneath are the sub-captions: "MRS. F.D.R. FOR ANTI-LYNCH BILL," "WAGE EQUALITY IS NEEDED SHE SAYS," "FIRST LADY AIDS MEMBERSHIP DRIVE WITH ADDRESS SUNDAY."

Directly under the column featuring her speech is a picture showing students coming out of the State University of Moscow, showing a burly Negro student grinning at his white girl companion, described as: "RUSSIAN STUDENTS leaving summer school of Moscow. Dr. A. L. Locke, professor of philosophy at Howard University, will attend this summer school as a student. American students are getting special invitations from Russia." . . .

The studied, insincere and obsequious flattery by the Roosevelts and their radical supporters of the Negro people is without precedent in any *American* political party. However, it is no accident but follows, as closely as other parts of the Roosevelt Socialist program, the old well-laid, well-thought-out plan of the Marxists to enlist and use the Negro to change the American system of government and the entire social order.

A Communist View of Right-Wing Conspiracy (1938)

EARL BROWDER

As in the past, the paranoid style was no monopoly of the right. Earl Browder joined the Communist party in 1919 and then rose to become General Secretary and the Communist nominee for President in 1936 and 1940. Although in 1934 he had attacked Roosevelt as the tool of big bankers and industrialists, two years later Browder was appealing for a united front against fascist reactionaries. By 1938, in line with international Communist policy, Browder had muted his criticism of the New Deal, interpreting the election of 1936 as a sweeping mandate for social reform which was now imperiled by a worldwide conspiracy of fascists and warmakers. In his report to the Tenth National Convention of the Communist party, he warned that fascist reactionaries had infiltrated the ranks of the Democrats in Congress and were secretly promoting divisions in the American labor movement.

There is ample cause for uneasiness and alarm. Reactionary forces, moving toward fascism, within our own land, are not accepting their

---

From Earl Browder, *Report to the Tenth National Convention of the Communist Party of the U.S.A. on Behalf of the Central Committee*, Special Edition for the Delegates to the Tenth National Convention (n.p., n.d. [1938]), pp. 7–8, 10–12.

defeat in the last elections. They do not admit the right of the majority of 27,000,000 Americans who voted them down in 1936, to direct the destinies of America. Using their enormous powers as the owners of American economy, they have proceeded to defeat the measures proposed by President Roosevelt, to sabotage those already enacted, to split away the Right-wing section of his party and unite it in a reactionary coalition with the Republicans, to combat and divide the rising labor movement, to cut wages and reduce living standards, and by all means to break up the growing unity of the masses of the people in their search for jobs, security, democracy and peace.

In world affairs, the reactionaries of our own land have succeeded in preventing the great potential power of America from being thrown into the balance on the side of democracy and peace. They carry through, in practice, the opposite of that policy enunciated by President Roosevelt in Chicago last October, of concerted action to quarantine the warmaking powers. They are carrying America in the wake of the Tory Chamberlain government of Britain, which is moving into the camp of the warmakers and betraying democracy into their hands. They are bringing the horrors of a new world slaughter, already begun in the invasions of Spain and China, each day closer to the shores of America.

Truly our country, together with the rest of the world, is threatened with chaos and disaster, with the destruction of the best heritage of our past, with the destruction of civilization itself.

The reactionaries, the fascists, the warmakers, have tremendous resources on their side. They have control of the great trustified industries, the heart of the national economy, in each of the capitalist nations. They are the economic royalists, the "sixty families." They control the bloody dictatorships of Germany, Italy and Japan, which regiment whole peoples into the military machine. They work internationally, in concert, despite their sharp struggle among themselves, on a worldwide plan, to gobble up and assimilate the world, piecemeal, bite by bite, leading toward world anarchy. They operate on the age-old principle of oppressors—"divide and conquer."

Democracy and progress, the camp of the plain people, the toiling masses, have the advantage of numbers—the overwhelming majority of the people. To it belongs the future. This majority spells power, but only to the degree that it is united and is aware of its enemies and how to defeat them. . . .

In 1936 the people won a brilliant victory over the reactionary camp, in the overwhelming electoral successes of Roosevelt and the New Deal—but the reactionary camp had smuggled into Congress, under cover of formal adherence to Roosevelt, a sufficient minority which, united with the Republicans, was able to sabotage and defeat the main program for which the people voted in the elections.

In 1936 and since, the workers have broken through the capitalist strongholds of the "open shop," the basic and trustified industries, have established a strong industrial union movement, have more than doubled the numerical strength of the trade unions, and begun to build independent political organizations—but the reactionary forces have been able to split the labor movement into two competing centers engaged in fratricidal struggle.

The workers, farmers, and middle classes were able to establish new measures of protection of their incomes and living standards, and thus ward off to some extent the miseries of a new economic collapse—but the economic royalists still retained such powers, and the Roosevelt administration proceeded with such hesitations, that a "sit-down strike of capital," with the slogan of "lack of confidence" in democracy, was able to plunge our country into a new economic crisis of unprecedented severity and swiftness of development.

The camp of democracy advanced its positions, through its assault against the stronghold of reaction in the Supreme Court, forcing some liberalization of its personnel and policies; through its fight for the anti-lynching bill; through its exposure and fight against local reactionary machines like that of Kelley-Nash in Chicago, responsible for the Memorial Day massacre, and of the infamous Hague in Jersey City—but the camp of reaction was able to sidetrack the Supreme Court reform, kill the Anti-Lynching Bill by filibuster of a minority, and postpone the break-up of the worst local reactionary powers or substitute for them others equally reactionary.

The progressive movement has been able brilliantly to penetrate into the territory of the old "Solid South," break up its solidly reactionary character, arouse the mass democratic movement, and already show the promise of a "New South"—but the reactionary camp still controls most of the main positions in the South, which they are trying to unite with the Northern reaction of the Republican Party.

Finally, the camp of progress and democracy has awakened to the realities of the world about us, emerged from its dreams of "isolation" in a world threatened with fascism and war, and found expression for its awakened conscience in Roosevelt's call to "quarantine the warmakers"—but the everyday practical policy in Washington continues along the reactionary line, giving aid and comfort to the bandit governments in their aggressions, and to Chamberlain's policy of surrender to and complicity with them.

We can sum up the main results of the past two years as follows: The camp of the people, of progress and democracy, has won some important battles and positions, has become conscious of its own existence, of its enemies, of its own potential forces, and of the main direction of the program which alone can fulfill its tasks and bring victory to the people; it has begun the first steps in the organization of its forces. The camp of reaction, of the economic royalists, has suffered some serious defeats; it is feverishly calling its reserves into action, uniting all its many armies under a single command, and preparing a desperate general attack, all along the line, against the living standards and democratic rights of the people. It follows a strategic line for division of the democratic camp and the defeat of its separate sections through concentration of the united forces of reaction, point by point, against a divided democracy.

The Trojan Horse (1939)

HOUSE COMMITTEE ON UN-AMERICAN ACTIVITIES

The growing fear of subversion which arose from opposition to the New Deal and from alarm over the rise of totalitarianism in Europe was institutionalized in 1938 by the creation of the House Committee on Un-American Activities. This new body was authorized to investigate "the diffusion within the United States of subversive and un-American propaganda that is instigated from foreign countries or of a domestic origin and attacks the principle of the form of government as guaranteed by our Constitution." While the Committee gave passing attention to pro-Nazi groups, it was primarily concerned with Communism, which it defined as being "diametrically opposed to Americanism."

Despite the traditional separation of church and state, the Committee defined Americanism in terms of religious belief, on the ground that man's inherent and fundamental rights came from God. The chief sin of totalitari-

---

From *Investigation of Un-American Activities and Propaganda. Report of the Special Committee on Un-American Activities* . . . *January* 3, 1939 (*Washington,* 1939*),* pp. 27–28.

anism was its denial of the divine origin of man, which opened the way for the state to obliterate individual rights. In the words of the Committee, "A scheme or philosophy of government or a teaching which embraces all or any essential part of the principles of Communism is un-American." This meant that it was un-American to promote class or racial hatred, to advocate a planned economy, or to weaken constitutional checks and balances.

The Committee was deeply embittered by the refusal of the President and his Cabinet to cooperate with their investigations. The first hearings emphasized the leftist penetration of federal projects and agencies. One of the main targets of the Committee's attacks was the American Civil Liberties Union, which it portrayed as supporting and protecting subversive movements that would destroy civil liberties. The ACLU had supposedly weakened America by working up sympathy for radicals and various protesting minority groups. By branding disturbing ideas as un-American and by focusing "the spotlight of publicity" on the activities of disruptive groups, the House Committee prepared the way for the more extreme suspicions and phobias of the post-World War II era.

In 1935 the Communists changed their strategy and tactics to what is now known as the "Trojan Horse tactics." Georgi Dimitrov, in an address to the Seventh Congress of the Communist International, held in Moscow in August 1935, said:

Comrades, you remember the ancient tale of the capture of Troy. Troy was inaccessible to the armies attacking her, thanks to her impregnable walls, and the attacking army, after suffering many sacrifices, was unable to achieve victory until with the aid of the famous Trojan Horse it managed to penetrate to the very heart of the enemies' camp. We revolutionary workers, it appears to me, should not be shy about using the same tactics. . . .

The new tactics have proven to be very effective and successful. Instead of conducting labor organizations of their own, as they formerly did, the Communists have found it much more effective to penetrate legitimate trade unions and to seize strategic positions and offices in those unions. Under the new policy, the Communists form units or fractions within labor unions especially in the heavy industries. These units work in complete unison and harmony under instructions. Their members were well trained in organizing work. In addition to this, they are actuated by a fanatical zeal. When the industrial unions sprang up like mushroom growths in the heavy industries, there was a scarcity of trained and skilled organizers. Having permeated the organizations, the Communists stepped into the roles of organizers and found it easy to seize strategic positions in the unions. Many of the

Communists became organizers, stewards, and members of the executive boards.

The same tactics of penetration or "boring from within" were used successfully in other organizations, such as political parties. Formerly the Communists had their own candidates and their own ticket which they actively and openly supported. Now the Communists either do not put up candidates or, if they do, it is for the purpose of deception. Actually the Communists actively support "left-wing" elements in other political parties.

Not only do the Communists penetrate other organizations, but they set up numerous organizations with high-sounding titles and laudable objectives. These are known as the "front" organizations of the Communist Party. The majority of members of these organizations are unaware of the Communist control or influence, but we invariably find outstanding Communists occupying strategic positions within the organizations. From these vantage points they are able to subtly shape or influence the policies of the "front" organizations and direct their activities. The ease with which Communists are able to infiltrate these organizations and seize important positions would be unbelievable if we did not have before us the most convincing proof. The explanation is that many of the non-Communist members are inactive and indifferent while the tightly organized group of Communists within the organization are well organized and fanatically zealous. It is the old story of a well-organized minority being able to outmaneuver an unorganized and indifferent majority. Herein is typified the genius of Communist strategy. They have simply put into effect what has been demonstrated time and time again; namely, that an active and disciplined minority is always able to outmaneuver a disorganized majority. The Communist influence in the United States cannot, therefore, be measured by its size. The Communist program does not call for large numbers. When the Communists seized control of Russia they comprised less than 1 percent of the population of Russia.

Their real influence must be measured in terms of their ability to direct or influence other organizations and groups who have many times the membership that the Communist Party claims. The effectiveness of the Communists in the United States must be gaged by their ability to infuse the poison of class hatred into the blood stream of the Nation. It is not the open and undisguised activity of the Communists that we need fear. It is not their direct influence which should occasion alarm. It is rather the subversive and insidious way in which they go about their destructive work; the penetration of other organizations; the seizure of strategic positions in other organizations and in the Government itself; the subtle and indirect influence which they exert—these are the things which constitute the Communist menace to America. If the Communists worked in the open there would be nothing to fear, but when through policies of deception and tactics that are cleverly concealed they pursue their destructive plans, it becomes important to reckon with them as menacing factors in our national life. Many of the activities and tactics of the Communists appear ridiculous to the average American and, by reason of this fact, he is prone to discredit the seriousness of these activities. He is apt to overlook the important fact that the minds of most Communists are diseased and that their thinking and process of reason are fantastic and often border on insanity. Indeed the very philosophy of communism is fantastic and unreal. There is nothing in the experience or reason of man to justify it; it is the product of mental warping. It is, therefore, natural that minds which can seriously entertain such a destructive philosophy, and such an unreasonable conception of man in the universe, should be productive of fantastic schemes and activities. It is strange but true that this irrationalism affords the Communists their most effective guise because the average American is inclined to "laugh it off." The Communist is cunning enough to take advantage of this attitude on our part so that he may prosecute his subversive work unmolested.

Communist Influence
in High Places (1940)

MARTIN DIES

The first chairman and guiding spirit of the House Committee on Un-American Activities was Martin Dies, a Democratic Congressman from Texas. A bitter enemy of the liberal and reform wing of the New Deal, Dies foreshadowed the tactics of Senator Joseph McCarthy by compiling tedious lists of individuals and groups with alleged Communist "connections."

From Martin Dies, *The Trojan Horse in America* (New York: Dodd, Mead & Company, 1940), pp. 285, 292–293, 294–295, 303.

Stalin baited his hook with a "progressive" worm, and New Deal suckers swallowed bait, hook, line, and sinker. . . .

The First Lady of the Land has been one of the most valuable assets which the Trojan Horse organizations of the Communist Party have possessed, due to the immense prestige which her sponsorship has conferred upon them. She has been a speaker for the following organizations: the American Youth Congress, the World Youth Congress, the League of Women Shoppers, the Daughters of the American Depression, the Southern Conference for Human Welfare, the American Communications Association, the Workers Alliance, the National Negro Congress, and the Southern Negro Youth Congress. She has otherwise lent her prestige to the Motion Picture Artists Committee, the China Aid Council of the American League for Peace and Democracy, the United Student Peace Committee, and the American Federation of Teachers, Local No. 5.

Following the lead of the White House, cabinet officers have done their part to add to the influence of some of the Communist Trojan Horses.

The Secretary of the Interior, Harold L. Ickes, has spoken for the National Negro Congress. He endorsed the meeting of the American Committee for the Protection of the Foreign Born, held in Washington in March, 1940. He permitted himself to be made the honorary chairman of the Spanish Refugee Relief Campaign which the Communist Party abandoned when it lost control of the organization by the narrow margin of one vote. He signed the "Call" of the American Youth Congress for its annual gathering in 1939. He contributed to the publication of the International Labor Defense. He wrote for the League of American Writers, and he sponsored the Descendants of the American Revolution. . . .

Archibald MacLeish, Librarian of Congress, has had one of the longest records of association with Communist-controlled groups to be found among New Deal appointees. His connections have included the following organizations: the American Friends of Spanish Democracy, the North American Committee to Aid Spanish Democracy, the Spanish Refugee Relief Campaign, the Friends of the Abraham Lincoln Brigade, Frontier Films, Writers and Artists Committee, Motion Picture Artists Committee, the *New Theatre*, the New Theatre League, the Workers Dance League. . . .

The Communist Party's highly synchronized and highly disciplined organization has been permitted to entrench itself deep in our body politic. It will not be rooted out until the powerful voice of the American people makes itself heard and demands effective action.

The Fascists' Conspiracy against the People (1938)

GEORGE SELDES

George Seldes is a left-wing journalist who carried the muckraking tradition into the 1940's. His work is best summarized by the title of one of his books, The Truth behind the News *(1929). As editor and publisher of the periodical* In Fact, *he portrayed a continuing picture of the American power elite manipulating the news as well as public policies. In Seldes' view, Red-baiting and superpatriotism were the classic devices of fascists and corporation leaders for dividing the people and thwarting the popular will. Since the fascist movements of Europe had originally been supported by bankers and industrial cartels, there was no mystery about the hidden backers of the Liberty League and other protofascist groups in America. Using tactics similar to those of the right, Seldes fully exploited the device of guilt by association. Like his conservative opponents, he also explained seemingly fortuitous events in terms of a hidden plot which demanded a renewed vigilance and unity among the common people.*

The final, and the desperate effort of any reactionary regime to preserve the economic-financial status-quo, can be called Fascism provided it acts according to the Fascist pattern—and that means, that to be Fascist it must employ violence, it must use armed force, it must if necessary impose itself through armed seizure of power and armed maintenance of power. This has been proved true elsewhere; it is the pattern for Fascism in America. The mass following is also a *sine qua non,* and so is a radical program by which the disinherited and dispossessed will be inveigled into following a dictator. . . .

It is always money and power that control Fascism. . . . The backers of Fascism everywhere are the industrialists, manufacturers, big businessmen, the bankers.

From George Seldes, *You Can't Do That: A Survey of the Forces Attempting, in the Name of Patriotism, to Make a Desert of the Bill of Rights* (New York, 1938), pp. 207, 209–211, 212–215, 238–239, 241.

The financing is always done secretly—until the movement succeeds. In America the one organization which is best adapted for financing a reactionary armed force is the one which has already proclaimed among its principles the salvation of private profits. The American Liberty League answers the description of the subsidizers of Hitler and Mussolini. It is at the moment in decidedly stale odor, but in Johnstown, Pennsylvania, and elsewhere similar groups are rivals for its succession.

I have already discussed the interests of the leaders of this organization. The United Press has made a survey of the industrial and financial empire which the members of the Liberty League direct or control, and places a money value upon it of $37,000,000,000. The directors of the League are affiliated with all the great corporations, including United States Steel, General Motors, Standard Oil, Chase National Bank, Goodyear Tire, Westinghouse, Baltimore and Ohio, Mutual Life Insurance Company, American T. & T., and scores of similar concerns. . . .

If Fascism comes to America, it must have the backing of an organization analogous to the American Liberty League.

Certain conditions necessary for Fascism exist in America as they did in Italy and Germany. We seem to have everything from economic distress to red-baiting hysteria to demagoguery to intolerant superpatriotism. The profit system is at last fighting in the open. As in Italy, the banner of nationalism, discipline, order, will be raised, and promises of share-the-wealth and social security will be made, and every means known to man will be used to obtain a mass following for a magnificently worded program. Although it will differ from Italian Fascism as German Fascism differs from the latter, the controlling forces will be the same.

These forces do not necessarily want civil war although they are willing, as history in other countries proves, to engage in bloodshed as a last extreme. They are usually willing to buy their peace. In the United States this means control of the two big political parties, and the corollary, the knifing of any and all third parties which might either get popular support or obtain the balance of power.

In the past it has been big business which paid the bills of both parties; at present it is still big business, but there is a decided leaning toward the Republican Party which is closer to Fascism than the Democratic, and in the future we may see a purely Fascist party—under a fine American patriotic Liberty-Boys-of-1776 name of course.

Potential sponsors for this party are the Liberty League and Mr. Hearst.

In connection with the latter, it is interesting to recall the following declaration on this subject: "We still maintain a republican form of government," wrote Mr. Hearst many years ago when he still favored a republican form of government instead of Hitler and Mussolini and the Liberty League, "but who has control of the primaries that nominate the candidate? The corporations have. Who control the conventions? The corporations. Who control the machinery of elections? The corporations. Who own the bosses and the elected officials? Are they representatives of the people or of the corporations? Let any fair-minded man answer that question truthfully. If the corporations do all this—and they surely do—can we any longer maintain that this is a government by the people? It is a government by a distinct class. . . ."

Well, it took Mr. Hearst a generation to make practical use of a truth he himself had announced. When he wrote the foregoing he was presumably devoting his press to the purposes and hopes of the working class against the corporations; today Hearst is openly on the side of the corporations. . . .

A more recent illustration has been given me by one of the foremost women of America, a famous journalist. During a crossing from Le Havre to New York, a group of great corporations heads—one of the greatest oil men in America, two of the biggest bankers, one of the most important industrialists—sitting daily at a table in the lounge, sought to disillusion my informant about politics and banish her naïve ideas about our Republican-Democratic olympiads. They explained to her exactly how the big businessmen of America finance the campaigns of both parties, including the "reform" party, whichever it may be, which promises the dear people it will end the iniquities of Wall Street, bust the trusts, drive the money-changers out of the temple, and what not.

"What about Franklin D. Roosevelt?" asked my informant.

"A slight error there," replied the oil king. "Of course, we had our money up on him as well as the opposition, and we expected him to make the talks about the money-changers, but we did not expect much action. He has, however, betrayed his class, and he has fooled us. Well, we had about five million dollars in the Democratic Party in that election and there is no doubt that Franklin Roosevelt has now got a large mass following. I do not think we can defeat him, but my friends here do. It will take more than five million, but they say they will do it. They'll do it if it takes twenty million. But make no mistake about it Miss——, we buy and control our presidents. And by *we* I mean the five men seated right here at this table and a few of our friends back home. We make mistakes sometimes, but usually big business wins no matter which party wins." . . .

The financial tie-up between the Republican Party, the corporations, the Liberty League, the superpatriotic organizations and the Fascist-minded Americans is much more apparent. The list of contributors to the Republican National Committee and the Liberty League is almost identical. The former reported Junius S. Morgan, H. P. Davison, George F. Baker, Lammot Du Pont, Alfred P. Sloan, W. L. Mellon, the Armours, Silas Strawn and others sending in between three and five thousand dollars each in January and February, 1936. By June, 1936 the committee gladly reported the Rockefellers had given $16,000, the Mellons $25,000, the Union League Club $15,000, and Messrs. William Woodward, George Whitney, Henry Du Pont, H. H. Timken and many others $5,000 each. Other heavy contributors included Hallock Du Pont, Silas H. Strawn, Hearst's lawyer, John Francis Neylan, William Bell of American Cyanamid, Sewell Avery of the Liberty League, Ernest T. Weir of the Liberty League, John N. Pew, Jr., and other big businessmen. . . .

In the civilized Scandinavian monarchies, in the Czechoslovakian Republic which is arming against the Fascist International, in Belgium where Fascism was soundly defeated in 1937, in Britain (where the Labor Party has too often stood by the Conservatives in the great hypocrisy of the Spanish crisis), and in many other nations where freedom still exists, the idea of a common front against the enemy is gaining ground. In fact, it has made such important gains that the frightened red-baiters have invented the charge that every such coalition is a Moscow plot. This fraud originated in Nuremberg at the 1936 Nazi congress; it was heard over the radio in the nightmarish voice of Doctor Goebbels, and it appears today in the self-styled objective press of the world, but nevertheless the Popular Front moves on, joining all good men, whatever their political views, in united action against those who wage war for profits. . . .

The question of Communism and Fascism has been clarified in Spain for everyone in America who is not blinded by propaganda or ingrown religious superstition. It is an obvious fact that for almost a generation the western world has been warned against the Communist Internationale, its "boring from within," its conspiracy, its plans to attack internationally—in fact against the very things which the Fascist International is doing today.

The Communist Internationale holds public congresses—I have attended them—where the hopes of winning the world to Karl Marx are reported and discussed, but the supposed documents of violent and military plans for that goal, such as the Zinovieff Letter, the Associated Press-Mexican red hegemony story of 1927, have without exception been exposed as forgeries and hoaxes. On the other hand there are no accusations of world plot against the Fascist nations, no forgeries and hoaxes, but there is the living and bloody evidence of Italian, German, Portuguese and Japanese cooperation throughout the world under the fraudulent banner of making the world safe from Bolshevism.

We who are interested in liberty and who fear dictatorship have convincing evidence that the enemy is international Fascism, that it is Fascism that not only conspires secretly but attacks first and openly; we have the proof in the Mediterranean and we can foresee it in the Far East. The four Fascist nations are united by treaties and blood. . . .

In America today, as in Germany many years ago, the enemy is Reaction. The enemy has the men, the guns, the money, the press, the power. They can beat us if we stand in separated groups. The friends of liberty and the enemies of liberty leagues cannot only maintain a democratic republic in America, producing the greater freedom which a few of the real libertarians among the founding fathers had in mind, but can surpass them by establishing economic liberty and eventually perhaps that maximum of liberty which comes with a minimum of government.

We must guard against the impostures of pretended patriotism, especially that patriotism which is the last refuge of scoundrels and which is so prevalent, so professional, and so well paid nowadays. Eternal vigilance must become more than the slogan for small associations desperately fighting almost overwhelming cases of infringement on individual liberties. We must realize that those who use red-baiting to attack every liberal and democratic movement today, are the armed cutthroats of reactionary Fascism tomorrow. Two facts emerge from any study of European turmoil and the new class alignment in our own land. The enemy is always the Right. Fascism and

Reaction inevitably attack. They have won against disunion. They will fail if we unite.

The Cold War a Product of Wall Street Conspiracy (1949)

WILLIAM Z. FOSTER

As part of the Alien Registration Act of 1940 (commonly known as the Smith Act), Congress made it a crime to advocate, advise, or teach the duty, necessity, or desirability of overthrowing the government of the United States or any of its states by force and violence. In 1949 the eleven top leaders of the Communist Party were tried and convicted under the Smith Act, whose constitutionality was upheld by the Supreme Court two years later. One of those convicted was William Z. Foster, who had been active in organizing the steel workers' strike in 1919 and had run as the Communist candidate for President in 1924, 1928, and 1932. In his defense of the Communist party, Foster pointed to a capitalist-fascist conspiracy which had counted on Hitler's armies to destroy Communist Russia. The defeat of Nazi Germany, in Foster's view, had brought widespread alarm among the reactionary forces of America, who finally triumphed by pushing Washington into an aggressive cold war abroad and the suppression of freedom at home.

World reaction watched with dismay the complete defeat of Hitler in the war and the rapid growth of democracy and Socialism in Europe and Asia after the end of the war. To the monopolists and exploiters it all amounted to the handwriting on the wall for their capitalist system. . . .

These capitalists were all the more scared because the reactionary forces in Europe and Asia, badly shattered and discredited because of their traitorous pro-fascist attitude during the war, could do little, except to launch abortive civil wars in Greece and China, to stem this elemental democratic-Socialist forward movement of the people.

It was in this spirit that the powerful American reactionaries,

From William Z. Foster, *In Defense of the Communist Party and the Indicted Leaders* (New York, 1949), pp. 54–56, 58–61.

deeply alarmed at the world democratic picture and also seeing a chance to feather their own nest in the disturbed situation, took it upon themselves to smash this tremendous progressive movement at any cost and with every means. When American imperialism went violently into action the world outlook immediately became ominous in Europe and elsewhere, and fresh fears were at once aroused among the peoples everywhere of a re-birth of fascism, the precipitation of civil war in many countries, and the outbreak of a still more terrible third world war. . . .

This country is dominated by the richest, most strongly organized, and most ruthless capitalists in world history. These exploiters not only own our great industries and national resources, but they also control the two big parties, as well as all major sources of public information, and they dominate the government from stem to gudgeon. These capitalist oligarchs are aggressive, fascist, imperialist, and warlike. Their ultimate objective is to establish a Wall Street mastery over the world, including the Soviet Union.

There are three major forces driving American capitalism on to its imperialist policy of world domination.

First, the tremendous, unhealthy expansion of American industry during the war makes it absolutely necessary for the United States to make a desperate effort to control the markets of the world in order to dispose of as much as possible of its vast surplus production and also to find fields for the export of its mountains of idle capital.

This urgent domestic economic situation is why, too, so great a proportion of American production is devoted to war armaments. Without the current armaments expenditures our economy would explode overnight into a devastating crisis. Fear of a tremendous economic crisis is the basic reason why the big capitalists of the United States are driven on to try to bring the whole world not only economically, but also politically, under their control, even at the cost of war.

Second, the broken-down condition of world capitalism gives added strength to the imperialist drive of American capitalism. The big trust-controlled government of this country, with great wealth, industrial power, and military force at its disposal, is impelled, by the very weakness of the other capitalist states, to secure control over them, both for the benefit of American capitalism and as the only possible way, they believe, to save ramshackle world capitalism from collapsing altogether.

Third, American imperialism is also impelled to fight for world domination out of fear and hatred of Socialism. It believes that it must suppress Socialism at all costs, or else the capitalist system is lost. And as the leading capitalist power of the world it takes over the job of organizing for an anti-Socialist war. Above all, it aims at subjugating the U.S.S.R., which it correctly understands to be the backbone of world Socialism and democracy.

Wall Street imperialism, in striving for world political domination, has most of the capitalist countries on its financial dole, and is able to force their political policies to conform to its militaristic, imperialistic aims. Whole groups of nations—France, Italy, Western Germany, Japan, Nationalist China, Latin America, etc.—are at present hardly better than puppet states to the United States. . . .

These capitalist oligarchs have long been calculating upon making war against the Soviet Union. Already during World War II they had this dangerous scheme definitely in mind. That was why, sabotaging the Allies' general war strategy, they did their utmost to have Germany and the Soviet Union cut each other to pieces, so that the U.S.S.R. in the postwar period would not be able to resist them. This was also why they delayed the opening of the Western war front for at least 18 months, thereby causing the Russians millions of needless casualties. This was why, too, they shipped only one-third as much lend-lease supplies to the U.S.S.R. as they did to the British, although the Russians were doing at least 20 times more actual fighting. . . .

The tragedy of the whole situation is that the monopoly capitalists, with their complete control of all the major means of public information in the United States, have succeeded in hiding their criminal war and fascist activities from vast masses of the people by making them actually believe that the Soviet Union, which lost 7,000,000 soldiers and 10,000,000 civilians killed in the war and had half of its industrial plants wiped out, is attacking the United States. They also have made many believe that Wall Street and its political stooges are the great champions of world peace and democracy.

All this is enough to make the late Mr. Goebbels turn green with envy, for he and Hitler never put over a greater deception than this upon the German people.

The Communist Party Is
a Secret Conclave (1949)

ROBERT H. JACKSON

*The belief that the Communist party posed a threat to American security
was by no means confined to demagogic Congressmen and right-wing extremists. Before being appointed an Associate Justice to the Supreme Court in
1941, Robert H. Jackson had been Solicitor General and Attorney General
under President Roosevelt; he was the chief war crimes prosecutor for the
United States at the Nuremberg International Tribunal, following World
War II, and was known as one of the more liberal justices in the postwar
court. The following selection is from his separate opinion in a case that involved the validity of a statute requiring union officers to file an affidavit
stating they were not members of the Communist party and did not believe
in or teach the overthrow of the United States government by force or any
illegal, unconstitutional methods.*

*In an opinion dissenting from the Court's majority, Jackson held that it
was a violation of free speech to prohibit the belief or advocacy of certain
ideas. However, Jackson upheld that part of the statute pertaining to membership in the Communist party. Jackson's view of the Communist party
was reminiscent of much earlier images of the Order of the Illuminati and
other foreign conspiracies against American liberty. He held that the party
could not be classed with or given the protections of native political associations.*

What constitutes a party? Major political parties in the United
States have never been closely knit or secret organizations. Anyone
who usually votes the party ticket is reckoned a member, although he
has not applied for or been admitted to membership, pays no dues,
has taken no pledge, and is free to vote, speak and act as he wills.
Followers are held together by rather casual acceptance of general

From the concurring and dissenting opinions of Mr. Justice Jackson in American Communications Association, C.I.O. *et al.* v. Charles T. Douds; United Steel
Workers of America *et al.* v. National Labor Relations Board, in *Cases Argued
and Decided in the Supreme Court of the United States*, October term, 1949,
contained in *U.S. Reports*, Vols. 338 (pp. 216–end), 339. Book 94 Lawyers' Edition, ed. by Ernest H. Schopler (Rochester, N.Y.: The Lawyers' Co-Operative
Publishing Company, 1950), 339 U.S. 431–433.

principles, the influence of leaders, and sometimes by the cohesive power of patronage. Membership in the party carries with it little assurance that the member understands or believes in its principles and none at all that he will take orders from its leaders. . . .

Membership in the Communist Party is totally different. The Party is a secret conclave. Members are admitted only upon acceptance as reliable and after indoctrination in its policies, to which the member is fully committed. They are provided with cards or credentials, usually issued under false names so that the identification can only be made by officers of the Party who hold the code. Moreover, each pledges unconditional obedience to party authority. Adherents are known by secret or code names. They constitute "cells" in the factory, the office, the political society, or the labor union. For any deviation from the party line they are purged and excluded.

Inferences from membership in such an organization are justifiably different from those to be drawn from membership in the usual type of political party. Individuals who assume such obligations are chargeable, on ordinary conspiracy principles, with responsibility for and participation in all that makes up the Party's program. The conspiracy principle has traditionally been employed to protect society against all "ganging up" or concerted action in violation of its laws. No term passes that this court does not sustain convictions based on that doctrine for violations of the antitrust laws or other statutes. However, there has recently entered the dialectic of politics a cliché used to condemn application of the conspiracy principle to Communists. "Guilt by association" is an epithet frequently used and little explained, except that it is generally accompanied by another slogan, "guilt is personal." Of course it is; but personal guilt may be incurred by joining a conspiracy. That act of association makes one responsible for the acts of others committed in pursuance of the association. It is wholly a question of the sufficiency of evidence of association to imply conspiracy. There is certainly sufficient evidence that all members owe allegiance to every detail of the Communist Party program and have assumed a duty actively to help execute it, so that Congress could, on familiar conspiracy principles, charge each member with responsibility for the goals and means of the Party.

To Secure the Existing Order against Revolutionary Radicalism (1950)

ROBERT H. JACKSON

When the Supreme Court reviewed the constitutionality of the Smith Act, under which the Communist party leaders had been convicted, the Court's majority utilized the concept of "clear and present danger" as a means of limiting the rights guaranteed by the First Amendment. Justice Jackson, however, questioned the applicability of the "clear and present danger" test, and instead extended his earlier arguments on the unique character of Communism. Thus he held that it was no violation of free speech to convict Communists for conspiring to teach or advocate the forcible overthrow of the government, even if no clear and present danger could be proved.

This prosecution is the latest of never-ending, because never successful, quests for some legal formula that will secure an existing order against revolutionary radicalism. It requires us to reappraise, in the light of our own times and conditions, constitutional doctrines devised under other circumstances to strike a balance between authority and liberty. . . .

The principal reliance of the defense in this Court is that the conviction cannot stand under the Constitution because the conspiracy of these defendants presents no "clear and present danger" of imminent or foreseeable overthrow. . . .

The Communist Party, nevertheless, does not seek its strength primarily in numbers. Its aim is a relatively small party whose strength is in selected, dedicated, indoctrinated, and rigidly disciplined members. From established policy it tolerates no deviation and no debate. It seeks members that are, or may be, secreted in strategic posts in transportation, communications, industry, government, and especially in labor unions where it can compel employers to accept and retain

---

From the concurring and dissenting opinion of Mr. Justice Jackson in Eugene Dennis *et al.* v. United States of America, **341** U.S. **494–592** in *Cases Argued and Decided in the Supreme Court of the United States,* October term, **1950,** contained in *U.S. Reports,* Vols. **340, 341.** Book **95** Lawyers' Edition, ed. by Ernest H. Schopler (Rochester, New York: The Lawyers' Co-Operative Publishing Company, **1951**) 431 U.S. **560–561, 564–565, 570, 577.**

its members. It also seeks to infiltrate and control organizations of professional and other groups. Through these placements in positions of power it seeks a leverage over society that will make up in power of coercion what it lacks in power of persuasion.

The Communists have no scruples against sabotage, terrorism, assassination, or mob disorder; but violence is not with them, as with the anarchists, an end in itself. The Communist Party advocates force only when prudent and profitable. Their strategy of stealth precludes premature or uncoordinated outbursts of violence, except of course, when the blame will be placed on shoulders other than their own. They resort to violence as to truth, not as a principle but as an expedient. Force or violence, as they would resort to it, may never be necessary because infiltration and deception may be enough.

Force would be utilized by the Communist Party not to destroy government but for its capture. The Communist recognizes that an established government in control of modern technology cannot be overthrown by force until it is about ready to fall of its own weight. Concerted uprising, therefore, is to await that contingency and revolution is seen, not as a sudden episode, but as the consummation of a long process. . . .

If we must decide that this Act and its application are constitutional only if we are convinced that petitioner's conduct creates a "clear and present danger" of violent overthrow, we must appraise imponderables, including international and national phenomena which baffle the best informed foreign offices and our most experienced politicians. We would have to foresee and predict the effectiveness of Communist propaganda, opportunities for infiltration, whether, and when, a time will come that they consider propitious for action, and whether and how fast our existing government will deteriorate. . . .

The authors of the clear and present danger test never applied it to a case like this, nor would I. If applied as it is proposed here, it means that the Communist plotting is protected during its period of incubation; its preliminary stages of organization and preparation are immune from the law; the Government can move only after imminent action is manifest, when it would, of course, be too late.

The highest degree of constitutional protection is due to the individual acting without conspiracy. But even an individual cannot claim that the Constitution protects him in advocating or teaching overthrow of government by force or violence. . . .

When our constitutional provisions were written, the chief forces recognized as antagonists in the struggle between authority and liberty were the Government on the one hand and the individual citizen on the other. It was thought that if the state could be kept in its place the individual could take care of himself.

In more recent times these problems have been complicated by the intervention between the state and the citizen of permanently organized, well-financed, semisecret and highly disciplined political organizations. Totalitarian groups here and abroad perfected the technique of creating private paramilitary organizations to coerce both the public government and its citizens. These organizations assert as against our Government all of the constitutional rights and immunities of individuals and at the same time exercise over their followers much of the authority which they deny to the Government. The Communist Party realistically is a state within a state, an authoritarian dictatorship within a republic. It demands these freedoms, not for its members, but for the organized party. It denies to its own members at the same time the freedom to dissent, to debate, to deviate from the party line, and enforces its authoritarian rule by crude purges, if nothing more violent.

The law of conspiracy has been the chief means at the Government's disposal to deal with the growing problems created by such organizations. I happen to think it is an awkward and inept remedy, but I find no constitutional authority for taking this weapon from the Government. There is no constitutional right to "gang up" on the Government.

Communism in Our Schools (1946)

GEORGE A. DONDERO

While the early anti-Communist crusade focused special attention on supposed Red infiltration of the federal government, a number of alarmists, such as Congressman George A. Dondero of Michigan, sought to explain why the general public had gone so far in accepting creeping socialism.

From the extension of remarks made by George A. Dondero in the House of Representatives, June 14, 1946, *Appendix to the Congressional Record, Proceedings and Debates of the Seventy-Ninth Congress, Second Session*, Vol. 92, Part 11 (Washington, 1946), A3516–A3518.

There was a growing tendency to attribute every form of social and cultural change to the subtle plotting of left-wing conspirators. Congressman Dondero was especially outraged by the corruption of the public school curriculum, which he blamed upon such allegedly "Communist-oriented radicals" as Charles A. Beard, Harold O. Rugg, and George S. Counts.

This country is being systematically communized, perhaps unconsciously, through its educational institutions.

These institutions are instruments through which left-wing theories and philosophies may be and are taught to large groups of young Americans by persons whom they respect and trust—their instructors.

That process has been going on for years, in an insidious manner.

As a consequence, we now have an entire generation of voters who do not appreciate our Constitution, or our national history, who believe the profit system is wrong and private ownership is undesirable, who are easy victims of demagogy, and who listen with credulity to false and misleading propaganda, of or from Russia.

If this program is not exposed and changed, it will soon be too late to save free enterprise and free government in the United States.

All of the prophets of un-Americanism are not Communists. A few of them are aliens, but all of them are carriers of the same disease—the disease of Marxism.

Such charges constitute a serious indictment and should not be uttered without proof. I feel that I would be remiss in my duties as a Member of Congress and faithless to my oath to uphold and defend the Constitution of the United States, against all enemies, foreign or domestic, if I did not offer what I believe to be reasonable and adequate proof. . . .

The so-called [Harold O.] Rugg textbooks, which ridiculed our national heroes, such as George Washington, and brought radical teachings directly to our American children, infiltrated into many State educational systems before their nature was discovered and they were gradually rooted out.

By 1941—and there is a long documentation of this—radicalism was rampant in teachers' organizations, one in particular—the Teachers Union in New York—reaching such an open blatancy that a legislative committee investigated it and took action to block its communistic aims. This was done only after radical organizations among the students in schools and colleges in at least six States showed the extent of the plot. It was proved that there were clubs on some school campuses openly teaching Marxism, and led by members of notorious Communist-front youth groups. . . .

Now, as we seek to revert again to peace, bring about mass production, and preserve the political and economic ideologies that twice made America great enough to save the entire world from chaos, steps must be taken—drastic steps—to trace communistic teachings to their source in America, and then eliminate them.

Hitler built his effort for totalitarian power on his ability to indoctrinate and fanaticize German youth from 1930 to the beginning of the war in 1939, 9 years. Our American youth have been under a sustained Communist indoctrination drive since 1935, 11 years.

Communism and the Colleges (1953)

J. B. MATTHEWS

A Kentuckian who graduated from Drew and Union Theological Seminaries and who received a Ph.D. degree from the University of Vienna, J. B. Matthews directed research for the House Committee on Un-American Activities from 1939 to 1945, and in 1953 became executive director of the Senate Permanent Subcommittee on Investigations. In Matthews' eyes, anyone who protested against investigations of un-Americanism automatically raised suspicions of his own Communist ties. He was also convinced that Charles Darwin and John Dewey had undermined the intellectuals' belief in eternal truth, and had thus prepared the way for the triumph of socialism and godlessness in American universities. Matthews went on to accuse the leading figures of American science and scholarship of furthering the designs of international Communism.

In the following selection Matthews emphatically denies that Thomas Jefferson's often-quoted words in favor of tolerating "error of opinion" could be applied to such a new and diabolical force as Communism; but ironically, as the selections in Chapter 3 of this book make clear, Jefferson's First Inaugural Address had been immediately preceded by charges and countercharges of conspiracy that were as shrill and vehement as the ideological debates of the mid-twentieth century.

For more than seventeen years, the Communist Party of the United States has put forth every effort to infiltrate the teaching profession of

From J. B. Matthews, "Communism and the Colleges," *American Mercury* (P.O. Box 1306, Torrance, Calif. 90505), May 1953, pp. 111–115, 134.

this country. In this endeavor to corrupt the teachers of youth, the agents of the Kremlin have been remarkably successful, especially among the professors in our colleges and universities. . . .

Congressional committees, which are now investigating Communists in the colleges, are on the track of a national scandal.

If all the colleges and universities in the United States had been closed for the past thirty-five years, there is no reason to believe that our national situation would be any the worse, *insofar as an intelligent approach to the problem of Communism is concerned.*

In fact, a case can be made for the argument that we would be in a much better position in this respect, if they had been closed. We would have lost many things which are vital to our very existence, of course; but clear public thinking with respect to the world-wide Communist conspiracy would not be among them. To the extent that we have any clear thinking on this subject, it is not the gift of our colleges.

Here and there, it is obvious, a few colleges and a few professors have had the academic integrity and competence, not to mention the academic freedom, to assess correctly the gravest challenge that has confronted this nation since its birth. What these few have done, and done well, has been more than offset by the successful Communist infiltration of so-called higher education. In other words, when we audit and balance the academic books we have kept since October 1917, we find that we are *in the red.*

It cannot be said, in extenuation of this academic failure, that our professors of higher learning have been so busy with the task of transmitting our cultural heritage that they simply neglected to note the rising world power of a remorseless foe. Such neglect would have been bad enough; but large numbers of professors went out of their way to hail the appearance of the first Communist world state as a great human experiment. Others have shamelessly collaborated with its agents and have not ceased to participate in their subversive activities to this very day.

The failure of higher education to perform reasonably well had its reasons.

For Communism and its agents to have found any reception whatever among American educators, it was necessary that certain prior conditions, inviting revolutionary innovations, had to obtain. . . .

For one thing, the Darwinian hypotheses had only recently made their full impact upon educational philosophy, giving a new cloak of respectability to materialism and environmental determinism. Intellectual uncertainties multiplied like guinea pigs. Experimentation in morals, as well as in science, became an end in itself. The illusion of automatic human progress had not been wholly dissipated by World War I.

Then came pragmatism—a view of life so new in human thought that it is now barely fifty-five years since William James coined the word.

In educational circles, John Dewey's pragmatism, known as instrumentalism, replaced that of Harvard's William James.

With the ascendancy of Dewey in the classroom, Teachers College of Columbia became the Mecca to which tens of thousands of American teachers made pilgrimage to kiss the blackened stone of progressive education, as reverently and as superstitiously as any Moslem. From Morningside Heights, there spread across the entire land the intellectually envenoming and morally disintegrating view that how-to-teach is more important than what-to-teach and how-to-learn more important than what-to-learn.

Educators of the Dewey school of pragmatism began to profess a chilling fear of indoctrination. In most cases, this was sheer pretense, for what they actually did was to introduce their own new items of indoctrination for the older ones which they discarded. . . .

It is not suggested here that progressive education and Communism are the same, or that they have anything in common, unless it be a determination to eliminate completely the timeless verities and values around which western civilization had been so largely organized until the rise of the Soviet state, on the one hand, and the dominance in education of modern instrumentalism, on the other hand. Only juveniles playing at anti-Communism make the mistake of identifying Communism with progressive education, or progressive education with Communism.

The fact is that progressive education and Communism are at opposite poles in their basic philosophy. The former represents intellectual and moral anarchy, the latter the most rigid thought- and behavior-control ever known to man.

What, then, is the relationship of the late, mild-mannered philosopher of Columbia University to the Communist infiltration of education? To state it, in an over-simplified proposition, it was this: The relaxation of the old intellectual and moral disciplines and loyalties, encouraged by Dewey's progressive education, became *Communism's opportunity.*

The agents of the Kremlin always find it easier to move into a situation of chaos, intellectual or social, than they do to move into a situation of stability. That is why, in the preliminary stages of the Communist conspiracy, prior to the seizure of power, Communists welcome all the chaos which they or others (even the anti-Communists) can produce. Stability thwarts, and chaos aids, the motivation of Communism, just as they thwart and aid, respectively, any other drastic innovation, whether it be Fascism, the New Deal, Upton Sinclair's EPIC, or Townsend's old-age pension scheme.

Pragmatism and its educational high priests reject the concept of any timeless truths. . . .

The ordinary day-to-day work of the Communist Party is many-sided, ranging all the way from open propaganda to espionage. In whatever it wanted done, the Party has always been able to draw upon members of the academic profession for the running of its subversive apparatus. The intellectual uncertainties and moral chaos of the past quarter of a century have contributed to this achievement of the Kremlin agents in the colleges and universities. . . .

On the subject of conspiratorial secrecy in concealing or denying their Communist Party membership, *The Communist* of May 1937 had the following to say about its teachers: "Communist teachers are, therefore, faced with a tremendous social responsibility. . . . They must take advantage of their positions, *without exposing themselves. . . .*" Along the same conspiratorial line, we read: "Only when teachers have really mastered Marxism-Leninism will they be able *skillfully to inject it into their teaching at the least risk of exposure. . . .*"

Sooner or later, many of the pro-Communists and fake liberals among educators get around to quoting from Thomas Jefferson's First Inaugural Address. . . . What Jefferson said has become the principal smoke screen for subversion. Here are his words: "If there be any among us who wish to dissolve this union, or change its republican form, let them stand undisturbed, as monuments of the safety with which *error of opinion* may be tolerated where reason is left free to combat it." It does not take a university education to understand that these words of Thomas Jefferson have no conceivable applicability to the members and stooges of the Communist Party. *Acting as part of a conspiratorial fifth column in the interests of a foreign state is not the same thing as "error of opinion."* Reason is not free to combat the activities which are plotted in the dark cellars of Communist conspiracy.

Modern Art Shackled
to Communism (1949)

GEORGE A. DONDERO

Congressman Dondero achieved his greatest notoriety by attacking all modern art as Communist-inspired. In a speech before Congress on August 16, 1949, he named nearly all the greatest painters and sculptors of the twentieth century, as well as a galaxy of leading novelists, playwrights, and poets, as the supposed tools of a Communist plot to disrupt traditional values and modes of aesthetic perception. While Dondero had considerable difficulty explaining why Soviet Russia allowed only highly conventional and standardized art, his hostility to cultural change and experimentation— which reflected the bitterness of traditionalist painters and sculptors who were rapidly being displaced in American museums and exhibitions—gives insight into some of the psychological sources of the antiradical crusade. For minds that could not accommodate to new aesthetic values, the belief in a Communist conspiracy became a simple and satisfying answer.

Mr. Speaker, quite a few individuals in art, who are sincere in purpose, honest in intent, but with only a superficial knowledge of the complicated influences that surge in the art world of today, have written me—or otherwise expressed their opinions—that so-called modern or contemporary art cannot be Communist because art in Russia today is realistic and objective.

The left-wing art magazines advance the same unsound premises of reasoning, asserting in editorial spasms that modern art is real American art. They plead for tolerance, but in turn tolerate nothing, except their own subversive "isms."

The human art termites, disciples of multiple "isms" that compose

From the speech of George A. Dondero, August 16, 1949, *Congressional Record, Proceedings and Debates of the Eighty-First Congress, First Session*, Vol. 95, Part 9 (Washington, 1949), 11584, 11586.

so-called modern art, boring industriously to destroy the high standards, and priceless traditions of academic art, find comfort and satisfaction in the wide dissemination of this spurious reasoning and wickedly false declaration, and its casual acceptance by the unwary.

This glib disavowal of any relationship between communism and so-called modern art is so pat and so spontaneous a reply by advocates of the "isms" in art, from deep, Red Stalinist to pale pink publicist, as to identify it readily to the observant as the same old partyline practice. It is the party line of the left wingers, who are now in the big money, and who want above all to remain in the big money, voiced to confuse the legitimate artist, to disarm the arousing academician, and to fool the public.

As I have previously stated, art is considered a weapon of communism, and the Communist doctrinaire names the artist as a soldier of the revolution. It is a weapon in the hands of a soldier in the revolution against our form of government, and against any government or system other than communism.

From 1914 to 1920 art was used as a weapon of the Russian Revolution to destroy the Czarist Government, but when this destruction was accomplished, art ceased to be a weapon and became a medium of propaganda, picturing and extolling the imaginary wonders, benefits and happiness of existence under the socialized state.

Let me trace for you a main artery from the black heart of the isms of the Russian Revolution to the very heart of art in America.

In 1914 Kandinsky, a Russian-born Expressionist and nonobjective painter, who found it safer to live in Germany, returned to Russia, and 3 years later came the revolution. He is the man who preached that art must abandon the logical and adopt the illogical. He dominated a group of black knights of the isms, who murdered the art of the Russian academies. They were Cubists, Futurists, Expressionists, Constructionists, Suprematists, Abstractionists and the rest of the same ilk. Kandinsky was a friend of Trotsky, and after the revolution founded the Moscow Institute of Art Culture. He was Communist leader in Red art—the commissar of the isms. . . .

The Communist art that has infiltrated our cultural front is not the Communist art in Russia today—one is the weapon of destruction, and the other is the medium of controlled propaganda. Communist art outside Russia is to destroy the enemy, and we are the enemy of communism. Communist art in Russia is to delude the Russian workers.

The art of the isms, the weapon of the Russian Revolution, is the art which has been transplanted to America, and today, having infiltrated and saturated many of our art centers, threatens to overawe, override and overpower the fine art of our tradition and inheritance. So-called modern or contemporary art in our own beloved country contains all the isms of depravity, decadence, and destruction.

What are these isms that are the very foundation of so-called modern art? They are the same old lot of the Russian Revolution, some with transparent disguises, and others added from time to time as new convulsions find a new designation. I call the roll of infamy without claim that my list is all-inclusive: dadaism, futurism, constructionism, suprematism, cubism, expressionism, surrealism, and abstractionism. All these isms are of foreign origin, and truly should have no place in American art. While not all are media of social or political protest, all are instruments and weapons of destruction. . . .

We are now face to face with the intolerable situation, where public schools, colleges, and universities, art and technical schools, invaded by a horde of foreign art manglers, are selling to our young men and women a subversive doctrine of "isms," Communist-inspired and Communist-connected, which have one common, boasted goal—the destruction of our cultural tradition and priceless heritage. Many of our museum repositories of art treasures are now under the guidance of judgements that have been warped, and eyes that are blinded, seeing not the inevitable destruction that awaits if this Marxist trail is not abandoned.

A Conspiracy of
Blackest Infamy (1951)

JOSEPH McCARTHY

As the previous selections have indicated, by 1950 there was nothing new about sweeping and irresponsible charges that Communists had infiltrated the federal government and had corrupted the values of American society. However, it was not until 1950 and 1951 that Senator Joseph McCar-

From the speech of Senator Joseph McCarthy, June 14, 1951, *Congressional Record, Proceedings and Debates of the Eighty-Second Congress, First Session,* Vol. 97, Part 5 (Washington, 1951), 6601–6603.

thy of Wisconsin fully exploited the growing suspicions of a bewildered and frustrated people, and gave his name to a new and virulent form of the paranoid style.

In a Lincoln Day speech at Wheeling, West Virginia, in February 1950, McCarthy made the sensational statement that he possessed a list of 205 subversives who were still employed by the State Department. Although McCarthy quickly scaled down the number and was unable to verify a single charge, his accusations struck a public nerve that had been sensitized by the Alger Hiss case, by the detonation of the first Russian atomic weapon, by the revelation that Klaus Fuchs had delivered atomic secrets to Soviet agents, and by the inexplicable loss of China. To add to the public's sense of confusion and betrayed expectation, the Korean War erupted in June 1950, and within six months the American armed forces had been driven twice into the southern end of the Korean peninsula, the second time with disastrous losses at the hands of the Chinese. When General Douglas MacArthur insisted on extending the air war to China itself and openly rebelled against the policies of President Truman and the Joint Chiefs of Staff, he was relieved of his command and subsequently returned to the United States to denounce the strategy of limited war, or as McCarthy termed it, "the strategy of defeat," which was dictated by a fear of World War Three.

It was the investigation of MacArthur's dismissal by a Joint Senate Committee on Foreign Relations and the Armed Services that furnished the background for McCarthy's marathon sixty-thousand word speech of June 14, 1951. Excoriating the "no-win policy" in Korea, McCarthy reviewed the entire strategy of World War Two in an attempt to prove that General George C. Marshall, who had been Army Chief of Staff and then Secretary of State, was responsible for the spread of world Communism. It was Marshall, according to McCarthy, who had misled and manipulated President Roosevelt, who had joined with Stalin in thwarting Churchill, who had abandoned eastern Europe to the Red army, and who had surrendered China to the Communists. Few theories of conspiracy had been as extravagant and all-embracing as McCarthy's version of World War Two and its aftermath. Despite the wild and ill-founded character of his allegations, McCarthy presented a simple explanation for America's seeming decline from omnipotence to relative powerlessness in a hostile world. His basic thesis, interwoven with the old themes of American destiny and infamous betrayal, would serve as the foundation for later right-wing rewritings of American history and for appeals for an all-out war against Communism at home and abroad.

Six years ago this summer America stood at what Churchill described as the "highest pinnacle of her power and fame." . . . Only the United States among the great powers found its economic strength undiminished, its Territories uninvaded and unswept by war, its full powers still unflexed. Everywhere America had friends, everywhere its power suggested friendship to others. In terms of the division of the world into spheres of interest, the United States, at the head of the coalition of the West, exercised friendly influence over nearly all the masses of the earth. The Soviet Union's own people and the few millions in the bordering satellites upon which it was already laying its hands constituted a small minority of the earth's peoples.

What do we find in the summer of 1951? The writs of Moscow run to lands which, with its own, number upward of 900 millions of people—a good 40 percent of all men living. The fear of Russia or the subservience that power inspires inclines many hundreds of other millions, as in India, toward Moscow. The fear of Russia, plus other reasons, the chief of which is the supine and treacherous folly of our own policies, places other hundreds of millions in a twilight zone between the great poles of Moscow and Washington. . . .

The will to resist Russia here at home is vitiated. Gone is the zeal with which we marched forth in 1941 to crush the dictatorship. The leftist-liberals who preached a holy war against Hitler and Tojo are today seeking accommodation with the senior totalitarianism of Moscow. Is this because we are today arrayed against, to recall the phrase of General Bradley, "the wrong enemy" in the "wrong war"? We were on Russia's side in the last war—our strategy after the first Quebec conference might as well have been dictated in the Kremlin and teletyped to the Pentagon—and is that why the [General] Marshall who prosecuted World War II with bloodthirsty zeal, eager to order Americans to storm fortified shores, is sitting this one out? . . .

During all this time the administration preaches a gospel of fear and [Secretary of State] Acheson and Marshall expound a foreign policy in the East based upon craven, whimpering appeasement. The President and his palace guard go on a Nation-wide broadcast and threaten the American people with Russian-made atomic bombs. What is the purpose of such craven actions and utterances? Is it to condition us to defeat in the Far East, to soften us up so that we shall accept a peace upon the Soviet empire's terms in Korea; a peace which would put the enemy one step nearer to Alaska? And how, may I ask, did Russia acquire the technical secrets, the blueprints, the know-how to make the bombs with which the administration seeks to terrify us? . . .

How can we account for our present situation unless we believe that men high in this Government are concerting to deliver us to disaster? This must be the product of a great conspiracy, a conspiracy on a scale so immense as to dwarf any previous such venture in the history of man. A conspiracy of infamy so black that, when it is finally exposed, its principles shall be forever deserving of the madedictions of all honest men.

Who constitutes the highest circles of this conspiracy? About that we cannot be sure. We are convinced that Dean Acheson, who steadfastly serves the interests of nations other than his own, the friend of Alger Hiss, who supported him in his hour of retribution, who contributed to his defense fund, must be high on the roster. The President? He is their captive. I have wondered, as have you, why he did not dispense with so great a liability as Acheson to his own and his party's interests. It is now clear to me. In the relationship of master and man, did you ever hear of man firing master? Truman is a satisfactory front. He is only dimly aware of what is going on.

I do not believe that Mr. Truman is a conscious party to the great conspiracy, although it is being conducted in his name. I believe that if Mr. Truman had the ability to associate good Americans around him, he would have behaved as a good American in this most dire of all our crises.

It is when we return to an examination of General Marshall's record since the spring of 1942 that we approach an explanation of the carefully planned retreat from victory. Let us again review the Marshall record, as I have disclosed it from all the sources available and all of them friendly. This grim and solitary man it was who, early in World War II, determined to put his impress upon our global strategy, political and military.

It was Marshall who, amid the din for a "second front now" from every voice of Soviet inspiration, sought to compel the British to invade across the Channel in the fall of 1942 upon penalty of our quitting the war in Europe. . . .

It was Marshall who, at Tehran, made common cause with Stalin on the strategy of the war in Europe and marched side by side with him thereafter. . . .

It was Marshall who sent Deane to Moscow to collaborate with Harriman in drafting the terms of the wholly unnecessary bribe paid to Stalin at Yalta. It was Marshall, with Hiss at his elbow and doing the physical drafting of agreements at Yalta, who ignored the contrary advice of his senior, Admiral Leahy, and of MacArthur and Nimitz in regard to the folly of a major land invasion of Japan; who submitted intelligence reports which suppressed more truthful estimates in order to support his argument, and who finally induced Roosevelt to bring Russia into the Japanese war with a bribe that reinstated Russia in its pre-1904 imperialistic position in Manchuria—an act which, in effect, signed the death warrant of the Republic of China. . . .

What can be made of this unbroken series of decisions and acts contributing to the strategy of defeat? They cannot be attributed to incompetence. If Marshall were merely stupid, the laws of probability would dictate that part of his decisions would serve this country's interests. If Marshall is innocent of guilty intention, how could he be trusted to guide the defense of this country further? We have declined so precipitously in relation to the Soviet Union in the last 6 years. How much swifter may be our fall into disaster with Marshall at the helm? Where will all this stop? That is not a rhetorical question: Ours is not a rhetorical danger. Where next will Marshall carry us? It is useless to suppose that his nominal superior will ask him to resign. He cannot even dispense with Acheson.

What is the objective of the great conspiracy? I think it is clear from what has occurred and is now occurring: to diminish the United States in world affairs, to weaken us militarily, to confuse our spirit with talk of surrender in the Far East and to impair our will to resist evil. To what end? To the end that we shall be contained, frustrated and finally fall victim to Soviet intrigue from within and Russian military might from without. Is that farfetched? There have been many examples in history of rich and powerful states which have been corrupted from within, enfeebled and deceived until they were unable to resist aggression.

The United States first ventured into world affairs a bare half century ago. Its rise to world leadership was almost unprecedentedly sudden. We call this a young country. It is in terms of the tenure of the settlement by Europeans on these lands. It is also in terms of the spirit and daring of its people. Yet the United States belongs to, is the last great example of, the farthest projection of an old culture. The vast and complicated culture of the west, which bloomed with the spread of the Gothic cathedrals and the universities, which has carried science and technology and art and the humane values to lengths nowhere else dreamed of and whose sway covered the earth only a few years ago, is in manifest decay. We see the symptoms of decay in Western Europe. We find evidences of it here. . . .

The time has come to halt this tepid, milk-and-water acquiescence which a discredited administration, ruled by disloyalty, sends down to us. The American may belong to an old culture, he may be beset by enemies here and abroad, he may be distracted by the many words of counsel that assail him by day and night, but he is nobody's fool. The time has come for us to realize that the people who sent us here expect more than time-serving from us. The American who has never known defeat in war does not expect to be again sold down the river in Asia. He does not want that kind of betrayal. He has had betrayal enough. He has never failed to fight for his liberties since George Washington rode to Boston in 1775 to put himself at the head of a band of rebels unversed in war. He is fighting tonight, fighting gloriously in a war on a distant American frontier made inglorious by the men he can no longer trust at the head of our affairs.

The America that I know, and that other Senators know, this vast and teeming and beautiful land, this hopeful society where the poor share the table of the rich as never before in history, where men of all colors, of all faiths, are brothers as never before in history, where great deeds have been done and great deeds are yet to do, that America deserves to be led not to humiliation or defeat, but to victory.

Interlocking Subversion
in the Government (1953)

In the early 1950's Senator McCarthy was by no means alone in charging that Communists had infiltrated all levels of government and had played a decisive and disastrous role in shaping American policy. The Senate Subcommittee on Internal Security, which was chaired by Senator William E. Jenner of Indiana, and which included such figures as Senator Pat McCarran of Nevada, Senator James Eastland of Mississippi, and Senator Herman Welker of Idaho, drew heavily on the testimony of former Communists like

From *Interlocking Subversion in Government Departments: Report of the Subcommittee to Investigate the Administration of the Internal Security Act and Other Internal Security Laws, To the Committee on the Judiciary, United States Senate, Eighty-Third Congress, First Session* (Washington, 1953), p. 49.

Elizabeth Bentley and Whittaker Chambers in an attempt to substantiate the general picture drawn by McCarthy.

Conclusions

1. The Soviet international organization has carried on a successful and important penetration of the United States Government and this penetration has not been fully exposed.

2. This penetration has extended from the lower ranks to top-level policy and operating positions in our Government.

3. The agents of this penetration have operated in accordance with a distinct design fashioned by their Soviet superiors.

4. Members of this conspiracy helped to get each other into Government, helped each other to rise in Government and protected each other from exposure.

5. The general pattern of this penetration was first into agencies concerned with economic recovery, then to warmaking agencies, then to agencies concerned with foreign policy and postwar planning, but always moving to the focal point of national concern.

6. In general, the Communists who infiltrated our Government worked behind the scenes—guiding research and preparing memoranda on which basic American policies were set, writing speeches for Cabinet officers, influencing congressional investigations, drafting laws, manipulating administrative reorganizations—always serving the interest of their Soviet superiors.

7. Thousands of diplomatic, political, military, scientific, and economic secrets of the United States have been stolen by Soviet agents in our Government and other persons closely connected with the Communists.

8. Despite the fact that the Federal Bureau of Investigation and other security agencies had reported extensive information about this Communist penetration, little was done by the executive branch to interrupt the Soviet operatives in their ascent in Government until congressional committees brought forth to public light the facts of the conspiracy.

9. Powerful groups and individuals within the executive branch were at work obstructing and weakening the effort to eliminate Soviet agents from positions in Government.

10. Members of this conspiracy repeatedly swore to oaths denying Communist Party membership when seeking appointments, transfers,

and promotions and these falsifications have, in virtually every case, gone unpunished.

11. The control that the American Communications Association, a Communist-directed union, maintains over communication lines vital to the national defense poses a threat to the security of this country.

12. Policies and programs laid down by members of this Soviet conspiracy are still in effect within our Government and constitute a continuing hazard to our national security.

Communist Pressure by Transmission Belts (1954)

LOUIS F. BUDENZ

While Senator McCarthy and his co-workers were notably unsuccessful in turning up genuine subversives, their sweeping accusations gained significant support owing to the testimony of a small group of ex-Communists who won publicity as experts on the techniques of subversion. Louis F. Budenz, a graduate of Xavier University and Indianapolis Law School, had been a member of the Communist party National Committee and had edited Communist newspapers from 1935 to 1945. After switching over to the side of the radical right, Budenz asserted that anyone who objected to McCarthyism was in effect following the Communist party line. It is clear that Budenz' real target was the American liberals.

With the overthrow of the United States government, a major goal of the Red conspiracy, the agencies of that government are logically a chief target for infiltration. In this the Stalinites have been unusually successful, as the record, which is only half disclosed, has revealed. Stalin's "law of conspiracy"—that "it takes a thousand men to build a bridge but one to blow it up"—applies neatly. If one or two Communists, or persons influenced by the Communists, work themselves into positions of trust and responsibility in any federal agency, they can create havoc. Working in non-Communist garb and always under directions from Soviet agents, they can bring about vacillation, uncer-

From Louis F. Budenz, *The Techniques of Communism* (Chicago: Henry Regnery Company, 1954), pp. 278–279, 298–299.

tainty, and even downright betrayal of the interests of the United States. If they are in very high places, they can suggest those recommendations which will betray, and have betrayed, millions of people to the Kremlin. . . .

It would have been much more difficult for Alger Hiss and his associates to betray the United States—and the biggest part of that betrayal consisted in what happened to the Chinese and the Poles—had it not been for a sympathetic attitude toward Soviet Communism created in many organs of American public opinion after the recognition of Soviet Russia in 1933. The reader should constantly remain aware of the relation between views helpful to the Communists expressed in certain newspapers, and on television and radio, and the ease of infiltration of the government by Soviet agents. . . .

Work within the government is accompanied by pressure from without, through the stimulation of "crusades" by either Communist fronts or captive organizations or both. The Communists are always aware that they must make all "mass organizations," religious, labor, educational, and scientific groups, "transmission belts" for the Communist line. During the first six months of 1953, they made great gains in this respect, inducing many organizations, newspapers, and other agencies of opinion to forward the Communist line in relation to government. The campaigns against "McCarthyism," "book burning," and alleged "attacks on religion" were all Communist initiated and Communist stimulated. They arose from the order given by Joseph Stalin in October, 1952, that the Communist Parties "in imperialist countries" should raise higher "the banner of bourgeois civil liberties." The arrogance of that order from a man who had crushed all liberties is colossal. And yet, transmitted in the form of cries against "McCarthyism" and the other slogans issued by the Party through the *Daily Worker*, the dead Stalin is able to control the opinion of a great segment of vocal America. The average American, the so-called common man, was least affected by these outcries, but self-appointed groups and some stable organizations, penetrated or influenced by concealed Communists, took up the Communist line and plugged it day after day. Newspapers gave them publicity notices far beyond their actual representation of American thought, and the government was induced, in part at least, to retreat and in some instances even to sanction the Communist line, making America's security more unstable.

The "Independence" Maneuver (1956)

LOUIS F. BUDENZ

The Soviet bid for peaceful coexistence, the so-called "new look" promoted by Khrushchev at the Twentieth Congress of the Russian Communist Party, presented a new challenge to the American radical right. One response was a compilation by the House Committee on Un-American Activities of a series of essays and documents entitled Soviet Total War, *which emphasized the deceit and deviousness of all Communists, and which warned that Khrushchev's peaceful overtures were part of a plot to lull America into lowering her guard. One of the contributors to the House Committee's volume was Louis F. Budenz, who argued that non-Communist front organizations were more vital to the Communist conspiracy than the Communist party itself.*

To many, the Communist-front organization or enterprise is something *less* than Communist or at least a much milder form of the virus, as it were; and to aid or support it is, therefore, to be considerably less implicated in Communist activity than to hold membership in the Communist Party. It is not sufficiently well understood that many of the most effective supporters of the Communist movement do their work for it entirely outside the so-called discipline of Communist Party membership. A prominent supporter of the Communist-front apparatus may, in given instances, aid the Communist conspiracy in more subtle and important ways than a hundred rank-and-file Communists who pay dues to the party. More and more, as the cadres of the Communist Party go deeper underground, the Communist fronters become the principal agents of Communist propaganda. . . .

The belief that ultimate control of the entire revolutionary apparatus resides in the Communist Party ignores the established fact that the real boss of the movement in any given country is an individual

From Louis F. Budenz, "The 'Independence' Maneuver," *Soviet Total War: "Historic Mission" of Violence and Deceit*, Vol. I, prepared and released by the Committee on Un-American Activities, United States House of Representatives (Washington, 1956), pp. 115–117.

whose dictatorial power is not necessarily related to any title which he may hold within the organizational structure of the party but in turn derives solely from the whimsical and irresponsible pleasure of the man who happens to be on top in Moscow. . . .

It is unfortunately a common error to ascribe conscious disloyalty to all Communist Party members on the one hand, and to ascribe nothing more than misguided idealism to all supporters of the Communist-front apparatus on the other. There are unwitting dupes, as well as witting subverters, among both party members and fronters.

In the case of the overwhelming majority of professional groups—educators, clergymen, lawyers, artists, novelists, and the like—who have been affiliated in one way or another with the Communist movement in the United States, the Communist-front apparatus has been their only point of contact. . . .

Clergymen and educators, whose integrity in the pursuit of truth is supposed to be of a purer mold than that of most mortals, present a striking incongruity when they support the fraud of the fronts.

The essence and most distinctive characteristic of the Communist-front organization is its deceitfulness.

Behind an often impressive façade of non-Communist notables who serve as sponsors, signers, or nonfunctioning officers of a front organization lurk unseen directors, manipulators, and functioning executives who are agents of the Communist conspiracy. For its deceptive purposes, a clergyman is the ideal national chairman of a Communist front; and the record discloses that at least a score of the party's front organizations have been headed by clergymen.

Behind the title of a front organization coils a conspiratorial reality which strikes savagely at the ideals of those who neglect to immunize their humanitarian impulses with sound judgment and a healthy skepticism.

Behind announced objectives which may be wholly praiseworthy lie unannounced and shrewdly concealed aims which are calculated to advance—however slightly—the cause of the Communist conspiracy.

Up against the masters of deception, the sentimental liberal is a babe in arms.

The conspiring totalitarian entices the unsuspecting humanitarian into his web, and fattens on the gullibility of his victim. The spider-and-fly analogy is weak at one point: the humanitarian cannot be held altogether blameless for his credulity.

The Communist-front organization, to change the figure, is a whited sepulcher, outwardly beautiful but full of dead bones within. The façade belies the interior.

Communist America,
Must It Be? (1960)

BILLY JAMES HARGIS

*Although many educated Americans have assumed that religious funda-
mentalism virtually died with William Jennings Bryan after the celebrated
"monkey trial" at Dayton, Tennessee, in 1925, there is abundant evidence
that "the old-time religion," far from being in decline, has spread from the
rural Bible Belt to such cities as Tulsa, Oklahoma, where it has gained renewed power. The fundamentalist attack on modern secular and scientific
culture reflects deep cleavages in education, social values, and attitudes toward racial and ethnic minorities. Many fundamentalists have gained contemporary relevance by assimilating the rhetoric of anti-Communism, which
has provided them with a clear-cut explanation for the sophisticated secu-
larism of the universities, the communications media, and various governing
elites.*

*Billy James Hargis, the leader of the "Christian Crusade," attended Ozark
Bible College and then resigned from the ministry at the age of twenty-one
to devote his life to the struggle against Communism. By the early 1960's
Hargis was director of a massive enterprise, based at an "international headquarters" in Tulsa, and including weekly and monthly papers, lectures and
conferences, an "anti-Communist summer school" in Colorado, and a membership of around a hundred thousand. Convinced that "God ordained segregation" of whites and Negroes, Hargis interprets current racial conflict as
the bitter fruit of Communist plotting. Voicing the comforting belief of
many southerners, he holds that American Negroes were happy with segregation until they were misled by godless radicals.*

Regardless of what the Negroes think, regardless of what the entire
South thinks, segregation and racism have become one of America's
great "social crises," one of the most artificial of all such social crises

From Billy James Hargis, *Communist America, Must It Be?* (distributed by
Christian Crusade, Box 977, Tulsa, Oklahoma), pp. 102, 104–105, 111–112, 115,
121–122, 130–132. Copyright, 1960, Christian Crusade.

instigated by the Communists within America to add racial hatred to class hatred, and thus betray America into Communist hands through betrayal of the American Negro. . . .

"The National Association for the Advancement of Colored People," Manning Johnson revealed, "set up the situation that erupted into racial violence at Little Rock . . . the main danger and handicap to the Negro is not the southern school, but the persecution and hate complex the NAACP and the Reds are trying to create." That the Reds are behind it, and within the NAACP, there can be no doubt. The Communist *Daily Worker* on September 2, 1957, scooped the press of the nation with screaming headlines about "ARKANSAS TERROR." "Stirring up race and class conflict is the basis of all discussion of the Communist party's work in the South," Manning Johnson revealed . . . "leaders in Moscow ordered the use of all racial, economic and social differences . . . to start local fires of discontent, conflict and revolt . . . black rebellion was what Moscow wanted. Bloody racial conflict would split America."

Manning Johnson climbed to the highest governing body of the Communist Party in America, the National Committee. He was placed on the National Negro Commission, an important subcommittee of the National Committee on direct orders from Moscow to facilitate the subversion of the Negroes. Like Mrs. [Helen Wood] Birnie, his intelligence made him see through the stupidity of the Communist doctrine, and his courage made him willing to confess his sins in public. His patriotism and religious upbringing triumphed, and he became an outstanding citizen performing invaluable service to his country and his race. The NAACP, which Manning Johnson warned against, has been overloaded with Communist-front supporters. . . .

The people of the United States have ceased to be their own rulers —and the government now ruling them is heavily pro-Communist. Not only is America financing its enemy, and welcoming its treacherous enemies as honored guests, but America is legislating itself into enemy hands with the "blessing" of the Supreme Court. So long as they don't spell out exactly how to do it, Communists can take over America and there isn't anything in the world which the American people can do about it. Communists have more freedom in America than do the non-Communist, patriotic Christian-American people of America.

Because of rulings of the Supreme Court of the United States, congressional committees are denied the right to determine whether the questions asked of pro-Communist witnesses are pertinent. Congressional committees are denied sufficient freedom to investigate Communists and pro-Communists.

Because of rulings of the Supreme Court, the states are not permitted to enforce their own anti-subversive laws. For the same reason, it is no crime in America to teach or advocate the violent overthrow of the government. . . .

One of the Supreme Court Justices, Felix Frankfurter, testified as a character witness in the trial of Alger Hiss, who eventually went to prison for the minor crime of perjury. According to Steven Paulsen, writing in the *American Mercury* of January, 1959, "Felix Frankfurter is the third member of the Supreme Court who has served continuously since 1943. He participated in 72 cases and his record shows pro-Communist votes, 56; anti-Communist, 16." When Warren came into power in the Supreme Court, wrote Paulsen, he "lost little time demonstrating that he was embarked upon a one world career. Warren later told how Frankfurter made him feel at home on the Supreme bench, took him in hand socially and helped him to secure qualified assistants. One of the Frankfurter hallmarks has always been to plant his own men in key positions under other top governmental executives. One of them was Alger Hiss, as Hiss himself admitted."

In decisions involving the Communist conspiracy, President Eisenhower's appointees to the Supreme Court have voted 92%, 90%, 58% and 36% in favor of the enemies of America. Chief Justice Earl Warren has voted 92%! . . .

The United Nations is not an organization of free nations, but is an organization which attempts to mix free nations and slave nations, peaceful nations and aggressor nations, into an harmonious relationship. Such, of course, is impossible. . . .

Congressman John T. Wood on October 18, 1951, said, "UNESCO is the greatest subversive plot in history. It is my sincere hope that every parent of every child in America may be able to read the inroads that this infamous UNESCO plot has already made in the educational system of America, and reading, may feel impelled to do something about it."

Left-wing educators plan to alienate children from their families, and they are doing it while American parents sleep. UNESCO literature refers to the love of America as "the poisoned air of nationalism."

Pro-UNESCO teachers are told that such "errors" taught in the home can be overcome or corrected in the "infant school," or "kindergarten."

UNESCO urges teachers to "demand . . . complete liberty of action"!

On Halloween night, American children knock on the doors of America and instead of the usual "Trick or Treat" they request a contribution for the United Nations Children's Fund! . . .

The people of America should be reminded that God gave us victory in two great world wars. God granted America every blessing which we now enjoy. We have the greatest opportunity of any nation in history to lead the nations of the world in righteousness and strength. But America cannot lead free nations into paths of victory by association with organizations like the United Nations, with its mixture of evil with good. "Our Pilgrim Fathers," as the Virginia Legislator Jessica Wyatt Payne has written, "would not approve our membership in any world organization, such as the UN, which could or would jeopardize our national sovereignty and solvency—an organization that can, and will out vote us when the chips are down and our money out; an organization which keeps us involved in, and a party to, every dispute between nations, large and small, from civil war to global combat."

The United Nations bears the curse of God for its inclusion of godless nations. From its beginning, the United Nations has deliberately ignored the Lord God Almighty and the Lord Jesus Christ. In fact, the Communist co-creators of the United Nations saw to it that there should be no mention of God, nor any sign of God, anywhere in the United Nations headquarters nor in any United Nations deliberations. God is not mentioned in the United Nations Charter. United Nations meetings are not opened with prayer.

Civil Rights Myths and
Communist Realities (1963)

MEDFORD EVANS

During the civil rights confrontations of the early 1960's, a growing liter-
ature pointed to Communist conspirators as the force behind both American
Negro protest and the worldwide movement for freedom from political and
economic colonialism. The following selection, for example, claims that
Martin Luther King was a tool of the Communists and that the relatively
conservative NAACP was a Communist-front organization. The accusation
is based on the fact that the civil rights leaders have been praised by var-
ious Communist writers.

"The Negro situation is being exploited fully and continuously by
Communists on a national scale."

> —J. Edgar Hoover, Director
> Federal Bureau of Investigation
> January 16, 1958

Attorney General Robert Kennedy on July 25, 1963, issued a statement in which he said that "based on all available information from
investigation and other sources" he had found no evidence that "any of
the top leaders of the major civil rights groups are Communists or
Communist-controlled." In his all-inclusive statement Attorney General Kennedy thus displayed his ignorance of the background of racial agitation in this Nation.

An editorial in the July 21, 1963, issue of *The Worker*, official organ
of the Communist Party, U.S.A., has this to say: "The Communist
Party of the United States wholeheartedly and selflessly supports the
just struggle of the Negro people for freedom and integration in the
political, economic, and social life of the Nation." . . .

William Z. Foster, Communist leader, in his book, *Toward Soviet
America*, published in 1932, discussed the role of Negroes by stating:
"The Negroes constitute a great potential revolutionary force. . . .

The Negro masses will make the very best fighters for the revolution." . . .

In view of continuing failure to "sell" the American Negro on a Negro Soviet republic in the South, the 17th National Convention of the Communist Party, U.S.A., in December, 1959, announced an about-face on its long-established policy which advocated the formation of a Negro nation within the United States. This marked a fundamental change in the line of the American Communist Party which had dated back to 1930. Moscow-trained Negro Communist leader James Jackson, in explaining to the party faithful the turn-about on Communist policy stated that "it has been misconstrued as a form of segregation."

Because of this policy change in the Red line, white and Negro members of the CPUSA reverted to an alternative official program of action regarding racial agitation which had been spelled out in 1932 by Communist leader William Z. Foster in *Toward Soviet America* as follows:

The Communist Party actively promotes . . . organizations to defend the rights of Negroes. . . . Where no mass organizations exist in these fields, the Party takes the initiative in forming them; where such are already in existence, and are headed by conservative officials, the Party follows the policy of building an opposition within them and fighting for the revolutionary program and leadership. This is the so-called boring-from-within policy.

A column by Ray Cromley, appearing in the Birmingham, Ala., *Post-Herald* of August 8, 1963, reveals that the Communist Party, U.S.A., is now sending out Communists with specialized training, instructing them to infiltrate local branches of Negro civil rights organizations and to arrange for Party members to participate in local demonstrations. According to Mr. Cromley, "this grass-roots attempt to infiltrate the civil rights movement is currently, at least—one of the major activities of the Communist Party, U.S.A." . . .

In a pamphlet entitled *Turning Point In Freedom Road*, by Negro Communist Claude Lightfoot, published in October, 1962, the screws were turned tighter when Lightfoot, calling for a step-up in agitation, stated: "The Negro movement has, by and large, broken with gradualism, and seeks revolutionary solutions to its problems."

This new Red line admittedly promoting revolution in the U.S. was accentuated by Negro leader Benjamin J. Davis, national secretary of the CPUSA, in the August, 1963, issue of the Communist publication, *Political Affairs,* when Davis, in an article entitled "The Times Is Now!" screamed:

The whole country—north, east, south and west—is in the throes of a peoples' revolution. . . . The Negro Freedom movement—American counterpart of the national liberation movements in Africa, above all, but also in Asia and Latin America—has, since Birmingham—entered a new stage.

Here is proof positive of Communist direction and control of such movements as the FLN (National Liberation Front) which took over Algeria, as well as Communist guerrillas such as the FALN (Armed Forces of National Liberation) in Venezuela.

Communist Davis, declaring that "the movement aims to demolish so-called moderation," went on to say that "the struggle" will be "fought out and won by the American people within the framework of the present capitalist system." Davis further said:

Birmingham brought the simmering upsurge of the people to a revolutionary pitch. . . . Communists believe that the "freedom now" aims of the program answer the pressing democratic needs of the people and . . . (are) the central domestic issue before the country. At the same time, Communists believe the achievement of this program will lay an indispensable basis, not only for the further social program of the country, but for its Socialist and Communist future when U.S. imperialism . . . will be no more.

Promising Communist support of the so-called Negro Freedom movement led by organizations other than the Communist Party itself, Davis exulted:

The Communist Party greets with boundless joy the present revolutionary freedom movement of the Negro people, and will spare no sacrifice to help bring about its total victory now. . . . There is a wide area of agreement between the Communist Party and the Negro Freedom movement on program, aims and tactics.

Following several months of feverish planning which manifested itself in a solid front of cooperation between the most important Negro civil rights groups in the country, more than 150,000 Negroes marched on Washington, D.C. on August 28, 1963. The disciplined, placard-carrying marchers, swarming over Constitution Avenue, bore a sinister resemblance to May Day scenes in Moscow's Red Square.

Who were the leaders and participants of this tightly-organized show of strength with its threatening overtones?

Among the Negro leaders in the forefront were, of course, Roy

Wilkins, executive secretary of the National Association for the Advancement of Colored People; Rev. Martin Luther King, Jr., president of the Southern Christian Leadership Conference; A. Philip Randolph, president of the AFL/CIO Brotherhood of Sleeping Car Porters; and Whitney M. Young, Jr., executive director of the National Urban League.

At the beginning of the ceremonies in front of the Lincoln Memorial, one of the speakers, paying tribute to W. E. B. DuBois, who had just died in Accra, Ghana, asked for a moment of silence. The huge crowd immediately complied, with bowed heads.

Who was this man, W. E. B. DuBois, whom the speaker referred to as "the father of the modern freedom movement," and what were his views?

DuBois, who is listed by Congressional investigating committees as having had 96 Communist front affiliations, was a founder of the NAACP. In 1959, DuBois was a recipient of the Lenin Peace Prize.

The Communist official publication, *The Worker*, of September 1, 1963, in mourning the passing of W. E. B. DuBois, referred to a letter DuBois wrote to Communist leader Gus Hall when he, DuBois, joined the Communist Party, U.S.A., in 1961. Wrote DuBois: "Capitalism is doomed to self-destruction. . . . In the end Communism will triumph. I want to help bring that day." . . .

An article appearing in the March, 1935, booklet entitled "Party Organizer," issued by the Central Committee of the Communist Party, U.S.A., stated: "In the United States there are five million of the Negro population organized in fraternal organizations, ten million in churches. . . . We must systematically study how to penetrate among the millions of organized Negro workers."

In *International of Youth*, published under the authority of the Young Communist International, headquarters in Moscow, March, 1935, appears the following:

. . . In the South, especially for the Negro youth, the church is the center of all cultural and social activity. It is here that we must work. By building our units in the church organizations, we can improve our work. . . . In Alabama there are certain places in which we can in a short while take over the church organizations of youth under our leadership, and these can become legal covers for our work in the South.

By a strange coincidence, the leader of the riots in Birmingham, Ala., in April, 1963, was a Negro minister by the name of Rev. Martin

Luther King, Jr. According to an article appearing in the New Bedford, Mass., *Standard-Times:*

Mr. King was quoted as telling a Chicago assembly last year, "it (the Montgomery, Ala., boycott, in which there was much violence) is a part of something that is happening all over the world. The oppressed people are rising up. They are revolting against colonialism and imperialism and all other systems of oppression."

When Martin Luther King, Jr., draws a parallel between the situation of the American Negro and "oppressed people's" rights against "colonialism" and "imperialism" he is following exactly, to the word, the Communist line. . . .

Again, it is no coincidence that with increasing frequency Negro churches are becoming the assembling areas for mobilizing the Negro masses to pour into the streets in Negro demonstrations.

The activities of Martin Luther King, Jr., have met with beaming approval by members of the Communist Party, U.S.A. In the pamphlet entitled *Turning Point In Freedom Road* published in 1962, the Negro Communist Claude Lightfoot praises Rev. King by describing his activities as "the healthiest sign in the whole Negro struggle."

King conducts most of his racial agitation activities in his capacity as president of the Southern Christian Leadership Conference. The national secretary of King's organization is a Negro by the name of Rev. Fred L. Shuttlesworth. An article in the June, 1963, issue of the *Cincinnati Enquirer* identified Shuttlesworth as also the new president of the Southern Conference Educational Fund. According to the article, both the Senate Internal Security Subcommittee and the House Committee on Un-American Activities have described the SCEF as an organization set up to promote Communism throughout the South. The field secretary of the SCEF is an identified Communist by the name of Carl Braden, of Louisville, Kentucky. . . .

It is not surprising that Martin Luther King, Jr., associates himself with characters tagged with Communist-front labels when King's own views are coming nearer and nearer to those of the Communist Party itself. In addressing the March on Washington participants in August, 1963, Rev. King promised that there would be "neither rest nor tranquillity in America" and that "the winds of revolt will continue to shake the foundations of our Nation" until his aims are met.

The "revolt" or "revolution" which was so frequently referred to by the speakers in Washington is not really one for so-called Negro "rights," but is, instead, a revolution to seize political power in this Nation in order to first hoist the flag of Socialism—and ultimately, Communism—over the United States of America.

The Need for Black Power (1967)

STOKELY CARMICHAEL AND CHARLES V. HAMILTON

If reactionaries pictured both anticolonialism and the domestic civil rights movement as part of a worldwide conspiracy against the established order of white supremacy, American radicals increasingly saw racial discrimination as a domestic form of colonialism, closely related to America's economic and military dominance of the so-called developing nations. The early advocates of Black Power did not accuse a small group of whites of consciously conspiring to keep the Negroes in subjugation. Rather, they affirmed that the lives of Negroes were wholly controlled, both physically and psychologically, by a power structure that systematically favored the interests of whites at the expense of blacks. All American whites, in other words, stood in the position of colonial masters; whites automatically closed ranks whenever Negroes dared to defend their own interests. This view of the totalitarian character of white power bears a striking resemblance to the "enslavement" which countersubversives have long held up as the ultimate penalty for public apathy. Whether the enemy was identified as the Catholic Church or international Communism, the end product of subversion was conceived as a total subordination much like that of Negroes to whites. According to Stokely Carmichael and Charles V. Hamilton, the blacks could never bargain successfully with whites until they had acquired an independent power base and a unifying sense of group self-identity.

Colonial subjects have their political decisions made for them by the colonial masters, and those decisions are handed down directly or through a process of "indirect rule." Politically, decisions which affect black lives have always been made by white people—the "white power structure." There is some dislike for this phrase because it tends to ignore or oversimplify the fact that there are many centers of

From Stokely Carmichael and Charles V. Hamilton, *Black Power: The Politics of Liberation in America* (New York: Vintage Books, 1967), pp. 6–7, 9–10, 22–23. Copyright 1967, by Stokely Carmichael and Charles Hamilton; reprinted by permission of Random House, Inc., and Jonathan Cape, Ltd.

power, many different forces making decisions. Those who raise that objection point to the pluralistic character of the body politic. They frequently overlook the fact that American pluralism quickly becomes a monolithic structure on issues of race. When faced with demands from black people, the multi-faction whites unite and present a common front. This is especially true when the black group increases in number: ". . . a large Negro population is politically both an asset and a liability. A large Negro populace may not only expect to influence the commitments and behavior of a governor, but it also may expect to arouse the fears of many whites. The larger the Negro population, the greater the perceived threat (in the eyes of whites) and thus the greater the resistance to broad civil rights laws." [1]

Again, the white groups tend to view their interests in a particularly united, solidified way when confronted with blacks making demands which are seen as threatening to vested interests. The whites react in a united group to protect interests they perceive to be theirs—interests possessed to the exclusion of those who, for varying reasons, are outside the group. . . .

The black community perceives the "white power structure" in very concrete terms. The man in the ghetto sees his white landlord come only to collect exorbitant rents and fail to make necessary repairs, while both know that the white-dominated city building inspection department will wink at violations or impose only slight fines. The man in the ghetto sees the white policeman on the corner brutally manhandle a black drunkard in a doorway, and at the same time accept a pay-off from one of the agents of the white-controlled rackets. He sees the streets in the ghetto lined with uncollected garbage, and he knows that the powers which could send trucks in to collect that garbage are white. When they don't, he knows the reason: the low political esteem in which the black community is held. He looks at the absence of a meaningful curriculum in the ghetto schools—for example, the history books that woefully overlook the historical achievements of black people—and he knows that the school board is controlled by whites. He is not about to listen to intellectual discourses on the pluralistic and fragmented nature of political power. He is faced with a "white power structure" as monolithic as Europe's colonial offices have been to African and Asian colonies. . . .

[1] James Q. Wilson, "The Negro in American Politics: The Present," *The American Negro Reference Book*, ed. John P. Davis (Englewood Cliffs, N.J., 1966), p. 453.

This is why the society does nothing meaningful about institutional racism: because the black community has been the creation of, and dominated by, a combination of oppressive forces and special interests in the white community. The groups which have access to the necessary resources and the ability to effect change benefit politically and economically from the continued subordinate status of the black community. This is not to say that every single white American consciously oppresses black people. He does not need to. Institutional racism has been maintained deliberately by the power structure and through indifference, inertia and lack of courage on the part of white masses as well as petty officials. Whenever black demands for change become loud and strong, indifference is replaced by active opposition based on fear and self-interest. The line between purposeful suppression and indifference blurs. One way or another, most whites participate in economic colonialism.

Indeed, the colonial white power structure has been a most formidable foe. It has perpetuated a vicious circle—the poverty cycle—in which the black communities are denied good jobs, and therefore stuck with a low income and therefore unable to obtain a good education with which to obtain good jobs. . . . They cannot qualify for credit at most reputable places; they then resort to unethical merchants who take advantage of them by charging higher prices for inferior goods. They end up having less funds to buy in bulk, thus unable to reduce overall costs. They remain trapped.

In the face of such realities, it becomes ludicrous to condemn black people for "not showing more initiative." Black people are not in a depressed condition because of some defect in their character. The colonial power structure clamped a boot of oppression on the neck of the black people and then, ironically, said "they are not ready for freedom." Left solely to the good will of the oppressor, the oppressed would never be ready.

More Stately Mansions (1964)

ROBERT WELCH

With Robert Welch, the founder of the John Birch Society, our study of countersubversion comes full circle. It is an incredible stroke of irony that Welch should discover John Robison's Proofs of a Conspiracy Against All the Religions and Governments of Europe, and that he should take seriously the lurid account of Adam Weishaupt's Bavarian Illuminati, which had brought panic to the New England clergy of the 1790's. Not only did Welch accept the fantasy of a European secret conspiratorial society, but he concluded that the Illuminati, after probably engineering the French Revolution, had survived until the nineteenth century as an underground organization, and had finally given birth to modern Communism.

Indeed, for Welch all history can be interpreted as a struggle between the children of light and the children of darkness; he believes that from the earliest times there has been a direct continuity between the subversive, collectivist forces of evil. Unfortunately, the children of light, being dedicated to individualism and instinctively opposed to organization, have never learned to benefit from historical experience, at least until the formation of the John Birch Society. According to Welch, if there had been a John Birch Society in ancient Athens, Greece would have been spared the Peloponnesian Wars; similarly, a John Birch Society would have helped France avoid the turmoil of her Revolution. Thus for the first time in history the diabolical forces represented by Sparta, the Illuminati, and the Communists have met their match in a secret society of committed individuals who, in Welch's words, reject "debating-society" tactics in favor of "a monolithic body . . . under completely authoritative control at all levels."

Now this eternal war between good and evil has been fought on many fronts, in many ways, and with many weapons. We wish to

From Robert Welch, "More Stately Mansions," speech delivered in Chicago, June 5, 1964, and reprinted in *The New Americanism and Other Speeches and Essays* (Boston: Western Islands Publishers, 1966), pp. 117–121, 124–128, 130–132, 135–140. Seymour Martin Lipset and Earl Rabb point out that Robison was revived in the 1930's by Gerald B. Winrod, who saw the Illuminati as a Jesuit-Jewish alliance that gave birth to modern Communism. For uses made of the Illuminati by Winrod, the Coughlinites, and the John Birch Society, see Lipset and Rabb, *The Politics of Unreason: Right-Wing Extremism in America, 1790–1970* (Harper & Row: New York, 1970), pp. 161, 181, 252–255. Unfortunately, this study appeared too late to be of use in the present work.

deal tonight with just one front. This is the area in which the forces of evil have fought under the banner of collectivism, and the forces of good have defended themselves as well as they could under the banner of individual rights and responsibilities. . . .

By the time of Solon . . . in the first half of the sixth century B.C. a new theory was being accepted, that government owed its power to the consent of those governed. This was the basic theme of democracy, and in many ways it represented a huge advance over the Asiatic principle of governmental power resting on sheer might. But unfortunately, the forces of evil early recognized that the consent of the governed could readily be reduced in practice to the whim of the mob; that it could be made to derive from the bigotry of the ignorant, the enviousness of the irresponsible, the greed of the shiftless, the self-righteousness of the *unco guid,* and even from the manipulation by clever agents of the quite temporary passions of a volatile people. The consent of the governed soon became merely the mechanics by which demagogues put themselves in power.

Since these demagogues, to obtain the support of the mobs and masses, usually made the natural pitch of promising to take from the haves and give to the have-nots, and since increasing agencies of government were always necessary to handle and effectuate these transfers, the meshing of demagoguery and collectivism was as inevitable as sunrise. And so the forces of evil, which appeal to the laziness, the selfishness, the rapacity, and to all of the criminal tendencies of man, early become the continuing matrix of these recurrent alliances between demagogues and the rabble. For the forces of evil sought always to destroy or weaken man's slowly building traditions of morality, of property rights, of the rights and responsibilities of the individual. And there was no surer nor quicker way to damage these *mores* than through the government of tyrants who derived their power from mob instincts, which placed no value on the individual. . . .

In fact, most of the demagogic ideological appeals which are used by the collectivists as their strongest weapons to this very day were already commonplace by the time the Roman republic itself had been converted by successive criminal tyrants into a democracy. The principle of "agrarian reform," which is a fancy liberal name for stealing land from its owners and distributing it to the far more numerous tenants, was used by the Gracchi in the second century B.C. as opportunistically as by Mao Tse-tung twenty-one hundred years later, and by dozens of equal scoundrels in between. And the extension of the vote to new classes in order to dilute the influence of the solider citizenry and increase the weight of the rootless mobs was advocated by the Gracchi with the same arguments used by those who wish to reduce the voting age today to include youthfully irresponsible college pranksters who set "records" by piling forty-five of themselves into one bed.

By the turn of the first century B.C., Gaius Marius could have given Charles de Gaulle lessons in how to murder and imprison his anti-collectivist enemies by quasi-legal means; and by 50 B.C. that tribune of the pee-pul Gaius Sallust could have taught economic demagoguery to Huey Long and simultaneous personal fortune grabbing to Eleanor Roosevelt. By now the forces of evil had learned well, from massive experience, to use government as the instrumentality through which to achieve their ambitions, and to use the demagogic appeal of bread and circuses for the masses as a means of controlling that instrumentality. . . .

The price controls and wage controls and all of the similar procedures of economic regimentation for burying the rights and responsibilities of individuals under the huge palimpsest of government's rights and responsibilities, as inaugurated by Diocletian in around 300 A.D., were necessarily changed in scope, but not at all in principle, when reestablished as Franklin Roosevelt's New Deal sixteen hundred years later. . . .

The precedent had been set, however [by the collectivism of Sparta], and the vision obviously reoccurred to many evil men during those two thousand years. There were many small sects and heresies and societies and associations of which we catch fleeting glimpses now and then from the early centuries of the Christian era until they proliferated into numerous clumps of unsightly or even poisonous intellectual weeds after 1700. How many of them there were, each of which intended to be the embryo of an organization that would grow in power until it ruled the world, we do not know. How many revolutionary coups or insurrections, or how many more gradual and more peaceful impositions of tyrannical power by ambitious criminals mouthing the hypocrisies of collectivism, may have been "masterminded" by such esoteric groups, we do not know. How extensive or long lasting was the once well-established cult of Satanism, which incorporated into its beliefs, methods, and purposes practically all of the foulness now associated with our contemporary tyranny, Communism, we do not know. For a high degree of secrecy was not only essential to any even temporary success on the part of any of these nefarious collections of criminal con men, but the thrill of belonging to some mysterious and powerful inner circle was one of the strongest appeals any such group could offer to prospective recruits.

We do know, however, from hundreds of small leaks and published accounts that the doctrines which gave many of these secret groups their cohesiveness and continuity would fall clearly, and by the most tolerant classification, into the category of evil. Also, that by the eighteenth century A.D. these various doctrines had pretty much coalesced into a uniformly Satanic creed and program, which was to establish the power of the sect through the destruction of all governments, all religion, all morality, all economic systems; and to substitute the sheer physical force of the lash and the bayonet for all other means by which previous governments, good or bad, had contrived to rule mankind. And a most important one of these groups, which is now generally meant when we use the term *Illuminati*—although many others had called themselves by that same name—was founded on May 1, 1776, by Adam Weishaupt.

Despite the extreme secrecy with which this group cloaked itself from the very beginning, one early raid by the Bavarian government, another raid about three years later, the partial confessions at one arraignment of four men fairly high up in the conspiracy—all of whom, incidentally, were professors—and a few more or less accidental discoveries or disclosures from other sources have made the original nature, purposes, and methods of the *Illuminati* quite well known. Since by 1800 they were able to pull the veil of secrecy over themselves almost completely and permanently, we do not know to what extent Weishaupt's group became the central core or even one of the main components of a continuing organization with increasing reach and control over all collectivist activities after 1776. But that there have been one or more such organizations, which have now been absorbed into the top echelons of the Communist conspiracy—or vice versa—is supported by too much evidence of too many kinds to permit much doubt. Both because of the strong probability that Weishaupt's *Illuminati* has been the dominant factor in this development, therefore, and because if there has been some even more secret and more successful group to fill the role it is bound to have had an extreme degree of similarity to the Weishaupt clique, it is worthwhile for us to take a few paragraphs to examine some of the clearly established facts about this particular sect of *Illuminati*. For a mere recital of these facts will show, among other things, how inevitable is the conclusion that the present worldwide Communist conspiracy has evolved out of some such earlier organization. . . .

(1) Selected neophytes were brought into the order in the conviction that its general object was "the happiness of the human race." After about three years of receiving intensive instruction and observation as a novitiate—such lesser members were called Minervals—those selected to be taken further were given a fuller explanation. The aim of the order was "to make of the human race, without any distinction of nation, condition, or profession, one good and happy family." Does that sound familiar?

(2) By this time, also, the Minerval, if accepted to go on to becoming an *Illuminatus Minor*, was being taught that all religion was merely superstition, which should be abandoned in favor of enlightenment—in other words, illumination—and the triumph of reason. One of the idealistic inducements which brought many recruits into the Order was the assurance that it would help to spread the purest and noblest form of Christianity. Many Protestant ministers, during the initial three years of brainwashing to which they were subjected, then actually came to equate the doctrines and purposes of the Order with the purest form of Christianity, and were ready to shift their allegiance to the worship of *reason* by the time they were called upon to do so.

(3) Loyalty to the temporal powers of the time was solemnly promised by the Order, and was understood by new members to be a firm principle of the Order when they took the oath as Minervals. By the time one came, however, to take the far more serious oath as an *Illuminatus Minor*, he was already accepting the doctrine that the happiness of the human race required the uniting of all the inhabitants of the earth into one great family; that the abolition of national differences and animosities being requisite to this end, patriotism was a narrow-minded sentiment incompatible with the more enlarged views and purposes of the Order; and that consequently all ruling princes were to be regarded as unnecessary and expendable. Loyalty to the Order was represented as morally far superior to loyalty to the ruling powers. . . .

As a corollary to these instructions, it is to be noted, Weishaupt's

Illuminati contrived to place their members as tutors to youths of great rank or importance. They managed by influence and intrigue to get dignitaries favorable to themselves appointed to higher offices. And the diligence and skill with which they worked at promoting each other is illustrated by the fact that within a comparatively few years all of the chairs at Weishaupt's own University of Ingolstadt, with two exceptions, were occupied by *Illuminati*. When you thus realize that the Communists today may have had a hundred and fifty years of cumulative experience at these tricks, you cease to marvel at what they accomplish with such comparatively small numbers.

(4) Sensual pleasures were to be given high rank among those to be pursued for the happiness of mankind. This was gradually to be made clear to the Minervals; and the release by enlightenment or "illumination" of the restrictions on such pleasures, as formerly imposed by their consciences, was to be one of the subconscious appeals leading them to the worship of reason instead of religion. And any similarity of this process to the motivations which have produced the disgusting beatniks of both sexes that now overrun Harvard Square may not be at all coincidental. . . .

All of the above, and a great deal more, the Minerval had learned and promised by the time he really became a fully accepted member of the Order. The training, the disillusionment, the gradual acceptance of the real purposes of the Order continued until one who was properly qualified became at last a member of the inner circle. By that time the following facts had been made crystal clear to him, and he was a party to all that they signified:

A. The purpose of the Order was to rule the world.

B. In order to accomplish this, it would first be necessary to destroy contemporary civilization. This specifically included the overthrow of all existing governments; the merging of all nationalities and races into one people under one government; the abolition of all private property; the destruction of all religion; and the abrogation of all morality.

C. Any and all means were to be used to achieve this end. Whatever helped the Order was good, whatever hindered it was bad.

D. A philosophical front glorifying equality, and a new kind of "morality" were to be utilized wherever they would serve. The essence of the "morality" was that the world should come to be ruled only by able men and good men, in all positions and at all levels. But the important and undisclosed catch was that who qualified as good men and able men was to be determined solely by the Order.

E. Any and all persons, of whatever rank or character, who could forward the purposes of the Order in any way were to be utilized as much as possible, without any necessity for them to be members and perhaps without their even knowing of the Order's existence.

F. This incredibly ambitious undertaking was to be conducted as a conspiracy, and secrecy at every point and at all times was of utmost importance. . . .

It is not our duty nor our need tonight to explore the extent to which the *Illuminati* were responsible for, or contributed to, bringing on the French Revolution with all of its excesses and reign of terror. The evidence increases that their influence was powerful and extensive. More important, if there were time, would be a discussion of the methods used, especially to excite and manipulate the Paris mobs—on which mobs the successful destructiveness wreaked on the state, on religion, and on all morality depended. All was lies, planned agitation and mob action, murders carefully plotted to appear as spontaneous "vengeance" by the people, incredible terror used as a political weapon—all in the name of reason and of liberty, equality, and brotherhood. . . .

The further truth is that the French people under Louis XVI had as little cause to let themselves be led by conspiratorial destructivists into insane horrors and a murderous clamor for "liberty" as the Negroes in America have today in a demand for "freedom." Both are being stirred and led into the same kind of cruel idiocy by exactly the same kind of revolutionary criminals, for exactly the same megalomaniacal purposes on the part of the real instigators of these monstrous crimes against God and country. If the march on Washington had been more successful from the point of view of the Communists; if the common sense and basic morality of the American people—white and black—had already been sufficiently eroded by Communist wiles and propaganda so that the marchers could have been whipped up into the same kind of frenzy as were a smaller contingent of three hundred such marchers recently in the city of Chester, Pennsylvania; and if carefully planted armed goons of the Communists within the ranks of the marchers on Washington could have arranged for the burning of the city, and for murders and atrocities to be perpetuated on a number of loyal congressmen and senators, all to look like the spontaneous actions of an infuriated, resentful mob seeking freedom, then you might easily have seen the date of *that* great lie established in due course as the new national holiday of a "liberated" United States. And at least you would have seen an almost exact parallel to the sack of the Bastille.

The French Revolution turned out to be, in fact, a rehearsal in almost every particular of what the whole world is facing today. Compressed into one city and a period of six years, 1789 through 1794, were all of the lies and crimes and horror and propaganda and destructiveness which are now being applied to the whole world over a period of about six decades.

Whether the top command of the international Communist conspiracy is simply a continuing part of Weishaupt's *Illuminati* under whatever names and in whatever forms it may have perpetuated itself, we do not know. As Dr. Oliver has pointed out, we do know that Karl Marx wrote the *Communist Manifesto* in 1847 simply as an agent employed by one such group, the so-called League of Just Men, which already had branches in many countries long before it was renamed as the League of Communists. My own lesser researches clearly indicate that the infamous so-called German Union, and other revolutionary bodies with exactly the same purposes and methods as the *Illuminati,* which helped the identified Weishaupt *Illuminati* mightily in bringing on the French Revolution, were nothing more or less than divisions or branches of the *Illuminati* which had been set up separately for purposes of deception, protection and convenience. It could easily be that the League of Just Men was just a division of the *Illuminati;* that Karl Marx and, after him, Trotsky and Lenin and Stalin and Malenkov, and de Gaulle and Castro and Nehru and Betancourt, and hundreds of other leftist leaders elsewhere throughout the world, and a dozen in this country whom we had better leave unnamed, have all been working for such an inner group, or in some cases, have been members of it.

We do not know. For most purposes and in most respects it does not matter enough to deserve more than passing attention or speculation. What does matter, and the point to which this whole speech has been leading so far, is that forces of evil, which work through collectivism, are always organized; while the opposing forces of good, which support and defend the rights and responsibilities of individuals, are always disorganized. And this seems to me the primary reason, above all other reasons, why it sometimes takes so long for the forces of good, with all truth on their side, to come out from under the slavery or suppression or ignominy to which they are recurrently subjected for a generation or a century by the forces of evil.

Throughout all of the history which we reviewed so briefly at the beginning of this talk, the forces of evil have been organized for every fray; the forces of good have never been organized except during those last-ditch, often suicidal, but sometimes successful spasms of effort to throw off a collectivist tyranny, when enough individuals had finally come to recognize it as unbearable. And now we face an extension of this principle which makes it tremendously more important. For in our contemporary world the forces of evil are not only more elaborately and tightly and lastingly organized than ever before; and not only do they have the benefit of an organization which has visibly been continuous and growing for many decades; but whether or not this organization is merely a continuation of one which has been active for nearly two hundred years, it has obviously taken full and remarkable advantage of the accumulated knowledge and experience of collectivist groups which *have* been active throughout that period.

The Communist party of Khrushchev does not have to be a direct organizational descendant of Weishaupt's *Illuminati* to be able to benefit from everything the collectivists learned from their manipulation and use of that incredibly slimy hypocrite Mirabeau, or of the equally nauseating though far less brilliant traitor the duc d'Orléans, in steering the French Revolution onto the course they had designed. . . . While the anti-Communists of the world simply do not have, and never have had, any organizational continuity which gives the slightest chance of their even learning about, and much less utilizing, the experiences from past encounters which are repeated over and over.

As one of my associates has said, the Communists have missed *nothing*, absolutely nothing, among all the possibilities for deception, propaganda, and aggression in any and all situations which may arise. While the anti-Communists appear to have learned absolutely nothing from the past. I have never seen an anti-Communist who even recognized the similarities between the characters, careers, and utterly false historical legends of Cornelia, the mother of the Gracchi, and of Eleanor Roosevelt. I have never seen one that recognized in Alcibiades such an instructive prototype of Dwight D. Eisenhower. I have never seen one who pointed out the unbelievably numerous and extensive parallels between the Spartan state during the Peloponnesian War and the USSR during the war we are fighting today. . . .

And it is the very fact that the individualists will learn nothing from history, have no organizational means or opportunity of learning anything from history, which so helps the collectivists to perpetrate repetitions of tragic history on us again and again. All of which discussion and background leads us, as you are certain to have been surmising, to The John Birch Society. For we feel that it is clearly our duty, and may be our destiny, to fill this void. . . .·

In the last pages of the Blue Book, as simply a transcript of what was said at the founding meeting of The John Birch Society, it is pointed out that I think we are something new in history. I still think so, and this speech has been intended partly to explain and support the thought. Because this is the first time in history, so far as we know, that any sizable group of truly good men and women of all religious beliefs, and of all races and colors, has ever been brought together in any permanent voluntary organization to work, as a group, for those things which they believe in common . . . For this reason and in this manner The John Birch Society can become a new force in human history—one that has been very badly needed, especially for the past two hundred years; and . . . as such a new force, it can become a very effective factor on the side of the forces of good in making this a better world. For at least not *all* of the advantages of organization and of continuity will now be left on the side of the forces of evil.

The Truth about Vietnam (1967)

ROBERT WELCH

In the famous Blue Book of the John Birch Society (1958), Robert Welch described Communism as "a gigantic conspiracy to enslave man-

From Robert Welch, *The Truth About Vietnam* (Belmont, Mass.: *American Opinion*, 1967), pp. 1, 2, 4, 5, 7–8. © Robert Welch 1967.

kind; an increasingly successful conspiracy, controlled by determined, cunning, and utterly ruthless gangsters, willing to use any means to achieve its end." Convinced that America's danger "remains almost entirely internal," Welch argued that the American people had been systematically deluded into thinking that the primary threat of Communism was posed by the Russian armed forces. American leaders used this fabricated danger as an excuse for defense spending, for creeping statism and socialism, and for a gradual surrender of sovereignty to the Communist-controlled United Nations. It is perhaps to be expected that a man who saw the civil rights struggles in the South as being fomented "almost entirely by the Communists," should also see America's involvement in Vietnam as part of a subtle plot to weaken the country and drain its resources. It was, after all, but a short step from Senator McCarthy's charges against General Marshall to Welch's assertion that Henry Cabot Lodge, a liberal Republican who had played "a leading role" in turning Algeria over to the Communists, was now helping the Communists win in Vietnam.

The lead editorial of *The Boston Herald,* on Saturday, January 21, 1967, began as follows: "Last week in Vietnam 144 Americans were killed, 1,004 were wounded and six were reported missing."

It is the sad purpose of this article to raise the question: Did the death of those hundred and forty-four Americans constitute deliberate, conscious, and coldblooded murder on the part of the Johnson Administration? . . .

Why fight 'em in Vietnam and help 'em everywhere else? And if you do not believe we *are* helping the Communists everywhere else, you need only to read your daily papers. In fact, the Administration is right now moving heaven and earth to bring about more so-called trade with Soviet Russia and all of its satellites. Most of this trade turns out, in any final analysis, to be simply gifts in one form or another from the United States. Yet Moscow and these satellites are supplying most of the war matériel to be used by the Viet Cong in Vietnam against our soldiers there, while Washington helps to keep these Communist regimes in power and in position to do so. . . .

This is just the same old road show enacted in Korea, where MacArthur was fired for even trying to win the war. The road show has now been moved south a thousand miles and reopened at a new stand, with the same plot, the same management, and a very similar cast. Once again we are sending our men to fight against the Communists, in a war which is actually being controlled on both sides by Communists or Communist influences. Why are we stupid enough to allow it all a second time? . . .

Does anybody have any doubts as to who is really running things in Washington today, or that our actions in Vietnam are being conducted exactly according to Communist plans and wishes? . . .

The most obvious [question] is: Then why pick Vietnam, *and Vietnam alone,* for this opposition? We first went into Vietnam, or made it theoretically our protégé nation, in 1954, by throwing the French out and putting the Communists in. As so-called "observers" at Geneva in 1954, but really running the show, we turned the top half of the country over directly and officially to the Communists, and set up an anti-Communist government in the bottom half, exactly as we had done in Korea in 1948. In both cases we thus prepared the way for the Communist aggression from the northern part into the southern part, and for the war that would follow, exactly as the Communists were already planning. . . .

Now since 1954 there has been vicious and vital Communist aggression all over the world. In Ghana, in the Congo, in Indonesia, in Algeria, in Cuba, in the Dominican Republic, the Communists have proceeded by guerrilla action, mass murders and cruelties, treasonous subversion, and diplomatic pressures, to set up one Communist tyranny after another. And in every case the Administration in Washington, whether headed by Eisenhower, Kennedy, or Johnson, has been visibly and actively on the side of the Communist aggressors. Basically it has been the same Administration all of the time, of course, controlled by the same influences, carrying out identically the same policies, with politically hermaphroditic characters serving alike in so-called Republican or Democratic administrations, and with bi-partisan treason rampart everywhere. But this treason to the United States and treason to the human race has taken the form of brazenly helping Communist aggression everywhere else, until we come to Vietnam. Why the change? Or the pretended change?

There are circumstances about this war, deriving from its geographical, historical, and ethnological background, which are palpably disadvantageous to the United States. To these circumstances there have been added many others, carefully and cunningly created by somebody, which serves the same purpose of "stacking the cards" against us. The combination produces a situation in which the United States is fighting a war under the cumulative weight of the greatest possible handicaps which could be contrived anywhere on this planet at this time. Is that why Vietnam was picked as the battleground?

The Internal Threat Today (1964)

EZRA TAFT BENSON

The assassination of President John F. Kennedy unleashed a swarm of wild theories of conspiracy; many had nothing to do with ideological conflict, but were simply ingenious responses to the unexplained discrepancies connected with the shocking event. But for many conservatives, the most striking fact was the initial assumption of liberals, including many writers in the national press, that an assassination in Dallas had to be the work of the extremist right. Ezra Taft Benson, who was Secretary of Agriculture under President Eisenhower and who is a member of the Council of Twelve of the Mormon Church, felt that it was highly revealing that the national press followed the Communist line in its first response to Kennedy's assassination. It should be noted that Benson also considered the John Birch Society to be "the most effective nonchurch organization in our fight against creeping socialism and godless communism."

To have the President of the United States suddenly torn from his high office by the violent hand of an assassin was an insidious and dastardly act which struck at the very foundation of our Republic.

All of us felt the impact of it. All of us caught the ominous spirit of tragedy and sorrow which accompanied it. Each of us sensed in a very personal way the heartbreak which had come to the Kennedy family.

But after the services and burial were over, we also realized something else. There was the cold, stark reality that the accused assassin's murder of President Kennedy was just one more mon-

From Ezra Taft Benson, "The Internal Threat Today," in *Title of Liberty*, compiled by Mark A. Benson (Salt Lake City: Deseret Book Company, 1964), pp. 22–24. Copyright 1964 Deseret Book Company.

strous treachery in the long list of crimes against humanity which have been inspired down through the years by the godless philosophy of communism.

It was communism that sowed the seeds of treason in the mind of President Kennedy's accused assassin. This is something which must not be forgotten.

In fact, this harsh historical fact should have served as a shock therapy to that segment of our population who like to call themselves "liberals." America is big enough to make room for many different kinds of thinking, but many liberals have claimed to see virtues in socialism and communism which I, for one, have not been able to find. To promote their ideas, American liberals have become a highly organized, hardcore establishment in the United States and they have been excusing their appeasement and coddling of communism on the ground that they were being "tolerant," "broadminded," and "working for peace."

But the assassination of President Kennedy should have jolted them into a realization that they have been pampering, protecting, and promoting the very nest of serpents which produced Lee Harvey Oswald. The diabolical spirit of murder and violence which struck down the President is that same spirit of communist violence which has been allowed to spread its terror into the heart of every continent on the face of the earth. Perhaps those who have been apologists for this conquering Marxist socialist-communist movement might now agree to reconsider the fatal delusion they have been following.

Two additional things happened in connection with this recent tragedy which are worthy of comment.

First was the speed with which the communist leaders spread the word that the slaying of the President must have been the work of American conservatives. Moscow has conducted a three-year propaganda campaign to make American conservatives look like hysterical fanatics. It has called them "rightists," "extremists," and even "fascists." Within an hour after the assassination, and before Oswald was captured, Moscow was assuring the world that this crime was a product of the "rightist" movement in the United States.

The second thing which happened was the amazing rapidity with which American liberals took up the Moscow line. They too were quick to fix the blame even though there hadn't been the slightest hint as to who had committed the crime. I wonder what would have happened if Oswald had not been captured and identified as an active communist who was in direct contact with party headquarters in New York City? Undoubtedly the liberal element would be blaming this tragedy on conservative Americans to this day.

And even after Oswald was captured and identified as a Moscow-associated communist, there were those who insisted that any who had opposed the President during his term of high office was guilty of that same "spirit of hate" as that which led to the President's death. This line of thinking was expressed by a number of prominent persons through the press, radio, and TV. To me it was incomprehensible.

Marxmanship in Dallas (1964)

REVILO P. OLIVER

Writing for the John Birch Society's American Opinion, Revilo P. Oliver, who taught Classics at the University of Illinois, went far beyond the intimations of Ezra Taft Benson. Oliver had no scruples about branding President Kennedy, Chief Justice Warren, and the entire liberal "establishment" as being agents of international Communism. Since Kennedy himself was working for the Soviet Union, it followed that the Communists had murdered him only because he was not subverting America fast enough. The Communists plotted to make the assassination appear to be the work of patriotic conservatives, thus causing, they hoped, mass persecution and slaughter. Fortunately the country had been saved by the timely intervention of Officer J. A. Tippit.

We all know what happened in Dallas on the twenty-second of November. It is imperative that we understand it.

Lee Harvey Oswald was a young punk who defected to the Soviet, taking with him the operational codes of the Marine Corps and such other secrets as a fledgling traitor had been able to steal while in military service. He not only forfeited his American citizenship by his

---

From Revilo P. Oliver, "Marxmanship in Dallas," *American Opinion: An Informal Review,* February 1964, pp. 13–24.

acts, but also officially repudiated it under oath in the American Embassy in Moscow. He was then trained in sabotage, terrorism, and guerrilla warfare (including accurate shooting from ambush) in the well-known school for international criminals near Minsk, and while there he married the daughter of a colonel in the Soviet military espionage system (and probably also in the Secret Police). In 1962, after he had been trained for three years in Russia, the Communist agent and his Communist wife were brought to the United States, in open violation of American law, by our Communist-dominated State Department.

On his arrival in this country, Oswald took up his duties as an agent of the Conspiracy, spying on anti-Communist Cuban refugees, serving as an agitator for "Fair Play for Cuba," and participating in some of the many other forms of subversion that flourish openly in defiance of law through the connivance of the Attorney General, Robert F. Kennedy. In April of 1963, he was sent to Dallas, where he tried to murder General Edwin Walker. The failure does not reflect on the assassin's professional training: General Walker happened to turn his head at the instant the shot was fired. According to a story that has been neither confirmed nor denied officially at the time that I write, Oswald was arrested as a suspect, but was released through the personal intervention of Robert F. Kennedy, and all inquiry into the attempted assassination of a great American was halted.

In November, Oswald was sent back to Dallas, where a job in a suitably located building had been arranged for him. He shot the President of the United States from ambush, left the building undetected, and would have escaped to Mexico but for some mischance. He was stopped for questioning by a vigilant policeman, whom he killed in a moment of panic. Arrested and identified, he, despite his training, was so vain as to pose for photographs while triumphantly giving the Communists' clenched-fist salute; he asked for a noted Communist attorney, who had been a member of the little Communist cell that included the noted traitor, Alger Hiss; and he began to tell contradictory stories. He was accordingly liquidated before he could make a complete confession. . . .

It is highly significant that, after Oswald was arrested, you learned the facts. That proves that the Communist Conspiracy's control over the United States is not yet complete.

I firmly believe that in our nation as a whole the overwhelming majority of local policemen, whom we shamefully neglect and take for granted, are brave and honorable Americans. But I know nothing of the police in Dallas. It is quite possible that, as is usual in our large cities, they are subject to great pressures from a corrupt municipal government. I shall not be greatly astonished if, in the course of the Conspiracy's frantic efforts to confuse us with irrelevancies, it should be disclosed that pay-offs had been made by Jakob Leon Rubenstein, alias Ruby, and other members of the underworld that pander to human vice and folly. It is by no means impossible that crypto-Communists have been planted in that police force. But paint the picture as dark as you will, it remains indisputably true that, at the very least, there were enough honest and patriotic men on that police force to bring about the arrest of Oswald, to identify him, and to prevent both his escape and his "assassination while trying to escape." It required a gunman from outside to do the job.

It is quite true that the Communist Conspiracy, through the management of great broadcasting systems and news agencies, through the many criminals lodged in the Press, and through many indirect pressures (such as allocation of advertising and harassment by bureaus of the federal government), has a control over our channels of communication that seems to us, in our moments of discouragement, virtually total. As was to be expected, a few moments after the shot was fired in Dallas, the vermin, probably in obedience to general or specific orders issued in advance of the event, began to screech out their diseased hatred of the American people, and, long after the facts were known to everyone, went on mechanically repeating like defective phonograph records, the same vicious lies about the "radical right" until fresh orders reached them from headquarters. But the significant fact is that there were enough honest American newsmen, in the United States and abroad, to make it impossible to conceal the Conspiracy's connection with the bungled assassination. That is very encouraging. . . .

The assassination of Kennedy, quite apart from consideration of the office that he held, was an act of violence both deplorable and ominous—as ominous as the violence excited by the infamous Martin Luther King and other criminals engaged in inciting race war with the approval and even, it is said, the active co-operation of the White House. It was as deplorable and ominous as the violence of the uniformed goons (protected by reluctant and ashamed soldiers) whom

Kennedy, in open violation of the American Constitution, sent into Oxford, Mississippi, to kick into submission American citizens, whom the late Mr. Kennedy had come to regard as his subjects. . . .

Rational men will understand that, far from sobbing over the deceased or lying to placate his vengeful ghost, it behooves us to speak of him with complete candor and historical objectivity. Jack was not sanctified by a bullet.

The departed Kennedy is the John F. Kennedy who procured his election by peddling boob-bait to the suckers, including a cynical pledge to destroy the Communist base in Cuba. He is the John F. Kennedy with whose blessing and support the Central Intelligence Agency staged a fake "invasion" of Cuba designed to strengthen our mortal enemies there and to disgrace us—disgrace us not merely by ignominious failure, but by the inhuman crime of having lured brave men into a trap and sent them to suffering and death. He is the John F. Kennedy who, in close collaboration with Khrushchev, staged the phoney "embargo" that was improvised both to befuddle the suckers on election day in 1962 and to provide for several months a cover for the steady and rapid transfer of Soviet troops and Soviet weapons to Cuba for eventual use against us. He is the John F. Kennedy who installed and maintained in power the unspeakable Yarmolinsky-McNamara gang in the Pentagon to demoralize and subvert our armed forces and to sabotage our military installations and equipment. He is the John F. Kennedy who, by shameless intimidation, bribery, and blackmail, induced weaklings in Congress to approve treasonable acts designed to disarm us and to make us the helpless prey of the affiliated criminals and savages of the "United Nations." . . .

Why was Kennedy murdered by the young Bolshevik? . . .

Now it was generally suspected for some time before the assassination that Khrushchev and Kennedy were planning to stage another show to bamboozle the American suckers just before the election next November. According to this plan, a fake "revolt" against Castro would be enacted by the Communist second team, which has long been kept in reserve for such an eventuality. (Cf. *American Opinion*, March, 1962, p. 33.) The "democratic revolution" was to be headed by a Communist agent who differed from Fidel only in being less hairy and less well known to Americans, so that the *New York Times*, the State Department, the Central Intelligence Agency, and our other domestic enemies could swear once again that the vicious criminal was an "agrarian reformer," an "anti-Communist," and the "George

Washington of Cuba." (It is confidently believed in conspiratorial circles that the dumb brutes in the United States will never learn—until it is much too late.)

What is not certain is the script for the third act of the comedy. Most (but not all) informed observers believe that this performance in Cuba was to accomplish two things: (a) the re-election of Kennedy and most of his stooges in Congress, which would, of course, be impossible without some seasonably contrived and major "crisis"; and (b) the endlessly repeated and trite device of making the tax-paying serfs in the United States, who have financed every important Communist conquest since 1917, work to provision and fortify another conquest under the pretext that by so doing they in some mysterious way "fight Communism."

Now, if those observers are correct in their projections, the scenario called for the "success" of the "democratic revolution." And that would involve, if the play was to be convincing, the liquidation of Fidel and a few of his more notorious accomplices. And that, as is well known to everyone who has made even the slightest study of Communism, would be merely commonplace and normal.

The rabid rats of Bolshevism devour one another—and no one knows that better than the rats themselves. Almost all of the Conspiracy's most famous murderers—Trotsky, Zinoviev (Apfelbaum), Kirov (Kostrikov), Kamenev (Rosenfeld), Yezhov, Beria, and a hundred others, possibly including Stalin—were murdered by their insatiably blood-thirsty confederates. Indeed, it is a general rule that only accident or disease can save a Communist "leader" from assassination or execution by other Communists as soon as his usefulness to the Conspiracy is ended or his liquidation will provide an opportunity for useful propaganda.

Cornered rats will fight for their lives. Castro, of course, knew of the planned "revolution," and if the dénouement was correctly foreseen by American observers, he also knew that, whatever solemn pledges may have been given him by his superiors, he would not survive. It is possible, therefore, that Fidel arranged the assassination of Jack in the hope of averting, or at least postponing, his own. Now that Oswald is silenced and superiors who gave him his orders are unidentified, it may never be possible completely to disprove that hypothesis, although there are a number of considerations that weigh against it. . . .

. . . The Conspiracy ordered the assassination as part of systematic preparation for a domestic take-over. If so, the plan, of course, was to place the blame on the "right-wing extremists" (if I may use the Bolsheviks' code-word for informed and loyal Americans), and we may be sure that a whole train of "clues" had been carefully planted to lead or point in that direction as soon as Oswald was safe in Mexico. These preparations were rendered useless when Oswald was, through some mischance, arrested—probably in consequence of some slip-up of which we as yet know nothing. He may, for example, have missed connections with some agent of the Conspiracy who was to transport him to the airport, and it may be significant that, when observed on the street, he was walking directly toward the apartment of the Jakob Rubenstein (alias Jack Ruby) who later silenced him.

Two objections to this explanation are commonly raised, but neither is cogent.

The first is the assumption that, if the International Conspiracy had planned the assassination, there would have been no slip-up. That is absurd. The degenerates are not Supermen. Their agents make blunders all the time—blunders that could destroy whole segments of the apparatus, if the Conspiracy did not have so many criminals planted in communications and politics to cover up the blunders and to paralyze the normal reactions of a healthy society. . . . For that matter, a potentially serious and quite unnecessary mistake was made when the Communist Party's *official* publication, *The Worker*, yelled for the appointment of Earl Warren to "investigate" the assassination *before* the appointment was made—or at least, before the appointment was disclosed to the public. Nothing was gained by that mistake in timing, which serves only to give away the whole show.

The second argument is that the Conspiracy could not have wanted to eliminate Kennedy, who was doing so much for it. But that is a miscalculation. For one thing, the job was not being done on schedule. A few measures had been forced through Congress, but not, for example, what is called "Civil Rights," a very vital part of the vermin's preparations for the final take-over. Virtually nothing was done to speed up national bankruptcy and the total economic collapse that is doubtless scheduled to accompany the subjugation of the American people. The Congress was, on the whole, the most American Congress that we have had for many years, and it blocked the measures most cunningly designed to destroy the nation. It was not the fault of any one man, to be sure, but the record for 1963 was, for all practical purposes, a stalemate. Our "Liberals," always impatient for open dictatorship and terrorism, were beginning to feel frustrated; some of them were screeching in our more prominent daily, weekly, and monthly liepapers about the "standpatism" of Congress and hinting that that nasty relic of the Constitution must be abolished in the interests of "effective democracy." Others were beginning to lose confidence. . . .

Careful observers were aware of the feeling of crisis in conspiratorial circles before the assassination. In June of 1963, an experienced American military man made a careful analysis of the situation at that time, and in his highly confidential report concluded, on the basis of indications in Communist and crypto-Communist sources, that the Conspiracy's schedule called for a major incident to create national shock *before Thanksgiving*. . . .

But aside from the Conspiracy's obvious need for some drastic means of checking the growth of American patriotism, there is the consideration that Kennedy was rapidly becoming a political liability. Despite the best efforts of the lie-machines, it was clear that his popularity was diminishing so rapidly that some observers doubted whether even the most cunningly contrived and timed "crisis" could procure his re-election. His conduct was exciting ever increasing disgust even among the credulous; and what was worse, the vast cesspool in Washington was beginning to leak badly.

The bandits of the New Frontier, of whom Billie Sol Estes was but a puny specimen, had operated a little too openly. . . . There are rumors that an even more filthy scandal, involving both sadistic sexual perversions and the use of governmental powers for the importation and distribution of hallucinatory narcotics, is simmering dangerously near to the surface. I am told that documentary evidence of secret shipments of secret munitions of war to the Soviet by the Administration in treasonable defiance of law is available in a place in which it is secure from both burglary and bribery. . . . For aught I know to the contrary, the assassination of Kennedy may have been necessary as the *only* means of avoiding, or even long deferring, national scandals so flagrant as to shock the whole of our brainwashed and hypnotized populace back to sanity.

In summary, then, there is not a single indication that the Conspiracy did not plan and carry out the assassination of Kennedy. On the other hand, there is evidence which very strongly suggests that it did.

First of all, there is the suspicious celerity with which the broadcasting agency sardonically called Voice of America, Tass of Moscow, Earl Warren, and many publicists and politicians noted for their services to the Conspiracy in the past, began to screech that the murder was the work of "right-wing extremists" almost as soon as the shot was fired. One is justified in asking whether the leaders of this chorus went into action as soon as they received news *that they were expecting.* Or, if they did not know the precise moment, were they not prepared in advance for news of that kind? Is it conceivable that the same story would have occurred independently to so many different persons, however intense their hatred of the American people, or that they would have dared to announce *as fact* a malicious conjecture, if they had no assurance that their statements would be confirmed by "evidence" to be discovered subsequently? . . .

Persons whose business it is to tamper with the news are naturally accustomed to lying, but even they do not lightly take the risk of being caught promptly in a particularly improbable and offensive lie. The case of Earl Warren is even more puzzling. No one would suspect him of concern for truth, but surely the Chief Justice of the Supreme Court must be shrewd enough not to make allegations without some reason to believe that he will be able to produce some shreds of "evidence" to support them.

It seems that preparations had been made for rioting and murder throughout the country. Americans known to be opponents of the Conspiracy, including General Walker, prominent members of the John Birch Society, and leaders of other conservative organizations, began to receive threats of death by telephone from creatures who somehow knew that Kennedy was dead *before* he reached the hospital. In many communities, mobs composed of the dregs of humanity and openly proposing to burn the homes and murder the families of known conservatives began to form in the evening, as though in obedience to orders that had not been countermanded to all sectors. I do not suggest that the local vermin were entrusted with a foreknowledge of precisely what was to happen in Dallas, but it seems very likely that they had been prepared to respond to a signal and told what to do when the signal came.

Who Killed Kennedy? (1964)

THOMAS G. BUCHANAN

Revilo P. Oliver not only referred to the Order of the Illuminati but discussed the thesis that a "Force X" might be the inner core of the Communist conspiracy, in addition to directing the world traffic in drugs, homosexual rings, and organized crime. Curiously enough, Thomas G. Buchanan, who approached the Kennedy assassination from a diametrically opposite point of view, suggested that the conspiracy had been directed by a mysterious Texas oil millionaire, whom Buchanan called X. Both theses indicate the growing conviction that events are never what they seem to be, that behind even apparent conspiracies lurk still darker forces of intrigue and evil. Like many critics of the Warren Report, Buchanan was troubled by Oswald's apparent lack of motive. Surely, at most Oswald could only have been a front for a far more systematic and malicious force. Whereas Oliver had seen Officer Tippit as the martyred savior of America, Buchanan suspected he was really Oswald's intended executioner. After Tippit bungled the job, the assignment fell to Jack Ruby.

Few Americans suspect the dominant position oil assumes in the American economy. Most of us probably would guess that steel or auto-manufacturing were the chief industries of the United States, with chemicals not far behind them. Oil investments are, however, more than these three industries combined—more than 50 billion dollars. Almost half of this enormous wealth is owned in Texas. . . .

Now and then, when the effects of the decisions of the oil men challenged the economy of the whole country, efforts have been made to stop them from demanding an unreasonable profit. Such, for instance, was the case in May, 1958, when a Federal grand jury indicted 29 oil companies for a conspiracy to charge outrageous prices. . . . The *New York Times* financial expert J. H. Carmical estimated, at that time, that this price rise cost the United States consumer half a billion dollars, and the public protest was so great that the oil com-

Reprinted by permission of G. P. Putnam's Sons from Thomas G. Buchanan, *Who Killed Kennedy?* (London: Secker and Warburg, 1964), pp. 162–164, 165–166, 171–174, 184–187, 189–191. Copyright © 1964 by Thomas G. Buchanan.

panies were brought to court and charged with a conspiracy to violate price-fixing legislation. But a sympathetic judge decided that "the evidence in the case does not rise above the level of suspicion," and concluded, "I have an absolute conviction personally that the defendants are not guilty." . . .

Since 1926 a special supplementary deduction has been granted to the oil men when they pay their taxes. In addition to the standard tax deductions to which other people are entitled, they receive a 27½ per cent "depletion allowance" which they can retain from their gross income. . . . Thus, the income saved by Texas millionaires by this "depletion allowance" is now 30 times what it was back in 1926 when the concession was granted.

This huge concession is, however, only the beginning. It will be recalled that it was justified by the oil industry upon the ground that oil men take more risks than other businessmen, and so cannot be as assured of making any profit at all. But they have simultaneously demanded, and were given, other tax concessions to reduce these risks until—for the big operators who have capital enough to take advantage of the risk-proof tax provisions—any chance of losing money in sustained oil operations has been almost totally eliminated. . . .

The Texas oligarchy shared with all right-wing groups in America a deep hostility to measures undertaken by the Kennedy Administration, in the months before the President's assassination, to improve relations with the Soviet bloc. The majority opinion in the U.S.A. has been that efforts by the President to find a basis for negotiations with the Russians ought to be encouraged. When we use the word "negotiations," we imply a willingness to yield on some points, in return for similar concessions. Otherwise, we are not asking our opponents to negotiate; we are demanding unconditional surrender; we must be, accordingly, prepared for the eventuality that they will choose to fight. This is a gambler's choice; it is not a choice which would recommend itself to any cautious leader or to any responsible section of the business community. The Kennedy Administration in the U.S.A., Khrushchev in the U.S.S.R., and the most influential leaders in the two armed camps, conscious that any new world war, as Khrushchev said in 1962, "would be thermonuclear from the beginning," had come to an agreement, just before the President was murdered, to renounce the testing of atomic weapons. It was understood that this was just the first step to eventual disarmament.

There was immediate and vocal opposition to this treaty, and it came from the minority in both camps. The Chinese and the Albanians said that any treaty made with Wall Street would be worse than useless; it would mean the Russians had placed peace above the independence movement of colonial peoples and revolutionary movement of the workers. It would mean, in short, that they had made concessions—and the Chinese said that this was treason. . . .

In the U.S.A., the argument proceeded along similar lines, with the majority of businessmen, like other sections of the population, feeling that the Kennedy Administration should continue cautiously exploring possibilities of stabilizing the world situation. By an overwhelming margin, Congress ratified the Moscow Pact. And yet there was extremely bitter opposition from such right-wing groups as the John Birch Society which, taking a position analogous to that of the Chinese, denied that there was any difference between the Communists of China and of Russia; they were all the same; the moment that they had the chance, they would attack us. These men proclaimed that a President of the United States who bothered to negotiate with the Communists was crazy; worse than that, he was a traitor. He was probably pro-Communist himself.

Right-wing groups were already championing the Southern cause against desegregation. Kennedy, they said, was sending Northern troops into the South to violate States' rights, and to grant Negroes equality with white men—which, they said, was a Communist objective. The double animosity combined; the streams formed one channel, and a violent campaign of personal abuse was directed at the President. The nature of this campaign may be judged from the leaflet passed out among students at a university near Dallas the day before the President was assassinated. A front and side view of the President are shown, in the manner normally associated with escaped criminals, below which is the line, "Wanted for Treason." . . .

Another pamphlet being circulated said, "Impeach the Traitor John F. Kennedy for giving aid and comfort to the enemies of the U.S.A." —and on this pamphlet, was a hangman's noose.

The centre of this campaign of abuse was Dallas. The President knew this quite well; he chose to meet his enemies upon their own ground and reply to them. . . .

Rather than waste our time in psychoanalysing Oswald, who was nothing but a minor member of the plot, it will be much more fruitful to establish the real motive for the crime. For what has been most lacking in official explanations of the crime which Oswald is alleged to have committed is the reason for his action. I cannot pretend to know it. Was it simply that the man was poor and desperate and disillusioned—willing to do anything to make a living? Or was he in sympathy with the political objectives of extreme right-wing groups? Mark Lane, the New York attorney who at one time represented Oswald's mother, makes a strong case for supposing Oswald was innocent of all guilt. I cannot accept this thesis. I find no way to explain his purchase of the rifle or his return to his apartment to pick up a pistol except on the ground that Oswald was involved in the conspiracy. But the motivation of Lee Harvey Oswald will not lead us to solution of the crime, since he did not plan its beginning and he obviously was not consulted in the planning of its ending. What then was the motive of the conspirators?

I believe the murder of the President was provoked, primarily, by fear of the domestic and international consequences of the Moscow Pact: The danger of disarmament which would disrupt the industries on which the plotters depended and of an international *détente* which would, in their view, have threatened the eventual nationalization of their oil investments overseas. . . .

How could the President's assassination *automatically* benefit the authors of the murder plot? It is clear, certainly, that they employed Lee Harvey Oswald for the purpose of increasing tension between the United States and Cuba, and above all the Soviet Union. This must be regarded as a maximum objective, from which they were willing to be forced back into a prepared position that the murderer was just a solitary madman—though of Marxist leanings. But the only element that would be automatic, if the President were killed, is that the Vice-President would take his place. What, then, are the major differences between Kennedy and Johnson? . . .

On foreign policy, the difference between the President and his successor starts to be important. It is premature, at this time, to assert that Johnson will reverse the progress Kennedy had made to a *détente*. What is important, though, is that the right-wing groups in the United States *believe* that he will do so. The John Birch Society's General Walker predicted, after Kennedy's death, "There will be considerable changes, even if they are not immediately apparent." And *U.S. News & World Report,* using almost identical language, summed it up this way: "There will be important changes, but gradual, in behaviour, personalities and politics. Intellectuals will not be favoured. Businessmen will be guaranteed a good rest. Khrushchev will find Johnson a hard man."

The one field in which Kennedy and Johnson were in total disagreement was the one which Texans feel to be the most important: Kennedy was an opponent of the tax concession for the Texas oil men; Johnson was the man whom Texas millionaires selected to succeed Sam Rayburn to defend their interests in Washington. . . .

I suggest the author of this crime, therefore, is a Texas millionaire named X, a man whose height, weight, age and physical appearance I ignore, but whose profession may be stated: Mr. X is now, and has been all his life, a gambler. He has made a bet—the biggest wager that he ever made—and so far, he has won it. He considered Kennedy to be pro-Communist, and he sincerely thought that Kennedy's assassination would, in some way, serve the interests of the United States; in addition, for the reasons which have just been stated, he felt it would bring him an immediate and personal advantage. Most of all, though, he looked on the plot as a manner of relieving his own personal and fatal boredom, just as Teddy Roosevelt did when he said, "The clamour of the peace faction has convinced me that this country needs a war. . . . I rather hope the fight will come soon." Mr. X had no more worlds to conquer in the State of Texas; he was anxious to find out if there was any limit to his power. . . . Everything would point to the original planned explanation: Oswald was a Communist who had been trained in Russia. When, through the bad luck that Oswald managed to outdraw his executioner, he was brought back alive to the Police Headquarters, there was only one thing left to do: Find someone who would kill him, before he could see a lawyer or discuss his case with newsmen. At all costs, a trial had to be averted, where he could have named his fellow-plotters. So Oswald was killed; the Dallas law-enforcement officers proclaimed that very day the whole case was closed, and there would not be an investigation. Oswald was a Communist, but *could* not have been working with accomplices, and there was no use looking for them—so they all insisted. Each time a new fact was brought forth to refute this thesis, the official story was revised; new "evidence" was found, like the remarkable shreds of clothing on the murder weapon, which were not discovered until dozens of investigators had their hands on it.

I charge the following additional conspirators assisted Mr. X, and I list them in the order of their culpability:

1. The police official who ordered the arrest of Oswald at a time

when there had been no reason to suspect him. He is guilty, as accessory before the fact to both assassinations—Kennedy's and Oswald's. Next to Mr. X himself, this is the key conspirator, and there are no extenuating circumstances for him. The police of Dallas know the name of this man, and they know how soon he gave the order.

2. An assassin who fired at least one shot from the unguarded railroad bridge directly at the Presidential car as it approached him. He is probably a gangster and escaped on foot. No doubt this murderer took refuge in a nearby building. . . . Any honest officer upon the scene knows that a weapon was found, on or near the overpass, and doubtless other evidence as well; he knows this evidence has disappeared since then. An investigator could determine why that railroad overpass was left unguarded—an irregular procedure. Who was meant to guard it? Who reversed the order?

3. Another assassin, who fired at least two shots from the Texas School Book Despository. Since one of these shots hit the President, he is no doubt an expert marksman. And since he was not detected leaving the building after the assassination, when that building was surrounded by policemen, one must assume that he passed unnoticed because he was himself in uniform. If not, then the policeman who permitted him to leave the the building must be regarded as a probable accomplice.

4. Accomplice Seven [Officer Tippit], who was meant to murder Oswald in cold blood. He failed to do so. He is now beyond man's power to judge him.

5. Lee Havery Oswald, ex-Marine, ex-friend of Russia and ex-F.B.I. informer. Charged with three crimes. On the first charge, murder of the President of the United States: Not guilty. On the second charge, murder of Patrolman Tippit: Not guilty. Justifiable homicide, in self-defense and in immediate peril of his life. On the third charge, complicity to murder John Fitzgerald Kennedy. Of being an accessory before the fact: Not guilty beyond reasonable doubt, although I personally feel he shared this knowledge. Of being an accessory after the fact: Guilty as charged. But, like the last accomplice, Oswald is beyond our power to condemn him.

6. Accomplice Four, who let Oswald leave the Texas School Book Depository after orders from Police Chief Curry to surround the building; and Detective Six, who followed Oswald for an hour and did not arrest him, despite the general order which had been sent out for his arrest.

The Ku Klux Klan as a Subversive, Conspiratorial Organization (1966)

IRVING KALER

Although the House Committee on Un-American Activities has been mainly preoccupied with liberal and left-wing influences, it was authorized early in 1965 to conduct a full-scale investigation of the Ku Klux Klan. A wave of brutal murders of civil rights workers in the South had led to a public demand for laws curbing terrorist organizations. The investigation revealed the existence of a genuine conspiratorial network dedicated to the violent suppression of civil rights work in the South. The following selection is from the testimony of Irving Kaler, a member of the Atlanta bar and the Southeastern Regional Board of the Anti-Defamation League of B'nai B'rith.

Here in the privileged confines of this room, it may be difficult to imagine the extent to which the Klan can undermine a community, a State, a Nation. To illustrate, let us suppose that you are a lieutenant colonel in the Army Reserve. You have been at Fort Benning, Georgia, for summer training—training essential to your military career, training necessary for service in Vietnam or wherever you might be sent.

Your training completed, you are in a hurry to get home to your family. So you drive through the night with two fellow officers toward Washington, D.C., where you live.

Suddenly, just outside of Athens, Georgia, home of the University of Georgia, you are overtaken by a car of nightriders. A shotgun fires. Your journey ends on a lonely highway in Georgia.

Why did this happen to Lt. Col. Lemuel Penn of Washington, D.C.? Simply because of the color of his skin, he innocently became the focal point of Klan hatred.

As a result of this brutal murder, four Klansmen were indicted. Two were tried in a State superior court and acquitted.

But later six Klansmen were indicted by a Federal grand jury and

---

From the statement of Irving Kaler before a subcommittee of the Committee on Un-American Activities, *Hearings Before the Committee on Un-American Activities, House of Representatives, Eighty-Ninth Congress, Second Session* (Washington, 1966), 1439–1432.

two men—the same two acquitted in the State superior court—were found guilty. This time the charge was conspiracy in violation of a Federal statute. And this time the trial was in Federal court.

The facts were essentially the same. In the State court, the Klansmen were acquitted; in the Federal court, two were convicted.

We may well ask ourselves how the different results occurred. I believe much of the answer lies in the annihilation of free will that occurs when the Klan is operating in a community.

We saw the same thing in Hayneville, Alabama, where four Klansmen were charged with murdering Mrs. Viola Liuzzo. Again there was no conviction in the State court. It would not do so despite the fact that one of the four was an FBI informer and provided detailed testimony about the murder. Klansmen roamed the courtroom. During a break in the trial, one came forward to inspect the evidence that had been presented.

In both the Georgia and Alabama cases, the Klan oath became a means of subverting the judicial process. In both cases, key witnesses were accused of violating their Klan oaths by testifying in courts of law. In the Alabama case, the FBI informer was charged by the defense with dishonoring his Klan oath. In the Georgia cases, a witness who had been a Klansman was able to point out that his Klan oath had expired and, therefore, he was relieved of this burden and could testify. . . .

Mr. Chairman, from the time he served as an Assistant Attorney General more than 21 years ago, Judge Duke of the criminal court of Atlanta had been one of the most vigorous opponents of the Klan in the Nation. Last October he wrote a letter in which he outlined information which had come to him of a recent Klan conspiracy. This included secret plans to assist Klansmen arrested and prosecuted and steps to prevent witnesses and jurors from carrying out their duties in courts of law.

This is a portion of the official letter that he wrote:

The most insidious evil growing out of the Ku Klux Klan conspiracy is the one which teaches its fellow members and travelers to prevent and subvert public justice and disrupt the oath of truth and the oath as a juror in any instance where the interest of the Ku Klux Klan or a fellow member may be at issue.

In October of 1965, Judge Duke called upon Governor Sanders to revoke the charters of Klan units operating in Georgia. Further quoting Judge Duke:

Proof is available in abundance that the Ku Klux Klan carries on its affairs for the purpose of disseminating racial and religious prejudice, intolerance and hatred, that it spreads false propaganda for the purpose of inciting its members and fellow travelers to acts of violence which disrupt and destroy the public peace and tranquility of the state.

It is a well-documented fact, Mr. Chairman, that the Klan has succeeded in infiltrating law enforcement agencies and courts. A famous KKK photograph of the 1960's shows a Klansman opening his robe wide to display the police uniform underneath. In some southern communities, the police station or sheriff's office has been known to be the local Klan headquarters. More than one judge, prosecutor, or juror—as Judge Duke has noted in his letter—has been known to be friendly to the Klan. And where the influence of the Klan is heavy—usually out of proportion to its actual size—witnesses and juries and elected court officials are apt to be cautious about offending an organization whose members may be packing the courtroom.

Said a bold young Methodist minister in Philadelphia, Mississippi, where Klansmen have been implicated in the murder of three civil rights workers:

For all practical purposes, the Klan has taken over the guidance of thought patterns in our town. It has controlled what was said and what was not said.

The coercion applied by the Klan often cuts deeper than is suspected. It can even put an end to constitutionally guaranteed free speech.

Thus, the citizens of Bogalusa, Louisiana, were warned in leaflets that anyone who attended an address by former Congressman Brooks Hays, "will be tagged as integrationists and will be dealt with accordingly by the Knights of the Ku Klux Klan." . . .

The Ku Klux Klan is at war with the United States. It is the avowed enemy of U.S. laws and traditions. It is an underground organization with the frank goals of subverting individual rights, terrorizing groups of people and whole communities, and promoting strife. Around the world, the hood and robe are symbols of bigotry in its ugliest form.

Suppression of
Antiwar Protest (1966)

Mounting opposition to the Vietnam War has led a new generation of radicals into openly defiant acts of public protest and civil disobedience. While these new forms of protest have generally been spontaneous and disorganized outbursts of disillusion and frustration that have had little, if any, connection with previous radical movements, they have often been interpreted as evidence of a well-planned and highly coordinated movement to aid the cause of international Communism. In 1966, after the Berkeley Vietnam Day Committee had attempted to stop troop trains in California, the House Committee on Un-American Activities held hearings on a bill to amend and strengthen the McCarran Internal Security Act of 1950, which requires Communist-front organizations to register with the Attorney General, and which provides, in the case of war, for detention camps for Communists and other subversives. Thus far the government has moved slowly in prosecuting antiwar protestors, but J. Edgar Hoover, among others, has warned that various student organizations constitute a new and widespread threat of conspiracy against the American way of life.

The investigations of this committee reveal that:

(1) There exists a widespread and well-organized effort initiated within the United States by Communist groups, and their affiliated organizations, involving thousands of adherents, who render various forms of aid and assistance to Communist forces engaged in armed conflict with the United States.

(2) The immediate purpose of this activity is to obstruct the Government of the United States and its Armed Forces in the execution of their commitments in Vietnam, so as to facilitate the seizure of South Vietnam by Communist agencies.

(3) The long-range objective of such Communist groups is to destroy the Government of the United States and to install a Communist totalitarian dictatorship, consistently with the ideology of Marxism-Leninism.

(4) The efforts of such Communist groups have been exhibited in

From *Obstruction of Armed Forces, Report From the Committee on Un-American Activities, Eighty-Ninth Congress, Second Session,* August 29, 1966 (Washington, 1966), pp. 2–6, 8.

various ways and forms, including activities pertinent to H.R. 12047; namely, the solicitation, collection, and delivery of money or property to and for the use of North Vietnam and the Vietcong, and the obstruction of the movement of personnel and supplies of our Armed Forces within the United States.

(5) Despite the repeated and notorious occurrence of such activities described in the preceding paragraph, with the promise of more to come, the Department of Justice had not, prior to the commencement of these hearings, initiated a single prosecution to prevent or punish this conduct which has shocked the conscience of the Nation. This failure has raised grave misgivings in the minds of many citizens whose sons are being called upon to die, if necessary, in the performance of their duties. . . .

The committee investigation has made clear that the various Communist organizations, and their affiliated groups, within the United States have instituted and participated in a nationwide campaign to induce the United States to withdraw from the defense of South Vietnam. The variety of forms this campaign has taken cannot be related within the confines of this report. We shall only briefly relate a few of the instances of those activities which the bill seeks to reach to illustrate their nature and occurrence.

With regard to the collection of money and medical aid for North Vietnam and the Vietcong, a principal organizer was the Progressive Labor Party, a Peking-oriented Communist group, which has established cells or clubs on several campuses and which, through a now dissolved front, the May Second Movement, with affiliated chapters on at least 20 campuses, undertook a widespread effort to solicit money and medical aid for this country's enemies. This campaign was supported by the Moscow-controlled Communist Party and its affiliates, and a number of Marxist-oriented organizations. . . .

The Vietnam Day Committee, organized at the University of California at Berkeley in May of 1965, and controlled by members of various participating Communist and Marxist-oriented organizations, has lent support to the campaign for the collection of money and medical aid for North Vietnam and the Vietcong. However, the Vietnam Day Committee has been concerned, as to matters relevant to the bill, principally with the "Stop the Troop Train" incidents which took place in the bay area of California. . . .

The troop train incidents, which are probably the best known activities of the Vietnam Day Committee, took place on the 5th, 6th and

12th of August 1965. Although troop train movements are unscheduled, the Vietnam Day Committee, by a system of spotters and observers, together with a communication network, was aware of the movements and on hand to press its program.

On the 5th of August, about 100 demonstrators, and about 100 more observers, congregated at the Santa Fe station on University Avenue in Berkeley. Several of the pickets jumped in front of the train, which proceeded slowly at that point, and jumped away when it became obvious that the train would not halt. No one was hurt and the train was not actually stopped although there were some narrow escapes.

The effort to stop a troop train was repeated on the following day, August 6. The activity had been elaborately planned. A network of observers had been set up by the Vietnam Day Committee along the track of the Santa Fe system in southern California. To warn of the approach of the train, telephone communications were set up in northern California to advise those on hand in Berkeley. Demonstrations occurred in the Emoryville station of the Santa Fe and at the Berkeley station. The pickets were stopped from massing themselves on the track only as a result of flying wedges of police officers and sheriff's deputies. . . .

On October 15, 1965, following a rally on the Berkeley campus after a half-day teach-in, well in excess of 10,000 people marched from the University of California with the avowed purpose of reaching the Oakland Army Terminal. Following a denial of a parade permit through Oakland, the group nevertheless endeavored to reach it but were prevented by the Oakland police from doing so, and the group then camped overnight at a Berkeley park. . . .

What we witness today is, we believe, but a prolog of what may be anticipated. We cannot dismiss the activities of Communists as "eccentric," which the Deputy Attorney General [Ramsey Clark] has indicated we should do. The people of more than one nation have done so to their regret. If we are not prepared to suppress hostile activities in their infancy, we shall be faced with greater problems as they mature. If we value our liberties, as we do, we shall not permit any impairment of our national security while powerful forces, avowedly hostile to our society, are preparing to make us their victim.

Afterword

IN LOOKING back over the diverse selections in this book, we clearly see that American fears of conspiracy must be regarded as something more than pathological aberrations. Even when false, the belief in hidden, systematic subversion has not always been an unreasonable interpretation of seemingly inexplicable events (see, for example, the quotation from Abraham Lincoln's speech at the beginning of the book). One could argue that hypotheses of conspiracy are not so different from other theoretical constructs that give an explanatory framework to discrete facts of experience.

One could even conclude that conspiratorial views of politics have played a positive role in various periods of American history. For example, it could be said that in the 1760's and early 1770's an exaggerated picture of British plots against American liberty helped awaken colonists to their own true interests and even to the importance of man's natural rights. As we have seen, anti-Masonry helped to diffuse egalitarian ideals and to democratize American politics. The image of a Slave Power conspiracy may have been necessary to alert northern public opinion to the genuine moral evils of Negro slavery. Without the crusade against Communism, the American public might not have abandoned its traditional isolationism or accepted its responsibility toward the less affluent peoples of the world (in the form of foreign aid, for instance).

On the other hand, genuine conspiracies have seldom been as dangerous or as powerful as have movements of countersubversion. The exposer of conspiracies necessarily adopts a victimized, self-righteous tone which masks his own meaner interests as well as his share of responsibility for a given conflict. Accusations of conspiracy conceal or justify one's own provocative acts and thus contribute to individual or national self-deception. Still worse, they lead to overreactions, particularly to degrees of suppressive violence which normally would not be tolerated. Nothing demonstrates a "clear and present danger" better than the discovery, within the supposedly secure walls of society, of a Trojan Horse.

The sudden spread and intensification of the paranoid style has been symptomatic of severe social and political strains in American society. And while hysteria over subversion has been particularly pronounced in limited periods—such as the late 1790's, the mid-1830's, the 1850's, the 1890's, the early 1920's, and the 1950's and 1960's—we must conclude that there has been a remarkable continuity in the themes, values, and expectations of countersubversion. There is an ironic significance in the fact that Robert Welch can trace the conflict with America's Great Enemy back to the Order of the Illuminati, and then create an Illuminati-like countersociety (the John Birch Society) to do battle with the forces of darkness.

We have suggested that in a fluid, competitive, and heterogeneous society there has been a continuing fear of hidden, monolithic structures which would at once *exclude* the majority of people and impose a purposeful pattern on otherwise unpredictable events. Such "Monster Institutions" seem to account for the disturbing divisions and disunities of American society, since the strategy of Illuminati, Freemasons, Catholics, and Communists has been seen as identical—to divide and conquer. At the same time, the very presence of such subversive forces is a cause for closing ranks and regaining a sense of national purpose. Movements of countersubversion have thus been a primary means of restoring collective self-confidence, of defining American identity by contrast with alien "others," and of achieving unity through opposition to a common enemy.

One would hope, however, that there are better ways to promote social unity and to define national purpose. For it seems clear that in the later twentieth century America cannot afford the infantile luxury of collective ego-building through self-deception and aggression. We have said that the paranoid style leads inevitably to overreaction. In the future, overreaction at home will surely erode the democratic process; in the world at large it can lead only to annihilation.

Index

The Fear of Conspiracy
Designed by R. E. Rosenbaum.
Composed by Vail-Ballou Press, Inc.,
in 10 point linofilm Caledonia, 2 points leaded,
with display lines in Bulmer and Caledonia Bold.
Printed by offset by Vail-Ballou Press
on Warren's 1854 Text, 60 pound basis,
with the Cornell University Press watermark.
Bound by Vail-Ballou Press
in Columbia Bayside Vellum
and stamped in All Purpose foil.